CRISIS
IN EDUCATION

Barry A. Farber

with Contributions by
Leonard D. Wechsler

CRISIS
IN EDUCATION

Stress and Burnout in the American Teacher

Jossey-Bass Publishers

San Francisco • Oxford • 1991

CRISIS IN EDUCATION
Stress and Burnout in the American Teacher
by Barry A. Farber

Copyright © 1991 by: Jossey-Bass Inc., Publishers
350 Sansome Street
San Francisco, California 94104

&

Jossey-Bass Limited
Headington Hill Hall
Oxford OX3 0BW

Library of Congress Cataloging-in-Publication Data

Farber, Barry A. (Barry Alan), date.
    Crisis in education : stress and burnout in the American teacher /
Barry A. Farber, with contributions by Leonard D. Wechsler.
        p.   cm.—(The Jossey-Bass education series)
    Includes bibliographical references and index.
    ISBN 1-55542-271-3
    1. Teachers—United States—Job Stress.   2. Burn out (Psychology).
3. Education—Social aspects—United States.   I. Wechsler, Leonard
David.   II. Title.   III. Series.
    LB2840.2.F37   1991
    371.1'001'9—dc20   90-19770
                                                        CIP

Manufactured in the United States of America

The paper in this book meets the guidelines for
permanence and durability of the Committee on
Production Guidelines for Book Longevity of the
Council on Library Resources.

JACKET DESIGN BY VARGAS/WILLIAMS/DESIGN

FIRST EDITION

Code 9134

A joint publication in
The Jossey-Bass Education Series
and
The Jossey-Bass
Social and Behavioral Science Series

Contents

Foreword

Over the past two decades, *burnout* has become a catchall term, pervasively used but ill defined (along with *low morale*), to describe one of the most common and serious afflictions of our nation's teachers. The term has been used to describe and often excuse the inability of many teachers to persist effectively in the classroom.

In assessing the meaning and significance of the burnout phenomenon, we must remember that the 1960s, 1970s, and early 1980s were times of great disappointment and discouragement in American education, times in which much of the blame for the perceived failings of education fell upon teachers. These were times when the turmoil of desegregation and busing produced new political conflicts around the schools; times in which a youth culture flourished and then faded; times in which new curricula, notions of open education, and other aspects of the romantic movement in American education sprang up and withered. The period witnessed times of serious financial hardship for the schools and diminishing financial rewards for teachers, times when collective bargaining agreements began to govern the working arrangements of the majority of American teachers. Many of the reform movements launched in the 1970s concentrated on minimizing or avoiding the perceived shortcomings of teachers rather than building on their strengths. Thus we had a quest for teacher-proof curricula, then for alternative schools. It is little wonder that teachers, faced with this onslaught of misfortune and blame, were increasingly demoralized and that teacher burnout became a common phenomenon. The entire profession of teaching was in trouble.

Given this background, one surprising aspect of the educational reforms proposed in the 1980s was the rediscovery of the teacher. While the many national reports and proposals for reforms contained criticism of the teaching profession, they nevertheless stated that teachers were an essential part of the solution, assuming that teachers could improve their performance and become more effective. Indeed, they came to the important, if obvious, realization that no improvement in educational outcomes of students was likely without more effective teaching. Thus, during the 1980s many of the dismal trends of the 1970s began to be reversed. Teachers' pay began to rise as did regard for teaching by both college students and those seeking to escape from other professions. A series of initiatives designed to enhance the status and performance of teachers emerged: proposals for merit and incentive pay, for master teachers and mentor teachers, for career ladders, and, more recently, for the development of new roles for teachers in decision making and for the restructuring of schools to accommodate and encourage these new roles. Withal, though, teacher burnout persists, accompanied by a hefty skepticism among teachers about the proposed reforms and their purported intent to improve the conditions of teaching.

As we come to recognize this dilemma of reform, Barry A. Farber's research tells us a vital tale. Until now, teacher burnout has been a widely misunderstood concept, with little specific explanation as to its occurrence, its variations and symptoms, or its solutions. It has connoted merely a generalized state of hopelessness and exhaustion, impossible for policy makers and managers to deal with in any specific way. Barry A. Farber remedies all of this. He carefully lays out the etiology of teacher stress and burnout, helping us to understand the varieties of burnout arising in different circumstances and requiring different responses. He reviews the context and history of the development of burnout with great thoroughness and care, enabling us to understand how it is the consequence of many of the rapid social and educational changes of the 1960s and of the subsequent attacks upon teachers and the schools, of low pay, urban social disintegration, lack of parental-community support, and student apathy. Farber discusses the alternatives available to combat teacher burnout, noting perceptively that the initial educational reform proposals of the mid-1980s, in imposing higher standards and requirements, did nothing directly to address the issue and had the potential, in fact, to make it worse. He notes too that individual coping strategies may ameliorate the local classroom conditions but can never solve the problems that lead many teachers to the burned-out state. He concludes that the best hope lies in the kinds of school-level and school-based improvement strategies that are now surging forward under the heading of "restructuring." In this, he adds a significant and clinically based psychological perspective to the various proposals for this sort of reform.

Burnout, with all its symptoms, is itself symptomatic of the seemingly intractable problems present in many American schools. No one should think that it will be quickly or easily diminished or erased, since it is the consequence of each burned-out teacher's profound and complicated psychological conclusion that his or her work is not efficacious. As such, burnout will itself be a substantial obstacle to educational reform and improvement, at least for several years. The situation calls for careful diagnosis and treatment for all affected individuals and groups in the schools. Nostrums—whether organizational, rhetorical, or therapeutic—will not suffice.

January 1991   P. Michael Timpane
President
Teachers College
Columbia University

To my parents—
For their love of education

Preface

Background of the Book

When I was training to be a public school teacher in the late 1960s, I was assigned books in teacher education courses that were strongly critical of teachers (for example, those by Holt and Kozol). When I became a teacher, community groups and the popular press were strongly critical of teachers. When I left teaching, in the mid-1970s, university experts were busy writing curricula, textbooks, and subject guides that, while not explicitly critical of teachers, clearly assumed that most teachers could not think for themselves and would be entirely ineffective if left to their own devices. In 1979, when I became a psychology professor in a college of education, the most pressing issue was the decline in quality of American teachers. This book grew out of a feeling that teachers have been maligned in this country for too long. From this perspective, the emergence of teacher burnout as a significant social and educational phenomenon is evidence not of the failings of teachers but rather of how difficult teaching has become in this day and age.

I started my own teaching career in a New York City public school in 1968, where I spent four often difficult, often rewarding years teaching both special and regular education. I spent my last year as a public school teacher in an elementary school in an affluent suburban community. Over these years, I became somewhat accustomed to many inexplicable bureaucratic practices and became better at handling many student problems as well. But what I could never get used to, nor entirely understand, was the seemingly constant belittling of teachers by parents, media, school personnel, community leaders, and the public at large. Along with many of my colleagues, I grew increasingly bitter over the widespread accusations that teachers were racist, incompetent, dull, and oppressive. Most teachers I knew were, in fact, kind, decent, and personally committed to helping children, especially the underprivileged. Perhaps this now smacks of naivete, but it was a sincere belief in the late 1960s when idealistic feelings made teachers of many of us.

Many of us struggled even as we made our curriculum more "relevant," "opened up" our classrooms, established precise goals, systematically rewarded small achievements, and fed breakfast to our needy students. Not achieving the successes we strove for was difficult to accept. Equally difficult was the attitude we felt from a public that seemed intent on criticizing rather than understanding, on condemning failures rather than acknowledging hard work or success. In the late 1960s and early 1970s, many teachers were beginning to feel exasperated by the criticism, the lack of public support, the bureaucratic interference, the increasingly violent nature of schools, and the pressures placed on them to educate all children equally effectively.

Many teachers, myself included, began feeling that the satisfactions of teaching were no longer commensurate with the stresses. Some left the field, and others continued to teach without the enthusiasm or commitment they had once had. And many began to identify with a concept that seemed to reflect many of their feelings about work: *teacher burnout.* "I've had it, I don't care, and I have very little left to give" are the feelings underscoring teacher burnout—a phenomenon that reflects both the difficulty of the work and the lack of available support and rewards to offset the stresses.

Teacher burnout is not an excuse that poor teachers invoke. It is a work-related disorder to which even the best educators sometimes succumb when faced with the nature and circumstances of teaching. Moreover, teacher burnout is not just a cluster of stress-related symptoms; it is a disorder that must be placed in a certain historical and social context. The perspective taken here is that teachers, traditionally a much criticized group, have been especially maligned since the mid-1960s and that it is far from coincidence that the "discovery" and frequency of teacher burnout have occurred in an era that has been particularly critical of teachers' efforts.

Overview of the Contents

There are several other books and a plethora of articles on teacher stress and burnout, but my sense is that this book differs from the vast majority of such literature in several essential ways. First, as noted above, it provides a social and historical context for the emergence of teacher burnout within the past two to three decades. That is, it goes beyond a mere enumeration of the immediate causes and symptoms of this problem to a consideration of those factors—including teacher strikes, the civil rights movement, the women's movement, and changing demographic patterns—that have provided a fertile soil for its emergence. Second, it provides multiple perspectives on the issues of teacher stress and burnout, at times employing the language and viewpoint of educators, at times those of sociologists, and at times those of psychologists. Third, it offers the voices of teachers themselves, talking not only about their classroom experiences but about the personal consequences of their work as well. Fourth, this book identifies several subtypes of burnout, providing a degree of specificity to this phenomenon that has heretofore been absent. Fifth, it provides no faddish answers as to how to deal with this disorder, no package of solutions; its recommendations are more cautious and its forecast for change more respectful of the seriousness of the problem. Sixth, and perhaps most important, this book is a rarity in the literature of either education or psychology—it is supportive of teachers.

Chapter One reviews the history of the burnout concept and the various ways that it has been defined. A fictional teacher manifests the varied symptoms of burnout as described by several prominent theorists. Chapter Two looks at the prevalence of burnout in different groups of teachers and examines its sources at both the individual and organizational levels. In Chapter Three, the focus is on symptomatology and the three different types of burnout that seem to occur. Chapter Four addresses the teacher shortage, especially these questions of concern: Who teaches and why? Who leaves and why? Three profiles of former teachers are offered. In Chapter

Five, the origins of modern-day teacher burnout are traced to several events and trends in the 1960s, including the general iconoclastic tone of that era, the unintended and unforeseen consequences of the civil rights movement, and the infusion of male teachers into education as a consequence of the Vietnam War. Chapter Six reviews some of the antiteacher books published in the 1960s and 1970s; it also looks at the way television and the movies have portrayed teachers over the years. Chapter Seven focuses on the ways teachers have historically been treated in this country; in addition, it discusses three prime aspects of the general lack of respect accorded contemporary teachers: public opinion, low salaries, and day-to-day treatment by parents, students, and administrators. Chapter Eight takes a close look at the particular problems of teachers in urban schools and their special vulnerability to the phenomena of stress and burnout, examining the issues and problems through a discussion of a "typical day" in an urban school. Chapter Nine addresses the specific problems and vulnerabilities of suburban, rural, private, and special education teachers. Finally, Chapter Ten is a wide-ranging discussion and critique of the solutions that have been offered for teacher stress and burnout at the individual, school, and societal levels.

Crisis in Education is based on empirical data that I and other researchers in the field have collected over the years. It is also based on critical reviews of the growing literature in the field and on the impressions gleaned from the approximately one hundred interviews that Leonard Wechsler and I have conducted with teachers over the past five years. This book is intended for teacher education courses, professional educators, and that growing segment of the public interested in education and the plight of teachers.

Acknowledgments

I'd like to thank several individuals for the enormous help they have provided me on this project. I'm grateful to Leonard Wechsler, whose experience as both a teacher and an administrator has provided me with a number of insights about the ways schools function. His interviews with teachers greatly complemented my own; our regularly scheduled discussions about the issues contained in this book were both informative and motivating. He provided research help, comments on unfinished drafts, and the case studies of different teachers used throughout this book. Moreover, he essentially coauthored Chapters Six, Eight, and Nine.

I'd also like to thank several very talented graduate students: Melissa Kretch and Susan Schachner for their research assistance, and Laura Markham for her support, advice, political insights, editing abilities, and all-around helpfulness. Laura, who will surely one day write her own books, was an invaluable resource and someone whom I relied upon as a colleague. I'd like to thank Seymour Sarason, who taught me how to think about schools and the problems of education; there is no better source. I also benefited greatly from talks with Howard and Judi Aronson, April Farber, Isaac Friedman, and Stephen Suffit. I'm grateful also to the many teachers who so graciously contributed their time and views to this project, and to the Spencer Foundation, whose support for my early empirical studies provided the foundation for this book.

A special thanks goes to Gracia Alkema, former editor at Jossey-Bass, for her extraordinary patience and support. She has become a friend as well as a colleague. Thanks also to Mary White, her editorial assistant, who provided friendly pushes toward completion, and to Lesley Iura, Jossey-Bass education editor, for her vital help in the final stages of the publication process.

For their thoughtful and detailed comments on early drafts of the manuscript, I'd like to thank three anonymous reviewers as well as one not-so-anonymous reviewer—Bob Ancowitz, a fine and not-burned-out teacher at Central School in Larchmont, New York.

Finally, to my family: Thank you, dear April, Alissa, and David, for your encouragement and love. I promise to wait a while before the next book.

New York, New York Barry A. Farber
January 1991

The Author

BARRY A. FARBER is director of the clinical psychology program and associate professor of psychology and education at Teachers College, Columbia University. He received his B.A. degree (1968) from Queens College (City University of New York) in psychology, his M.A. degree (1970) from Teachers College in developmental psychology, and his Ph.D. degree (1978) from Yale University in clinical-community psychology.

Farber taught in the New York City public school system from 1968 to 1972 and in the Edgemont School System (Westchester, New York) in the 1972–73 school year. He has published a number of articles in professional journals on teacher burnout, on psychotherapist burnout, and on the ways in which the practice of psychotherapy affects psychotherapists. He maintains a part-time private practice in Manhattan and Westchester. His previous book, published in 1983, was *Stress and Burnout in the Human Service Professions.* His current research focuses on how patients construct images of their psychotherapists.

CRISIS
IN EDUCATION

1

What Is Burnout?

IN RECENT YEARS, THERE HAS BEEN A SHARP RESURGENCE OF interest in our nation's public schools. According to a multitude of local and national reports, our schools are so replete with problems that education has come to a standstill for many children. Only 40 percent of this nation's seventeen-year-olds can comprehend, summarize, and explain what they have read; no significant progress has been made since 1971 in raising the reading levels of our students. High school seniors in this country have lower mean scores on a test of mathematical abilities than those of fifteen other industrialized nations. The high school dropout rate is estimated to be about 30 percent, with about one million students dropping out annually. *A Nation at Risk,* the report by the National Commission on Excellence in Education (1983) warned us pointedly about the "rising tide of mediocrity" in American schools. And John Goodlad (1984) asserted that the problems of American schools are of such crippling proportions that "it is possible that our entire public education system is nearing collapse" (p. 1).

But it has also become apparent to many who have studied the educational system in this country that teachers, as well as students, are victimized by problem-laden schools. A substantial proportion (26 percent) of all current teachers are seriously considering giving up teaching as a career within the next five years (Harris

1

and Associates, 1988). Attrition rates for new teachers during their first five years on the job average between 40 and 50 percent (Olson and Rodman, 1988). And nearly half the teachers in this country (49 percent) believe that morale within the profession has substantially declined since the school reform movement began in 1983 (Boyer, 1988). Too many teachers have become stressed or burned out. The primary aim of this book is to examine the nature of these phenomena in teachers—to investigate the reasons and ways that teachers are dysfunctionally affected by their work and to examine the solutions that may be available.

The impact of teacher stress and burnout on our educational system is easily imagined and clearly serious. Current teachers will pursue alternative sources of satisfaction and continue to seek career changes. New teachers will be difficult to recruit and retain, even with more attractive salaries. However, the most critical impact of teacher stress and burnout will surely be on the teaching process itself, particularly in urban schools with children who can ill afford a further deterioration of an already troubled educational system and who are unable to gain access to private schooling.

Although teacher stress has certainly existed as long as teaching, recognition of a serious morale problem among teachers in this country has become more explicit in the last twenty to thirty years. A series of autobiographical accounts of disillusioned teachers in the late 1960s first sparked public interest in teaching and the problems of teachers. Several years later a resurgence of interest in these issues was generated by the introduction of an evocative new term to describe a particular type of demoralization occurring among human service workers: *burnout.* As conceived originally by Freudenberger, burnout occurs in highly motivated workers who react to stress by overworking until they collapse. Subsequent definitions have attributed burnout to the discrepancy between a worker's input (what he or she invests in the job) and output (feelings of satisfaction and gratification derived from the work); a worker's perception of a mismatch between the two results in feelings of detachment, emotional exhaustion, and a loss of concern for those with whom one works. But regardless of the exact meaning of the term—and there is no consensus as to its definition—teachers quickly became the professional group most identified with this phenomenon. As

I noted in an earlier paper, "the word 'teacher' modifies the word 'burnout' all too well" (Farber, 1984b, p. 321).

Moreover, the association of burnout with teachers did not occur in spite of teachers or over the protests of their professional associations but seemingly in accord with their own view of the state of their profession. In 1979, Willard McGuire, then president of the National Education Association, ominously acknowledged the emergence of teacher burnout. "A major new malady," he wrote," has afflicted the teaching profession and threatens to reach epidemic proportions if it isn't checked soon" (p. 5). Several years later, Albert Shanker (1982) pointed to the burgeoning literature on teacher burnout as one indicator that teachers were finding their jobs less rewarding and more stressful than ever. In general, then, teachers did not refute the characterization of many of their colleagues as burned out, and, indeed, many teachers themselves adopted this label—even flaunted it—as the most accurate reflection of their feelings toward a job that no longer commanded public respect nor engendered self-respect. For many, there appeared to be a wish for the public to know just how onerous conditions for teachers had become and just how tired teachers were of being blamed for social conditions beyond their control. Surprisingly, to many teachers, *burnout* was not a term of opprobrium. To be unabashedly "burned out" offered an Ancient Mariner-like opportunity to explain, justify, complain, and moralize about everything from parental responsibilities (or, more typically, the lack thereof) to school discipline problems to the lack of administrative support provided to teachers. If *burnout* was a "buzz word," it was also a rallying cry around which teachers could actively and angrily protest their situation. It is likely that by now most Americans are acquainted with the deep dissatisfaction of at least one teacher who dreams of leaving the profession to open a restaurant or go into real estate, computers, or small business.

Both the educational community and the public at large have shown enormous interest in the concept of teacher burnout, a common concern of both being the potential adverse effects of stressed and burned-out teachers on the quality of education. As Sarason (1982) noted several years before burnout became a focal point for teachers' dissatisfaction, "If teaching becomes neither terribly interesting nor exciting to many teachers, can one expect them to make learning interesting or exciting to children?" (p. 200). In recent years, the causes, symptoms, and treatment of teacher burnout have been frequently described in popular magazines and professional journals. National television news programs have run several features on this topic. The National Education Association (NEA) made teacher burnout the central theme of its 1979 convention, and teacher trainers report that burnout is often the highest-rated subject on needs-assessment measures designed to identify major teacher concerns.

Despite the attention and concern paid to the phenomena of teacher stress and burnout over the last two decades, there is a good deal of confusion regarding the nature of these terms as well as the difference between these and other, related terms. *Stress, burnout, depression, demoralization, disillusionment,* and *alienation* have all at times been used to refer to a similar constellation of work-related symptoms, and differentiation between these terms has often been made haphazardly, if at all. *Stress* is used as both cause and effect, at times referring to oppressive conditions (the stresses *of* work) and at other times to the dysfunctional consequences of these conditions (feeling stressed *by* work). The word *burnout,* as one researcher in the field has pointed out, has become a "verbal Rorschach test," assuming an idiosyncratic meaning for virtually every individual writing or thinking about this topic (Jackson, 1982).

Our knowledge of teacher stress and burnout has been compromised by methodological limitations in assessing these concepts and conceptual confusion in writing about them. Given this state of affairs, it is no wonder that there are those who view burnout, for example, as an epidemic of tragic proportions while others think that the term itself is an overused, convenient excuse for the lazy and self-indulgent. The balance of this chapter will attempt to clarify some of these terms, especially as they relate to teachers, including a short history of the concept of burnout, emphasizing the views of the major theorists and researchers in the field; it will propose a working definition of burnout; it will review the criticisms of the concept of burnout; it will explain the differences between burnout and several related concepts (including depression, alienation, and teacher stress); and, finally, it will discuss the process of burnout—its progressive course.

A Short History of the Concept of Burnout

Freudenberger: A Clinical Approach. Herbert Freudenberger, a New York-based clinical psychologist, was the first professional to describe (and label) a case of burnout. In 1973, in a professional psychology journal, he gave an account of what he called the "burnt out" syndrome. Even before Freudenberger, however, Graham Greene (1961) wrote a novel about a "burnt-out case." Greene's protagonist was a spiritually tormented, disillusioned, and despondent man who found an appropriate metaphor for his condition in a leper colony; the symptoms of this fictional character fit the current descriptions of burned-out individuals. Although Greene's book was a best-seller, it did not make *burnout* a household word in the 1960s. It was primarily Freudenberger, as well as Christina Maslach and Ayala Pines (colleagues for several years at the University of California, Berkeley) and Cary Cherniss (at the University of Michigan), who popularized the concept and legitimized its status as a critical social issue.

Freudenberger took a term that was used primarily in the 1960s to refer to the effects of chronic drug abuse ("burned out" on drugs) and used it rather ironically—to characterize the physical and psychological states of certain volunteers working with drug abusers in alternative health care agencies. In fact, Freudenberger's first description of someone suffering from this syndrome was of himself:

> One serious consequence of working in a free clinic which I have personally experienced is the "burnt out" syndrome. Just consider for a minute what it can do to one working in a free clinic. Such work requires that most of what you do there you do after your normal professional working hours . . . and you put a great deal of yourself in the work. You demand this of yourself, the staff demands it of you, and the population that you are serving demands it of you. As usually

happens, more and more demands are made upon
fewer and fewer people. You gradually build up in
those around you and in yourself the feeling that they
need you. You feel a total sense of commitment. The
whole atmosphere builds up to it, until you finally
find yourself, as I did, in a state of exhaustion. . . . If
one wants to work in a free clinic or therapeutic community, one cannot permit oneself to so overextend
his personal and emotional resources that he collapses
[1973, p. 56].

The original notion of burnout, then, emphasized a state of
exhaustion brought on by working too intensely and without regard to one's personal needs. Freudenberger posited that this condition occurred most frequently among the "dedicated and
committed—those who work too much, too long and too intensely"
(1974, p. 161), who regard their own needs and wants as secondary,
and who feel pressure to give coming from three sides: from within
themselves, from needy clients, and from harried staff administrators. This pressure may engender guilt, which, in turn, may spur
these workers to expend even greater energies. Burnout, Freudenberger would later note in one of his books, was a result of "excessively striving to reach some unrealistic expectation imposed by
one's self or the values of society" (1980, p. 17). The problem, as he
realized, was that there could be no end to the work required; the
clients with whom human service professionals often work are *in-
satiably* needy. As he put it, "the population which we help is often
in extreme need, and because of this they continually take, suck,
demand. Let us be honest about it, and admit that the people I am
referring to require a continuous giving on our part. And our feeding supplies appear both to us and to them to be endless. We soon
learn, however, that this is a mistaken notion. The supply can—and
often very quickly does—dry up" (1975, p. 75).

To Freudenberger, burnout was essentially the product of an
unfortunate interaction between overzealous helpers and overneedy
clients. This formulation may seem unremarkable now. But then—
in the mid-1970s—it was notable for at least two reasons. First, at
a time when it was popular to emphasize the neglect, needs, and

virtues of the underserved and to rail at the putative failings of professional helpers, the concept of burnout was implicitly sympathetic to the plight of helpers. Workers, Freudenberger told us, were burning out primarily because they were working too hard and caring too much. In this sense, public interest in and acceptance of the concept of burnout helped refocus attention on the problems and needs of human service professionals (such as teachers) and probably helped restore some balance to the nation's sympathies. Second, the notion of burnout suggested that to the extent that a helper was having difficulties fulfilling his or her role (helping or curing or teaching), these difficulties could be understood, at least in part, in terms of the severe nature of *clients'* problems. Freudenberger noted that it was difficult, if not impossible, to be successful or feel gratified as a helper if one were working with chronically needy, demanding, and troubled individuals. As obvious as this now sounds—that a helper's effectiveness is partially a function of the problems he or she has to contend with—it was not a popular view in the late 1960s and early 1970s, when the problems of the poor, addicted, mentally ill, and educationally disadvantaged were largely attributed to the elitist, nonsympathetic, uncaring attitude of those professionals serving these groups. In this regard, it is interesting to note that Freudenberger saw fit to include the words "let us be honest about it" in formulating his views. Presumably he knew that any attempt at drawing attention to client problems— even severe, historically intractable problems—as a factor in understanding the frequent failure of either client or professional to benefit from a helping relationship was not going to be readily acknowledged by many of those exposed to his views.

Although Freudenberger has not written specifically about teacher burnout, his perspective would suggest the following profile of a burned-out teacher.

Rachel B., a single woman in her mid-twenties and the only daughter of a middle-class, dual-career, politically liberal couple, made the decision to become a teacher in her junior year in college. She felt she dealt well with children (having been a camp counselor for many summers), liked spending time with them, and, most important, felt that most kids responded well to her sensitivity, sense of humor, and

upbeat manner. She also felt that most adults did not really understand or appreciate the nature or problems of kids and that she could
do better than most of the teachers she herself had had. She felt
strongly about her ability to be an exceptionally good and helpful
teacher and made a distinction in her mind between her strongly
motivated career choice and the more passive ("I don't know what
else to do") way many of her friends had chosen to become teachers.
Following graduation and prior to her first classroom assignment (a
fifth grade class in an inner-city neighborhood), she spent most of the
summer preparing lessons and decorating her classroom. She was
excited, if a bit nervous, about teaching her first class but felt confident of her ability to "win over" even hard-to-reach students.

     She was surprised at first at how difficult it was to teach—that
there were so many distractions, classroom interruptions, behavior
problems, and administrative requests—but vowed to do whatever it
took to become an outstanding teacher. The children deserved an
effective education and she was going to provide it. She spent a good
deal of her after-school time planning lessons, individualizing assignments, and thinking about ways of dealing more effectively with her
less motivated students. Her students seemed to like her and many
responded quite positively to her energy and her obvious caring. Her
supervisor—one of the school's assistant principals—as well as the
other teachers in the school seemed to think she was a talented new
addition to the school staff and lauded her efforts. To her mind,
though, too many students in her class were still turned off to education and were interfering with the learning of the others in the
class. She couldn't feel successful unless this group responded to her
efforts as well. As she became friendly with other teachers in her
school, she began borrowing their curriculum materials and soliciting
their advice for dealing with troublesome students. She took suggestions from all quarters—from her supervisor, principal, fellow
teachers, helpful students, and involved parents. And, within that first
year, she improved herself greatly as a teacher, soon gaining a reputation as being among the hardest-working, most involved, and
most dedicated teachers in the entire school. And yet still she didn't
feel she was doing enough. Of a class of twenty-five students, three
or four rarely came, and another five or six couldn't or wouldn't stay

attentive in the classroom, dropping further and further behind academically. Their futures, to Rachel B., seemed increasingly bleak.

At the end of the first year, she promised herself that she would work even harder—these students' lives depended on her. That summer she took a quick break but later took a seminar in urban education at a local college. She went back to work the second year with a strong resolve that everyone in her class would make substantial academic gains. She was sure that, having learned from her first-year mistakes, this time she could really make a difference to all the students she had an opportunity to work with. And, in fact, early on things went better for her: She established an effective classroom routine earlier in the year, she managed problems and disruptions with less anxiety, and she had a clearer idea of how to set up individualized programs for her students.

Consistent with her resolve, Rachel B. did work harder. Increasingly, though, she became both angry and despondent as she realized that despite her best efforts the work of many of her students was still marginal at best and that in comparison to national norms some were actually losing ground. She became less sympathetic to her students and more critical of many of her colleagues, particularly the administrative staff, whom she thought of as incompetent and unhelpful. She became irritated if a supervisor suggested changes in her approach and felt that only someone working as hard as she had a right to comment on her work—and that certainly didn't include any of the supervisors she knew. She began to feel that she was by far the most competent and serious teacher in her school and if only others would abide by her ideas a great deal could be accomplished. This sense of grandiosity extended also to her insistence on taking risks on her job—for example, making home visits, often at night, in dangerous areas of town. By the end of her second year, she was aware of feeling exhausted and realized how much of her life she had been giving to teaching; she saw that she was neglecting her health, her friends, and her social life. She wasn't sure whether or not she was going to return to teaching in the fall, but she was quite certain that she needed to take a long vacation that summer—an idea that her friends and family endorsed wholeheartedly.

Rachel B., like most of Freudenberger's cases, is depicted here as a tragic hero, burning out because her idealism and background predestined her to give too much to others and too little to herself. As appealing as this notion is now to many professionals, and as influential as Freudenberger's work has been, this view of burnout is subject to criticism on several grounds—most notably that it substitutes an unrealistically romantic and noble view of the helper for a previously overly romantic and noble view of the helper's clientele. Many burned-out teachers, as we shall see, do not suffer from a surfeit of dedication or enthusiasm and do not push themselves "ever onward to work even harder" (Freudenberger, 1975, p. 74).

Essentially, Freudenberger took a clinical approach to understanding burnout. He described its etiology, symptoms, clinical course, and recommended treatment (focusing on greater awareness of one's needs and values); he also placed the entire phenomenon of burnout within a particular social context. "Value shifts in our society," he noted, have "contributed to the ambiguity in our lives, which, in turn, has created a fertile ground for the growth of burnout" (1983, p. 25). Primarily, though, his work focused on individuals who, in either their personal or professional lives, have paid a "high cost" for "high achievement."

Maslach and Pines: A Social-Psychological Approach. In contrast to Freudenberger, Maslach and Pines investigated the phenomenon of burnout from a social-psychological perspective. Maslach was influenced by Philip Zimbardo's work in the early 1970s on dehumanization and depersonalization; in fact, the same year (1973) that Freudenberger first wrote about burnout in a professional journal, Maslach presented a paper at the American Psychological Association meeting that pointed out how role-related stress in professionals—especially work overload—could lead to dehumanized treatment of clients. Before coming to the United States, Pines did research on stress for the Israeli army. Working individually as well as collectively, they collected data on several thousand workers across many types of human service jobs. Their approach was to study burnout from a more research-oriented perspective, attempting to identify specific environmental conditions that give rise to burnout, specific mediators (most notably social support) that mitigate the impact of stressful events, and specific symptoms (most notably various types of emotional distancing) that characterize burnout across a wide variety of professional groups. Using both questionnaires and interviews, they identified three central dimensions of burnout: emotional exhaustion (feeling drained, used up), depersonalization (feeling "hardened" emotionally, treating recipients as if they were impersonal objects), and lack of personal accomplishment (feeling ineffective and inadequate). The most widely used measure in the field, the Maslach Burnout Inventory (Maslach and Jackson, 1981, 1986), assesses these three factors in measuring burnout in individuals.

In contrast to Freudenberger, who hypothesized an intensified work effort as a response to frustration and stress ("the only way to stem the flood of demands . . . is to put in more hours and more effort"), Maslach emphasized emotional exhaustion and worker detachment. Both viewed heavy emotional involvement and overextension as precursors to burnout, but whereas Freudenberger saw increasingly greater stress leading to greater effort on the part of human service professionals (up to the point where the person "breaks"), Maslach saw stress leading to greater worker withdrawal. (Pines seems to have taken a middle stance by focusing on the gradual loss of caring in burned-out professionals but by noting too that an initial flight into "workaholism" may be typical of the process.) "Professionals who work intensely with others," noted Maslach in her original article in 1976, "tend to cope with stress by a form of distancing that not only hurts themselves but is damaging to all of us as their human clients" (p. 17). The constant emotional stress of human service work leads to burnout, a condition in which workers "lose all concern, all emotional feeling, for the persons they work with and come to treat them in detached or even dehumanized ways" (p. 17). Maslach noted that burned-out professionals become cynical toward those with whom they work, blaming them for creating their own difficulties or labeling them in derogatory terms; furthermore, burned-out professionals attempt either to withdraw physically from the incessant demands of direct service work (by opting for administrative work) or, if the job situation makes this impossible, to withdraw emotionally and psychologically, for example, by communicating with clients in impersonal or overly formal ways or viewing them in more intellectual terms. Burnout is also marked by the development of a negative self-concept in workers; they come to feel guilty, inadequate, and incompetent and find it difficult to feel good about themselves either at work or at home (Pines, 1983). Their physical health deteriorates and they increasingly complain of sleep disorders, headaches, loss of appetite, nervousness, backaches, and stomachaches. They also experience increased marital and family conflicts as a result of coming home too stressed to interact comfortably with others; many burned-out individuals come home from work not wanting to be with others at all. Most seriously, Maslach and Pines found that burnout is significantly correlated with alcoholism, hopelessness, and suicidal potential.

Like Freudenberger, Maslach and Pines stressed that burnout is most likely to afflict those who start out being the most idealistic and caring. And, like Freudenberger, they took a very sympathetic view toward service providers. Maslach, for example, while acknowledging the criticism that human service work has become impersonal and dehumanizing, noted too that such criticism "fails to take into account the heavy psychological burden that is placed on the providers of such services" (1977, p. 2). "It should be recognized," Maslach wrote in a later paper on the client role in staff burnout, "that clients can dehumanize staff just as staff can dehumanize them" (1978, p. 111). And Pines noted that the "client-centered" orientation of a helping professional leaves too little room for the legitimate expression of the helper's needs and feelings (Pines and Aronson, 1981, p. 52).

What might a burned-out teacher look like from the perspective of Maslach or Pines? Let's go back to the case of Rachel B. The initial scenario was that Rachel B. continued to extend herself as her frustrations in the classroom mounted; she worked harder and became more involved with her students even as she became more embittered and resentful. An alternative script (beginning with the second paragraph) might suggest the following:

She was surprised at how difficult it was to teach—that there were so many distractions, classroom interruptions, behavior problems, and administrative requests—and she found herself becoming increasingly annoyed and frustrated. She knew she was sincerely committed to helping these children and it disturbed her greatly that the children weren't responding to her. She found herself caring less as she continued to feel that she was getting less back from the children than she deserved. She really didn't understand how others continued to work hard in light of the conditions of work and the seemingly limited gratification they received for teaching.

She began to detach herself from the work. If students weren't working, she no longer bothered to figure out why; if students were misbehaving, she attributed the behavior to the lack of adequate parenting and decided that she could do little to remedy what she imagined were years of neglect or abuse. She started distributing a great deal of dittoed material to the entire class and cut back greatly on individualized lessons; she spent increasing amounts of time at her desk, avoiding, when possible, close interaction with the children. She continued to care for a few "favorites" but increasingly resented those who seemed uninterested in school and made only perfunctory attempts to engage them in classroom activities. Although she was dismayed at the thought, she found herself convinced at times that many of the children in her class—and the school—were getting what they deserved. These kids, she thought, do not really care about school, do not care about others, and barely care about themselves. Her impressions of several kids were that they were "unsalvageable" and that the sooner they could be "kicked out" of the classroom the better off everyone would be; she made several referrals to the school psychologist and the Committee on the Handicapped, hoping they would send several of her children to special education classrooms.

She began to complain about her job to her friends, and in describing her daily life in the classroom she resorted to sarcasm and even ridicule. She also complained about frequent headaches and a constant feeling of exhaustion. She felt bad that she wasn't as successful a teacher as she once imagined, but she also felt determined not to define her whole life in terms of her teaching job. Rather than staying in her classroom after 3 P.M. to straighten up or do administrative work, she fled the building immediately. Rather than going home feeling energized by her work, she often went home, drank some wine, and slept; rather than planning for her class at night, she made a point of going out whenever possible. Rather than making it a point to come in even when she was not feeling well, she decided to take her whole allotment of sick days, sometimes calling in sick because she simply didn't feel she could cope well that day. Rather than taking another graduate course in education, she decided—and felt defiant in doing so—to take a film appreciation course. And rather than contemplating whether or not she should return for another year of teaching, she vowed not to come back at all.

Clearly, this is a very different view of teacher burnout. Despite some similarities in symptoms (for example, resentment, disillusionment, anger at students for not performing better) and ultimate outcome (physical and emotional exhaustion), these two views of burnout offer contrasting images of teachers' responses to frustration. And while the proponents of either of these approaches would almost certainly agree with the view that the pattern of burnout is unique for each individual (Mattingly, 1977), it is also true that, in general, the picture of the burned-out professional that Maslach or Pines depicts is harsher, less idealistic, and far more problematic for society. For while Freudenberger sees burned-out individuals as still "conscientious and hard-working" (albeit in a mechanical, cut-off way), both Maslach and Pines see these same individuals as having "nothing left in them to give" (Pines and Aronson, 1981, p. 15) and not giving a damn anymore (Maslach, 1976, p. 16). My view is that while both patterns occur among teachers, it is, unfortunately, the latter picture of burnout that is more typical of teachers in our society.

Cherniss: An Organizational Perspective. Maslach and Pines both contended that job characteristics are prime determinants of an individual's proneness toward burnout. Their research found, for example, that both high client-to-staff ratios and long hours of continuous direct contact with clients are positively correlated with various indices of stress and burnout. This approach to understanding the etiology of burnout—of attempting to link it to specific features of the work environment—was prominently carried forward and widely studied by Cary Cherniss.

Cherniss, influenced by his graduate work with Sarason at Yale, focused on both the nature of organizations and the sociocultural environment in which they function to show how these contextual features may affect a person's response to work. Concomitant with the work of Freudenberger, Maslach, and Pines, Cherniss and his colleagues did research in the mid-1970s on the specific job stresses of "public professionals"—those who provide services requiring a high degree of skill and/or formal training and who work in public institutions. According to Cherniss, the psychological stress inherent in such work is inevitably exacerbated by two factors: social changes that keep the nature of professional roles in flux and "the challenge of existing in a bureaucracy while trying to provide a basic human service" (Cherniss, Egnatios, and Wacker, 1976, p. 430). In regard to the first point, Cherniss wrote that, as society changes its views regarding the "appropriate" degree of authority professionals should assume vis-à-vis their clients, so too must these professionals, particularly new professionals, find a role comfortable for them—one that is neither too distant nor too close and informal. In addition, the vast amount of criticism directed toward virtually all professional groups since the early 1960s can make it more difficult for some individuals to feel good about their work, or to experience the status and prestige they assumed their work would engender. In regard to the second issue, Cherniss noted that in large, bureaucratic public institutions, conflicts between administration and staff are almost inevitable and professional staff members must learn to manipulate the system in order to function effectively. Public school teachers, for example, "must learn how to acquire supplies they need from a system that frequently is stingy and complicated" (1976, p. 430).

Moreover, Cherniss suggested that many individuals' expectations regarding professional work are unrealistic and, therefore, conducive to subsequent feelings of disillusionment and burnout. These individuals believe in a "professional mystique" that assumes that human service work is (1) invariably interesting, (2) a skill one has been well prepared for, (3) performed by sympathetic and compassionate people, (4) flexible and autonomous, (5) conducive to feelings of collegiality, and (6) responded to with feelings of gratitude and appreciation. While some of these assumptions are certainly true for some individuals, they are "not as typical as many people in our society believe" (Cherniss, Egnatios, Wacker, and O'Dowd, 1979, p. 6). More often than not, for example, professionals employed in public service bureaucracies experience low autonomy in their work. Teachers cannot choose their clients (students), cannot refuse administrative or even clerical duties, and cannot, except in the most limited ways, affect educational policy. As Cherniss, Egnatios, Wacker, and O'Dowd (1979) noted, "bureaucracy tends to limit individual autonomy and to resist change, no matter what one's formal credentials and training happen to be" (p. 7). Another example of the way in which expectations are refuted by the actual conditions of work is the assumption of many teachers-in-training that schools foster collegiality, collaboration, and mutual support; in fact, as Sarason (1971) and Lortie (1975), among others, pointed out, teaching tends to be a rather lonely profession, and many teachers have relatively few contacts with adults during the school day.

Like most other workers in the field, Cherniss felt that burnout is essentially caused by a mismatch between what workers feel they are giving and what they feel they are getting in return (1980a, 1980b). This mismatch, he noted, may be catalyzed by two very different situations: an environment in which the individual is overstimulated (for example, a teacher with too many students) or one in which the individual is faced with only limited stimulation and challenge (for example, the teacher who has taught the same grade or subject for years). Burnout begins, Cherniss said, "when the helper experiences stress and strain that cannot be alleviated through active problem solving" (1980b, p. 18).

The symptoms he associates with burnout are similar to those proposed by Freudenberger, Maslach, and Pines. In particular, he noted three patterns of change in professionals that burnout tends to induce: They lose sympathy and tolerance for clients and tend to both "objectify" them and blame them for their own difficulties (Ryan, 1971); they lose their own sense of idealism and optimism regarding change; and they increasingly look outside their work to find fulfillment in their lives. And much as Maslach posited that the three factors included in the burnout phenomenon (emotional exhaustion, depersonalization, and lack of personal accomplishment) are independent and cannot be summed to produce one central burnout score, Cherniss felt that the three patterns he has identified do not necessarily co-occur. They simply represent three possible responses to stressful, frustrating, or monotonous work in a helping profession. On the other hand, Cherniss and Krantz (1983) disagree—as I do—with Freudenberger's view that burnout is a disease of overcommitment. Instead, they suggest that burnout is caused by "the loss of commitment and moral purpose in work" and that, therefore, the advice to reduce one's commitment to work as a means of ameliorating symptoms of stress or burnout "is not only wrong, it probably increases the potential for burnout" (pp. 198–199). Indeed, it is Cherniss's contention that committing oneself to a cause or a formal ideology may go a long way toward preventing burnout.

What might a burned-out teacher look like from Cherniss's perspective? Again, we go back to Rachel B., beginning with the second paragraph:

She was surprised at first at how difficult it was to teach—that there were so many distractions, classroom interruptions, behavior problems, and administrative requests. She had majored in education and spent two semesters in a classroom as a student teacher, and so she didn't expect to feel unprepared or inadequate. She did feel competent in preparing lessons and working directly with the children but felt as if she had very little sense of how to organize a classroom— her experience was in working in classrooms that were already functioning and well established. Moreover, she felt entirely unskilled in terms of dealing with the adults around her—no one had taught her how to deal effectively with administrators nor how to talk to parents. Her supervisor was not particularly interested in discussing these "political issues" but preferred instead to focus on lesson plans, curriculum ideas, and classroom design (bulletin boards, seating plans, decoration). She felt that all his advice was well intentioned and that much of it, in fact, was quite helpful. What was discouraging, though, was the constant sense of intrusion into her classroom: the supervisor going over her lesson plans, the administration deciding on the books she was to use, the principal's decision on how her children were to walk down the halls of the school, the new kids who were assigned to her already overcrowded classroom, the monitors coming in with notices and announcements several times a day, the incessant forms she was required to fill out. Somehow she was oblivious to these aspects of a teacher's work while she was student teaching.

Another phenomenon she had been oblivious to was the limited time available to her to get to know other teachers. Over time, she became acquainted with them all, of course, and liked many of them; in turn, she felt as if she gained their respect as a caring, motivated, well-prepared teacher. But during the school day the only real opportunities to socialize, or learn from others, were during her "prep" (preparation period) and during lunch. Like most other teachers in her school, she ended up spending her prep periods by herself, often in her classroom, either preparing lessons or filling out some form or another. And while lunch was pleasant and friendly, again it didn't meet her needs or expectations of a community of mutually supportive professionals. Even dismissal surprised her a bit— she hadn't realized how many teachers were as anxious as most of the children to leave the school immediately after 3.

Initially, she responded to these surprises and disappointments by taking solace in the fact that her work, at least the actual classroom work with the students, was gratifying and challenging. Unfortunately, by the end of her first year, these feelings began to erode. Students she first saw as challenging she now perceived as threatening and resistant; gratifications seemed greatly outweighed by disappointments and frustrations. Lesson plans, once seen as an opportunity to be creative, now became an oppressive, routinized, only marginally useful task. She felt that both her students and administration had taken advantage of her good nature and willingness to give. The "good" kids in her class—and there were many—appreciated and liked her, but it wasn't enough; overall, she felt unappreciated by too many of the kids and virtually all the parents. Although the administration seemed to like her work, she felt she was being paid lip service; she was appreciated by them because she was a hardworking teacher who didn't cause them any trouble. Even her friends and family generally failed to appreciate how difficult teaching was and how much it took out of her to do a good job.

She began withdrawing from the work—giving less, planning less, and feeling less as if she could make a difference. The more she withdrew, the fewer gratifications she derived from the work, the fewer moments there were of feeling fulfilled as a teacher. And though intellectually she knew that as her investment in the work decreased so would the satisfactions, she was willing to pay the price and forgo additional rewards. During her second year, these feelings turned to despair, and she began to disparage the children as well as herself for having decided to become a teacher. Despite finding other sources of satisfaction in her life, she could no longer tolerate waking up each morning to face another day at school. She made up her mind to leave teaching but to try to stay in education at some administrative level. Even this decision, though, was fraught with self-deprecation. She wished she could leave education entirely but felt that she had no other marketable skills or ability.

Cherniss suggested that there are sources of burnout at the individual, organizational, and societal levels. By examining the interaction of individual helpers' expectations and goals (their ideal notions of the helping relationship), the institutional constraints of working in and for large bureaucracies, and the public's perceptions of the nature of such work (the "professional mystique" that many professionals accept), Cherniss developed an unusually comprehensive model of burnout.

Sarason and Others: Social and Historical Perspectives. One of the common elements of all the views noted above is the notion that social conditions may influence the occurrence of burnout. This theme—that the possibility of finding fulfillment in one's work is necessarily determined, at least in part, by the traditions, values, and history of a given society—is one that has been explored most fully by Seymour Sarason at Yale University. As Sarason noted, "burnout is never a characteristic of or within an individual but rather, it is a complex of psychological characteristics that reflect features of the larger society" (1983, p. vii).

While many others in the middle and late 1970s were investigating the issue of burnout per se, Sarason's work at that time was more broadly focused on the work-related consequences of rapid social change following World War II. According to Sarason, the aftermath of the war precipitated an era of general optimism based on the dual perceptions of unlimited national resources and unlimited individual potential. It was a time of rapidly rising expectations, of hopes for economic success, social mobility, and personal growth. At the same time, this new emphasis on individual needs helped establish a mythology of the individual as separate from the community and unneedful of a network of mutually supportive, self-validating relationships. The value of a "psychological sense of community" in mitigating the impact of stress and loneliness at work was overlooked by individuals in their choice of a career and a work setting. It was only *after* dissatisfaction with work had set in that individuals began to recognize its importance. "After a person becomes aware that he cannot continue to make a strong commitment to work, that an impersonal society has rendered him impotent and dependent and has frustrated the desire for personal growth, the resulting alienation and loneliness bring to the fore the absence and need for a sense of community" (Sarason, 1977, p. 287). This need, argues Sarason, is central to the positive experience of work and has become ever stronger as "the centrifugal forces in our society have whirled with increasing speed" (p. 283).

Sarason (1981) also strongly emphasized considering the history of the human services movement in this country as a means of understanding the current condition of individuals working in the field. He (as well as Levine and Levine, 1970) noted that when the human services became a profession for the first time in the 1920s, the small number of individuals involved in this work (mostly social workers) were a close-knit group, possessed of a common missionary zeal to help others. They had "the word," they had each other, and, for the most part, they were unconstrained by governmental regulations or bureaucracy. They understood the disparity between what they wanted to do, what needed to be done, and their ability to do it; according to Sarason, they were in no way burned out. In the 1930s, as a result of the Depression, government unwillingly had to get into the business of supporting people. It was a decade when social work became important, and government projects and programs proliferated. Still, there was no burnout; human service workers still keenly felt a sense of opportunity and a sense of mission.

The experience of such work began to change dramatically, however, following World War II, as the relationship between the government and human service workers grew closer. Although this connection was initially pursued enthusiastically by professional groups as a way of expanding their influence, it was not without its unintended consequences. Human service work, noted Sarason, became professionalized, bureaucratized, credentialized, and isolated. A growing sense of professionalism served to increase the distance between the helpers and the helped. Furthermore, an increasing demand for services coupled with government support for these services created a widely held perception that the human services could solve all of society's problems. The stage was now set for burnout: Large numbers of relatively isolated human service workers with great expectations and little autonomy worked as part of an impersonal, bureaucratized system of organizations and agencies where policies over which they had no control were formulated. As government interference increased (more paperwork, more cases, more agencies, more levels of bureaucracy), and as clients became needier and more entitled, the possibility for finding fulfillment in human service work grew markedly dimmer.

Drawing upon Sarason's work, as well as that of Lasch (1979), Packard (1972), Slater (1976), and Yankelovich (1981), I attempted in an earlier work (Farber, 1983) to link the emergence of the burnout phenomenon to changes in family, work, and social structures that have occurred in post–World War II American society. These changes include the following: a shifting emphasis from production of commodities to consumption; the growth of large organizations and bureaucracies; urban renewal and flights to suburbia; frequent mobility of families and industry; a rising divorce rate; and increasingly transient, impersonal, and disconnected social relationships. In turn, our culture has fostered the development of substantial numbers of narcissistic, self-absorbed, manipulative individuals who demand immediate gratification but who live "in a state of restless, perpetually unsatisfied desire" (Lasch, 1979, p. 23). Such individuals are indifferent to community events, are reluctant to become involved in others' lives, exhibit an uncertain sense of self, and experience a resolve to "live for the moment" (Packard, 1972).

As I pointed out, individualism not only leads to general feelings of alienation and disconnectedness but also, by its very nature, impedes the formation of a psychological sense of community or even collegial support systems, either of which can mitigate stress and prevent burnout. In addition, as a result of social fragmentation and uprootedness, each opportunity for gratification and fulfillment grows increasingly important to individuals. Work, then, especially work that holds the promise of a "noble calling," is invested with great meaning and expectations. The combination of these trends has produced workers with higher expectations of fulfillment and fewer resources to cope with frustrations—a perfect recipe for burnout. Moreover, economic conditions in our society have made career shifts increasingly difficult. Burned-out professionals, particularly those with many years of experience, may find few, if any, economically comparable opportunities in other fields. Thus, they may feel "stuck" and increasingly resentful at remaining in their present jobs. Their sense of frustration grows, and feelings of burnout increase.

What emerges from these perspectives is a clear indication that social and economic conditions—including broad, pervasive social changes, changes in the circumstances under which a particular occupational group functions, and changes in the way that society views the status, domain, and authority of a particular profession—exert a strong, if sometimes unarticulated, influence upon workers that affects their perceptions of work and their propensity toward stress and burnout.

How might the case of Rachel B. be viewed from this perspective? Again, beginning from the second paragraph:

She was surprised at first at how difficult it was to teach—that there were so many distractions, classroom interruptions, behavior problems, and administrative requests—but vowed to do whatever it took to become an outstanding teacher. In truth, this was a difficult time for her and she was glad for the opportunity to devote herself to a cause she believed in. She was not teaching in the town in which she attended college but rather in another part of the city in which she grew up. Many of her college friends were either still on campus or working near the college town; some were in Europe or traveling cross-country, taking a year or two off before making further career decisions. Some of her old friends from the neighborhood were still around, but she didn't feel as close to them and didn't have much desire to get together with them. She was single and enjoyed dating but didn't enjoy the ways in which people were now meeting each other in the city. Instead of going to bars or joining singles' clubs, she stayed home, and instead of visiting her parents' house and feeling as if she were always getting in the middle of their marital difficulties, she stayed home. Of course, she'd call her best friends at least once a week, get together with her parents or old friends sometimes, and occasionally go out with a man someone had introduced her to, but, in truth, she didn't feel very attached to anyone in her life.

What was somewhat surprising and aggravating too was how little support she got from all these people for her career choice. No one seemed to understand why someone "as bright as you are" would go into teaching. "Why do you want to do it?" they'd all challenge. "Isn't the pay lousy? Won't you get burned out?" She vacillated between feeling defensive and wondering whether they might be right. She was a quite competent and personable young woman with a number of artistic skills, but at this time in her life being a good teacher was central to her sense of identity. She decided teaching was the right thing for her, at least for now, and so most of her time was spent at school, planning for her class, and taking graduate education courses.

Unfortunately, she found it difficult to experience an emerging sense of professionalism at school. The administrative staff hardly treated her in a professional manner, often ignoring her needs for supplies, saddling her with piddling requests and duties, and providing little help for the problems she encountered in her classroom. Parents, when they came in at all, seemed to want only to complain about what she hadn't done; rarely, if ever, did they compliment or thank her for her efforts. And while she genuinely enjoyed teaching many of the children, she was also outraged at times by the lack of respect shown her by some of them. She wouldn't have dreamed of talking to her teachers the way some of her children (or their parents) talked to her. Most disconcerting, however, was the attitude of many of her colleagues, who seemed uncaring and unmotivated; they seemed to do only what was absolutely necessary and even those tasks were performed in a perfunctory, mechanical manner. The prevailing attitude seemed to be "punch in, do what's required, punch out, collect a paycheck." *Somber* and *gray* were the words she used to describe the atmosphere of her school.

She felt as if her enthusiasm and motivation were looked at in a bemused, somewhat condescending fashion by many of the older teachers. When someone in the teachers' room commented on how hard she was working, someone else was sure to reply, "She'll learn." No one—not the children, not the parents, not her fellow teachers, not the administrative staff, not the board of education—seemed to care very much or believe anymore that education was really going to make a difference. She felt a long way from her college classes, where they used to argue the merits of different teaching methods and curriculum materials and reading programs, and where everyone seemed to have a resolute belief in the value of good teaching. Here, the feeling was, "It doesn't matter." Or, more accurately, it matters very little what books one chooses, what methods one uses, what materials are available. She hated them all for giving up but, in fact, she felt she would give up soon, too.

What this perspective emphasizes, then, is how difficult it is to maintain a commitment to human service work when social conditions fail to provide a context conducive to personal concern for others. One cannot be expected to sustain one's ideals in a vacuum. In a system where everyone else—clients, colleagues, administrative staff, workers down the block, and friends around the corner—seem to be "in it for themselves," the decision to distance oneself from clients and to relinquish one's sense of caring may be painful but also necessary to maintain a sense of equilibrium.

A Definition of Burnout

Burnout is a work-related syndrome that stems from an individual's perception of a significant discrepancy between effort (input) and reward (output), this perception being influenced by individual, organizational, and social factors. It occurs most often in those who work face to face with troubled or needy clients and is typically marked by withdrawal from and cynicism toward clients, emotional and physical exhaustion, and various psychological symptoms, such as irritability, anxiety, sadness, and lowered self-esteem.

Inconsequentiality: The Critical Component. None of the four perspectives discussed above is, of course, the "right" one. Most burned-out professionals embody some elements of each of these views. However, one of the common assumptions of virtually all views of burnout is that this state is essentially triggered by feelings of "inconsequentiality"—a sense on the part of professionals that their efforts to help others have been ineffective, that the task is endless, and that the personal payoffs for their work (in terms of accomplishment, recognition, advancement, or appreciation) have not been forthcoming (Farber, 1983). Their work—and by extension, they themselves—have simply not mattered. For teachers, this sense of inconsequentiality lies in the lack of student responsiveness to their efforts. Human service workers, indeed, all workers, need to feel competent and effective in their work. We are all driven by what Robert White (1959) has called "effectance motivation," and we seek situations that allow us to feel that we are the cause of observable, positive outcomes. This need to feel effective and special is also related to what a prominent psychoanalyst has called "healthy narcissism" (Kohut, 1971), a trait that enables us to realize our basic ambitions in life (our "nuclear program"). For most human service professionals, this nuclear program includes the need to help others and to feel helpful in the process. Deprived of the opportunity to realize these goals, workers suffer from a loss of self-esteem and feel inconsequential, burned out.

A particularly well-articulated model of burnout encompassing this point of view was developed by Heifetz and Bersani (1983). "It is not the heavy emotional investment per se that drains the provider; rather, it is an investment that has insufficient dividends" (p. 58). Their particular model emphasized two key needs of professionals: a need to promote growth in others and a need to grow personally on the job. When feedback from the system fails to produce evidence of progress in either area (often because the service provider has not established realistic, short-term goals), most professionals withdraw from work—"attempts to render service have been extinguished" (p. 58). I concur with their views, particularly in regard to their sense that most professionals react to the lack of positive feedback in their work by working *less* hard. (Freudenberger would posit that burned-out workers are distinguished by virtue of their working harder in response to frustration.)

This sense of inconsequentiality in burned-out professionals is similar to Seligman's (1975) notion of "learned helplessness." Both concepts refer to a state in which individuals feel that their actions can no longer effect desired changes in the environment and, therefore, there is no point in continuing to try; both concepts also posit cognitive and emotional consequences of the condition, namely, hopelessness regarding the future, depressed affect, lowered self-esteem, and self-blame. In Seligman's original experimental paradigm, a dog who initially could not escape a mild electric shock would not attempt to escape later even when conditions were changed so that it was now able to do so. The dog had been conditioned to "believe" that his actions would not make a difference in changing his condition. A teacher who feels her work-related behaviors are inconsequential asks herself, "Why should I spend three hours at home lesson-planning for my class when one hour (or no time spent at all) will produce the same disappointing results?" Many teachers feel that the job is well beyond their (or the school's) capabilities.

Parameters of the Burnout Syndrome. At times *burnout* has been used in a very broad sense to describe feelings that may occur in almost any setting. Freudenberger (1980) referred to people burning out in relationships, Edelwich and Brodsky (1980) discussed burnout in artists and lovers, and Chance (1981) extended the concept to include runners. Other researchers, however, have supported a narrower definition of the term, applying it (as I have above) only to workers in the helping profession. Pines and Aronson (1981), for example, distinguished between burnout and "tedium," a similar constellation of feelings that affects workers in nonhuman service jobs. Restricting the definition of *burnout* to human service workers acknowledges the unique pressures of utilizing oneself as the "tool" in face-to-face work with needy and demanding clients.

Criticisms of the Burnout Concept

In reaction to the frequent use of the term in everyday speech, the concept of burnout has been criticized in the popular press as a convenient explanation of individual malaise or lack of will. Paul Quinnett (1981), writing in the *New York Times,* contended that "we have stumbled upon a worthy and thoroughly modern concept with which to label our discontent. . . . [It] covers our personal failures much better than ordinary forms of irresponsibility to ourselves and others. It gives us, as I see it, the perfect out" (p. A23). Similarly, Lance Morrow (1981), in *Time,* viewed burnout as a peculiarly American "hypochondria of the spirit," arguing that labeling oneself as burned out provides an easy escape from life's pressures. "The idea contains a sneaking self-aggrandizement tied to an elusive self-exoneration" (p. 84). William Safire (1982) felt that the term had become so overused that "the locution is now undergoing linguistic burnout" (p. 16). In short, there are those who see burnout simply as a currently acceptable excuse for failure and who question whether the invocation of "burnout" as a description of behavior has any diagnostic, predictive, or therapeutic value.

There are also those who feel that the methodologies employed for studying stress and burnout have been entirely inadequate. For example, the Maslach Burnout Inventory has often been criticized for confusing cause and effect—that is, including items that describe both stressors ("I feel recipients blame me for some of their problems") and symptoms ("I've become more callous toward people since I took this job"). Others have suggested that all survey methods "fail to take into account the fact that different teachers may interpret the meaning of the questions differently, that their responses may be affected by ego-defensive processes, and that teachers may genuinely lack insight into their situation" (Kyriacou and Sutcliffe, 1977, p. 305). In addition, much of the research on teacher stress and burnout has failed to include physiological measures, even though physical symptoms are invariably regarded as an important component of these disorders.

Differences Between Burnout and Other Concepts

In psychological circles, it has often been noted that the symptoms of burnout overlap with those of depression: feelings of hopelessness, helplessness, emptiness, and sadness; psychosomatic complaints; and neurovegetative signs (sleeping and eating disturbances, lack of energy, loss of sexual drive). In fact, as Meier (1984) noted, "depression has been listed as a symptom of burnout . . . as

the final state of burnout . . . and, as a synonym for burnout"
(pp. 212–213). The results of Meier's own research are equivocal: He
states that his data support the notion of burnout as a separate
construct (in relation to depression and a neutral trait, that of
"orderliness"), but he also notes a "substantial relationship" between burnout and depression. He concludes, "It is quite likely that
measures of burnout would show moderate to high correlations
with any other measures of so-called negative emotional states. . . .
Burnout and depression, which may be experienced by many individuals as similar [feeling] states, may . . . have different aetiolo-
gies" (p. 217). Freudenberger (1980) goes even further, suggesting
that symptoms of the two are distinct. He contends that depression
is most often accompanied by guilt, whereas burnout generally occurs in the context of conscious anger. I have suggested too (Farber,
1983) that the symptoms of burnout, at least initially, tend to be
situation-specific rather than pervasive. In other words, a person
may be burned out in one sphere of his or her life and functioning
quite well in another. In classic depression, on the other hand, a
person's symptoms tend to be manifest across all situations. It
should be noted, though, that burnout, if left unchecked, will invariably affect nonwork situations. For example, a husband who
feels burned out from work is likely to have less energy and sympathy for his wife and children; nevertheless, that same husband
may be generally more optimistic and future-oriented than the person suffering from depression.

Burnout has also been confused with the notion of "worker
alienation." Whereas some authors prefer to reserve the term *burnout* for those who work in human service jobs and *worker alienation* for those who work in industry, others, including Karger (1981)
and Dworkin (1987), suggest that these are virtually the same phenomenon: a cluster of anomic symptoms arising out of a dehumanizing process that affects workers in both industrial and human
service settings. Cherniss takes the position that worker alienation—the process of withdrawing one's energy from work and investing it elsewhere—is one of the *results* of burnout.

Is *burnout* no more than a current word for what used to be
referred to in the political science literature as worker alienation?
Marxist theory suggests that people are invariably alienated from

their work (and, thus, their essential natures) in any but a communist state. This alienation, he thought, was the result of several divisions: the division of people from products they make but cannot distribute, the division of people from each other as a result of class antagonisms, and the division of people from their work as a source of personal identity. In 1844, Marx described worker alienation in a manner foreshadowing current descriptions of burnout: "[Because] labor is external to the worker . . . he does not affirm himself but denies himself, does not feel content but unhappy, does not develop freely his physical and mental energy but mortifies his body and ruins his mind. The worker therefore only feels himself outside his work, and in his work feels outside himself" (cited in Ollman, 1971, p. 136). In terms of a Marxist model, professional dissatisfaction and burnout can be viewed as reactions to the fragmentation of work, to competition within the workplace, and to the loss of worker autonomy. As Dworkin (1987) pointed out, teachers are not directly involved in setting policy that determines the nature of their labor. Furthermore, as Sakharov and Farber (1983) noted, teacher burnout may be considered expectable in a society that continues to devalue women and withhold necessary resources from children, especially minority children.

Nevertheless, although insights into the impact of capitalism on the experience of work can prove useful in understanding burnout in the helping professions, a class analysis of the role of professional workers is inadequate in and of itself. Human service work is, in many ways, unique and does not fit neatly into Marxist doctrine. First and foremost, human service professionals are exceptional in that they *are* their own tools and means of production. In this sense, they are entirely unalienated, and their work, activity, and source of creativity largely overlap. Their work is not external to them but rather perceived as "ego syntonic" (consistent with their self-images and life plan). Their work affords them the opportunity to experience directly the satisfaction of seeing it make a difference. Gratification at work—in the form of promoting growth and change or achieving a sense of intimate involvement in the lives of clients—is an unpredictable yet profoundly moving experience for human service professionals. Satisfaction and fulfillment may occur suddenly in the midst of an otherwise chaotic day and may provide instant affirmation of the wisdom of one's career choice. A teacher who is feeling burned out may be suddenly heartened by a sense of having finally reached a difficult child or may become rejuvenated through the successful completion of a class activity. Feeling that one has made a significant difference in the life of another human being is at the heart of human service work, and such moments can provide an emotional fix that may carry the physician, psychotherapist, or teacher through months of doubts or disillusionment. Thus, being one's own tool and means of production creates opportunities for fulfillment that are largely unavailable to those who do not work directly with others. And while this situation can also leave professionals vulnerable to significant doubts in regard to competency, power, and control, these issues, although of critical significance to an individual's experience of work, are largely unrelated to Marxist thought (Cherniss, 1980b). Worker alienation, then, is an inexact synonym for professional burnout. Though it includes similar elements of disillusionment and despair and though, like burnout, it is a by-product of social conditions, its exclusive focus on socioeconomic determinism fails to address those particular tensions in the helper-helpee relationship that help define burnout.

Finally, it should be noted that both the popular press and the professional literature have often confused or equated "stress" with "burnout." Though these two concepts are similar, they are not identical. Burnout is more often the result not of stress per se (which may well be inevitable in the helping professions) but of *unmediated stress*—of being stressed and having no "out," no buffers, no support system (Farber, 1984b). What is often overlooked is that stress can have both positive and negative effects—a fact that Selye (1956) noted over thirty years ago. Stress occurs when there is a substantial imbalance (perceived or real) between environmental demands and the response capability of the individual. As environmental demands increase or an individual's response capability decreases, the likelihood of stress becoming a negative experience—and ultimately effecting a burned-out state—becomes more probable.

It is no wonder though that these two concepts become confused. In several theories, certain stress reactions are referred to in terms that are quite similar to those used to describe burnout. Hackman (1970) noted four general types of strategy for coping with stress: (1) explicit movement against the stressful situation, for example, aggression, attack, or hostility; (2) movement away from the source of stress, such as avoidance, withdrawal, resignation, inaction, or escape; (3) submission, or collaborative movement toward the source of stress, such as ingratiation or undue cooperation; and (4) distortion of the situation through traditional psychological mechanisms such as denial, displacement, reaction formation, or intellectualization. In this context, burnout may be seen as the final step in the progression from active problem solving to submission and distortion (strategies three and four, above) to anger and depletion (strategies one and two, above). When earlier steps in this progression fail to alleviate stress, more severe reactions (such as those seen commonly as part of the burnout syndrome) become manifest. In a similar vein, Lazarus (1966) noted that efforts to reduce stress can take the form of active problem solving (for example, increased information seeking), psychological defense, or withdrawal. And Selye (1956, 1976) proposed a stage theory of stress which he terms the "General Adaptation Syndrome." In stage one, "alarm reaction," the body mobilizes forces to defend itself against stress; in stage two, "resistance," a person is able to function in what appears to be a normal fashion; but in stage three, "exhaustion," the cumulative effects of damaging stress have become too severe to allow for adaptation. The symptoms in this last stage are, again, similar in many respects to those of burnout.

Perhaps nowhere is the confusion between stress and burnout more evident than in the literature on teachers. Too often these articles treat teacher stress and burnout as if they were interchangeable terms or attempt to explain burnout simply by enumerating all of the many stressors teachers encounter. The first error is perhaps motivated by the desire for data: Since there is a relative paucity of hard data on teacher burnout, data on sources of teacher stress are substituted. Behind the second error lies the implicit and erroneous assumption that a stressed teacher inevitably becomes a burned-out teacher. Ignored in either form of this confusion is the myriad number of variables that mediate between stressful environmental conditions and the subjective perception of being burned out. These include, for example, constitutional vulnerability to stress; cognitive appraisal of stressful events (how one thinks about and makes sense of noxious environmental events); personality type; other life events; and knowledge and availability of coping mechanisms, including social support. These factors explain why there is considerable variation in the ways that individuals react to identical or nearly identical stressful situations.

Popular accounts of teacher burnout, however, have opted not to explain the process of burnout but rather to simply list its most observable and immediate precipitants, implicitly attributing teacher burnout in urban schools, for example, to the presence of disruptive students. While in some sense this is not entirely inaccurate, it is rather akin to explaining World War I by referring to the assassination of Archduke Ferdinand while omitting discussion of the entire social, historical, and political context within which this event was embedded. In short, the assumption that stress necessarily leads to burnout is simplistic and misleading. Burnout is better regarded as the final step in a progression of unsuccessful attempts to cope with a variety of negative stress conditions.

Nevertheless, while stress and burnout are theoretically distinct phenomena, in the absence of empirical data or extensive observational reports they are *practically* difficult to distinguish. Indeed, there is a good deal of overlap. Brown (1985), for example, used the two most common measures of each of these variables— the Teaching Events Stress Inventory (Cichon and Koff, 1980) and the Maslach Burnout Inventory (MBI)—in order to study the statistical relationship between job stress and burnout in teachers. She found that teacher perceptions of stress were significantly correlated with both the emotional exhaustion subscale and the depersonalization scale of the MBI. Thus, the boundaries between these two concepts cannot be made with any degree of practical certainty, and it is quite likely that on the way to becoming burned out, individuals experience intense stress. For all these reasons—because chronic stress is typically a less severe variant of burnout, because it may, if left unchecked, progress to the end state of burnout, and because both are clearly debilitating on both a personal and professional level—this book will deal with both phenomena in discussing the plight of teachers in this country.

The Course of Burnout

Viewing burnout as a final step implies that burnout is a process, not an event, and does not usually occur in reaction to a specific, identifiable precipitant. Instead, "it emerges gradually over a period of time in response to low intensity ongoing events" (Savicki and Cooley, 1983). But just as the determination of whether or not a worker is burned out is not easily made (because there is no common definition, and, relatedly, because the specific symptoms of burnout are unique to each person), the designation of a typical sequence of burnout is also made with great uncertainty. The process of burnout, as well as its pattern, varies considerably across individuals. Furthermore, as Cherniss (1980b) suggested, "Burnout is not necessarily total or permanent. Job stress need not lead to severe strain. Even if it does, this strain need not lead to burnout. Finally, even if strain produces some of the changes associated with burnout, the changes may be mild and temporary" (p. 20).

The process of burnout is not inexorable; nevertheless, halting the process once it begins may be difficult. Burnout tends to be self-perpetuating inasmuch as exhaustion and withdrawal lead almost inevitably to even less success, which, in turn, leads to even greater withdrawal, ad infinitum. Switching to a new teaching situation, or finding new sources of social support, or committing oneself to learning a new curriculum module may all serve to halt the downward spiral—but none of these comes easily once discouragement and resentment set in.

There are three prominent models that describe the progressive course of burnout; none is especially comprehensive or entirely satisfactory. Edelwich and Brodsky's (1980) has been most widely cited. It specifies four stages in the burnout process: enthusiasm (high hopes, high energy, unrealistic expectations); stagnation (still doing the job but putting greater emphasis on one's personal needs); frustration (feeling ineffective, resenting others, and beginning to experience emotional, physical, and behavioral problems); and apathy (doing the minimum work required, avoiding challenges). Edelwich and Brodsky note that no sharp line can be drawn between the stages of stagnation and frustration; nevertheless, my

experience in working with burned-out teachers (as well as the
views of most of those writing on the topic) suggests that, more
often than not, frustration precedes that loss of momentum and
hope that they term stagnation. In addition, the lack of empirical
support of this model and its least-common-denominator approach
limit its usefulness for understanding the process of burnout in any
one professional group.

Spaniol and Caputo (1979) looked at the process of burnout
by focusing on the nature and intensity of symptoms, likening each
stage in the process to a different degree of burn trauma. According
to their model, the symptoms of first-degree burnout (irritability,
worry, frustration) are transient and easily reversible; second-degree
symptoms (exhaustion, cynicism, concern over one's effectiveness,
fluctuations in mood) are more regular, enduring, and difficult to
overcome; and third-degree symptoms (psychological and physical
problems such as reduced self-esteem, withdrawal from work and
interpersonal contact, headaches, digestive problems, consideration
of leaving work) are pervasive, intense, and difficult to treat. Like
the model of Edelwich and Brodsky, this perspective offers a com-
monsense notion of burnout as a progressively more pernicious set
of stress-related symptoms; the problem is that it isolates these
symptoms, failing to consider the intrapsychic, interpersonal, and
social context in which they originate and develop.

Finally, Golembiewski, Munzenrider, and Carter (1983) and
Golembiewski and Munzenrider (1984) used the three factors on the
Maslach Burnout Inventory (MBI) to advance an empirically derived phase model of burnout, arguing that depersonalization invariably occurs first, followed by diminished personal accomplishment, and then by emotional exhaustion. My acceptance of the
validity of their model for human service professionals is tempered
by the fact that their research was conducted with workers in a
commercial company (a product line division of a multinational
firm), that they modified the item composition of some of Maslach's
original factors, and that their treatment of MBI scores (dichoto-
mizing scores on each factor into high or low) resulted in a far too
crude categorization system. Moreover, their hypothesis that burnout begins with feelings of depersonalization is contrary to my sense
that in human service professionals, particularly teachers, burnout

begins with and is most prominently marked by feelings of incon-sequentiality (lack of personal accomplishment). My own work with teachers strongly suggests that depersonalization (treating clients callously, feeling hardened emotionally) and emotional ex-haustion *follow* the perception of personal ineffectiveness and lack of accomplishment.

On the whole, then, my understanding of the course of teacher burnout is based on a modified version of Edelwich and Brodsky's model. The general process, I believe, takes the following form: (1) Enthusiasm and dedication give way to (2) frustration and anger in response to personal, work-related, and societal stressors, which, in turn, engender (3) a sense of inconsequentiality, which leads to (4) withdrawal of commitment and then to (5) increased personal vulnerability with multiple physical (headaches, hyperten-sion, and so on), cognitive ("they're to blame"; "I need to take care of myself"), and emotional (irritability, sadness) symptoms, which, unless dealt with, (6) escalate until a sense of depletion and loss of caring occurs.

Ordinarily, teachers begin their work with enthusiasm and dedication, with a sense that their work is socially meaningful and will yield great personal satisfactions. The inevitable difficulties of teaching (the specifics of which will be noted in the following chap-ter) interact with personal issues and vulnerabilities, as well as so-cial pressures and values, to engender a sense of frustration and force a reassessment of the possibilities of the job and the investment one wants to make in it. The task (educating the children) seems overwhelming and one's efforts insignificant, virtually useless. With less investment in the work, fewer rewards accrue and greater withdrawal occurs; one attempts to balance investment in work with the perception of available rewards. The demands of teaching begin to feel more debilitating, the distractions more annoying, the classroom disturbances more aggravating, the pupils less caring, the parents more demanding, the administrators less sensitive, and the colleagues less supportive. Caring fades; energy is depleted; at-tempts to recruit support grow more infrequent and haphazard. Anger comes easily; patience becomes a scarce commodity. The children, once perceived as innocent victims, are now viewed as spoiled, or undersocialized, or lacking in values. Their needs, even when seen as legitimate, are no longer of greater priority than one's own. Headaches, backaches, and stomachaches abound and are resentfully attributed to the job; too often they're treated with alcohol or inappropriate drugs. Absences increase and are viewed as "mental health days." Increasingly, one thinks of quitting; the idea of spending one's whole life in a classroom becomes intolerable. The job has become devoid of its original meaning; ultimately, paychecks alone serve as motivation to come to work. Burnout is now apparent to others and even personally acknowledged—but where to go and what to do are difficult issues, and so preparations to teach another day are resignedly and perfunctorily undertaken.

2

Sources of
Teacher Stress and Burnout

CHAPTER ONE PROVIDED AN OVERVIEW OF THE BURNOUT SYN-
drome. In the present chapter, the focus is on two specific aspects
of teacher stress and burnout: the prevalence rates of these conditions in different groups of teachers and their sources at individual
and work-related levels.

Prevalence Rates of Burnout, Stress, and Dissatisfaction

What Proportion of Teachers Are Burned Out? It is more
than likely that teacher burnout has always been around, masquer-
ading in the past under names such as job dissatisfaction and
demoralization. Close to sixty years ago, Waller (1932) described
how community pressure, the need for constant vigilance to control
large numbers of students in classes, and loneliness and isolation
could combine to lower a teacher's morale. More recently, many of
the critics of education in the 1960s—Kozol and Holt, for example—
took fellow teachers to task for their presumed lack of concern for
students.

Stress and burnout in teachers, then, are not new phenomena. What is new, though, is the extent to which at least some
teachers claim a defiant notoriety in declaring just how stressed or
burned out they feel. Teachers are, in effect, saying to one another:

"You think *you're* burned out . . ." The problem here is one that Edelwich and Brodsky (1980) aptly termed "staff infection." When enough teachers in a school spend their lunch hours denigrating students, complaining about administrators, regretting their choice of careers, and planning for new ones, burnout begins to feel less like a shameful emotion and more like a battle wound worthy of showing off.

What may also be new is the magnitude of the teacher burn-out phenomenon. Teacher burnout has become a widely publicized issue and its causes and symptoms are well known to virtually every teacher. Compared to several decades ago, it is now far easier for a teacher to identify with this problem and to attend to and label previously ignored symptoms. As with every disease or disorder throughout history, publicity greatly increases the numbers of those who believe they are victims. In addition, as I will argue in the next chapter, attitudes toward teachers have changed dramatically in the last twenty to thirty years, leaving them far more vulnerable to the impact of work-related pressures.

There is no way of comparing the percentages of teachers burned out twenty or fifty years ago with the number burned out today. We do know, however, from surveys conducted by the National Education Association, that the percentage of teachers reporting considerable *stress* in their work has increased dramatically over a forty-year period: from 37.5 percent in 1938 and 43 percent in 1951 to 78 percent in 1967 and 1976 (Holt, Fine, and Tollefson, 1987). Moreover, it is clear that a determination of the seriousness of the current teacher burnout problem is a direct function of the way we choose to operationally define the term. For example, *Learning* magazine, by leaving the term *burnout* undefined and by simply asking teachers to state whether they had experienced feelings of burnout, found that 93 percent of respondents to their survey had experienced such feelings. Similarly, the results of my study (Farber, 1984b) could be interpreted to mean that 77 percent of urban teachers and 70 percent of suburban teachers are burned out. These figures represent the percentages of teachers who responded with any answer other than "never" when asked the extent to which they had experienced burnout during the preceding month. It should be clear that feeling burned out "rarely" during a given month (one of the response options on the measure I used) should not define a teacher as burned out. The point is that whatever percentage we derive is neither inherently right nor wrong, because there is no agreed-upon definition of what constitutes teacher burnout. The Maslach Burnout Inventory, which is most often used, specifically advises against combining the three subscale scores into a single measure of burnout. "Burnout . . . is not viewed as a dichotomous variable, which is either present or absent" (Maslach and Jackson, 1986, p. 2). Nevertheless, at least one study (Belcastro and Hays, 1984) has utilized the MBI to derive a percentage of burned-out teachers. By considering a teacher burned out if his or her scores on each of the three subscales exceeded Maslach and Jackson's mean scores for all human service professionals, Belcastro and Hays identified 20 percent of the teachers in their sample (a large school district in Alabama) as burned out. However, not only is this operational definition of burnout extremely loose—the criterion being scores above the average on each of the three subscales—but the sample used in this study excluded all teachers with less than two years' experience at their current school site. Birmingham (1984) compared her sample (319 Minnesota public school teachers in grades K–12) to Maslach and Jackson's norms and found that 18 percent scored in the high range (upper third) in terms of emotional exhaustion, 14 percent in the high range of depersonalization, and 26 percent in the high range of lack of personal accomplishment.

We are thus left in a situation analogous to that of psychotherapy research, wherein a determination of the efficacy of psychotherapy is based directly on an arbitrary definition of "improvement." What constitutes improvement? Or, more to the point of the present discussion, what constitutes teacher burnout?

In an earlier group of studies (Farber, 1984b, 1985) I attempted to determine the extent of teacher burnout by surveying 693 public school teachers from both urban and suburban school districts in the New York metropolitan area. The measure used with these teachers—the Teacher Attitude Survey (TAS)—was a modified version of the Maslach Burnout Inventory. As noted earlier, this latter instrument has been used extensively to assess burnout in a wide variety of human service professionals. It consists of twenty-five statements about professional work—for example, "I feel de-

pressed at work." For the purposes of investigating the specific
nature of teacher burnout, I augmented the twenty-five items on the
MBI with forty additional items of exclusive relevance to teachers,
chosen to represent the range of satisfactions and stresses in teaching most often noted in the literature. I also modified the instructions on the MBI for this research. The original instructions request
those filling out the survey to read each statement and decide if they
have *ever* felt this way about their job (0 = never; 1 = a few times
a year or less; 2 = once a month or less; 6 = every day). I felt that
this time framework was too vague, making it virtually impossible
to accurately gauge the *current* status of a person's feelings of burnout or to trace the process over the course of a few months or a year.
Therefore, I modified the instructions so that respondents were
asked to evaluate the extent to which they felt a certain way "during
the last month" (0 = never; 1-2 = rarely; 3-4 = occasionally; 5-6 =
frequently). The data obtained from this research were analyzed
separately for suburban and urban teachers. I felt that working conditions (especially sources of stress) might be perceived dissimilarly
by suburban and urban teachers and that pooling the data from
these two groups might well obscure important differences in the
ways they experience and are affected by their work.

In this study, rather than comparing respondents' scores on
the three MBI scales with Maslach and Jackson's national norms—
a practice that does not allow for specification of a single estimate
of the proportion of teachers who may be burned out—a direct
attempt was made to operationalize burnout in a way that would
allow for such computations. Although Maslach and Jackson contend that burnout is a multifaceted, nondichotomous variable, so
too are many other dysfunctional conditions (for example, depression and anxiety disorders) for which prevalence rates are nonetheless estimated. The calculation of such prevalence rates, even if
subject to some unavoidable error, can at least begin to allow policy
makers to gain some sense of the magnitude of a problem.

Given the methodology of this study, teacher burnout was
defined in two different ways. The first method simply involved a
determination of the percentage of teachers who, in response to the
statement "During the last month I have felt burned out from my
work," answered "frequently" (points 5 or 6 on the 0-6 frequency

scale). On this basis, 10.3 percent of suburban teachers and 21.6 percent of urban teachers could be considered burned out.

A second, more conservative way of defining burnout required consideration of a subject's overall score on an eighteen-item subscale of the Teacher Attitude Survey that measured physical and emotional symptoms of burnout (for example, "I have felt used up at the end of the workday," "I have resented the paperwork and other nonteaching duties that eat up my time and energy," and "I have been impatient with my students' lack of progress"). This subscale seems to tap the essence of what is called "teacher burnout," inasmuch as the items making up the subscale reflect many of the aspects of this syndrome noted in the literature. By operationally defining teacher burnout as a score of 72 or more—an average of 4 or more on the 7-point scale across each of the items—12.9 percent of urban teachers and 6.9 percent of suburban teachers can be considered burned out. Using either method, then, a substantial minority of teachers was found to be burned out.

These percentages were derived from surveys of these teachers conducted in the fall (October–November) of the school year. Do the percentages of teachers who are burned out remain relatively constant over the course of the school year? In general, longitudinal studies of teacher stress or burnout have been inconclusive. On the one hand, Fleischut (1983) found a significant variation in the intensity of stress experienced by teachers at five different intervals during the school year: Stress increased from September to November, decreased in January, and increased in March and again in May. And Makinen and Kinnunen (1986) indicated that teacher stress increased considerably during the second half of the fall semester. On the other hand, Brenner, Sorbom, and Wallius (1985) found that "most teachers change very little in perceived general strain over the school year" and that those who do change usually move from higher to lower stress (p. 6). The results of my earlier research suggest that these apparently contradictory positions may both be accurate—that variations in patterns of stress and burnout may be quite different in different settings. Thus, I found that the relative stability of burnout rates is different in urban schools than in suburban schools. In urban schools, the percentage of teachers who are burned out remains fairly constant; on the other hand, in suburban settings, the proportion of burned-out teachers decreases substantially over the course of the school year. As defined by a score on the entire subscale, the percentage of burned-out teachers drops from 6.9 to 3.4 percent. In terms of a single item score, the percentage of burnout among these teachers drops from 10.3 to 5.5 percent. Thus, during the course of the school year the ratio of urban teacher to suburban teacher burnout rises from, at most, two to one to approximately three to one or four to one. Depending on the type of community and the time of assessment, therefore, between 5 and 20 percent of all teachers in this country are burned out at any given time.

What Proportion of Teachers Are Stressed or Dissatisfied?
Assessing the extent of teacher stress or dissatisfaction poses similar methodological problems as assessing rates of teacher burnout. As Table 2.1 indicates, studies utilizing different methods and different populations yield variable results in regard to the proportion of teachers who are purportedly stressed or dissatisfied with their work or who regret their choice of careers.

The percentage of teachers who find their work very or extremely stressful ranges from 16.5 percent in Feitler and Tokar's (1981) study of teachers in sixty school districts in northeastern Ohio and western Pennsylvania to 53 percent in Brown's (1983) study of elementary school teachers in Missouri. The percentage of teachers who feel that they would not choose to teach if they had to make a career decision again ranges from a low of 31 percent in Goodlad's (1984) national survey to a high of 55 percent in both the *New York Times* sample (Fiske, 1982) and my (Farber, 1984b) sample of urban teachers in the New York metropolitan area. The percentage of teachers who have reported feeling dissatisfied with their work has varied from the 13.1 percent noted by Kottkamp, Provenzo, and Cohn (1986) in their study of Dade County (Florida) teachers to 44 percent in the national NEA (1979) survey to 83 percent of the middle school teachers in Birmingham's (1984) Minnesota-based survey. A tentative conclusion here is that in addition to the 5-20 percent of teachers who are burned out (viewing this condition as an end state), another 30-35 percent are strongly dissatisfied with the teaching profession.

Table 2.1. Percentage of Teachers Assessed as Stressed, Dissatisfied,
or Regretful of Their Career Decision.

Study	Sample	Variable	Percentage
Birmingham (1984)	319 (Minnesota)	satisfaction	58% dissatisfied; 81% of middle school teachers dissatisfied
Broiles (1982)	314 (California)	stress	33%: work very/extremely stressful
Brown (1983)	271 (Missouri)	stress	53%: work decidedly/extremely stressful
Carnegie Foundation (1988a)	2,000 (nationwide)	satisfaction	23% dissatisfied
Farber (1984b)	693 (New York)	choose teaching again?	55.5% no (urban) 47.5% no (suburban)
Feistritzer (1985)	1,592 (nationwide)	satisfaction	16% dissatisfied
Feitler and Tokar (1981)	3,789 (Ohio, Pennsylvania)	stress	16.5%: work very/ extremely stressful
Fiske (1982)	5,702 (New York)	choose teaching again?	47% no (overall); 55% no (New York City); 35% no (suburbs)
Goodlad (1984)	1,350 (nationwide)	choose teaching again?	31% no
		career expectations fulfilled?	26% no
Harris and Associates (1987)	1,002 (nationwide)	satisfaction	14% somewhat/very dissatisfied
		leave teaching	52% have considered it 23% likely within five years
Harris and Associates (1988)	1,208 (nationwide)	satisfaction	13% somewhat/very dissatisfied
		leave teaching	26% likely within five years
Kottkamp, Provenzo, and Cohn (1986)	2,700 (Florida)	job satisfaction school satisfaction	13.1% dissatisfied 20.1% dissatisfied
Moracco, D'Arienzo, and Danford (1983)	691 (a middle Atlantic state)	choose teaching again?	52% no
NEA (1979)	1,738	choose teaching again? satisfaction	41% probably not/ no 44% dissatisfied/ very dissatisfied

A question that might be raised at this point is: How do these percentages of stressed or burned-out teachers compare to those in other occupations? On the one hand, the data clearly show that teachers are hardly unique in their experience of work-related stress. In a 1985 survey of 40,000 workers in various occupations, the National Center for Health Statistics found that more than half their sample had experienced either "a lot" of or "moderate" stress from work during the previous two weeks (Miller, 1988). Even such well-remunerated and highly respected professionals as doctors and lawyers are not immune to dissatisfaction or regrets. A 1989 poll of doctors found that 39 percent felt they would definitely or probably not enter medical school if they had the choice again (Altman and Rosenthal, 1990); a survey of lawyers under the age of thirty in the state of Washington showed that 85 percent would not reenter the profession (Margolick, 1990). Furthermore, several studies have found that teachers' scores on the three subscales of the Maslach Burnout Inventory tend to cluster right around the combined means of heterogeneous samples of human service professionals. Pines and Aronson (1981), as well as Anderson and Iwanicki (1984), found that teachers' scores on the MBI were slightly below group averages; Maslach and Jackson (1986) found that teachers' scores on these subscales were slightly higher than the average scores of other health and service occupations. On the other hand, Cox and Brockley (1984) found that, when matched for age, sex, and socioeconomic status, more teachers reported work-induced stress than did nonteachers. Overall though—and somewhat surprisingly—it appears that, when compared to other professionals, teachers, as a group, are not especially vulnerable to stress or burnout. However, two qualifications must be made to this statement: First, teachers in urban schools do constitute a subgroup that is at particular risk for stress and burnout; and second, teachers do deserve special attention and consideration even if they are no more stressed and burned out than other professionals. It is to teachers that we entrust our children and thus our future.

Individual Risk Factors: Who's Most Likely to Feel Stressed or Burned Out?

As noted in the previous chapter, sources of burnout can be found at the individual, organizational, and societal levels. When these factors combine to produce a perception of inconsequentiality in workers, burnout is likely to result. In this section, the focus is on those individual variables, especially personality characteristics and demographic factors, that seem to affect the probability of an individual's becoming a severely stressed or burned-out teacher.

Personality Factors. The literature on teacher burnout suggests that teachers who are idealistic and enthusiastic are most vulnerable to feelings of burnout. These are the teachers who have something to lose. Pines (1982) noted that burnout is more likely the more individuals value and attempt to meet their work ideals. And Bloch (1977) has shown that teachers who are obsessional, passionate, idealistic, and dedicated are more prone to "battered teacher syndrome," a disorder that Bloch describes in much the same ways as others describe teacher burnout. These teachers, committed as they are, involve themselves intensely in their work and feel severely disappointed when payoffs for their efforts are not forthcoming. This scenario may be an especially common one for those who have brought a sense of idealism and commitment to their work in inner cities. Working with students whose chronic social and economic difficulties often interfere with learning, teachers in this environment may find it difficult to garner rewards commensurate with their idealistic expectations. But the dysfunctional implications of extravagant idealism are not restricted to inner-city teachers. The strains of idealism and commitment may be experienced by all those teachers who base their self-esteem too exclusively on the attainment of unrealistic, albeit humane and worthy, educational goals. As Pines noted, "while losing touch with one's goals is a symptom of burnout, having goals that are too high or unrealistic is a common pitfall of professional helpers and a powerful antecedent of burnout" (1982, p. 21).

In a similar vein, studies have suggested that "Type A" persons are particularly prone to developing physiological symptoms in reaction to stress (for example, Glass, 1977). Type A personalities are aggressive, competitive, intense, and moody, less able to tolerate frustration than their Type B counterparts, and more likely to get angry and stressed when they perceive their efforts to be unsuccessful or unfairly compromised by others' interference. Type A personalities have a greater need to feel in control, an objective that cannot always be realized in running a classroom. Although these arguments would suggest a specific link between personality type and teacher burnout, this association has not been confirmed empirically. For example, Nagy (1982), in studying 227 teachers at the elementary and junior high school levels, failed to find a significant relationship between personality type (A or B) and burnout. He did, however, find that "workaholism" was a significant factor in explaining susceptibility to burnout.

Burnout has also been shown to be related to such "higher-order needs" of teachers as self-actualization and self-esteem (Anderson and Iwanicki, 1984; Malanowski and Wood, 1984). Self-actualization includes the need for success, achievement, and working at full potential; self-esteem includes the need for self-respect and respect by others as a person and as a professional. Research findings point to an "obvious" but nevertheless critical fact: When teachers' needs to feel respected and fulfilled through their work are thwarted, burnout becomes more likely. These findings also provide some support for the argument I will take up in later chapters, that the rise of burnout as a critical phenomenon in teaching over the last twenty to thirty years can be understood at least partially in terms of the loss of respect suffered by teachers over this time period.

Studies have found a number of other psychological variables that influence teachers' vulnerability to stress or burnout. For example, teachers with an "external locus of control"—those who feel that their destiny is not in their own hands but rather is controlled by external events—are more likely to suffer from burnout (Cadavid, 1986; Fielding, 1982; McIntyre, 1984; Marlin, 1987; Meehling, 1982; Stone, 1982; Zager, 1982). This finding is consistent with much recent research in psychology suggesting that, of all factors explaining stress, controllability may be most important (Taylor, 1990). In addition, it has been shown that teachers who are characterologically tense and anxious and who exhibit "low ego strength" (feel unsure of themselves) are more prone to burnout (Williams, 1982; Zager, 1982); also, teachers who are relatively intolerant of ambiguity report more stress and burnout than other teachers (Fielding, 1982). On the other hand, teachers who are personally "hardy," who see themselves as having a positive capacity to cope with and mediate stress (Kobasa, 1979), are less likely to suffer from burnout (Holt, Fine, and Tollefson, 1987; Schoenig, 1986). Even when studies control for demographic variables such as age, sex, race, years of teaching, school level, and marital status, personality variables such as locus of control, anxiety, and self-esteem remain significant predictors of teacher stress (Meehling, 1982).

In general, therefore, how a person reacts to job stress is a function of both the stress encountered and individual personality characteristics. It is the "goodness of fit" between job demands and personal abilities that determines the amount of stress experienced (French and Caplan, 1972). In other words, individual perception of and reaction to stress are a subjective matter and vary significantly from person to person; indeed, an individual can react dysfunctionally to the perception of stress, regardless of its objective existence. Two teachers undergoing the same degree of stress may react quite differently to the situation. For example, the teacher whose expectations are more realistic and who better understands and accepts the erratic nature of children's social and educational progress is less likely to overreact to one student's failure to grasp algebraic equations or another's sensitivity to mild criticism. The teacher who is more sure of him- or herself may feel less threatened by the lack of available textbooks. Many of the studies of risk factors in teachers have confirmed this pattern, finding that those with greater response capabilities (reflected in high degrees of self-esteem, self-confidence, or hardiness) are better able to withstand the typical rigors of a classroom (administrative disruptions, student fights, dilapidated equipment, and so on) and are less likely to become severely stressed or burned out. But while this makes intuitive sense, it is also a statement that needs to be interpreted rather cautiously. First, it is far from true that stress and burnout are restricted to teachers with low self-esteem. Second, the correlational nature of these studies makes it impossible to determine the direction of cause and effect; it is entirely possible that low self-esteem is an outcome of burnout and not a causal factor. (It may, of course, be both.) Lastly, the attribution of burnout in teachers to personality deficiencies such as lack of self-esteem resonates all too well with the notion of "blaming the victim." The feeling here is that such attributions (that this or that is wrong with teachers and that they are essentially responsible for their plight) have contributed substantially to the stress, demoralization, dissatisfaction, and early retirements that currently plague the profession.

The Effect of Life Changes. Life changes may make workers especially susceptible to job-related stress or burnout. Consistent relationships have been found between the numbers and types of changes in a person's life and the onset of illness or disease within as little as one year (Holmes and Rahe, 1967). Both positive changes (such as marriage) and negative changes (such as death or divorce) are considered stressful, inasmuch as both types demand adjustment by the individual to new patterns. Life changes may also be viewed from a developmental perspective. Theorists such as Erikson (1963, 1968), Levinson (1978), and Vaillant (1977) have all proposed models of adult development that include normative crisis periods involving significant reevaluations of an individual's personal or professional life, which may dramatically affect self-esteem, marital relationships, or faith and investment in one's work. Though "normative," these transitional periods are nonetheless stressful and may leave an individual with less capacity to cope successfully with other daily stresses. Again, though, while these arguments regarding the impact of life changes on vulnerability to job-related stress seem compelling, they have not been validated with respect to teachers. In fact, at least one study (Birmingham, 1984) has shown that the occurrence of significant life change events within a given year of a teacher's life is unrelated to job satisfaction or burnout.

Demographic Factors. A number of demographic variables have been linked with the occurrence of stress and burnout in teachers. Studies have consistently found that both are more likely to occur in men than women (for example, Anderson and Iwanicki, 1984; Birmingham, 1984; Burke and Greenglass, 1989; Rottier, Kelly, and Tomhave, 1983), in those under forty rather than older (for example, Anderson and Iwanicki, 1984; Birmingham, 1984; Farber, 1984a; Gold, 1985; J. M. Martin, 1988; New York State United Teachers Research and Education Services (NYSUT), 1979), and in those who teach in a junior high, middle, or senior high school (for example, Anderson and Iwanicki, 1984; Burke and Greenglass, 1989; Farber, 1984a; Goodlad, 1984; Malanowski and

Wood, 1984; Martin, 1988; Schwab and Iwanicki, 1982; Taton, 1983). Similarly, the *New York Times* survey of New York State teachers (Fiske, 1982) found that male teachers, those in the thirty- to thirty-nine-year-old age bracket, and those teaching in either a junior or senior high school were most likely to regret their career decisions. In fact, Schwab and Iwanicki (1982) went so far as to contend that these factors (sex, age, and grade level taught) are the only background variables that are useful in predicting level of burnout among teachers. Other studies have, however, provided some evidence to suggest that being single (Farber, 1984a; Gold, 1985; Holt, Fine, and Tollefson, 1987), teaching in a large school (Goodlad, 1984; Moracco, D'Arienzo, and Danford, 1983), working with large numbers of students (Malanowsi and Wood, 1984), and teaching in an urban rather than suburban or rural environment (Farber, 1984a; NYSUT, 1979) also put one at risk for feeling stressed or burned out.

Perhaps the most consistent finding in these studies is that men are more vulnerable to stress and burnout than women. At first glance, one might simply conclude that women are more resilient than men, either better prepared or temperamentally better able to deal with the myriad pressures of teaching. And there may be some truth to this interpretation—especially if one gives credence to the-ories suggesting that women, because of their developmental histo-ries, are more interpersonally sensitive, have better relational skills, and are better able to use support networks than men (Greenglass and Burke, 1988). A more parsimonious, less psychological inter-pretation may, however, be more accurate: that a disproportionate number of male teachers work in junior and senior high schools in classes that are generally larger than those in elementary schools and are populated with students who are generally more difficult. These students may themselves feel worn down as a consequence of the pressures and lack of rewards in their own lives, and teachers may feel especially powerless and inconsequential in confronting the students' sense of alienation and hopelessness.

Several studies have shown that teachers under the age of forty are most at risk for stress-related disorders. Teachers in their twenties are more likely to be saddled with unrealistic expectations, and those in their twenties and thirties are more likely than older teachers to be actively involved in the process of establishing a stable and committed professional identity. Both groups, then, may be especially vulnerable to stresses that make them question the wisdom of their career choice. Cognitive dissonance theory—one of the guiding principles of social psychology—would suggest that older teachers, having made a decision to stay in education, are less inclined to attend to work-related stressors or personal symptoms that would make their decision seem less attractive or judicious. According to this theory, teachers who have made a resolute commitment to the field are more likely to scan their environment for satisfactions than for stresses, and less likely to acknowledge stresses as personally salient. An important factor here, too, is that those older teachers who have felt extremely dissatisfied have already left the field.

What also needs to be addressed is the fact that during the last twenty or thirty years many teachers have stayed in teaching longer. Increased financial needs, greater social acceptance of working women, and a depressed job market have contributed to this situation. According to Elsbree (1939), for most of this country's history teachers typically stayed no more than two or three years. Because teachers are now staying in education longer, they have greater opportunities for feeling stressed and burned out out than their counterparts from earlier historical periods.

Organizational (Work-Related) Factors of Stress and Burnout

"The search for causes [of burnout]," commented Maslach (1978), "is better directed away from identifying the bad people and toward uncovering the characteristics of the bad situations where many good people function" (p. 114). This viewpoint emphasizes the importance of work-related features—for example, the nature of one's role, the nature of one's interactions (with students, colleagues, supervisors), and the nature of the work setting—in the etiology of teacher burnout.

As the litany of complaints and stressors of teachers is described, it bears remembering that these experiences do not *necessarily* lead to burnout. They certainly make teaching less pleasant and the cumulative impact of these experiences *may* cause burnout in those individuals who are garnering insufficient rewards from work and/or are especially vulnerable (for example, those who are extremely idealistic or characterologically anxious or lacking in coping mechanisms). Still, many teachers endure these stresses and continue to function effectively. The most common stressors teachers complain of include the following.

Student Violence, Classroom Discipline, and Apathy. As the examples in Table 2.2 show, managing disruptive students is invariably among the top-ranked items in teacher stress surveys. In most teacher surveys, the various manifestations of school discipline

Table 2.2. The Most Highly Ranked Sources of Stress According to Teachers.

New York State (NYSUT, 1979)	*Chicago* (Cichon and Koff, 1980)
1. Managing disruptive students	1. Involuntary transfer
2. Incompetent administration	2. Managing disruptive children
3. Maintaining self-control when angry	3. Notification of unsatisfactory performance
4. Overcrowded classrooms	4. Threat of personal injury
5. First week of school	5. Overcrowded classrooms
6. Disagreeing with supervisor	6. Lack of books and supplies
7. Dealing with community racial issue	7. Colleague assaulted in school
8. Preparing for a strike	8. Reorganization of classes or program
9. Target of verbal abuse by students	9. Implementing board of education
10. Theft and destruction of teacher property	10. Denial of promotion or advancement
Nationwide (High School) (Goodlad, 1984)	*Nationwide* (Gallup and Elam, 1989)
1. Lack of student interest	1. Lack of parent interest/support
2. Lack of parent interest	2. Lack of financial support
3. Student misbehavior	3. Lack of student interest
4. Drug/alcohol use	4. Lack of discipline
5. Size of school/classes	5. Lack of public support
6. Inadequate resources	6. Use of drugs
7. Student language problems	7. One-parent households
8. Poor teachers/teaching	8. Lack of respect for teachers/other students
9. Administration	9. Large schools/overcrowding
10. Organization	10. Problems with administration
	11. Low teacher salaries

problems—disruptive students, threats of personal injury, verbal
abuse, assaults on colleagues—are represented three or four times in
the list of the top ten stressors. Parents tend to concur with teachers'
sentiments regarding the seriousness of this problem: When parents
were queried as to why teachers burn out, the greatest number (63
percent) mentioned school discipline problems (Elam, 1984).

In 1979, a National Education Association poll found that
nearly three-fourths of all teachers felt that discipline problems impaired their teaching effectiveness at least to some extent. Each year
an estimated 70,000 teachers nationwide are beaten, robbed, raped,
or assaulted. Moreover, the majority of such attacks probably go
unreported (E. Muir, cited in Liff, 1980). The *New York Times* poll
of New York State teachers (Fiske, 1982) found that for nearly 40
percent of those polled, violence was a "daily concern"; an aston-
ishing 25 percent reported that they had actually been physically
assaulted by a student while on school premises. The federally
funded National School Safety Center suggests that three million
crimes a year occur on school grounds. Sutton (1984) found that of
all sources of stress for teachers, the problem of student discipline
was most highly correlated with an overall measure of job
dissatisfaction.

Said one teacher in a junior high school in the Bronx, "You
don't have the time to help the best kids because you spend 25
minutes in every class dealing with the trouble-makers, and you
can't really deal with them. You can only suspend a kid two times
for five days, and the kids know this. It's tough being 37 years old
and dealing with 13 year olds who are laughing in your face" (Fiske,
1982, p. A52).

Bloch (1978), a psychiatrist at UCLA, studied the effects of
violence on teachers and compared their symptoms to those of combat neurosis. These teachers, many of whom referred to their schools
as "battle zones," suffered from anxiety, insecurity, nightmares, fatigue, irritability, headaches, ulcers, hypertension, and a number of
other emotional and physical symptoms. Ianni and Reuss-Ianni
(1983) pointed out that while crime in schools is not increasing, the
fear of becoming a victim is. Teachers do not have to be directly
assaulted to be fearful—the atmosphere of a school can affect their
feelings, increasing their fears. In this regard too, Lazarus (1966)

pointed out that anticipation of a threat may be as stressful as an actual threat.

That the problem of student discipline ranks at or near the top of teacher stress surveys is not surprising; my experience is that nothing gets teachers so worked up and so ready to leave the profession as this issue. Virtually every teacher in urban schools (and many in suburban schools as well) has his or her own horror stories. Sometimes these stories involve real (or at least threatened) violence against teachers—a teacher being attacked by a student or a parent, a teacher being threatened by someone, or a teacher's car (or classroom) being vandalized. Sometimes these stories involve student-to-student violence—fights in the classroom or hallways, shakedowns in the bathrooms, sexual harassment in or around school. Sometimes too these stories do not refer to violence per se but rather emphasize a certain tone that seems to permeate a school: a tone reflected in the frequency with which students insult or attempt to intimidate each other, in the ways in which students talk to teachers or administrators, in the graffiti on school buildings, in the number of lockers broken into. And sometimes teachers don't even attempt to illustrate their feelings with specific examples but refer instead to an attitude toward learning that they sense in students, an attitude that, according to some teachers, ranges only from indifferent to contemptuous. The pervasiveness of what many teachers (and students) call "attitude problems" may dramatically lessen a teacher's sense that he or she can make a difference. It can also lessen a teacher's desire to invest in the work or even return to it the following day.

The metaphors used by angry, outraged, and frustrated teachers speak to their feelings about the issue of school violence. Schools are seen as "prisons," or "zoos," or "mental institutions"; acting-out students are seen as "hoodlums," or "animals," or "crazies"; and teachers themselves are seen as "policemen," "wardens," or "gatekeepers." Teachers who confront violence too often or for too many years speak of their own craziness in regard to their willingness to continue to do it. Having to constantly deal with violent or disruptive students reduces teachers' status in their own eyes. As Waller (1932) noted, being forced to play the role of Simon Legree may corrupt the best of teachers. Many do not feel professional,

complain they have not been prepared adequately for the conditions
under which they must now teach, and detest the role they now feel
forced to play. Keeping control is difficult and personally exhausting, yet failing to keep control results in a still worse outcome.
Lortie (1975) observed that "teachers who fail to keep control over
students soon find that teaching is intolerable work" (p. 151).

A related issue is that of student apathy. Goodlad (1984), in
fact, reported that "lack of student interest" was the most frequent
response of teachers to the question "What is this school's one biggest problem?" Although not responding as viscerally as to the
problem of student violence, teachers do feel enormously frustrated
and deprived of a crucial sense of gratification when working with
students who seem uncaring and unconcerned about learning. Although one of the reactions to this situation—a sense of "If they
don't care, why should I?"—is neither particularly rational nor professional, it does reflect accurately the degree of vexation that some
teachers feel in working with apathetic students. These students are
not only personally frustrating, thwarting the best efforts of some
very fine teachers, but they also contribute to a class tone often
leading to further discipline problems that make it considerably
more difficult for a teacher to infuse a positive sense of learning into
a classroom. Continuing to work enthusiastically and with a sense
of effectiveness in an urban high school with a dropout rate of
somewhere between 30 and 40 percent is, for most teachers, an enormously trying task.

Controlling Oneself When Angry. This source of stress, related as it is to the issue of student discipline, is highly ranked in
several surveys. Teachers' options for dealing with disruptive students are often quite limited, and the search for effective ways of
dealing with classroom frustrations can in itself be exasperating.
Yelling at students is neither a mature response nor a particularly
effective one (though it may temporarily suppress some inappropriate behavior); not infrequently, in fact, it is counterproductive. Nevertheless, the inclination to lash out or get angry at disruptive
students can be quite powerful so that attempts to control such
impulses are necessarily formidable. Many teachers acknowledge
that they at least occasionally fantasize about being able to really

"give it" to a "well-deserving" student. Leonard Wechsler, who interviewed many teachers for this book, defines teacher stress as "the effect of holding yourself back from strangling some abusive student who richly deserves it."

Administrative Insensitivity. This complaint is usually linked to the dual issues of student violence and school discipline. According to many teachers, administrators are neither supportive nor sensitive to their fear of violence and do little or nothing about enforcing rules or promoting a secure learning environment. Teachers feel that administrators are too content doing paperwork in their offices and avoiding, if at all possible, dealing with problem students. To teachers, administrators have "graduated" from the rigors of teaching and prefer "keeping their hands clean," and when pressed to help with discipline problems they will often resort to "there's not much I can do," or "do the best you can," or "everyone's got the same problem," or "the board (or district office or superintendent) has tied my hands too." Student suspensions, indeed any disciplinary action, are often seen as reflecting badly on a school's administration and are, therefore, often avoided. Said Saltzman (1988) in the *New York Times*, "Instead of attacking the problem [of student violence] head-on, supervisors and administrators hide behind the bureaucratic hierarchy that keeps track of only the most serious offenses and tries to keep even these figures from the public. Meanwhile, the psychological damage being done to children and educators is incalculable. . . . What can be more basic to a free society than the absolute right of teachers to teach and students to learn, free from fear?" (p. A27). The message these teachers contend they get is that everyone would be better off if the incident were not reported, that there's nothing much to be done, too much paperwork to fill out, too much negative publicity for the school, and too much ill-will created in the community.

In general, teachers see administrators in an adversarial role, as upholders of bureaucratic rules and regulations that undermine teachers' authority and effectiveness; as having no useful feedback to provide; as not being either supportive, inspiring, or appropriately "challenging." The data of my earlier studies underscore these points. In both suburban and urban schools, most teachers perceive administrators as contributing more to the problems that teachers face than to the help they need. Ideally, administrators should be working with teachers to reduce stress and facilitate optimal working conditions; unfortunately, they are seen as part of the problem, not the solution. Stress and burnout have been found to be significantly related to principals' lack of participatory management, lack of sensitivity to school- and teacher-related problems, and lack of support for teachers (Adams, 1988; Blase, Dedrick, and Strathe, 1986; Hanchey, 1987; Jackson, Schwab, and Schuler, 1986).

Bureaucratic Incompetence. In the late 1980s, when the Oakland, California, school system was threatened with bankruptcy, school officials were accused of patronage and arrested for embezzlement. In New York City in the late 1980s, one could scarcely go a week without reading about a new scandal implicating the board of education. The board, it was found, required an average of *eight years* to build a school; one particular high school was found to be eleven years behind schedule and $55 million over budget. Time Inc., and CBS magazines, angry over the board's lackadaisical efforts, withdrew their support from a program aimed at establishing a writing skills high school in New York. A school dropout prevention program collapsed when only a few hundred students of a total of 7,000 who applied received the part-time jobs they had been promised. In discussing the results of the *New York Times* poll, Fiske (1982) noted that "running through many of the responses [of teachers] was the theme that the system in which they must operate got in the way of the things that attracted them to teaching in the first place" (p. A52). Of course, all school bureaucracies are not as inefficient or cumbrous as that of the infamous 110 Livingston Street in New York City. Nevertheless, akin to their feelings for school-based administrators, many teachers nationwide feel that those who work at central headquarters are either indifferent to their plight or actually working against their best interests. The image of many educational bureaucracies—as incompetent, inefficient, overly concerned with cost, and scarcely concerned with education—does little to make teachers feel respected or supported. Nor does it make teachers feel as if they are being led by those who have either educators' or students' best interests in mind.

Unreasonable or Unconcerned Parents. Most educators believe that parents are an integral part of the educational process and that parental support of children's work strongly influences school success. Teachers, therefore, generally welcome parental involvement in schools. It is all the more unfortunate then that parents are viewed as a significant source of stress for many teachers in the public schools. In both the 1984 and 1988 Gallup Poll of Teachers' Attitudes Toward the Public Schools, the school problem mentioned most frequently by teachers was lack of parental support and interest.

Unsupportive parents come in two major varieties: not at all involved and far too involved. In the "not involved" category are those who are unavailable (working too many hours or being preoccupied with their own careers or new marriages or new children); those who are incapable (incapacitated by illicit drugs or alcohol or mental disturbance); those who are simply uninterested in their children's education; and those who have simply washed their hands of behavior they themselves have had little or no success in controlling. There are also those parents who insist, often quite angrily, that their children's "problems" are directly attributable to teacher incompetence or inexperience or vindictiveness or racism and that they (the parents) are entirely blameless and hence will have nothing further to do with the issue. In the "too involved" category are those parents who have decided that the school is inadequate, that the teachers and administrators are incompetent, and that real education is only possible if parents constantly monitor what occurs in the school and classrooms. These are most often parents who feel that their child is being overlooked, insufficiently challenged, or "picked on" by the teacher or other children and that only constant vigilance and pressure on their parts will rectify the situation. Thus, they may want or demand justification for almost every rule and classroom assignment and feel that it is imperative for them to make their presence felt. Their feeling is that teachers will work hard for their children only if someone is watching.

Although these descriptions are somewhat hyperbolic and certainly not representative of the universe of parents with whom teachers have contact, they do represent a psychologically significant aspect of a teacher's world. Parents are perceived by many teachers as either unhelpful and unavailable or intrusive and demeaning.

   Public Criticism. According to teachers, parents are not alone in their lack of sympathy or support for teachers. "Teachers are not respected as professionals by students, parents, administrators, and society" ("Former Teachers in America," 1986, p. 39). Among former teachers, 64 percent noted that their professional prestige was worse than they had expected it would be before they began to teach (Metropolitan Life Insurance Company, 1986). Apparently, those who have never taught have difficulty empathizing with those who do. Typical comments (understandably irksome) about teachers include: Teachers have it easy, teachers have summers off, teachers get paid too much for the little they do, teachers complain too much, teachers teach because they can't "do" anything else.

   Related to the lack of respect shown teachers is a noticeable lack of appreciation for their efforts. Charged with the task of educating, and sometimes socializing, millions of children in this country, teachers are continuously reminded of and excoriated for their failures, but they are rarely praised for their successes. Of course, one may contend that this is typical of all occupations: The public tends to focus on workers' limitations and failures. But one would be hard-pressed to find another professional group that has been so often and so severely evaluated by the popular press in the last two decades. As Grant (1983) noted in an excellent essay, "although the halo of authority dimmed for many in public roles in the 1960s and 1970s, teachers came in for special criticism" (p. 600). Doctors and lawyers are criticized but their accomplishments are often noted and they are rewarded well in terms of money and prestige. Where, teachers wonder, is the recognition for *their* accomplishments and hard work?

   How dissatisfied are teachers with their public image? My data show that about 80 percent of teachers have never or only rarely felt satisfied with teachers' standing in society. Though stress and burnout may be more prevalent in urban schools, teachers in both urban and suburban communities are united in their agreement that teachers are not well regarded by the public at large.

Involuntary Transfers. This source of stress has actually been ranked first in some teacher surveys. These surveys were, however, conducted at a time when many schools were either under court orders to desegregate faculty or attempting to reduce faculty as a result of declining student enrollment—policies that are no longer as common now as they were ten years ago. It is doubtful, therefore, that this source of stress would be rated as highly now as it was in the late 1970s; in fact, in more recent surveys it is not among the more frequently named or highly rated sources of stress. Still, it is worth discussing the fact that teachers have, in the recent past, reacted to the idea of involuntary transfers so strongly. In addition, involuntary transfers still occur. In many school districts, senior teachers have the right to "bump" less experienced teachers, especially those with temporary teaching licenses, from their assignments. Moreover, budget cuts, necessitated in many districts by taxpayers' refusal to support increases in the school budget, continue to leave teachers feeling unsure about job security. In Massachusetts in 1990, 9,000 teachers, one-fifth of the entire public school teaching staff, received layoff notices.

When professional athletes are traded against their wishes, they may be consoled by the size of their paychecks. (Even so, athletes have protested vehemently the notion that they are "chattel" who can be traded away or kept by a team against their will. Star players often have "no-trade" clauses in their contracts.) Teachers, however, have neither a substantial paycheck nor an adoring public to cushion involuntary transfers or layoffs. Both violate teachers' sense of professionalism and also deny teachers two primary sources of coping with stress: a sense of collegial support and a sense of control over one's life and job. Particularly for younger teachers, who are the usual targets, involuntary transfers or layoffs may come just when they are establishing themselves in a school, putting down professional and personal roots. Transfers, layoffs, and even layoff notices that are later rescinded invariably demoralize teachers and stir up fantasies of leaving forever.

Overcrowded Classrooms. Classrooms of twenty or twenty-five reasonably well-behaved children can be difficult enough to plan for and manage. Classrooms generally require structure, children generally require attention, and the most effective classrooms are generally those in which teachers can individualize lessons to meet the needs of each child. Obviously, this task becomes increasingly difficult as the size of the class increases. Because large class size provides fewer opportunities to interact individually with each student, the teacher may feel less involved and less effective—two critical sources of satisfaction. Moreover, as class size increases, classroom management becomes more difficult. Similarly, many teachers feel that as their roster size increases so too does the probability of having another seriously disruptive child in their class. Overcrowded classrooms, then, are seen as aggravating the problem of student discipline and weakening the likelihood of effective teaching. As Pines (1984) noted, "when caseloads are exceedingly heavy, professionals who try not to compromise the quality of the care they provide can get extremely discouraged and frustrated" (p. 19).

In 1990, the average class size in a U.S. public school was twenty-four. According to a policy statement from the National Association of Elementary School Principals (Kelly, 1990), teachers should be assigned no more than fifteen students per class up to grade three in order to ensure a good learning environment. Nevertheless, the U.S. Department of Education estimates that even lowering the average number of students to twenty in all grades would require 335,000 extra teachers and cost $22.8 billion.

Mainstreaming. Mainstreaming handicapped children into regular classes whenever possible is a practice mandated by Public Law 94-142 (the Education for All Handicapped Children Act). Though motivated by the best of intentions, that of achieving the least restricted, best education possible for handicapped students, among the unintended consequences of this law was making teaching and classroom management more difficult, increasing greatly the amount of paperwork teachers have to cope with, and creating role conflict among the variety of educational personnel charged with serving the handicapped.

Most critical is the fact that the normal stresses of teaching are necessarily exacerbated by having one or two or several emotionally or physically handicapped children in the classroom. Justifications, such as "the price is worth it" or "that's what teachers get paid for," overlook the inevitable costs of this action, not just in terms of the amount of teacher work or teacher stress but in terms of the attention that teachers can focus on others in the classroom. In this regard, "lack of time to spend with individual students" was recently rated as the single highest source of stress by a group of teachers in California (Broiles, 1982). Although both handicapped and nonhandicapped students may benefit psychologically from new opportunities to interact with each other (the argument usually invoked), another reality is that most teachers, at least occasionally, simply do not have the resources to cope with the added responsibilities and attention that handicapped children demand and deserve. Like it or not, it must be acknowledged that although adding handicapped children to a class is a humane act, it is also a source of additional stress (albeit also rewards) for most teachers.

Public Demands for "Accountability." It appears reasonable that the public should hold teachers accountable for the success of their work. After all, the public, through taxes, pays teachers' salaries and should have a right to expect certain performance levels. However, from the perspective of teachers, the demand for accountability is too often the means by which teachers' autonomy and sense of professionalism are trampled upon by those who know little about education and even less about educational evaluation. Accountability is too often seen as synonymous with student performance on a single set of standardized tests and too rarely measured by realistic criteria established for a particular group of students. Most troubling to teachers, however, is their feeling that society expects them to educate, socialize, and graduate virtually every student who comes to school, regardless of the social, economic, familial, or psychological difficulties some of these students bring with them. Even if parents, psychologists, social workers, and various public and private helping agencies have failed, teachers are still expected to succeed and will be held accountable if they do not. For many teachers, the public cry for accountability is no more than a new, more sophisticated way of expecting schools and teachers to cure all the ills of society.

Excessive Paperwork. On the face of it, one would not imagine that this issue should exist as a significant source of stress for teachers, and yet on virtually every survey, it is ranked high. In both Corpus Christi, Texas, and Wichita, Kansas, teachers actually rated excessive paperwork as their number one concern. The National Center for Education Statistics released figures in 1989 indicating that the typical teacher works 50.4 hours per week, split almost equally between time in the classroom (25.5 hours) and time spent at home with paperwork (24.9 hours). The following is a list of paperwork duties in Oakland, California: "Teachers not only have to prepare a report card, but must document in several ways the reason for each grade; prepare intervention strategies; prepare documentation for and write up parent conferences; record test scores; submit lesson plans; perform lunch counts; maintain financial records; prepare applications for free or reduced meals; complete state and federal surveys on bilingual, gifted, disabled, ill, and uninoculated students; fill out media and film orders and emergency reports; and provide extensive field trip justifications" (Newell, 1987, p. 8).

Paperwork is burdensome (it is a source of stress), wasteful (it takes time away from teaching duties per se), insulting (in excess it reduces the role of teachers to that of clerical workers), and frustrating (it prevents teachers from pursuing the more satisfying and important aspects of their job). Most teachers feel adamantly that schools are wasting precious teaching time by having teachers fill out forms that secretaries should complete. Given the enormity of problems in public school systems, time spent on paperwork is not just inconvenient but is an affront to both students and teachers.

The stress engendered by paperwork is almost certainly related to teachers' perceptions of a lack of professional respect accorded them. Rather than being left to concentrate on what they are trained to do and do best—teach their students—they are instead called upon to perform nonprofessional tasks. In addition, time spent on paperwork does not replace time necessarily spent on the essential tasks of teaching but is an additional burden on top of an already too busy day. Sometimes, in fact, a demand for paperwork comes in the middle of a day in the form of requests for "urgent information," interfering with class time or preparation periods.

Finally, teachers often react negatively to the nature of the paperwork itself: Much of it is seen as unnecessary (similar forms having been filled out in the recent past) or intrusive (essentially requesting justification of one's program or curriculum) or trivial (asking for information that could certainly be supplied by a school secretary). As Albert Shanker remarked, "When the day comes that teachers are getting $75,000 or $100,000 a year, nobody will want them to spend their time on a lot of paperwork anymore than you'd want a surgeon or a lawyer to be wasting his time on petty paper shuffling" (cited in Newell, 1987, p. 9).

Loss of Autonomy and Sense of Professionalism. As noted above, both excessive paperwork and demands for accountability are related to the concern that teachers' autonomy and professionalism are being expropriated by others. Pressure on teachers to improve schools through adherence to newly created local, state, and federal mandates (for example, Public Law 94-142) has been enormous in recent years, but decisions to institute new programs or policies, or to monitor old ones, are usually made with little or no input from teachers themselves. Teachers are given their students and supervisors, of course, but are also frequently assigned a curriculum they must follow, the books they must teach it with, and sometimes even the approach they must take (for example, a phonics approach to reading). As Phelan (1982) noted, "even if teachers are conceded the right to set the pace and timing of learning conditions, their selection of curriculum content or materials may be overruled by administrators or even school board members" (p. 3). Some teachers grant their students greater autonomy and responsibility than they themselves are afforded. The point is that too often teachers' sense of autonomy or professionalism is appealed to by others when convenient (for example, when dealing with disruptive students or during salary negotiations) but is otherwise overlooked.

Inadequate Salaries/Lack of Promotional Opportunities. Although teacher salaries are presently increasing, in some places dramatically, they still fall far short of those of many other professional groups. In most cities, beginning teacher salaries are lower than those of tolltakers or sanitation workers. Many salary schedules offer "professional salaries" (in the $45–50,000 range) only after fifteen or twenty years in the field. For many teachers, then, resentment over years of feeling grossly underpaid is a nearly impossible legacy to overcome.

The average beginning salary of teachers in 1986 was $16,500; the overall average annual salary was $25,257. At first glance these figures represent significant improvements over the 1976 figures of $8,700 and $12,600, respectively. Yet in 1986 dollars, $8,700 translates to $16,788 and $12,600 translates to $24,313. Thus, in real dollar terms the salaries of beginning teachers actually declined slightly during the 1976–1986 decade while the average teacher's salary increased only marginally.

Parents, and society at large, expect a great deal of teachers and invest them with an enormous degree of responsibility. Politicians continually declare that "our children are our nation's future." In response to such statements, teachers ask: "Where are the financial rewards commensurate with such a profoundly important task?" "Why, in comparison to friends with equal, or even lesser, amounts of education, do I earn significantly less money?" "Why, of all professional groups, do we have to fight so hard to justify salary increases?"

The fact of relatively low salaries is more than psychologically distressful for teachers. Many feel compelled by financial obligations to take second jobs—not just during the summer months or other vacation periods but after-school and/or weekend positions the year through. There are, of course, several possible ramifications of such decisions: extreme resentment at the perceived necessity of having to take on another job (and having less time to spend with family), less time available for school-related tasks, greater rewards (financial or emotional) in another line of work. The part-time job may ultimately take precedence over the full-time job, and, indeed, many teachers leave the field to pursue business opportunities that they once only "dabbled in." Many feel they have no choice—not only are their salaries low but there are few, if any, opportunities for promotion. "There's something troublesome," noted Frank Macchiarola, one-time chancellor of the New York City school system, "about a system where you hold people in the same position for 20 years without a promotion" (Fiske, 1982, p. A52). Actually,

advancement in education has typically meant leaving the classroom for administrative positions in education or, as one teacher
phrased it, "The further away from children you get, the more
money and prestige you receive" ("Teaching in Trouble," 1986, p.
55). But there are few high-level administrative positions in each
school, and landing any of these often demands not only a good deal
of extra education (often the doctorate in administration) but a fair
amount of political influence as well.

*Isolation from Other Adults and the Lack of a Psychological
Sense of Community.* Throughout the history of this country,
teachers have belonged to an isolated group, rarely enjoying social
or political influence. But even within the school building itself,
teachers' needs for affiliation and support are often unfulfilled. According to Eisner (1985), teachers live in a "world of childhood" and
spend about 90 percent of their workday exclusively with children.
They have little time for reflection or even friendly chatter, a problem magnified by the fact that, in comparison with other occupational groups, teachers are highly social and greatly value
opportunities to interact with co-workers (Holland, 1973; Super,
1970). Burke and Greenglass (1989) found that burnout was significantly correlated with teachers' perceived lack of social support.

Goodlad's (1984) study of teachers and schools focused in
part on the problem of teacher isolation. "The teachers in our sample had some association with others in college courses, inservice
classes and workshops, and meetings of educational organizations,
but rather brief and casual kinds of associations. They rather rarely
joined with peers in collaborative endeavors such as district committees or projects. Nor did they visit other schools or receive vis-
itors from them very often. There was little in our data to suggest
active, ongoing exchanges of ideas and practices across schools between groups of teachers, or between individuals even in the same
schools. . . . Inside schools teacher-to-teacher links for mutual assistance in teaching or collaborative school improvement were weak
or nonexistent" (p. 187). For the most part, then, teachers are terribly alone in their helping roles. They not only function independently but, within the confines of their classrooms, they become the
sole repository for skills, stamina, and enrichment—a role that can-

not long be endured by a single individual. Schools are settings where learning and change are goals for someone other than the helping professional. Thus, in spite of the obvious impact of teacher satisfaction on pupil performance, schools are inadequately designed to meet the needs of teachers. Teaching is indeed a "lonely profession" (Levine, 1966; Sarason, 1982).

Inadequate Preparation. Many teachers, particularly new teachers, feel that their formal education has ill prepared them for the realities of a classroom, much less of a school and its culture. Their contention is that undergraduate and even graduate education courses emphasize curriculum and technology and greatly underestimate teachers' needs to master issues related to classroom management, administrator-teacher relationships, parent-teacher relationships, and so on. Many now angrily dismiss the "fluoride" premise taught in their teacher prep courses—that good curriculum is an effective preventive against student discipline problems. The reform reports of recent years—particularly those issued by the Carnegie Commission and the Holmes Group—have argued strongly for reforming teacher education, proposing to abolish the four-year education major in favor of a five-year program, which would have prospective teachers learning pedagogical skills only after they completed a typical four-year college experience with a traditional academic major.

Sarason (1982) spoke to the issue of teacher training as articulately as anyone. He emphasized that "the student teacher obtains an extraordinarily narrow view of what a school and school system are—[a view that is] more in keeping with the role of the narrow technician than it is of the professional practitioner who has a broad conceptual *and* institutional framework within which his or her activities take on meaning and justify actions" (p. 47). The acceptance by beginning teachers of this circumscribed view, says Sarason, "tends to produce self- and role-derogatory attitudes" (p. 47). It is only a slight exaggeration to suggest that teachers are prepared to teach as if their classroom were going to be covered by a glass bubble. Rarely, as Sarason (1985) pointed out, do teachers learn how and when to talk with parents, principals, or other teachers; rarely then can teachers see themselves as working in an interlocking setting with others who might provide service to both themselves and their students.

Even experienced teachers are often unprepared to deal with changes in their schools and communities. Many find themselves teaching students whose histories, values, and behavior they may not wholly comprehend nor sympathize with. To be sure, their anger is sometimes expressed at actual students or their parents, but it is also directed toward their graduate school teachers, administrators, or in-service instructors, who were "supposed to have" anticipated or prepared them for these changes but who, instead, too often underestimated the educational implications of a changing social structure. Ironically, the recommendations of some of the new reform reports, that teachers should be experts in specific subject areas rather than in pedagogy per se, conflict with the substance of current teacher complaints regarding adequacy of preparation.

Complaints Regarding the Physical Plant. Particularly in‐ urban schools, teachers are likely to feel at least occasionally distressed by the physical condition of their school. *Decaying* is a word teachers often use to describe their schools, even those that are not decades old. Crumbling walls and ceilings, graffiti inside and outside the school building, classrooms with peeling paint, playgrounds and parking areas that need cleaning, fixtures without light bulbs, windows that won't open, bathrooms without privacy, asbestos problems, heating problems—these are some of the complaints that teachers make, often futilely, to their principal, union representative, or custodian. The typical responses take the form of either "we don't have enough money/manpower to do it" or "it's on the list and someone will get to it eventually." In urban school districts, the proportion of the school budget spent on school maintenance decreased from 6 percent in 1983 to 3.5 percent in 1987 (Corcoran, Walker, and White, 1988). Poor working conditions in urban schools—from inadequate supplies to a shortage of desks, blackboards, and books—may wear down both teachers and students. Consider, for example, the daily environment—and its probable psychological effects—of one New York City school district: "At the 125-year-old red brick Pacific High School, across the street from the Board of Education headquarters in Brooklyn, students attend classes in rooms with boarded-up windows, the lone science laboratory is inoperable and one of just four toilets is usually not functioning. At Erasmus Hall High School, a few miles away, neglect has left the once graceful building, designed to resemble the Gothic architecture of Magdalen College at Oxford University, looking like a dilapidated subway station" (Perlez, 1987, p. A1).

Although not as egregious as some of the other factors noted above, a poorly maintained school can certainly feel oppressive and demoralizing, especially in conjunction with other stresses, for example, school discipline. Conversely, a new school or one kept in excellent shape can facilitate a positive attitude toward school in both teachers and students.

A similar issue concerns the lack of instructional supplies available to some teachers. In 1985, the California Commission on the Teaching Profession noted that one quarter of the state's teachers did not have a textbook for every student; more than a third of California teachers reported spending at least $100 of their own money annually to buy supplies for their students.

Role Ambiguity, Role Conflict, Role Overload

Teachers, then, have many specific gripes. My sense is that three issues in particular contribute most highly to teacher stress and burnout: inadequate salary, lack of respect and appreciation, and, perhaps most important, lack of a sense of efficacy (the feeling of inconsequentiality). From this perspective, the impact of many of the above-mentioned stressors—especially school discipline problems—is most debilitating in its power to thwart teachers' needs to feel effective in their work. When the rewards of teaching are absent, stress is magnified and burnout becomes a far more likely occurrence. Taken together, the complaints of teachers suggest that, like others who work in institutional rather than private settings, they struggle with issues of role ambiguity, role conflict, and role overload (Caplan and Jones, 1975; French and Caplan, 1972; Kahn, 1974; Tosi and Tosi, 1970).

Role ambiguity is associated with a lack of clarity regarding a worker's rights, responsibilities, methods, goals, status, or accountability. Although in some ways a teacher's role is defined quite explicitly ("teach your children well"), in other ways—notably in regard to school discipline and accountability—vagueness and conflicting opinions abound. "How much," many teachers ask themselves, "do I have to accomplish, and with how many children, before I can be considered effective and successful?" And, "Is it my job to discipline the children in my class if their parents haven't? Is it my job to feed them? to instill values?" Answers to such questions do not come easily to those who are thoughtful.

Role conflict occurs when inconsistent, incompatible, or inappropriate demands are placed upon an individual. Sutton (1984) pointed out two common sources of role conflict for teachers: They are expected to provide quality education to their students, yet they are not allowed to use the best instructional methods or curriculum material available; they are responsible for maintaining discipline but do not have the authority for doing so. Teachers may also experience role conflict when told to perform tasks (cafeteria duty, yard duty, bus duty) that are perceived as outside the domain of professional work. And role conflict may also occur when a teacher's values are at odds with those of colleagues or administrators. Teachers who have left to work in private schools have often done so for this reason—some, for example, over disagreements with administrators regarding the value of open classrooms.

In recent years, many teachers have complained that mainstreaming handicapped students forces a role conflict upon them, that they have to decide at certain times whether to attend to one or two handicapped children or twenty nonhandicapped children. Many teachers resent students who are discipline problems for a similar reason—these students are clearly needy but attending to them deprives other students of a teacher's time and attention. Teachers are constantly making such on-the-spot decisions about where their priorities lie, but they often feel the sword of Damocles hanging over them. Regardless of their decision, someone will soon question the wisdom of it. In Sutton's (1984) study of 200 Michigan teachers, role conflict bore the second highest correlation to job dissatisfaction; among thirteen sources of stress, only student discipline problems yielded a higher correlation.

Role overload is one of the most common complaints of those who work in schools. Twenty-five students in a class—each with his or her own needs, interests, motivation, and achievement level—"is a lot of children for any one person to handle" (Sarason, 1982, p. 187). Said one educator: "What I personally minded most about teaching was the inflexibility of the schedule, and the stamina required to face 100 students a day without allowing the frayed edges to show. The classes seemed to arrive in a loop; one filed in as the previous one left" (Standard, 1987, p. 32). Furthermore, role overload is becoming even more common in this era of budget cutbacks and job freezes. Teachers are being asked to teach larger classes, to cover classes outside their area of expertise, to make do without aides, to do the work that others (administrators, aides) should be doing. Role overload may also result from the effort necessary to work effectively with children who are seemingly unprepared or unmotivated to attend school. Of course, it is the teacher's job to make this effort, but if a fourth-grade teacher in California, for example, has to organize lessons to meet the needs of children from five different countries, none of whom speaks English well, and three children who will not sit in their seats for long and are likely to disturb others, and two other students who haven't learned to read yet, and two others who are well ahead of the other students in the class, and two or three others that come to school only intermittently, then the complaint of role overload should not be surprising. As noted before, few individuals can sustain this kind of effort for long, especially in the absence of suitable rewards. There is one other aspect of role overload that should be noted as well: Good teachers are those who are most often "rewarded" with more work.

        Sutton (1984) has pointed out two distinct, though equally dysfunctional, responses to overload. In the first case, teachers feel forced either to do low-quality work or to not finish the work at all; in this case, lower-quality teaching invariably results, which is psychologically (low self-esteem) as well as physiologically (high blood pressure, anxiety) distressing. In the second case, teachers may choose to try to keep up with the demand; this response, though, is likely to lead to family problems (insufficient time available for family members) as well as physiological problems stemming from lack of sleep and relaxation. Burnout may result from either response.

It bears keeping in mind, however, that there may be only a fine line between the stress of role overload and the satisfaction of new job challenges. For example, one computer teacher may find that keeping up with the constantly changing technology in the field is an excessive burden, while another may be energized by the same task; one sixth-grade teacher may regard the great range of student abilities in her class as beyond her effective limits, while her colleague down the hall, having taught a homogeneous group of students the previous year, may feel excited by this new prospect. For most teachers, though, the effect of role ambiguity, conflict, and overload is similar to that of school discipline problems: a far greater difficulty in feeling effective.

This is hardly an exhaustive list of the work-related stressors for teachers. In any given city, school district, or individual school, a number of idiosyncratic stressors impinge on teachers, their existence a function of the type of individuals who have set policy, who have taught, and who have learned in that particular setting. As Sarason (1982) has so well demonstrated, an appreciation of the historical context in which an institution has developed is necessary to truly understand its current functioning and problems. In this vein, Chapter Five will discuss the events and social currents of the 1960s as a way of understanding the current roots of teacher stress and burnout. First, however, Chapter Three will describe the general symptoms of stress and burnout in teachers and Chapter Four will discuss the factors leading to both teacher employment and teacher attrition.

3

Symptoms and Types:
Worn-Out, Frenetic,
and Underchallenged Teachers

THIS CHAPTER FOCUSES ON THE MANIFESTATIONS OF TEACHER burnout: its symptoms, of both a personal and professional nature, and its various subtypes. In describing burnout this way, I am guided by the principles of psychiatric classification and diagnosis wherein a disorder, such as depression, may be characterized in general symptomatic terms (low energy level, eating and sleeping disturbances, and so on) but may also be broken down into subtypes (acute versus chronic, unipolar versus bipolar, and so on).

Teachers burn out in different ways and for different reasons; thus it is difficult to generate a single, universal description of the etiology and symptoms of the disorder. In general, though, teachers who are burned out feel emotionally and/or physically exhausted and are often irritable, anxious, angry, or sad; furthermore, the emotional frustrations attendant to this phenomenon may lead to psychosomatic symptoms (for example, insomnia, ulcers, headaches, hypertension), alcohol or substance abuse, and increased family and social conflicts. Being burned out may mean planning classes less often or less carefully, teaching classes less enthusiastically and creatively, staying home from work more often, feeling less sympathetic toward students and less optimistic about their future, getting frustrated easily by classroom disturbances or lack of student progress, maintaining a greater distance from students, feeling more hostile toward administrators and parents, harboring a cynical view of the profession, viewing oneself in self-deprecating terms, regretting the decision to enter teaching, and fantasizing about (or actually planning on) leaving the profession.

Physical and Psychological Symptoms

Burnout in teachers is most often associated with feelings of emotional and physical exhaustion (Pines, 1982). "I've had it," "I can't take it anymore," "I have nothing left to give," and "I just don't care anymore" are the most common phrases one hears from burned-out educators. Many complain of chronic fatigue and talk of coming home from school and collapsing in bed for several hours; for others, though, restlessness and an inability to sleep are more common symptoms of their nervous exhaustion. Related symptoms include tension and the inability to relax or "decompress" after work (Kyriacou and Pratt, 1985). This exhaustion may well take on characteristics similar to those of depression. In fact, teacher ratings of work-related stress correlate quite highly with a widely used depression inventory, so much so that in one study (Hammen and DeMayo, 1982), 45 percent of a sample of urban high school teachers reached the cut-off score used to distinguish depressed from nondepressed individuals.

A second common feature of teacher stress and burnout is anxiety. Some teachers are constantly fearful and hypervigilant, worried about their personal safety or the safety, say, of their car in the school parking lot. Others are more prone to free-floating anxiety—a pervasive, nonspecific sense that "something" is wrong; still others are plagued by anticipatory anxiety, concerned not so much with what is happening now but "about what may happen in the future" (Fimian, 1982). Some individuals suffering from severe stress or burnout seem to vacillate between bouts of anxiety and depression; when one state becomes unbearable, the other comes to predominate.

Frequently, somatic complaints accompany these feelings of exhaustion, depression, or anxiety. Indeed, many teachers feel that their work has caused them physical illness—this proportion ranges from 41 percent in a study of teachers in New York State (NYSUT,

1979) to 53 percent of teachers in Chicago (Cichon and Koff, 1980) to 77 percent in San Diego (Wilson, 1979). When the teacher journal *Instructor* asked its readers whether health hazards were related to teaching, 84 percent of 7,000 nationwide respondents answered "yes." Clearly, a good number of teachers, burned out or not, have experienced physical illness as a result of their work. Moderate levels of stress, then, may cause a host of nagging physical complaints even when burnout per se (with its more comprehensive, dysfunctional symptoms) is not the result.

Studies have found that teachers can be accurately classified as burned out or not (burned out being defined as scoring above the mean on each of the three MBI subscales) on the basis of their somatic complaints (Belcastro, 1982; Belcastro and Hays, 1984). The frequency, as well as the intensity, of such disturbances as abdominal pain, nausea, difficulty in breathing, tachycardia (rapid heartbeat), headaches, dizziness, loss of appetite, tinnitus (ringing in the ears), muscle tightening, cold sweats, back pain, and occupational injury have all been found to be significantly higher in burned-out than non–burned-out teachers. In addition, ulcers, kidney disorders, gallbladder disorders, cardiovascular disorders, and depression have all been found to occur more frequently in burned-out than non–burned-out teachers, even when the onset of these conditions has been controlled for (Belcastro, 1982; Belcastro and Hays, 1984). Hypertension, gastrointestinal problems, tearfulness, nightmares, lingering illness, sexual problems (impotence, frigidity, lack of interest), loss of one's voice, and drug and alcohol problems have also been linked with stress or burnout (Freudenberger, 1974; Maslach, 1976; Kyriacou and Pratt, 1985; Kyriacou and Sutcliffe, 1978; Needle, Griffen, Svendsen, and Berney, 1980). In short, the vast research literature linking stress with a number of physiological symptoms is supported by the literature on teacher burnout. Teachers who are burned out, who have "had it" with their jobs, are likely to exhibit specific symptoms of physical and/or mental distress.

That teachers experience physical and mental distress as a result of the conditions of work should hardly be surprising. Work is necessarily a *transforming* experience, affecting an individual's feelings, thoughts, and actions in significant, if often subtle, ways.

Nor should it be surprising that the effects of these conditions extend to the personal lives of teachers. Teachers who feel physically and emotionally exhausted at work and who no longer feel committed to their work will find it nearly impossible to keep these problems contained within the classroom. As several researchers have shown, a crucial connection exists between a person's work and his or her behavior and self-identity outside of the work environment (Green, 1968; Sarason, 1977; Terkel, 1972).

Teachers may feel that their life has completely gotten out of their control, so that questions of personal competency and self-esteem may begin to haunt them. They may even second-guess the wisdom of choosing teaching as a career and may wonder whether they could pursue any occupation successfully. These teachers may question too whether they are sufficiently likable or caring or patient enough human beings, concerns that will certainly affect their sense of self. In addition, when, as a result of stress or burnout, these teachers pull back from work or become aware of their covert disparagement of students, they may experience guilt over the failure of their efforts or their apparent repudiation of their ideals and values. Of course, some teachers experience little guilt and remorse when they become burned out but may be filled instead with anger (at those perceived as having caused the problem—for example, unruly students) or anxiety (in regard to what the next day will bring). In many teachers, periods of guilt (blaming oneself) are interspersed with periods of anger (blaming others); at times, too, these feelings co-occur. The point is that feeling stressed or burned out brings out behaviors and feelings in individuals that are either difficult to accept (for example, rage, irritability, intolerance, apathy, cynicism, physical and/or verbal abuse of others) or simply acutely uncomfortable (for example, guilt or anxiety); in either case, these new behaviors and feelings invariably alter the ways in which teachers view themselves, often leading to significant reductions in general feelings of self-regard.

Here's how one teacher experienced the physical and psychological symptoms of burnout:

Phyllis was in her fourth year of work as a high school teacher of biology in a middle-class suburban school district. Because of the

retirements of several colleagues in her department, she was asked
to take on additional administrative responsibilities, which she agreed
to do. She was also asked to teach an advanced placement course for
which the newer teachers were considered too inexperienced. She
agreed to this as well, feeling that the challenge would balance the
need to plan for a new course.

After several weeks, however, the workload began to feel excessive and Phyllis began to experience a chronic sense of fatigue. At
first she didn't link the two, attributing her tiredness instead to a
"low-grade flu." But as the fatigue continued and as other ailments
developed, including frequent headaches and digestive problems,
Phyllis began to suspect that her physical symptoms were related to
the increasing pressure she felt at work. Soon too she found it difficult to fall asleep and realized that she felt frequently anxious, on
edge. She alternately blamed herself, her students, and her administration for her deterioration. In the teachers' room she bitched
about the administration; to her friends she complained about the
apathy of her students; and at home at night she couldn't help wondering whether a more competent, dedicated person would simply
cope much better than she. At times she felt quite confident that one
of these attributions was the correct one; at other times she felt that
the whole situation was too complex and multidetermined to ever
understand clearly. But the moment-to-moment determination of
whose "fault" this all was left her only momentarily satisfied—the
bottom line to her was that she couldn't continue to suffer through
headaches and nausea and anxiety and intermittent self-blame.
Teaching had become too physically and mentally painful.

The experience of work is, of course, "transforming" even
when it is going well. Psychotherapists, for example, are often self-
reflective, and they are therapeutic outside their professional offices
(Farber, 1985), just as lawyers are often analytical outside their work
environment. Exceptions of course abound, and it may be pointed
out that many such professionals were this way before they ever
formally entered their field; nevertheless, for most workers the experience of work continues to shape their overall behavior and style
even after their entry into their profession. Optimally, individuals
continually learn from their work and become more and more like

their "ego ideal"—their preferred image of themselves. And when individuals perceive their work as meaningful and fulfilling, some approximation to this process generally occurs. For example, the changes that occur in psychotherapists as a result of their practices are consonant with both their personal values and the changes they seek to promote in others (for example, increased self-reflection and self-confidence). But when work loses meaning, when the costs seem to greatly outstrip the benefits, the transformations that result from work are generally unwelcome. Thus, when teachers become burned out, they are no longer able to see themselves in terms that approximate their ego-ideal; they no longer believe in themselves or their students and no longer see themselves as helpful and concerned.

Interpersonal Problems

The effects of teacher stress or burnout include interpersonal problems. Physical and psychological distress are invariably brought home and interfere with the individual's relationships with family and friends. After a difficult, draining, anxiety-filled day in which one has repeated to oneself for the thousandth time, "I don't know why I'm doing this," coming home should be simply a relief, a place to immediately forget the troubles of the day; yet for many teachers the transition between school and home is a difficult one (Blase and Pajak, 1986). Many need an adjustment period before they can cope with others and would like nothing better than to wear a "please do not disturb" sign following work or take a long uninterrupted stretch on an easy chair with a newspaper and a drink. But often this kind of slow, gradual period of decompression is just not possible. Married teachers have spouses' needs to contend with and may also have children waiting to be cared for, played with, and talked to; all teachers have errands to run, food to buy, dinner to prepare, and personal lives to pursue. That teacher who feels entirely unable to cope at school, who feels overwhelmed by the demands and underwhelmed by the available support, will not surprisingly be testy and irritable with others even when the school day is over.

This kind of displacement of feelings manifests itself in various guises. The most typical and frequently caricatured form is the scene in which the teacher, at the slightest provocation, yells at his or her spouse and children, demanding that they immediately end their offensive behavior. "I put up with enough of this at work, I refuse to deal with this rudeness/fighting/helplessness/being talked back to at home. . . . Do it yourself . . . just stop it and leave me alone . . . dammit, can't I have five minutes to myself? . . . How about me, don't I count?" But other, more subtle effects of feeling burned out may surface as well. For example, such teachers may have less energy for their families, may not listen to their spouse or children as sensitively or intently, may take a more passive role in planning family events, and may be less emotionally available. Discussions with family members may more easily escalate into arguments. Interest in current events, charitable causes, or politics may fade or even give way to cynicism. Single teachers may feel too enervated to bother dating, and married teachers may feel that going out with one's spouse or being sexual with him or her is "more trouble than it's worth." And in severe cases, when a teacher's sense of burnout and resentment seems to be all but out of control, he or she may resort to behaviors at home (for example, physical abuse or neglect of children) that have been strongly considered but not acted upon at work. Unfortunately, the constraints that bind teachers' impulses at school may feel less binding at home. "Taking it out" on one's family is, of course, a common symptom of stressed or burned-out workers of all varieties.

The effects of some recent cultural trends—most notably the vast increase in the number of dual-career families and the rising divorce rate—may well increase the probability or virulence of many of these potential problems. When both partners in a relationship work outside the home (as is frequently the case with teachers), both may feel cheated of support or free time and a constant process of negotiation for who takes care of whom may go on. Arguments frequently develop over sharing of household responsibilities, autonomy, and power (Pepitone-Rockwell, 1980). When one member of this working dyad—in this case, the teacher—is feeling burned out, the partner may feel burdened with his or her own work, may further feel as if he or she has been given insufficient attention or credit, and thus may feel disinclined to be supportive or sympathetic. Without social support, a burned-out teacher may become even more symptomatic and bitter. Divorce inevitably adds to the woes of a burned-out teacher as well. Not only is this individual without a crucial element of social support (if he or she is still single) but for some the complications of divorce—alimony, stepchildren, visitation schedules—further strain an already burdened system.

Freudenberger (1984) has suggested that when the effects of burnout appear at home, as they almost invariably do, they are often "manifested through alcoholism, depletion of finances through drugs or cocaine abuse, periods of physical deterioration of the burnout victim, neglected and abused family members, significant uninvolvement with activities of the family, lack of communication, withdrawal from work, or eventual withdrawal and detachment from the family" (p. 102).

When work feels oppressive, the whole world may seem inhospitable. Friends, whose flaws have usually been overlooked or minimized, are now viewed more critically and the need or desire to get together with them may decrease greatly. Sometimes, too, friends are unexpectedly subjected to long, heated, critical accounts of the problems of schools or teachers. When asked how things are going for them, many teachers are apt to reply, "Don't start me," or "You don't want to know!" Nevertheless, many are anxious to tell their stories, to unload their guilt, anxieties, or anger. And those who are truly burned out seem almost obsessed with telling and retelling their side of the story, usually with little patience for those who might disagree or offer a different perspective on events.

But the need to make sense of what went wrong with teaching, to understand or to blame someone or something for the failure of work to provide meaning, competes with the opposite need—to forget as completely as possible about teaching and everything about it. Teachers who are burned out seem to need to reduce the importance of teaching, to relegate it to a lesser position in their lives. Many burned-out teachers vacillate between these opposing tendencies, leaving friends and family members perplexed as to whether to ask about work or not. Furthermore, when teachers do seem intent on forgetting (rather than understanding), they again are faced with a choice: to forget via fatigue and withdrawal or to forget via hypomanic energy invested in something completely different. Sometimes, a teacher may come home and want to shut the world out, feeling unable to do anything but climb into bed or watch TV. At other times, this teacher may come home determined to do something for him- or herself in order to forget the "awfulness" of the day or the perceived meaninglessness of the job—go shopping, for example, or go out for dinner, or socialize with friends. And at still other times, this same teacher may want desperately to share the details of an "unbelievable" day with a friend or spouse and get validation from a loved one that the work really is impossible. The unpredictability of the needs of burned-out teachers may well leave those who care about them shaking their heads in frustration.

Teacher burnout, then, often leads to increased marital and family conflict and increased vulnerability to outside stress, but clearly these effects are bidirectional and interactional. Family conflicts and responsibilities as well as the pressures of outside stress make it more difficult for a teacher to invest and find fulfillment in work. The teacher who has had a serious fight with his or her spouse the night before or the morning of a school day will be hard-pressed to concentrate at school, will have less patience for students, will teach less effectively, and will probably get less back from students, all of which may evoke in the teacher that "what's the use" feeling. Multiple roles (teacher, part-time worker, parent, spouse, and friend) can, and often do, result in work overload and role conflict, precipitants of burnout. In this regard, Cooke and Rousseau (1984) found that the interaction between family roles and work roles engenders progressively more strain for single teachers, married teachers, and those with children. Similarly, Claesson (1986) found that while the dual role of teacher and mother yields several benefits (for example, a greater ability to view children as multifaceted individuals), it may also create problems, for example, harboring unrealistically high expectations of pupils as well as parents of pupils.

Most commonly, work and home life constantly interact, the one situation affecting the other, which, in turn, affects the first situation. A hard day teaching with an inordinate number of bureaucratic demands and students who seem oblivious to one's demands and exhortations is likely to lead to some bitterness or frustration that is taken home. Interacting with family members then becomes tinged with some degree of anxiety, unease, or unreasonable expectations; one may look for family members to provide unconditional support or expect them to be perfectly empathic (as if they themselves may not also have had their difficult moments at work or school). And, as these expectations (mostly unspoken and often unconscious) of finding a warm, totally non-stressful haven at home are invariably dashed, the teacher feels even less ready to give his or her attention to students at school. But one does not have to fight with a spouse or even experience an especially difficult day at school in order to reach a state where either work or home life feels too much to cope with. Sometimes the sheer weight of multiple and constant responsibilities is sufficient to lead one to feel overwhelmed and undercared for.

It might be argued that family-career conflicts and constant responsibility are encountered by individuals at many high-level professional jobs. What makes teaching, then, any different from other forms of demanding work? Teaching is special in several regards. It demands virtually constant personal interaction with children or adolescents and further demands that such interaction be consistently tinged with helpfulness, patience, sensitivity, and expertise. It demands that such interactions be open to scrutiny, evaluation, and input from a variety of other, frequently competing sources. It demands that teachers work with individuals who may not want to work with them and who may not be benefiting from their style or expertise. It offers little opportunity to refer elsewhere those who seem to be refractory to one's best efforts. It offers little opportunity to relax with and profit from interaction with colleagues or other adults during the day. And the remuneration for this work is such that outside work is often necessary in order to meet expenses. Although other forms of human service work contain some of these features, no other job combines elements of constant work with children, high expectations of success from others, little opportunity for interaction with adults, and inadequate wages. It is no wonder that teachers are prone to work overload and role conflict, particularly those teachers with families and school-age children.

Of course, when things are going well at home—when one

feels on top of all the competing demands and when spouse and children express their appreciation for all one does—then one may feel particularly energized and ready to tackle difficult situations, even those that previously seemed intractable. And when things are going well at school—when students seem to be learning and when one feels confident in attributing these results to one's own efforts— then "miraculously" one has more time and energy for family, looks forward to time spent with others, and has greater patience for others' needs.

Professional Effects

Burned-out teachers exert less effort teaching than they once did (Schwab, Jackson, and Schuler, 1984), a finding consistent with data indicating that a substantial minority of both teachers and students acknowledge that *some* teachers in their school show no interest in their students (Harris and Associates, 1988). Burned-out or worn-out teachers are no longer as motivated, patient, or optimistic. Comments from teachers reflecting these themes include:

> "It's not worth the effort to keep trying . . . to be creative . . . to care . . . to attempt to educate everyone in the class."
> "I'd rather spend time doing paperwork than interacting with students; most of the kids don't try, why should I?"
> "The parents don't care; why should I?"
> "I'll try but it's a losing cause."
> "Most of these kids were lost by the time they started school."
> "They only care about themselves. They're spoiled and are only interested in instant gratification."
> "I've learned that I have to take care of myself first."

Burned-out teachers look for ways to reduce their direct involvement with students ("It should be the other way around: one period teaching and seven preps"; "I'll only stay in the profession if I can become an administrator"; "It's too much work to individualize curriculum"). In addition, because most forms of help are seen as useless, these teachers may also refuse to accept the advice or input of others. Administrators who want to help may be perceived as intrusive ("I wish he'd just stay out of my classroom and leave me alone") or unrealistic ("What does she expect me to be able to do?") or condescending ("He treats me as if I'd just graduated and never been in a classroom before"). With less invested in the job, there is less motivation on the part of burned-out teachers to be "good team players" and greater willingness to be stubborn ("I'll be damned if I'm going to do that for them") or even contentious with administrators ("Who the hell do they think they are?")

Although they will tell you they shouldn't, most teachers lose their patience at least occasionally. The burned-out teacher, however, loses patience more easily, more frequently, and more intensely. In an attempt to cope with anxiety, he or she may become rigid or authoritarian (Keavney and Sinclair, 1978). Incidents that may have once been handled with compassion or patience or wisdom are now reacted to with unabashed anger, threats, or selfish solutions. Burned-out teachers tend to lose perspective on the seriousness of certain offenses, taking some far too seriously and others not seriously enough. Intolerance of minor "offenses" is commonplace. The next student who talks out of turn is

> going straight to the principal's office
> having a note sent home
> missing gym
> staying after school
> getting extra homework
> getting a failing mark in my gradebook

Students are viewed cynically ("They're too far gone to work with"; "They're too spoiled to care about others"; "They expect me to entertain them every minute"), as are their parents ("They have no idea how to raise children or how to talk to them; I blame them more than the kids") and the teaching profession ("This job is absurd"; "I wasn't prepared for this and it's certainly not what I'm going to do the rest of my life"). And the content of one's thoughts and daydreams seems to shift dramatically away from professional issues. No longer do new curriculum ideas or projects dominate or even significantly occupy one's thinking. Burned-out teachers seem to become more solipsistic, concerned primarily with their own survival and needs. Questions like "What shall I do after school?" "Where should we go on vacation?" and "How can I earn some extra money?" replace questions like "What can I do with this class to make vivid the notion of the American Revolution?" and "What auxiliary services are available to help students with reading or math problems?"

In the teachers' lounge, stressed and burned-out teachers are much more likely to share "horror stories" regarding some student behavior or administrative indignity than they are to discuss some exemplary student achievement or administrative initiative. The cognitive set of these teachers has become attuned to negative events. Convinced that teaching and all its component parts (the school, the bureaucracy, the students, the parents) essentially constitute a disaster with few redeeming qualities, the teachers perceive and re-member more accurately the events that fit this perspective, while events that are dissonant with this perspective tend to be more easily overlooked or forgotten. Similarly, colleagues and friends who share this view are most often sought out while those who see teaching in more positive terms tend to be avoided. Thus, the burned-out teacher's view of teaching—as a job demanding much effort and producing too few social, financial, or even educational rewards—is confirmed and sometimes even strengthened. Disconfirmatory ex-amples—students doing well, colleagues extending support, admin-istrators providing supplies—are perceived as welcome but tempo-rary aberrations, exceptions that only serve to prove the rule.

Going to work may seem like a formidable, ominous task. "Sunday night dread" and "Monday morning blues" speak to the apprehension of stressed and burned-out teachers over returning to the scene of bad memories. Silent curses and a bad temper may usher in the new work week. Lateness and mental health day absences increase; Hammen and DeMayo's (1982) study of urban high school teachers found that stress per se caused these teachers to miss an average of 4.5 days of work per year. What was once a "calling" becomes a strict "punch in at 8:30, leave immediately at 3" kind of job. Moreover, the thought of leaving teaching is never too far away, even when the realistic chances of this occurring are slim to non-existent. "I'm just waiting for the right business opportunity"; "I'm thinking over my options"; "I'm planning on going back to school soon." For some, of course, these thoughts are far from mere fantasy; many teachers, once talented and dedicated, leave the profession each year. Those who stay may suffer a dramatic loss in idealism. Pines (1982) found that teachers perceived a significant decline in their level of idealism from the time they began teaching to the present.

The dysfunctional effects of teacher stress and burnout are also manifested on a school-wide level. I've noted before that the existence of a "critical mass" of such teachers may alter dramatically the tone and motivation of an entire staff. New teachers especially are affected by the climate and predominant mores of their school and may feel singularly odd and uncomfortably conspicuous if their views are discrepant from those of most of their colleagues. But more experienced teachers may also have difficulty with their burned-out colleagues, feeling as if they (the non–burned-out staff) may have to work even harder to cover for those who are apathetic and disillusioned. It is easy to see how those who still care would greatly resent the attitudes and work habits of those who have essentially given up. In addition, as Dixon, Shaw, and Bensky (1980) have noted, administrative roles are necessarily affected when schools suffer from a morale problem. In such cases, administrators have to spend more time recruiting and orienting staff as a result of high turnover rates and dealing with role conflict and interpersonal problems between different groups of teachers and between teachers and administration, and need also to deal with the resistance to bureaucratic forms and procedures that stress invariably generates.

Not surprisingly, then, stress and burnout affect every facet of a teacher's life—relationships with students, colleagues, administrators, family, and friends. From a societal point of view, the impact of teacher stress and burnout may be greatest in terms of its potentially devastating effects on pupil education, particularly the education of those in lower socioeconomic groups. Unfortunately, this is an area of investigation that has been largely neglected. Empirical studies on the effects of teacher burnout on pupil performance are clearly needed to test our assumptions regarding adverse effects. With hard evidence in hand, federal and private research money generally becomes more available, as does greater knowledge of where and how to intervene in the cycle.

Types of Teacher Burnout

As noted earlier in this chapter, certain emotional disorders, such as depression, manifest themselves in various forms. There are several types of depression as there are several types of anxiety disorders, thought disorders, and eating disorders. Burnout may also appear in different guises. The most common manifestation occurs in the teacher who gives up after years of feeling chronically stressed and emotionally spent. But there is also the teacher who feels underchallenged and understimulated, who cannot tolerate another day of teaching young learning-disabled children simple spatial concepts, for example. And there is also the teacher who gives up after spending weeks rather than years on the job and the teacher (the one that Freudenberger often writes about) who appears not to give up at all but rather to be consumed by his or her own passion for the job or commitment to students. Those familiar with teachers and schools have seen each of these types and more, including those teachers who seem to be a conglomeration of many of these categories. In the balance of this chapter, three major subtypes are described: the worn-out teacher, the frenetic teacher, and the underchallenged teacher.

Type I: Worn-Out Teachers. Freudenbeger's original conception of burnout was that workers found themselves under increasing pressure to succeed in helping others, demanded more of themselves than they were able to give, and ultimately burned out. These were overly committed and excessively dedicated individuals who ignored their own discomforts and preferences almost without respite. According to Freudenberger, these highly motivated workers reacted to stress by overworking until they collapsed. Such a description brings to mind an image of a supernova star consumed by its own power, destroyed by its own energy. The protagonist in Tom Wolfe's book *Bonfire of the Vanities,* a hard-driving, high-powered Wall Street investment broker with little time for his family and friends, describes himself and others like him as "masters of the universe." For such individuals, failure is simply inconceivable—the only solution to temporary setbacks and frustration is more work and greater effort.

But this is not the typical description of teachers who complain of burnout. Indeed, were this the case, although we might feel bad for a group of driven and unfulfilled teachers, we might well be delighted by the educational benefits generated by such a stance. More often than not, though, rather than overworking to the point of exhaustion, teachers turn off to the job and stop attempting to succeed in situations that appear hopeless. One worn-out teacher, who used to take it personally when he saw a student in his junior high school bullying others or cutting classes, now has a very different attitude: "I walk down the hall now and I don't see anything and I don't hear anything. And I feel better" (Cerra, 1980, p. B2).

Frenetic, overcommitted teachers (those whom Freudenberger would deem as burned out) are zealous in trying to get their students to learn and like what they are doing; worn-out teachers are those who regularly pass out mimeographed worksheets. Worn-out teachers react to stress not by working harder but rather by working less hard; they attempt to balance the discrepancy between input and output by *reducing* their input. In this sense, worn-out workers have quit before they become totally consumed by their work.

One of the most unfortunate aspects of such cases is that the symptoms tend to be self-reinforcing. As Cherniss (1980b) has pointed out, "discouragement and withdrawal most likely will lead to more failure because enthusiasm, optimism, and involvement are often necessary for success" (p. 19). Once teachers are worn out, renewing their sense of dedication and care is a difficult task. Worn-out teachers act as if they believe that regardless of how hard they work the classroom results will be disappointing. These teachers act in accordance with the learned helplessness paradigm: They no longer believe their actions can effect the intended goal. They have been worn down by the cumulative effects of dealing with situations that they perceive as beyond their control: disruptive students who seem not to listen to anyone, slow-learning students who won't try any longer, parents who seem to have given up on parenting or who seem simply overwhelmed by life, bureaucrats who seem more in-

terested in their own power than they are in student progress or
teachers' standard of living. The inner-city teacher may be worn out
from dealing with the classroom consequences of poverty and despair; the suburban teacher may feel worn out from dealing with the
entitlement and callousness that sometimes accompany affluence.
Both may be worn out from trying to get anything at all from short-
sighted and narrow-minded school boards.

A teacher best labeled as worn out had the following to say
about his job (as a high school teacher in a small, racially integrated
city):

> How many years can you expect me to work hard, to
> believe in what I am doing, to imagine that I am mak-
> ing a difference, when no one else—not psychologists,
> not the criminal justice system, not social agencies,
> not the federal government, not anyone—is dealing
> effectively with the problems I face? . . . Drugs, crime,
> apathy, teenage pregnancy . . . none of these problems
> are going to get fixed without massive amounts of
> help and we both know how likely that is. I'll be
> damned if I'm going to ruin my life trying to play the
> hero. I once thought I could, but I know now I can't.
> Or maybe I just won't. . . . Even when I've tried my
> best, the successes have been less than overwhelming
> and God knows never appreciated. I'm bombarded
> daily with demands and threats; sometimes I even get
> ridiculed, which I can't stand. I'm too old [forty-one]
> to take this anymore. The only way I can protect my-
> self is to stop caring. I know I get back less by giving
> less but I just can't give anymore.

Harvey Fischer, a psychoanalyst who originally drew the distinction between two types of burnout (1983), suggested that those
who are excessively driven and overcommitted (the Freudenberger
type of burnout) "cling tenaciously to a high sense of self-esteem"
(p. 42). According to Fischer, these individuals attempt desperately
to succeed against all odds, risking their physical health and neglecting their personal lives to maximize the probability of profes-

sional success. For them, the acknowledgment of failure is nearly impossible. inasmuch as it reflects on their personal worth as human beings. The job is an extension of their selves, their egos, and must be successfully performed. On the other hand, those who are worn out have incurred damage to their sense of self-esteem— they are no longer personally invested in performing well on the job. They have acknowledged their failure, have allowed that they cannot do the job they once thought they could. Some, perhaps many, still blame others for the failure but the bottom line is their willingness to face the fact that they cannot achieve the goals they had once set for themselves and that efforts in this direction are senseless and self-defeating. My sense is that this lack of ongoing personal investment, the withdrawal of damaged ego, is, unfortunately, more typical of those teachers who are *said* to be burned out than is the opposite stance of increasingly greater degrees of investment.

This contention is supported by the results of an earlier study I conducted (Farber, 1984b). I found that teachers' sense of dedication and commitment to the teaching profession (measured by such items as "If I had to do it all over, I would still choose to be a teacher" and "I see myself continuing to teach for the rest of my career") were not positively correlated with burnout. In fact, the data indicated that the more burned out a teacher is the *less* committed he or she is to the profession. The cause-effect relationship here is, of course, unknown and it is possible that those teachers who now appear burned-out were once the most dedicated teachers in their schools. Nevertheless, these data suggest that the prototypical burned-out teacher—at least at the time when symptoms of burnout are being manifested—is neither excessively committed nor dedicated to teaching.

It may be argued that frenetic overcommitment often precedes feeling worn out, that is, that teachers escalate their efforts, at least initially. when their "baseline rate" of effort has not succeeded in producing results and that only when their best efforts fail does "wearout" (or "brownout," as some call it) result. This may indeed occur, but my sense is that when it does, it is a rapid stage on the way to becoming worn out. Most teachers from the beginning feel they are putting forth a good and decent effort, certainly a good

enough effort that results should be forthcoming given even a minimal effort on the part of students (or parents). Thus, while some
teachers may increase their efforts somewhat in the face of failure,
most simply cut back (become worn out) when they sense their
reasonable efforts are of little or no avail.

Type II: Frenetic Teachers. In the face of adversity and anticipated failure, some teachers do indeed redouble their efforts and
do everything possible to make classroom success more likely. They
may well be the crusaders in a given school or district, campaigning
for greater effort on everyone's part, pleading for cooperation, supplies, patience, and optimism. At times, they seem to have sufficient
ideas and energy for the entire faculty, to be able to carry the whole
team on their shoulders. Individuals who fall in this category believe in maximum effort till success, with no letup allowable; failure is never attributed to the nature of the problem but is always
seen as a failure of will.

The quality that marks the efforts of frenetic teachers is that
of frantic energy marshaled on behalf of their students, an energy
that often cannot be sustained for long periods, so that the person
ultimately succumbs to exhaustion. But there is often a nobleness
to these efforts that is inspiring. These teachers are often "true believers" (in social justice or the ameliorative effects of education on
poverty or the therapeutic effects of simple caring) and thus have
the most difficulty accepting constraints on their vision. Though
others may chide them for their failure to perceive things realistically or for their refusal to shift perspectives on a problem, they
refuse to compromise the integrity of their values. When input fails
to achieve the hoped-for output, this type of burned-out teacher
does not narrow his or her goals, rationalize failures, or reduce
efforts (as a worn-out teacher is apt to do) but rather works harder
and harder in the belief that a point will be reached where efforts
will succeed. But the despair that accompanies the eventual realization that "this isn't going to work" (despite my best efforts, everyone's not going to be reading at grade level by June) may be
considerable. The disillusionment may be truly frightening; their
world view, based on a sense of their power and effectiveness, has
been shattered. The point at which the belief that efforts will nec-

essarily succeed is relinquished is the point at which burnout has taken over. It is often a sudden and dramatic fall, because these beliefs and efforts have often been sustained at an intense level for long periods of time. Whereas a worn-out teacher has gradually allowed cracks to form in her or his belief world and has become increasingly disillusioned, this other type of burned-out teacher often appears to hold on tightly to a seemingly impervious belief system until the whole system shatters suddenly.

The distinction between these two types of burned-out teachers—the worn-out individual and the frenetic, overcommitted one—lies essentially in their reaction to frustration and disappointment. The worn-out teacher is willing to concede at least partial defeat and withdraws his or her personal investment in work; the frenetic teacher cannot admit defeat (or be content with reasonable successes) and reacts by working harder and investing increasingly more of him- or herself until no more is possible and exhaustion sets in.

The classic example of Type II burnout is a young, well-educated, socially idealistic, politically involved young man or woman who comes to an impoverished inner-city or rural school brimming with ideas, enthusiasm, and confidence and who, after several months (or perhaps even years) of giving more and more—of depriving him- or herself of sleep and/or a relaxing social life, of trying to find new, creative ways to motivate and teach children—senses that these efforts are not paying off, that he or she is ineffective and perhaps even still mistrusted. But this type of burnout can occur in more propitious circumstances as well, even in a suburban school.

Jim S. was a high school English teacher in an affluent suburban community. Following graduation from college, he had taken a year off to travel, and he felt fortunate in being able to find such a good teaching position upon his return. He had dreamed of being an English teacher since his own high school days, imagining that he would be able to motivate his students far more easily and effectively than his own teachers had been able to do. Over the years, he had amassed a list of the books, plays, and poems he thought tenth and eleventh graders would easily relate to. Though he knew he might be faced with the prospect of a prescribed curriculum, somehow he didn't imagine he'd have trouble convincing the department chairperson that his new ideas would be exciting and beneficial to all. But it was a problem. Citing state regulations and the need for college-bound students to cover "traditional material," the department chairperson turned him down flatly. Jim was disappointed but nonetheless decided to teach the traditional material in as enthusiastic a way as possible. He was ready for the challenge.

During his first year at the school, he was assigned four classes, two of which were academically talented. For the most part, the students loved him. He was young, seemed to understand students well, joked around with them, respected them, challenged them fairly. During that year, he was asked to be on the prom committee and enthusiastically agreed; the second year he agreed to serve as the adviser to the school newspaper and agreed also to help with production of the school play. At this point, these assignments didn't seem burdensome; indeed, he felt more a part of the school and closer to the students. He loved the feeling of helping students and enjoyed greatly the adulation he was receiving. The third year was a turning point, though: As his reputation grew, students sought him out after school for advice. At first, this too was tremendously gratifying, but soon the pressure grew to be at school more frequently to help out a still greater number of students with even more serious problems. But they needed him, and the guidance counselor and school psychologist, overburdened themselves, encouraged his efforts. The school was beginning to consume him. Though he told himself he loved the work, he also felt that there was no respite— there was always something to plan, someone to meet with, some project that needed his help. Though his demeanor was almost always pleasant, he began to resent the constant intrusions on his life.

The turning point was one afternoon in his third year of teaching. As he was leaving school at 5 P.M., a student turned up at his room to ask for a few minutes of his time. He became angry, and though he quickly reversed himself and spent time with the student, he felt changed. Over the next few weeks he frequently felt angry at students for not respecting his boundaries, at other teachers for not being sufficiently available to students (thus leaving more work for him), at the chairperson for being rigid and for not helping him to protect his time better. He felt overworked and underappreciated and began wondering for the first time whether this was really going to be his life's work.

There is also another kind of Type II teacher, one whose energetic efforts to help are marred by an attitude of smugness and impatience with others. Whereas many Type II burned-out teachers exhort and help out needy colleagues, this subgroup is hard on colleagues (and on themselves as well). There is often a markedly narcissistic quality to these teachers, for they give the appearance that only they understand, only they are sufficiently caring, only they have the right answers. Note, for example, the spate of auto-biographical books written in the late 1960s by young, idealistic teachers, most of whom ultimately acknowledged that they couldn't succeed at the task they had been so zealously pursuing. These books, although sincere and well-meaning, are essentially self-serving heroes' tales—epic accounts of solitary, honest, persistent, and misunderstood teachers who struggle valiantly, but ultimately futilely, against petty bureaucrats, uncaring administrators, and racist colleagues in an attempt to save underprivileged children from the ravages of the system. On the one hand, this narcissistic aspect of burnout, this sense of "I must do it because no one else knows how or cares to help," serves students particularly well. Before they exhaust themselves entirely, these burned-out teachers give a great deal to their classes and their students, in fact, a great deal more than the average teacher. On the other hand, as this earlier group of authors well demonstrated, these teachers, both before and after reaching a state of total exhaustion, may well be self-righteous, self-justifying, and condemnatory of those who refuse to totally dedicate their lives and risk their health in the pursuit of noble goals. Burned-out teachers, then—at least this subgroup of self-righteous ones—are often good for their students (before their collapse, of course) and detrimental to their colleagues.

This last point perhaps requires clarification. Why should seemingly enthusiastic and dedicated teachers—assuming they don't write disparaging books—provoke animosity in their colleagues? Enthusiasm and dedication, after all, are generally positive and infectious qualities that facilitate staff functioning. On first

impulse, one might hypothesize that jealousy or envy is operative—
that some teachers feel upstaged or inadequate in comparison to
hard-working colleagues. But my sense is that most teachers are not
at all envious of this group. Instead, they feel put off by the intolerance for others' styles, values, and goals that seems to color their
enthusiasm and effort. This subgroup of burned-out teachers seem
certain that their way is right. In contrast, worn-out teachers are less
likely to be judgmental of colleagues and tend to be empathic
toward those who are struggling to find a comfortable professional
stance.

    Type III: Underchallenged Teachers. There is yet another
group of disenchanted teachers who appear to be neither excessively
driven (frenetic) nor excessively fatigued (worn out). These are the
teachers who feel dissatisfied not by the sheer amount of work that
needs to be done or even by the obstacles that must be encountered
in doing the work but rather by the sameness and lack of stimulation presented by the tasks that face them each day and each year.
These are the teachers who feel they can no longer summon any
enthusiasm for teaching simple multiplication to elementary school
students or the causes of the Civil War to yet another generation of
high school students. They are disinterested rather than fed up,
bored rather than intolerably stressed. They have not incurred damage to their self-esteem, nor are they attempting through work to
confirm an irrationally high level of self-esteem; instead, they have
begun to realistically sense that their self-esteem might well be damaged if they continue in work that they find unfulfilling and insufficiently demanding of their skills and abilities. For underchallenged teachers, the stresses of work are not especially great but
neither are the rewards, particularly those of a psychological nature.

    The plight of underchallenged teachers is not as dramatic as
those who fall into the other two categories of burnout, but they too
feel that they are getting insufficient returns from teaching given
the work they put in. They do not feel oppressed by the work as do
many worn-out teachers, and they do not have the missionary zeal
and frantic energy of the overcommitted burned-out teacher, but
over time the underchallenged teacher begins to perform the work
more perfunctorily, begins to question more whether this is the

right field, begins to withdraw energy and enthusiasm. Typically, all this occurs not out of desperation (as with the worn-out teacher) and not as a reaction to a feeling of sudden and total depletion (as with the burned-out teacher), but it nonetheless occurs. The underchallenged teacher continues to do a professional job, doesn't especially resent the work, but doesn't especially look forward to it either. Teaching has lost its meaning, its spark—once viewed as a means to personal fulfillment, it now feels like another assembly line job. This teacher begins to consider other work possibilities.

Underchallenged teachers often feel that their skills and talents are being insufficiently utilized. Working all day in a self-contained classroom of young children, or getting the opportunity only once or twice a day to work with a class of especially bright students, is not enough. In this vein, an eighth-grade English teacher in a fairly typical suburban area remarked: "Maybe, if I'm lucky, for an hour and a half in any given working day I'll feel stimulated and excited by what's going on in my classroom. It feels great while it's going on, but it's not enough for me. I know I sound a bit like a snob, but I *do* enjoy teaching brighter kids better than slower kids and, given the system, I can only do that one or two periods a day."

Underchallenged teachers often complain too that their other skills go unnoticed and unused in their schools. Many teachers are able administrators, planners, writers, community organizers, or public speakers; many are politically astute and/or active in local civic or political organizations. The point is that most teachers are highly educated individuals with skills and ideas that are only rarely called upon by administrators or other school officials. Underchallenged teachers represent a most unfortunate failure of the educational system, inasmuch as many who fall within this particular category of burnout seem to be among the brightest and most creative of our nation's teachers. Most local educational systems provide little or no means for talented teachers to express or try out innovative ideas beyond their own classrooms. Indeed, in some school systems, even within one's own classroom, new approaches or methods may have to be carried out in almost covert fashion. The following example describes how lack of challenge can affect a teacher.

Over her parents' protestations, during her junior year in college Joan decided to become an elementary school teacher. Her parents, noting her consistently excellent grades, leadership ability (she held numerous offices in student government), and interest in civic issues, had wanted her to go to law school. But citing her love for children, as well as her desire to have summers for herself, she decided on education as a career. For the most part, she enjoyed her education courses and was intrigued by many of the issues discussed in her classes. She looked forward to trying out her own curriculum and classroom management ideas in her own classes and was meanwhile learning a good deal from her teachers and supervisors.

Her first job was in the district in which she did her student teaching. Impressed by her ability and personable style, the school superintendent of this medium-sized college community offered her a position teaching second grade. For several years Joan was mostly content with her job. Her students were well-mannered children from a wide range of socioeconomic backgrounds, and with each passing year she felt increasingly able to meet their needs. She felt good about her ability as a teacher, a feeling confirmed by feedback from parents as well as school administration. But after her fourth year on the job, vague feelings of discontent began to set in. She wasn't angry at anyone, she genuinely enjoyed the children, and she felt that the administration was somewhat narrow-minded but essentially decent and quite fair in their treatment of her. She had none of the more debilitating symptoms commonly associated with teacher burnout—at most she felt unexcited about going to work and mildly depressed on coming home—but she used the word *burnout* to describe her state. Actually, the closest she could come to articulating what was wrong with any degree of specificity was a phrase she frequently used with friends: "I feel like I've outgrown my job." Later she said too: "I know it sounds conceited, but I feel smarter than my job. . . . I'm doing the same things over and over again. . . . I just don't feel like doing it anymore. . . . I'll miss the kids but I want new challenges. . . . I want to work with adults. . . . Intellectually, I know I'm doing something quite important but I feel like I'm stagnating."

She considered asking to be transferred to a higher grade level but anticipated that the same process would occur after a few years of teaching fifth or sixth grade. She considered going into school administration but felt daunted at the prospect of spending years in graduate school with no guarantee of finding a good job in the field; moreover, she felt put off by the politicized nature of school administration. She felt somewhat guilty leaving teaching (to go into public relations) but justified it by reminding herself that she'd given four good years to teaching and that she'd certainly done "her share" of public service.

Perhaps to call this teacher "burned out" is to extend the term too far. Her symptoms certainly do not correspond to the usual list proffered by researchers or expected by the public. Yet many teachers like Joan resign from teaching after only a few years on the job and many more seem to peak after teaching five to seven years. The loss of these usually talented teachers is an acute problem for a profession that desperately needs more of the "best and brightest." Often, these teachers attribute their resignation or their waning interest to "burnout" and in at least one critical sense they are right: They too perceive that they are receiving less from their work than they are putting in and refuse to continue with more of the same. On this basis, they constitute a significant, if relatively inconspicuous, part of what may be broadly conceived as the teacher burnout problem.

Combinations of Burnout. I have presented these three subgroups of teachers as if they constitute homogeneous types. Yet, as noted earlier, many burned-out teachers defy easy categorization. Some, perhaps many, vacillate among these descriptive categories, at times feeling so overwhelmed and pessimistic that they cut back on their involvement (worn out), at times feeling so energetic and optimistic—or so desperate to prove themselves and regain some measure of self-esteem—that they invest more than ever and more than is healthy in their work (frenetic burnout), and at times simply feeling uninterested in and unstimulated by the problems and issues of schools and children (underchallenged).

4

Idealism and Disillusionment:
Who Teaches, Who Leaves, and Why

Wanted: Men and women with the patience of Job, wisdom of Solomon and ability to prepare the next generation for productive citizenship under highly adverse and sometimes dangerous conditions. Applicant must be willing to fill gaps left by unfit, absent or working parents, satisfy demands of state politicians and local bureaucrats, impart healthy cultural and moral values and—oh, yes—teach the three Rs. Hours: 50-60 a week. Pay: fair (getting better). Rewards: mostly intangible.

Susan Tifft (1988, p. 58)

THE SPECTER, AND THE REALITY, OF TEACHER STRESS AND BURN-out are at least partially responsible for two critical educational problems: the recruitment and retention of teachers. In turn, teacher shortages and ill-qualified replacements make teaching more stressful for those who remain. As a recent (1986) Carnegie Task Force on Teaching as a Profession report aptly noted: "The many good teachers we have are being driven out of teaching by intolerable conditions, and it will be impossible to attract many new people of real ability to teaching until these conditions are radically altered." Moreover, cautions the report, unless we attract talented teachers to improve the quality of education, "the future prospects of this nation will be a lot dimmer." The focus in this chapter will be on the related issues of teacher shortages, recruitment, retention, and satisfaction.

The Teacher Shortage

The teacher shortage caught up with this nation rather abruptly in the early 1980s. After years of closing schools and transferring teachers as a result of declining school enrollments (between 1970 and 1984, the number of school-age children dropped by 6.2 million), schools found that they needed more teachers to keep up with their suddenly rising enrollments. Children of late-parenting "baby boomers" were entering the public schools in unexpectedly large numbers. The problem, though, was that there weren't enough teachers available: The number of newly prepared teachers had declined 60 percent from 1972 to 1985 as the need for teachers decreased, as teacher salaries failed to keep pace with inflation, and as the attraction and prestige of teaching ebbed. The current problem is exacerbated by the fact that through 1995 the number of teacher retirements is expected to increase. By 1992, for example, the demand for new teachers is expected to be 215,000 annually, while only 137,000 graduates are expected by then to be ready to enter teaching.

The problem is particularly acute when it comes to filling the need for math and science teachers, for minority teachers, and for any teachers at all in major urban centers. It has been difficult to recruit math and science teachers since the 1950s, but the situation appears to be worsening as the wage differential between education and private industry grows wider. According to Linda Darling-Hammond of the RAND Corporation, math and science teachers earn on average 30 to 50 percent less than equally trained peers employed elsewhere. "At present rates, graduates from undergraduate schools of education could be expected to fill about half of the 20,000 annual vacancies for math and science teachers" (Darling-Hammond, 1989, p. E21).

As for the need for minority teachers—whereas black and Hispanic students constitute more than 25 percent of the forty million children enrolled in public schools, black and Hispanic teachers make up only 10.5 percent of the teaching force. And although in 1988 blacks constituted 5 percent of those enrolled in teacher training programs—and Hispanics an additional 3 percent—these figures are in sharp contrast to those of 1980 when blacks and Hispanics represented 17 percent of the undergraduates majoring in education. Another way of looking at the need for more teachers from minority groups: Based upon the percentage of the population that is minority, there is a need for 50,000 new minority teachers annually; however, the number of minority college students graduating with degrees in education is approximately 14,000 annually (Council of the Great City Schools, 1987). As higher-paying, more prestigious professions in industry and other areas continue to recruit minority college graduates, the probability of greater numbers of minority students entering teaching remains remote. "A built-in time bomb" is what P. Michael Timpane, president of Teachers College, Columbia University, had to say about this situation. "If we don't get a reasonable number of minorities into the teaching profession, it's going to be difficult to provide a diversified staff and leadership for a country whose future is multicultural" (cited in Berger, 1988, p. A17). Not only, though, are we failing to attract minority students into teaching, but there are strong indications that there will be major problems in retaining minority teachers already in the field. The Metropolitan Life Survey of the American Teacher (Harris and Associates, 1988) found that 40 percent of minority teachers are very likely or fairly likely to leave teaching within the next five years—a figure fifteen percentage points higher than that of nonminority teachers. Less experienced minority teachers (those who have been teaching less than five years) are most likely to leave, with 55 percent indicating that within the next five years they will probably be ex-teachers.

It is difficult to recruit teachers, minority or otherwise, inexperienced or otherwise, to work in major urban centers. Working conditions in urban schools are often perceived by prospective teachers as inhospitable—unsafe, impersonal, and unsupportive—and teachers working in such settings are perceived as intolerably stressed and often burned out. According to the superintendent of the Paterson, New Jersey, school system, Frank Napier, Jr., "Because of all the negative publicity that urban districts are receiving, teachers are not anxious to come into such systems" (Olson and Rodman, 1988, p. 28). The fact is that while teaching is generally perceived as a stressful occupation, teaching in urban schools is seen as especially stressful. "Who needs it?" said one of the teachers interviewed for this book: "Teaching is hard enough in a 'good' school." Compounding the problem is the fact that salaries in many urban school districts have fallen behind those of neighboring suburban districts. Faced with their own staffing problems, and offering a combination of higher pay and better working conditions, suburban school districts have begun to more actively recruit experienced inner-city teachers. The bottom line is that teacher vacancies in urban areas are estimated to be two and one-half to three times as great as they are in suburban or rural districts.

According to one researcher, "the magnitude of the urban teacher shortage problem has been understated. There's no crisis in the suburban schools. The real crisis in education is in urban America" (Yarger, cited by Wells, 1988, p. A28). Yarger surveyed 900 undergraduates majoring in secondary education and found that 95 percent came from suburban areas, rural areas, or small towns and that nearly all these students planned to return to these areas after graduation. Less than 4 percent selected an urban setting as their first preference for a teaching position. The idealism of the sixties that prompted many college students to work with underprivileged children in poorer neighborhoods faded to a considerable extent in the seventies and early eighties. Urban schools are now seen as harsh rather than glamorous; urban neighborhoods are seen as threatening.

Some school districts have come up with creative solutions in attempts to recruit teachers for understaffed positions. For example, the Houston School Board has begun offering temporary housing to newly hired teachers and their families, and in Dade County, Florida, new teachers in English, math, or science receive a $5,000 "signing bonus." Teachers in Dade County who choose to work in inner-city schools receive an additional $500 bonus, renewable each year they choose to remain in that school. Whether these inducements will work on anything more than a very temporary basis is still an open question. Increased salary and the availability of housing may well attract a greater number of teachers to urban schools, but unless conditions in these schools allow them to feel effective in their roles, the likelihood of their remaining for substantial periods of time is small.

The Carnegie Task Force on Teaching as a Profession (1986)

cautioned strongly against dealing with the teacher shortage by lowering standards. "To make that strategy work now the country will have to scrape the bottom of the barrel to find its teachers." Nevertheless, this strategy has already been adopted by many school districts desperate to find new teachers each fall. According to one superintendent of a large school system in the Northeast, "Every Labor Day, when you're short 2,000 teachers, you lower the standard and let anyone in. They're known as 'Labor Day specials'" ("Teaching in Trouble," 1986, p. 52).

Furthermore, several sources of data suggest that a small but significant number of teachers are already in over their heads. Since 1978, SAT scores of high school seniors planning to major in education in college have averaged about 200 points below the scores of those planning to major in English or science. In addition, almost half of all college education majors have graduated from general and vocational high school programs not designed for higher-achieving, college-bound students. According to Bridges (1986), 5 percent of teachers in this country are essentially incompetent and impair the learning process for about two million public school students. They cannot maintain control over a classroom nor teach fundamental skills. Some confirmation of this view comes from the results of competency exams taken by experienced teachers in several southern states. The failure rate for these exams ranges from about 5 percent in Texas to 10 percent in Arkansas to 12 percent in Georgia.

To meet the problem of teacher shortages, the Carnegie Task Force recommended making the requirements for teaching more stringent while making the rewards more substantial. Their point, which has been echoed by other national reports, is that teaching must become more highly professionalized and more highly qualified students must be recruited for teacher training. Specifically, the report recommended national certification of teachers, a national proficiency exam, requiring a master's degree for entry into the profession, and providing substantially higher salaries for established teachers. There are, however, problems with this highly idealistic plan, including the fact that effective implementation would substantially reduce the number of minority students in the teaching profession.

Recruiting teachers from among the best and brightest was not always so difficult. Until the late 1960s, many bright women and minority students looked to a teaching career as a first choice. As a result, however, of both the civil rights and women's movements, many of these students began exploring more prestigious, considerably higher-paying options. Since 1973, there has been a huge increase in the number of college women preparing themselves for careers in professions that were once reserved nearly exclusively for men, most notably accounting, business, management, engineering, and law. In some ways, of course, this is enormously progressive, but as Albert Shanker (1986b) noted, "the impact on public schools may be devastating. . . . Now that other careers have opened up for them, it's clear they prefer these new opportunities . . . this large group of talented people has been lost to our schools. They obviously believe that other jobs offer more rewards—in prestige, salary and working conditions" (1986b, p. E9). From the mid-1960s to the mid-1980s, making money became increasingly important to a greater number of students. Whereas in 1967 43.5 percent of college freshmen believed it was very important to be well off financially, that figure had swelled to 71 percent by 1985. "Teaching," said one educator, "doesn't have that much future for a young person who wants to get ahead in life" (Fiske, 1982, p. A52).

Prospects for Alleviating the Teacher Shortage. There is convincing evidence that the teacher shortage is serious and will only grow worse. According to Darling-Hammond (1984), the "coming crisis in teaching" can be attributed to the retirement of many highly experienced and well-educated teachers and the concomitant departure of many younger teachers for more lucrative careers elsewhere. In her view, "the crisis now emerging in the teaching profession could preclude the attainment of the other reforms being urged" (p. 1).

On the other hand, there are also data available to suggest that the teacher shortage may be lessening in the late 1980s and early 1990s and that the allure of teaching may be reviving. Berger (1988) pointed to several indices that suggested as much. Prestigious schools of education, such as those at Harvard, Stanford, and Columbia, reported substantial rises in applications in 1988. According to the national annual surveys conducted by the Higher Education Research Institute at the University of California, Los Angeles, the percentage of college freshmen intending to become teachers, after years of decline, began to rise again in the mid-1980s. From a high point in 1968 when nearly 25 percent of freshmen stated their intention to become teachers, the rate of interest in teaching dropped to a low of 4.7 percent in 1982. Since then, however, there has been a slow but steady increase in the percentage of students planning to teach. The 1985 figure of 6 percent increased to 7.3 percent in 1986 and to 8.1 percent in 1987.

Not only are there more students planning on teaching and more students entering graduate schools of education, but apparently the quality of these prospective teachers—at both the graduate and undergraduate levels—is increasing. SAT scores of prospective teachers have been improving in recent years and in 1988 the average score on the math portion of the SAT for those high school seniors planning to become teachers reached an all-time high of 442. At the graduate level, there appear to be a greater number of applications from students from prestigious colleges with higher test scores.

The question, of course, is what accounts for this apparent turnaround in interest in educational careers. Higher salaries, for one. Although teacher salaries in all but a few experimental districts (for example, Rochester, New York, or Dade County, Florida) are still relatively low, they have improved dramatically. Average teacher salaries in 1989–1990 ($31,315) are nearly double 1980 levels. A factor that may be of equal importance, however, is that teaching may be beginning to regain the distinctive cachet it bore in the 1960s. As a result of the enormous attention brought to bear on the problems of education in the 1980s (particularly since 1983 when *A Nation at Risk* was issued), teaching has become important again. New teachers are needed, new ideas are being discussed, and new challenges to the profession seem to be constantly in the offing. In addition, "heightened press attention to troubled schools and the harm that implied for American economic power have seemed to lend the teaching profession the aura of a calling or crusade" (Berger, 1988, p. A17). Perhaps, too, the age of self-centered interest, which so marked much of the eighties, is beginning to give way to a renewed sense of altruism. A greater number of students may once again be considering careers that offer possibilities for personally meaningful, socially important work. In this regard, "Teach for America," a program aimed at recruiting noneducation majors into two-year teaching stints in some of the nation's most difficult school districts (both urban and rural), was launched quite successfully in 1990. The program, the brainstorm of 1989 Princeton graduate Wendy Kopp, began with a first class of 505 trainees selected from a pool of 2,500 applicants. The notion of this program as a sort of "domestic education equivalent of the Peace Corps" (Tiftt, 1990, p. 66) has, at least in its initial stages, attracted some of the best and brightest from the nation's top colleges.

The Impact of Teacher Shortages on Students and Teachers. It may be the case, then, that teacher shortages will not be quite as severe as predicted. More students, and perhaps a higher proportion of exceptional students, may be drawn to teaching over the next decade if school systems continue to raise salaries and deal effectively with issues affecting teachers' sense of professionalism. On the other hand, teaching is still perceived as an extremely stressful career, especially in inner-city schools, and unless working conditions change in ways that offer teachers greater opportunities for enjoying the intrinsic rewards of teaching—such as feeling effectively involved in the lives of children—it is likely that the field will continue to suffer from a paucity of dedicated and qualified applicants.

Even if student interest in education continues to rise, however, we are still faced with the prospect of serious teacher shortages, at least in the next few years. This prospect, one might imagine, can only create situations in which teachers are more heavily recruited, better paid, and more highly valued. And to some extent this situation has already occurred in nonurban environments where salaries have risen and teachers seem to have gained a greater sense of professional autonomy and a greater voice in school decision making. Teachers in nonurban areas, according to the Carnegie Foundation for the Advancement of Teaching (1988a), are three times as likely as their urban counterparts to feel involved in setting educational goals or selecting textbooks and classroom materials. Teacher shortages have also revitalized some schools by creating openings for new teachers. These individuals, many of whom come straight from their undergraduate educations, typically enter a school system with a great deal of spirit, enthusiasm, and new ideas.

But in many ways teacher shortages have also exacerbated teacher stress and burnout. It should not be hard to imagine how shortages of experienced teachers, frequent turnover, and understaffing can precipitate a decline in morale as well as a variety of educational and school management problems, regardless of the setting. Whatever gratification a new teacher might experience in being greeted warmly by a grateful principal or overburdened colleagues may soon be outweighed by the reality of working in an understaffed school with too few experienced role models. Whatever rewards and personal satisfactions experienced teachers may be deriving from their work may be threatened by the premature exodus of valued colleagues. As experienced teachers leave their jobs, those who remain are likely to find the work more difficult, social support less available, and their own commitment to the school or their classes more tenuous.

The typical scenario, then, is as follows. Teacher shortages force urban schools to scramble for even inexperienced, partially qualified personnel. These teachers invariably have a difficult time teaching (at least initially) and are left too often to cope by themselves with little supervisory help. To the extent that they have trouble controlling their classes, and to the extent that they leave to find better jobs (either inside or outside teaching), they contribute to the chaos and instability of a school, in turn making it more difficult—psychologically and educationally—for those teachers who remain. And to the extent that the students who most need the best teaching are least likely to get it, the problems of these students will be carried over from year to year, making the job of each teacher that much more difficult. As a study of New York City's teaching force by the Educational Priorities Panel found, inner-city schools are in a "double bind." They are not attractive to new teachers, who leave as soon as they are able, and "their ensuing high turnover rates make a sustained school-improvement program difficult, if not impossible." Some inner-city schools in Los Angeles have a 40 or 50 percent turnover each year (Olson and Rodman, 1988, p. 30).

A study in California by the state's Achievement Council found that at predominantly minority schools the largest concentration of teachers had zero to three years of experience. The next largest concentration in these schools included teachers with approximately twenty-five years of experience. The next generation of leadership was noticeably absent, a situation that must impact negatively on groups at both ends of the experience continuum. While the older teachers can serve as mentors to the younger group, it must be surmised that these more experienced teachers yearn for more qualified teachers in the next rank; in addition, the younger teachers must wonder and question why so few teachers of the generation before theirs have continued in the profession.

Staffing patterns in a school may create stress and burnout in other ways as well. Because even within schools experienced teachers tend to leave their classrooms for better teaching assignments, the least desirable assignments are left for the least experienced teachers. According to Darling-Hammond, "The experienced teachers, who are in great demand, are rewarded with opportunities to teach the kids who already know a lot. New teachers too often get assigned to the kids and the classes that nobody else wants to teach, which leaves them practicing on the students who would benefit most from the skills of expert, experienced teachers" (cited in Olson and Rodman, 1988, p. 29). This works out poorly for the students, of course, but also for inexperienced teachers in these schools, who are likely to feel stressed, unrewarded, and vulnerable to burnout in this kind of situation. The first assignments of these new teachers may well sour them on the prospect of a teaching career.

Who Teaches and Why?

As of 1986, there were approximately 2.2 million public school teachers in the United States. About 69 percent, or 1.5 million, were female. The average age of all teachers was forty-two, a substantial rise from 1976 when the average age for all teachers was thirty-three. Over 90 percent of these teachers (90.8 percent, precisely) had taught for five years or more, again a substantial increase from the comparable 1976 figure of 72.8 percent. Nearly one-third of all teachers (32.8 percent) enter the profession "late," that is, at least five years after their college class has graduated (Heyns, 1988).

According to a study by the National Center for Education Statistics, individuals choose to become teachers in order to help young people and in order to use their own abilities. Other factors noted in this study included a good salary and job security. But my sense, and also Lortie's (1975), is that these first factors are paramount: People enter the field and continue to teach because they feel they are making a difference in the lives of children, "reaching them" in some important way.

Other studies have confirmed this. Engelking (1986) found that the two greatest rewards of teachers were recognition from others and a sense of achievement. Similarly, two-thirds of the teachers in the *New York Times* poll (Fiske, 1982) suggested that the greatest reward for them was helping or motivating children. Said one teacher: "I love children. I enjoy watching them grow intellectually, socially and emotionally. Teaching is the most challenging experience that I've ever encountered." Another noted that he had entered the field because the job offered him a chance to "be among young kids and to influence and shape lives in positive ways"; a third stated that she took pride in knowing that she was "doing something worthwhile" (p. A52). Successful, dynamic, non-burned-out teachers, McEnany (1986) found, reported that their greatest reward was in seeing their students succeed: "Learning, making progress, and feeling good about themselves" (p. 84).

The Metropolitan Life Survey of the American Teacher (Harris and Associates, 1988) found that even among teachers who reported that they were "very satisfied" with their jobs, 21 percent of minority teachers and 12 percent of nonminority teachers felt it was very likely or fairly likely that they would leave the profession within the next five years. Of those who were "somewhat satisfied," 51 percent of minority teachers and 33 percent of nonminority teachers felt they would leave within five years. Many teachers, then, express considerable ambivalence about their jobs—on the one hand acknowledging that they enjoy teaching but on the other hand considering leaving the field. As Herzberg (1971) pointed out many years ago, the satisfactions and stressors of a job often exist independently of one another. Thus, some teachers report both high job satisfaction and high stress (Kyriacou, 1987). The problem in recent years is that working conditions have become such in many schools that satisfactions are fewer, especially in proportion to the increased strain. Nevertheless, for *most* teachers, there are apparently enough satisfactions to make the work bearable, even at times, enjoyable.

Despite the problems of stress and burnout, teaching still offers the opportunity to feel helpful, to feel worthwhile, to feel one is making a difference. Teaching still offers the opportunity, even in the midst of an otherwise dreadful day, of feeling that one is touching a student. All teachers have had the experience of feeling overwhelmed by stress, only to find themselves rejuvenated by the sudden look of understanding on a student's face, by the smile of appreciation, by the momentary but profoundly significant experience of knowing one has taught someone to read or reason or think about a problem in a significantly different way.

This poignant, powerful experience was well articulated in a 1988 *Time* magazine cover story on "Who's Teaching Our Children": "The moment the light bulb goes on—that, say teachers, is what they live for. That is why they are teachers and not plumbers or investment bankers. The look in a young person's eye: I got it! I understand it! In the average school year there may be only a handful of such moments, but to a teacher they are unforgettable" (Tifft, 1988, p. 64).

The most satisfied teachers, according to the *New York Times* study (Fiske, 1982) (those who would become teachers again), were women and minority group members, those less than twenty-nine or more than fifty years old, those less well educated, those who teach in elementary schools, and those who work with gifted students or who teach remedial education. The Metropolitan Life Survey of the American Teacher (Harris and Associates, 1988) found a far greater number of women (55 percent) than men (40 percent) "very satisfied" with teaching, and a greater percentage of elementary school teachers (54 percent) "very satisfied" with teaching than those working in junior high (44 percent) or senior high schools (47 percent). In addition, a somewhat greater percentage of those teaching twenty years or more (55 percent) were "very satisfied" than were those teaching less than five years (48 percent), five to nine years (49 percent), or ten to nineteen years (48 percent). What must be taken into account here, of course, is that experienced teachers who have been dissatisfied with their careers may well have already left the profession. In contrast to the *New York Times* survey, minority teachers in the Metropolitan Life survey did not seem more satisfied with teaching than nonminority teachers; 51 percent in each group reported that they were very satisfied with their profession.

Women have traditionally been drawn to teaching and perhaps still derive more satisfaction than men from the nurturing aspects of teaching. In this regard, it must be remembered that women are considerably more likely than men to teach at the elementary school level. Those who work in elementary schools, or with the gifted, or in remedial education programs probably have the best access to the rewards within education—that is, these are the teachers who may spend the most time working with and getting to know individual students. Heyns (1988) argued otherwise in regard to elementary schools, contending that secondary schools typically have greater resources and are more professionally rewarding places to teach. My sense, though, is that she is considering "ideals" rather than "realities" and that in many secondary schools the realities of drug abuse, discipline problems, and reluctant attenders mitigate greatly the potentially rewarding aspects of teaching.

Lending confirmation to this hypothesis is the fact that the *New York Times* study (Fiske, 1982) also found that those who would choose teaching again were more likely to feel positive about the quality of education in their schools and also less likely to have been assaulted or to fear they might be. That is, teachers feel good about their jobs and pleased with their career decision when they are working in schools that are effective, that are safe, and where they feel some sense of satisfaction that their input is making a difference. One other important factor affecting satisfaction must be mentioned as well: Teachers who have either entered the profession late (that is, not directly from college) or who have taken breaks during their teaching tenure appear to be more satisfied with teaching (Heyns, 1988). Perhaps teachers who have done other things prior to teaching or who take time out from teaching to pursue other interests feel less trapped and better able to escape the strains of the work when necessary. These feelings may in turn give rise to a greater sense of commitment, purpose, and satisfaction.

Who Leaves Teaching and Why?

In thinking about teacher shortages, most educators have focused on the politics and inducements necessary to recruit new teachers into the field. But recruitment is only half the story; the other half concerns retention. As Shanker (1986b) noted: "It would be foolish for us to crank up a massive teacher recruitment effort only to end, as we've done in the past, by losing a large number of those we hire to other occupations" (p. E9). Thus, who leaves, how many leave, and why people leave teaching are not just academic questions. The way we think about these issues affects policy decisions, staffing projections, and the level of morale in every teachers' lounge across the country. Several studies have examined these issues in detail.

How many leave? In a national sample of teachers who began teaching between 1976 and 1985, nearly half (44.7 percent) who had taught for at least one year were no longer teaching in 1986 (Heyns, 1988). Data from a RAND Corporation report (see Figure 4.1) are even more discouraging, reporting that while at least 80 percent of new teachers stay for a second year, there is steady attrition thereafter, with less than 30 percent of males and less than 50 percent of females still teaching six years after they've begun.

Attrition rates, however, are difficult to interpret, primarily because a substantial number of teachers take temporary breaks from the profession, only to reenter at a later point. In Heyns's (1988) sample, nearly one-fourth (23.7 percent) of those still teaching in 1986 had taken a break from the classroom sometime between 1976 and 1986. In addition, between two-thirds and three-fourths of attrition in a given school district is accounted for by "interdistrict mobility, temporary withdrawal, retirement, illness and death, and promotion and transfer to other education jobs" (Grissmer and Kirby, 1987). Furthermore, Heyns suggests that there is some good news regarding attrition rates in teaching—that they have actually declined since the late 1960s, at least among young teachers. She attributes the greater retention in recent years to several factors,

**Figure 4.1. Proportion of Teacher Cohort Remaining
During First Five Years.**

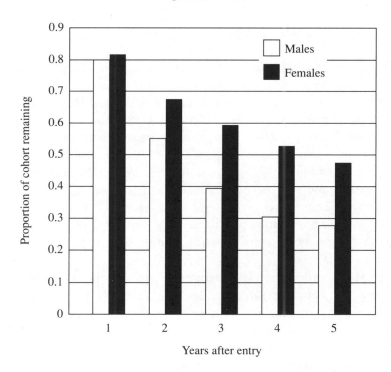

Source: Reprinted with permission of the RAND Corporation.

including the fact that couples have deferred both marriage and parenthood and the increased tendency for women to continue to work after having children. In fact, she notes, "the conventional portrait of the school teacher leaving the profession for marriage and family is distinctly outdated" (p. 26).

Much of the focus on attrition rates in teaching has centered on those who have newly entered the profession. The concern, apparently a valid one, is that too many young teachers leave the field in their first few years. Still, one must keep it in perspective. According to Feistritzer (1986), a turnover of even one-third of the teaching force within a five-year period is normative in comparison to historical turnover trends for teachers. Grissmer and Kirby (1987) point out too that concerns over large numbers of experienced teachers leaving the field are unsupported by research—this group is least likely to resign from teaching.

Who leaves teaching for employment outside of education? The most important findings that can be culled from the reports on who leaves and why are these: First, as mentioned above, inexperienced teachers are most likely to leave; second, many, if not most, who leave teaching are not burned out—the numbers who leave far exceed the numbers of burned-out teachers; third, and relatedly, the presence of stress increases the probability of leaving but the absence of rewards (both financial and emotional) is probably a more salient factor. Many, if not most, of those individuals who leave teaching (or who state they intend to) are reasonably satisfied with the profession and able to tolerate the strains of the work but seek greater rewards elsewhere.

An in-depth look at who leaves teaching and why was provided by the Metropolitan Life Survey of Teachers, conducted by Louis Harris and his associates (1985). This report found that most individuals who leave teaching do so early in their careers. Of those teachers who have left, 46 percent had less than ten years of classroom experience (compared to 22 percent of current teachers). In addition, twice as many men as women have left the profession despite the fact that twice as many current teachers are women. And while 45 percent of current teachers are at a junior or senior high school, 72 percent of those who left did so from positions in secondary schools, a finding that is confounded by the fact that a disproportionate number of men teach in the secondary schools. The Metropolitan Life Survey (Harris and Associates, 1985) attributed the greater proportion of men leaving to economic and social factors. Men, as the primary wage earners in most families, presumably feel more economic pressure to implement career changes; in addition, society typically affords men greater career opportunities and fewer child-care responsibilities. On the other hand, Heyns (1988) suggested that not only are the gender differences in attrition rates narrowing but that whatever differences exist can be understood primarily in terms of the different types of teaching men do. "For both sexes, the highest rates of attrition are among high school teachers; numerically men dominate the schools at that level"

(p. 26). It is difficult to determine, then, whether men are simply more likely to leave teaching than women or whether conditions at the secondary level result in higher attrition rates for whatever cohort teaches there.

The Metropolitan Life survey (Harris and Associates, 1985) found that those who moonlight (usually men) are more likely to leave the classroom: 28 percent of current teachers hold second jobs but 54 percent of former teachers worked after school hours during their last year on the job. The report also found evidence to dispel the widely held assumption that those who leave teaching are the most talented and qualified. Similar proportions of current and former teachers had received an advanced degree, had been asked to supervise other teachers, and had received a teaching award. Using a different data base, Heyns (1988) found that former teachers had but a "slight edge" on current teachers in terms of socioeconomic background and SAT scores. Offsetting these small differences, though, is the fact that former teachers who want to return to teaching scored higher on high school achievement tests and SATs than did teachers who have never left the profession and those who have left and do not want to return. Thus, concluded Heyns, "even if the most talented teachers are more likely to leave, they are also more likely to re-enter" (p. 28).

The Metropolitan Life report indicated that those teachers who perceive themselves as frequently working under stress are more likely to leave the profession than those who view their job stress as less chronic. It bears keeping in mind, though, that many teachers leave despite feeling generally satisfied. In fact, there is not much difference in the proportion of those former teachers who were dissatisfied with teaching (53 percent) and the proportion of those who left despite feeling generally satisfied (47 percent). Former teachers and "likely leavers," though, are more likely than current teachers to believe that other fields offer greater intellectual challenges than teaching. Those who do feel generally satisfied with teaching but leave because they feel they are not being sufficiently challenged exemplify what I've called Type III burnout: individuals who quit teaching not as a result of unbearable strains but rather as a result of feeling understimulated, underchallenged, or underrewarded by the work.

Another look at who leaves teaching was offered by Heyns (1988). Her unexpected conclusion was that "the teachers most likely to leave the profession are not those found teaching in the most troubled and troubling schools; they have taught in some of the most desirable settings" (p. 30). Specifically, she found higher rates of teacher attrition in private as compared to public schools, in suburban as compared to urban schools, and in large schools as compared to small or medium-sized schools. Most surprisingly, she found that a greater number of teachers who were working with high- or average-ability students (or with upper- or upper-middle-class students) left the profession than did those who were working with low- or mixed-ability students (or lower-middle-class or mixed-SES students). These findings are somewhat counterintuitive: One would assume that teachers working with the most difficult students in the most depressive surroundings would have the highest rate of attrition. Yet these findings are also consistent with a point highlighted above: Those who leave teaching are not necessarily those who are most stressed or those who are burned out, but instead are often those who are most determined to find greater career rewards for themselves. It may be that those teachers who find their way to better jobs in better schools are those who, if not better qualified on paper, have some sort of personal edge (energy, ambition, or creativity, perhaps) that leads them to eventually look for more lucrative, less stressful jobs elsewhere.

Why do teachers leave? The Metropolitan Life report found that poor salary was the most frequently stated reason. It was also the most frequently cited reason among current teachers considering leaving. Among former teachers, 60 percent cited inadequate salary as the chief reason for leaving; among current teachers who are likely to leave in the next five years, the figure is 65 percent.

The second reason for leaving teaching that was most widely cited in the Metropolitan Life Survey was "poor working conditions": too much paperwork, too many nonteaching duties, long hours, lack of input into professional decisions. Other reasons included student-related problems (lack of discipline, lack of motivation), administration-related problems (lack of support and general dissatisfaction), and lack of respect (from students, community, parents, society). Burnout was cited by 8 percent of former teachers and

6 percent of likely leavers as their chief reason for leaving education—significant figures in both cases but somewhat lower than expected. My sense is that the methodology of this survey accounts for these figures. That is, the question posed to teachers was: "What were the main things that caused you to leave teaching?" (or, to current teachers: "What were the main things that made you consider leaving teaching?"). Because the notion of burnout encompasses many of the specific factors already named (oppressive working conditions, student discipline problems, lack of administrative support, lack of respect), it can be assumed that many teachers were specific in their replies to this open-ended question rather than subsuming their answers under the more general term *burnout.*

Other surveys have also undertaken to find out the reasons that teachers leave. One study (Berry, 1985) found that of those teachers who left out of dissatisfaction (rather than for retirement or health reasons), most did so as a result of frustration with working conditions (for example, poor administration, poor student discipline, little teacher control) rather than as a result of unhappiness with salary. In two other studies (Bredeson and others, 1983; Frataccia and Hennington, 1982), the most widely cited reason was a perceived inability, due to organizational constraints, to deal effectively with students.

Taken together, these findings point to a familiar phenomenon: Teachers are able to tolerate relatively high doses of stress but may leave teaching (or burn out) when there are insufficient rewards available. These rewards may be monetary but may also take several other forms: respect or recognition from others, the intellectual challenge of the work itself, and the satisfaction that one is functioning as an effective educator. Indeed, research suggests that teacher attrition is strongly related to the tendency of schools to undermine teacher efficacy (Darling-Hammond, 1984; Darling-Hammond and Wise, 1983).

Both current and former teachers in the Metropolitan Life survey were in general agreement about what needs to be done to attract and retain teachers. Echoing familiar themes, these educators suggest that the following changes would be beneficial:

Higher salaries for teachers and increased budgets for school
   systems
Greater respect for teachers
Increased opportunities, such as teaching highly motivated
   students and taking advanced study sabbaticals
Reduced responsibility for nonteaching duties
Upgrading the status of teaching by tightening admission
   standards for education majors
Requiring prospective teachers to undergo a supervised in-
   ternship before certification

Teachers, it is clear, feel that they need "more" from their work—
more money, more respect, more intellectual stimulation, and more
opportunities for working with students who are most likely to
make them feel like effective professionals.

For former teachers who have left the field, the move seems
to have paid off handsomely. Ex-teachers are better remunerated in
their new jobs, receiving an average salary increase of 19 percent.
While 58 percent acknowledge missing teaching, an even greater
majority (83 percent) vow never to return to the classroom, at least
in the next five years. (The small number of those who say they
might return includes a disproportionate number of women who
last taught at an elementary school.) As a group, those who have
left teaching report a remarkable increase in their overall job satisfaction. Although 47 percent of them remember feeling satisfied in
their jobs as teachers, 96 percent report feeling satisfied with their
new jobs. These job satisfaction figures are probably somewhat misleading—the more positive, earlier memories of some of these
former teachers have likely been obliterated by memories of the
unpleasant events that preceded and provoked their leaving. In addition, it is highly unlikely that over time 96 percent of this group
will continue to feel satisfied in their new careers. These figures,
then, may be exaggerated, but they are nonetheless startling. From
a psychological standpoint, they represent the enormous discrepancy seen to exist between teaching and the universe of alternative
careers. Given the fact that virtually every teacher knows of and has
contact with at least one ex-teacher, these figures suggest that what

the current teacher is likely to hear is just how smart a decision it is to leave teaching.

In summary, then, who is most likely to leave and why? An example might be a young male suburban high school teacher who has been feeling stressed and unrewarded at work and who has been working after school at another job. After leaving, most often for a sales, executive, managerial, or other professional position, this young man is likely to believe that his salary, professional prestige, ability to control his work, and intellectual challenge on the job are all better in his new field. Will such a person return to teaching? Unlikely. Only 12 percent of men and 26 percent of women in the Metropolitan Life survey imagined they would return within five years. Heyns found that "the more teaching experience a respondent had, or the less exposure to any other job, the more likely he or she was to express a desire to return" (1988, p. 27).

Profiles of Three Ex-Teachers

Teachers leave the field at different times and for different reasons. In the next few pages are composite sketches of three types of leavers: the early-career teacher who leaves feeling burned out after giving it her all for two years; the mid-career teacher who leaves the classroom after ten years, not because she feels burned out but because she feels she needs greater intellectual challenges; and the experienced teacher who leaves feeling worn out.

Case I: A Young Burned-Out Teacher

Paula, twenty-six, left teaching after her second year of working in an urban elementary school. She left, she says, because she was "simply burned out" and felt she couldn't give anymore. (Her description of her experiences is in accord with what I've termed Type II [frenetic] burnout.)

Paula was a college education major but did not begin teaching immediately after graduation. Instead, she worked three years in business (public relations), a job she found "OK" but "lacking in the opportunity for personal satisfaction" and lacking also sufficient vacation time. She had thought in college that at some point she'd like to give teaching a try. During her third year on the job, she began taking graduate education courses and began also to make preliminary inquiries about teaching jobs (second grade) in her neighborhood schools. She got "no straight answers" from anyone regarding vacancies for the fall, only the suggestion to "check in" at the district office during the summer. In early August, she was asked whether she'd consider a position teaching science in a downtown junior high school about twenty minutes from where she lived. She refused. About two weeks later, she was told of a fourth-grade assignment in an elementary school in a section of the city that, while not quite "gentrified," had been changing for the better for several years. She hadn't intended to take a job in an inner-city school and had no experience at all in teaching in one but decided it was time for a change in her life and that she'd "give it a chance." One of the factors in her decision was that she'd heard that the school was run by a strong administrator who backed his teachers fully.

Her experience the first day, the first week, and the first month in this school was, as she puts it, "the typical horror story one hears about from beginning teachers." She felt she couldn't control the students in her class, couldn't round up enough books for the slower students, and couldn't find enough time or energy to make use of the support that some colleagues were offering. Her memory of teaching those first few weeks comprised primarily the following images: screaming incessantly at her class, feeling thankful for the handful of students who were listening to what she had to say despite the chaos going on around them, wondering why she was doing yard duty, and driving home feeling somewhat "beat" but also determined to "make a go" of the job. The principal (who she found later was a truly caring individual) had no time at all for her during the first few weeks of school.

Paula thought of herself as a quite competent person and believed that if she set her mind to it, she'd be an outstanding teacher. For the most part, she reacted to the strains at work by doubling her efforts at home, attempting to come up with creative lesson plans that would keep her students' attention. And this approach worked—to a point. She did engage more of her students in the work and felt more successful. She also began meeting and becoming friendly with a number of teachers at school. But in the middle of her second year she decided to leave. She felt she just couldn't keep up the pace of her efforts and was tired of screaming all day; besides, she said, she was having more and more trouble accepting the fact that her friends in other professions were beginning to make "serious money" and were being groomed for positions of increasingly greater prominence and responsibility in their fields. Her position was that if she gave as much to another profession as she did to teaching she'd be far more successful and ultimately happier.

It should not be surprising that so many new teachers leave the profession within the first few years. In any school district, new teachers are likely to get the most difficult assignments. New teachers, particularly those in an urban school system, require a good deal of extra support and assistance, qualities that are rarely forthcoming. According to Fran Bolin, director of the preschool program in childhood education at Teachers College, Columbia University, "new teachers are typically ignored on all fronts" (Olson and Rodman, 1988, p. 30).

New teachers in urban settings invariably feel unprepared for the tasks at hand. According to Martin Haberman, "what we have essentially are irrelevant schools of education that don't prepare people to work in urban schools" (cited in Olson, 1988, p. 19). Teachers, as well as an increasing number of education critics, are beginning to complain more vocally that colleges and universities prepare students to work only with homogeneous groups of non-transient, well-behaved, English-speaking students, all of whom come from two-parent, intact families and all of whom read on grade level. It should not be surprising that many feel they have been educated for an entirely different line of work, and their sense of helplessness and despair may be formidable. New teachers often reach out with a familiar cry: "Help, I just graduated from a credentialed program and I'm here in this inner-city school and I have no idea of what to do" (Olson, 1988, p. 19).

Why, we might ask, have schools of education been so lacking in their ability to prepare teachers for work in urban schools? Or, for that matter, to work in suburban schools with burgeoning numbers of minority students? Some would contend the primary factor is racism, an unwillingness on the part of colleges and universities to recognize the special needs of minority children. Some implicate geography, pointing to the fact that most schools of education are located in rural and suburban environments, unaffected for the most part by the urban educational crisis. Some suggest that the problem lies simply in the basic lack of status inherent in teacher training programs. Many point to tradition—the fact that colleges and schools of education have always been most knowledgeable about and comfortable with the 30 percent of students in this country who are most successful in school. The bottom line, though, is that many new teachers feel totally unprepared for the exigencies of the urban classroom; the energy they marshal to cope with the situation often cannot be sustained for more than a few years. They burn out and leave—or worse, they wear out (react to frustrations by investing less) and stay in the system, to the detriment of everyone.

Case II: An Underchallenged Suburban Teacher

Jill was thirty-eight years old when she stopped teaching for the second time. After college, she had gone to graduate school part-time for two years to get her master's degree in special education. Then she took a job in an urban elementary school where she taught a class of emotionally disturbed children for three years until the birth of her first child. She left teaching that first time with mixed feelings: She was delighted to be a mother for the first time but felt she'd miss being in the work world. She felt as if she had managed the strains of work relatively well and felt pleased at the job she had done.

Six years and one other child later she returned to work, this time as a resource room teacher at a local suburban elementary school. She was primed for a successful, fulfilling return to the work world. The family needed the extra income and she herself felt ready and even excited about her return to teaching. The first two or three years were fine: She enjoyed the children, felt excited about her new school, took a liking to several of her colleagues, and developed a reputation as someone who could be patient and creative with students who needed intensive tutoring. The bad days of yelling and feeling frustrated seemed greatly outnumbered by days in which she felt confident that she was doing good work. But some time during her fourth year back in teaching, she told her husband that she was considering another career. When asked why, she replied that she had begun to lose interest. No, the kids weren't giving her a hard time, or at least no harder than usual. And no, her pay was all right, if not great. She was just feeling that she wanted something more. She was having a hard time feeling motivated and wanted a new challenge. She wanted to be with adults more during the workday and wanted adult problems to occupy her time and challenge her.

This is the overlooked group of teachers who leave the field. Lost in the focus on overly stressed and burned-out teachers, this is the group who leave not to escape from too much stress but to find greater sources of stimulation—and often greater remuneration for their intelligence and ability. This is the group who flee teaching in their thirties and forties because they feel they want to make more of their lives. This is the group who feel stuck doing the same things every year and who, as a result, feel moribund, stale, left behind. It is this group who may benefit the most from the idea of career ladders in education.

Case III: A Worn-Out Older Teacher

Hal, fifty-six years old, recently left teaching after thirty years of service in an urban high school. By his own admission, he hadn't worked hard in the last ten years at least. Ask him why and he'll tell you, "It's not worth it. . . . Oh, every once in a while, I'll get turned on again by some superbright student or some exceptionally good class, but most of the time we'll all just play out the roles. They'll come to class because they have to and most won't listen at all because they think that's the cool thing to do. And I'll prepare some lessons—some pretty decent, some boring, I'm sure—and I'll yell a bit if they cut up too much but it's all so predictable and I just don't care very much anymore. Most of the public thinks teachers are the villains in this, but you'd have to be superhuman to take the abuse we do every day and still care a lot. I'm tired of reading about how bad teachers are. I'm tired of parents who are angry at me because their child isn't doing well in school. And I'm really tired of the entitled attitude the kids themselves have. As if they didn't have to work in order to get the rewards. I feel guilty sometimes about the good kids I'm not teaching as well as I should, but you know what? It's not really my fault. Ten or fifteen years ago society decided that everyone had to be educated and the good kids are now paying the price for that decision. Actually, I still like teaching—I just don't get a chance to do it that often.

"Why did I stop? Because I still wanted to get into another field before I got too old. I was also getting too old to take the crap anymore from all of them—the kids themselves, their parents, the school administration. In one sense I was used to it—used to being blamed, for example—and I didn't take it personally any longer. In another sense I felt my time was running out to be treated better. I wasn't a terrible teacher, but I could have been a lot better if I felt I was getting back anything from anyone."

It's this kind of teacher, of course, that the public resents the most. At the top end of the salary schedule, this is the kind of teacher whom everyone expects to be a role model for new teachers. But it's this teacher who has been worn out by years of dealing with the various strains of the profession. It's this kind of teacher who feels he's been cheated out of his "due."

These are the individuals who choose to take early retirement from a system that offers too many stresses and too few compensating rewards. Albert Shanker amassed some figures from the New York City school system that he believed are representative of many schools around the country. Comparing retirement ages from 1978 to those of 1985, these figures suggest that the average teacher is retiring about one to one and a half years earlier now than he or she might have done in the last decade. "What might appear to be a slight change in the figures really translates into the loss of literally hundreds of working years by experienced, highly trained personnel" (1986a, p. E7). Although administrators are often only too happy to lose these older, worn-out teachers and replace them with younger ones at lower salaries, Shanker's feeling was that "their cumulative loss is a devastating blow to our schools" (1986a, p. E7). According to Shanker, these teachers have not lost their love for teaching; their beef is with the system and circumstances that constantly impede the realization of their goals. Prematurely retired teachers, said Shanker, are a special subgroup. They do not leave the system, as do their younger colleagues, primarily because of financial issues; they have endured low salaries for many years. They leave because working conditions in too many schools have regressed to the point where teachers are not treated as respected professionals and are not provided with adequate supplies, well-maintained classrooms, or sufficient numbers of support personnel.

A Final Note on Teacher Shortages, Intentions to Leave, and Burnout

The problems facing the teaching profession today are indeed serious, with burnout affecting 10 to 20 percent of all teachers and an attrition rate that, while declining, still eliminates 30 to 40 percent of all new teachers before they've taught for five years. Moreover, even among those teachers who are neither burned out (viewing this condition as an end state) nor leaving the field, many feel chronically stressed. Yet, in the wake of such statistics and all the publicity surrounding burnout and teacher shortages, it is easy to lose sight of the fact that the majority of teachers working today are not burned out nor leaving; despite the strains of the job, they continue to care about their students, to be responsively involved in their work with students, and to perceive themselves as effective in their roles. In fact, over the five-year period from 1984 to 1988, the percentage of teachers who reported being either "somewhat satisfied" or "very satisfied" with their careers ranged from a low of 79 percent in 1984 to a high of 87 percent in 1988.

In an earlier study (Farber, 1984b) I found that although at least two-thirds of all teachers (in both urban and suburban schools) were strongly committed to their *students,* many were not so committed to their *profession.* As Kaiser (1981) wisely noted, "teaching itself is not stressful, it's everything that gets in its way." In my study, a substantial proportion of teachers, particularly in urban schools, indicated that they "never" or only "rarely" felt committed to the teaching profession. This is consistent with the figures of the 1985 and 1986 Metropolitan Life surveys of American teachers that indicated that more than half of this nation's teachers had seriously considered leaving the classroom.

The point here is that both effective involvement in the lives of students and lack of commitment to the teaching profession may play important roles in preventing burnout. Teachers, like everyone else, strive to maximize the rewarding aspects of their profession and minimize their stress and frustration. Thus, all but the most worn-out teachers continue to seek gratification in their work with children even as they distance themselves from a profession that has so frequently been criticized (often by those who should be most supportive, such as parents and politicians). One way of distancing oneself from the profession is to declare one's intention to leave at some indeterminate point in the future. Whether or not it actually occurs, this statement of intention may serve an important psychological function at the time. To announce, to oneself at least, that one is "not stuck" and will "probably leave at some point, perhaps in the next five years" is to allow oneself some necessary distance from a career that may be offering too little. For the many teachers who are in the middle of the burnout-enthusiasm continuum (stressed, but not burned out), a reduction in their sense of commitment and dedication provides the psychological means by which they feel able to continue to function. Without such a reduction in commitment, many feel intolerably taken advantage of by the "system." Decreased commitment restores a greater balance to the input-output equation, and while such a strategy may ultimately lead to decreased rewards and a greater desire to leave teaching, this is an interim price many seem willing to pay.

5

Blaming the Teacher:
The Troubling Legacy of the Sixties

IT WAS NOTED EARLIER THAT TEACHER STRESS AND BURNOUT
are not new phenomena, even if they are now known by different
names. As Sarason (1982) observed: "The phenomena that are so
troublesome about schools today were not created yesterday, or last
year, or a decade ago, but rather are the latest eruptions and disruptions that have long characterized schools in our social history" (p.
209). Acrimony and misunderstanding have long existed between
school and community, between teachers and administrators, between schools of education and prospective educators.

And yet some things have changed in the last two to three
decades. Rapid economic growth and community support for educational innovation have waned. In their place, we now have economic retrenchment and a call for a return to educational "basics."
We also have widespread middle-class flight from public schools.
Paperwork has increased, layers of bureaucracy have multiplied in
the larger school systems, and "student rights" have achieved a
prominence and legal status unthinkable in the 1950s. Teachers are
no longer as respected as they were in the 1950s and fewer parents
want their children to become teachers. And although the responsibilities and tasks assigned teachers seem far weightier now than
twenty or thirty years ago, no such proportionate increase in their
professional autonomy has occurred. In short, "to be an effective,

let alone outstanding, teacher . . . has become more problematic than ever before" (Sarason, 1982, p. 213) and therefore, I would argue, being a stressed or burned-out teacher has become far more understandable and easily accomplishable.

The particular configuration of ingredients that gives rise to current feelings of burnout—dedicated teachers working with needy children in settings offering limited support and yielding few rewards—has its roots, I believe, in the era that is called "the sixties." In particular, I will argue that five characteristics of the sixties provided the social context in which the origins of current teacher discontent are embedded:

1. A marked increase in the idealism of beginning teachers
2. Unrealistic expectations on the part of this group regarding student achievement, administrative support, and the need for personal rewards
3. An iconoclastic tone that became more extreme in the last years of that decade
4. A vast increase in civil rights legislation and social consciousness that, while long overdue and much needed, generated unintended dysfunctional consequences among both providers and recipients of social services
5. Widespread protest against the Vietnam War, leading to draft resistance and an infusion of male teachers into the educational system

In addition, teacher strikes in the late sixties were watershed events for the profession, dramatically changing public perceptions of teachers as well as teachers' perceptions of themselves.

Idealism and Expectations

My thoughts on these matters might well start with the phrase "once upon a time there was the sixties," for the magical and mythical qualities of that era, its promises of "radical" social transformation, its optimism, its good intentions, its surrealistic character, all contributed substantially to the eventual disillusionment of thousands of young men and women (myself included) who went into teaching and other helping professions. In the sixties, the typical idealism and fervor of youth were sharply heightened. This enthusiasm was, at times, excessive and misguided, leading to confrontations, some violent, that surely could have been avoided. But radical politics aside, the social and political feelings that characterized the sixties were primarily in the service of peacefully helping others. The stickers and posters proclaiming "peace" and "love" were backed up not only by peace marches and changes in sexual values but also by a change in attitudes that affected vocational decisions. As much as college students in the eighties were influenced by a *zeitgeist* embodied by the *Wall Street Journal,* students in the sixties were looking for alternatives to traditional materialistic values. The manifest pursuit of money was seen as crass and emblematic of the distorted values of the establishment; "inner peace" was considered a far more valuable and profound goal that could be achieved vocationally through practicing a craft, "working the land," or helping people or the global conditions affecting their lot. Many of these values were embodied in the work of such service organizations as the Peace Corps and VISTA. And though relatively few students actually signed up for stints in these agencies, many chose compromises—public service work that paid poorly—to reflect these values. Even those who did choose business-oriented careers often seemed to do so after considering other, seemingly more altruistic alternatives; moreover, most were supportive, sympathetic, and entirely respectful of those who pursued their humanitarian ideals.

There were, of course, many exceptions to this general state of affairs. But most of those who did go into the human services in the sixties and seventies were influenced greatly by new values that were experienced as both personally inspiring and historically significant. Many were convinced that the sixties augured a new age of respect and concern for others that would permanently change the nature of personal and international relations; a characteristic fantasy was of a global community linked by a common commitment toward spiritual and personal growth. The means for such an evolution (or revolution) was "consciousness-raising," with music and mind-altering drugs—both seen as making individuals more mellow, sensual, and accepting of others—playing important roles.

In retrospect, these ideas were, at the least, incredibly naive, but at the time they served as the guiding principles for many of those entering adulthood. A college student making an occupational decision in the sixties may well have done so under the influence of such self-statements as "My work should be personally meaningful," or "I can make a difference," or "I should be concerned with helping those less fortunate than myself." In short, many college students entering the work world in the sixties and early seventies were idealists, believing in their individual and collective potential to effect significant changes in the social order.

Those entering teaching during that time were certainly imbued with the idealism of the era and its fervent belief in "possibilities." Philosophically oriented novels (for example, those by Herman Hesse), politically oriented books (for example, those by Ivan Illich or Paulo Freire), psychologically oriented experiments in group dynamics (for example, encounter groups and t-groups), autobiography (for example, *The Autobiography of Malcolm X* or *Teacher* by Sylvia Ashton-Warner), direct critiques of American education (for example, Robert Rosenthal's *Pygmalion in the Classroom* or Paul Goodman's *Compulsory Mis-Education*), contemporary music (for example, the songs of Bob Dylan or the Beatles, beginning with "Sgt. Pepper"), film (for example, *To Sir with Love*), protest rallies, and endless discussions with like-minded others brought new ideas about teaching that suggested the need for a radical revision in the goals, methods, philosophy, and materials teachers would bring into classrooms. Traditional (tightly structured) classrooms were considered constraining and inimical to the full expression of a child's creative potential, traditional curricula were considered irrelevant to the needs of a changing world, traditional notions of teacher authority were considered elitist and condescending to children, and traditional assumptions about what children could learn were considered injurious, especially to minority group children. The human potential movement in psychology provided ideas and a semblance of theoretical support for new educational approaches emphasizing openness, mutuality, and, most of all, the enormous latent potential in virtually every child.

A host of beginning teachers who openly expressed disdain for the old ways and enthusiasm and optimism for their seemingly new approaches brought forth these values into the classroom. Students were going to learn more than they ever had, were going to feel better about school than they ever had, and were going to relate to their teachers more genuinely and openly than any traditional educator would have thought possible or desirable. Providing students with the warmth, love, and creative involvement that they had never adequately received would be sufficient to deal with the issue of "classroom control." These expectations, while laudable in intent, were often grossly unrealistic. The assumption that one teacher over a short period of time can accomplish any or all of these goals in the face of bureaucratic impediments, administrative indifference, collegial apathy, and, most of all, the cumulative dysfunctional impact on children of previous years of educational or familial neglect, abuse, or racism is one that inevitably leads to disappointment. To take but the most obvious example—classroom control—most teachers soon learned that "love was not enough," and that, indeed, paying attention to a misbehaving child often led to more of the same behavior. This irony, that idealistic teachers may be unintentionally victimized by their benevolence, is well expressed in *The Teacher's Survival Guide:* "Paradoxically, the teacher with a natural affection for young people and deep faith in their inherent goodness will be in for trouble . . . he is more likely to think that if he ignores such [disruptive] incidents they will go away. They won't. They will get worse" (Gray, 1967, p. 5).

But more generally, as Cherniss (1980a) documented so well, beginning teachers in this era, like other beginning public sector employees, were remarkably uninformed regarding the nature of the institutions in which they would have to work. Teachers were ill prepared to deal with education as anything more than a series of teacher-student interactions, and their expectations of collegiality, appreciation, and bureaucratic responsiveness were often greatly discrepant with reality. Moreover, as Sarason (1973) sensitively pointed out, teachers, as well as others who should know better, were naive and somewhat disingenuous in their thinking about educational change among disadvantaged minorities. Tackling an enormously charged and complex issue, Sarason suggested that the time frame we employ in thinking about improving the quality of urban education is unrealistically optimistic. What we failed to consider in the sixties, according to Sarason, was that cultural values emphasizing the primacy of education—so critical to real and enduring educational change—cannot be modified overnight or even within a year or two. And while it might be argued that, in the absence of opportunities, no culture *can* emphasize and encourage education, Sarason's point remains: Changes in the values, self-image, and educational aspirations of parents and children are rarely, if ever, accomplished in a short-term period. Not only, then, were teachers in the sixties unprepared for the nature of the educational system in which their hoped-for changes were to occur, but the process of change itself was construed unrealistically. In a related vein, few policy planners were willing to confront the fact that comprehensive efforts to more effectively reach culturally disadvantaged students and to retain in school those students who showed little interest in schooling or little evidence of academic skill were bound to have an impact on the nature of teachers' jobs. Although some teachers derived great satisfaction from the opportunity to make a difference to traditionally disadvantaged groups, others were overwhelmed by the task and failed to cope well with these new-found pressures.

New teachers in that decade seemed to have no trouble expecting a good deal from their students or administration but were curiously ambivalent about their need for personal rewards or comfort (at least until the late sixties when the whole profession became increasingly militant). On the other hand, as Cherniss, Egnatios, and Wacker, (1976) noted, they expected their efforts would lead to public appreciation and seemed disappointed and even angry when this didn't materialize. On the other hand, many seemed to be considerably more invested in improving conditions for students than for themselves; indeed, many seemed reluctant to acknowledge their own needs for job satisfaction. And many seemed caught in a trap fashioned by their own perceptions of this time period; their view of public service work such as teaching as an essentially selfless enterprise was incompatible with the notion of seeking personal rewards for the work. In retrospect, the late sixties presented a contradictory mixture of the solipsistic (the beginnings of the "me decade") and altruistic. Not surprisingly, though, those caught up in the magic of those years were more likely to base their self-perceptions and public behavior, at least, on its more virtuous aspect; in an age that prided itself on altruism, it was difficult to ask to be taken care of. Many new teachers, then, while acknowledging their desire to help others, denied or severely downplayed their own legitimate needs for personal satisfaction. And because continuing to work effectively under such circumstances for an indefinite period of time is nearly impossible, these teachers as well as their students ultimately suffered. Idealism, as many of the earlier burnout researchers noted, can contribute to an individual's motivation for doing public service work but, unrequited, it can also lead to disillusionment and burnout. In this regard, Schlechty and Vance (1983) found that although college students who are concerned with social justice and interested in community leadership positions are disproportionately represented among those who train to become teachers, they are also more likely than others to leave the profession within five years.

In short, teachers who entered the profession in the sixties harbored unrealistic expectations of several varieties: in terms of their expectations of virtually immediate and substantial student achievement; in terms of their anticipation that administrators, bureaucrats, and parents would smooth their way; and in terms of their assumptions regarding their ability to function in the absence of meaningful personal rewards. Together, these factors contributed to an atmosphere in which many teachers felt "wronged" by the system. They didn't want to have to ask for their due—it was antithetical to the values of many—but they also felt that a system that provided so little to teachers who gave so much was seriously flawed.

Iconoclasm and the Changing Nature of Protest

Iconoclasm is the action or doctrine of criticizing and/or destroying venerated institutions, practices, or attitudes. It is a word that describes particularly well the prevailing mood of the sixties. Others have preferred to characterize the age as "rebellious" or "revolutionary," but the point remains the same: It was an age of protest, of a mass of individuals, mostly young, rejecting older, presumably corrupt values and actively seeking new, presumably purer ways of living. Sarason (1982) suggested that the entire post-World War II era was one of redefinition and challenges in which "the authority-power basis of every major institution was questioned" (p. 183), an effort that certainly reached its zenith during the turbulent sixties. Government; religion; the law; the military draft; traditional gender, familial, and professional roles—all were subject to criticism and widespread rejection by those who came of age during this time. Idealism, with its focus on utopian possibilities of peace, love, and harmony ("the dawning of the Age of Aquarius") and its Jeffersonian goals of establishing institutions "by the people" and "for the people," was one manifestation of the iconoclastic attitude of the sixties.

But, as the decade progressed and as the nation moved ever so slowly, at times imperceptibly, toward realizing the idealistic aims of the young and disenfranchised, the folk-song spirit of the early years of this decade ("Blowin' in the Wind") gave way to a far angrier and more violent tone ("Sympathy for the Devil"); constructive, if insistent, criticism of traditional institutions yielded to destructive, no-holds-barred attacks on those perceived as impeding progress. Government, in all its myriad forms, was still seen as insufficently responsive to the rights and needs of individuals. Empowered by the apparent successes of campus protests and fueled by the legitimacy and rage of a rapidly growing civil rights movement, this angrier tone achieved a surprising influence in the late 1960s. Idealism may still have been part of the consciousness of influential activists during the later years of this decade, but the form it took was often far less benign than earlier. One can understand this escalation both as a reasonable response to frustration and as a justifiable response to more violent treatment of peaceful protests by the government (Kent State, for example). Still, the movement in this country toward more active, even violent confrontations against the war and racist policies, and against the paternalism and conservatism of the government, colleges, and industry seemed to ignite a form of protest that allowed little room for compromise or middle positions.

Divisive slogans abounded: "Don't trust anyone over thirty." "Non-negotiable demands." "All politicians are corrupt." "Schools are prisons." "Policemen are fascist pigs." "Teachers are poisoning the minds of the young." Such statements are, of course, distinguished by their exaggerated character and were likely representative of only a small minority even within that sector of disaffected individuals. Nevertheless, even though such views may not have received the unqualified endorsement of many people, they still received much attention and strongly influenced public attitudes, generally moving them toward a harsher, more cynical position. Thus, the *suggestions* in the early or mid-sixties that teachers needed to become more sensitive to the needs of minority children or that they needed to develop more relevant curriculum materials became, only a few years later, *indictments* of teachers' racial attitudes, *accusations* regarding their level of competence, and *demands* for immediate change. Teachers were certainly not alone as targets for the anger of those who wanted the world changed *now*, but (along with politicians, perhaps) they became the most resented and frequently criticized of all professionals during the last years of the sixties and well into the next decade.

Why teachers? Several reasons come to mind. First, teachers present a unique combination of visibility and vulnerability. Despite their vast numbers and their observable presence, they are often perceived by the public as lower-level professionals, distinctively less powerful and special than, for example, doctors or lawyers. A second, related reason is that virtually everyone fancies him- or herself as an expert on education and schooling; although critizing doctors or lawyers might necessitate having a specialized knowledge of their areas, many assume that their own experience as students suffices as a credential to criticize schools and teachers. Third, the implicit charge given to teachers—to educate students and to instill in them proper values—makes teachers a prominent focus of inquiry whenever flaws in society (from racism to the relative lack of mathematical aptitude in girls) are brought to national attention. Last, and perhaps most critically, teachers were denounced during those years because they were seen as a direct cause of the abject condition of much of this country's minority population. Unfortunately (for teachers), the equation generally accepted was not a complex one: Minorities are poor because they can't get jobs; they can't get jobs because they have not been taught well; they have not been taught well because schools and/or teachers are racist or incompetent or uncaring. Of course, schools were not and still are not doing well in terms of educating minority children, but as Sarason (1982) pointed out, "It is all too easy to pinpoint a problem *in* schools and to propose changes *within* schools, unaware that the problem did not arise only in the context of schools" (p. 12).

During the late sixties, teachers seemed to be catching flak from all sides. Not only were adults unconstrained in their criticism but so too were many of the students that teachers were working with. The mood of those years generated a rise in student militancy that reached down to the junior and senior high school levels. From November of 1968 through February of 1969, student protests erupted in 348 high schools in thirty-eight states and the District of Columbia; these protests occurred "in every kind of school in every kind of community in every part of the country" (Silberman, 1970, p. 13). Students were challenging traditional authority relationships and teachers were hardly exempt. Students complained of having their rights violated, of being subject to capricious policies and rules, of being taught irrelevant subjects by conservative teachers in oppressive surroundings. Again, the partial truth of these complaints should not obscure the point that teachers and schools were being made the focus of grievances of every sort and kind, even those that teachers had no direct responsibility for or bearing on.

The Civil Rights Movement

No one can doubt the need, legitimacy, or impact of the civil rights movement or its positive effects on the lives of millions of children both black and white. It resulted in greater access to quality education and decent job opportunities for members of minority groups, and in the process it changed the perceptions of many who were tied to long-held prejudices. But although there can be no argument with the basic premises or outcome of this revolution, it can be argued that along with all the good that the civil rights movement brought also came at least one seriously dysfunctional educational consequence. And I am not referring here to "quota systems" in higher education or elementary school classes for the gifted, the merits and problems of which can be, and seemingly have been, argued ad nauseum without apparently changing the mind of a single individual. Rather, I refer to the scapegoating or "trashing" of teachers. Made painfully aware of its virulent treatment of minorities, and of the lack of vocational opportunities available to minority youth, the nation seemed all too willing to project much of its guilt, regret, and anger onto the educational system, especially teachers. As the search for solutions to nearly two hundred years' worth of wrongs increasingly centered on the schools, teachers began to be viewed as impediments to minority progress and demands were made for much broader community-based participation in the schools. Placing blame on past leaders and old attitudes wasn't enough; politically, someone or some group needed to be blamed for the current lack of educational success experienced by minority children. Teachers were a convenient target. Thus, one of the most immediate and pervasive by-products of the grievously belated enfranchisement of minority groups was the withdrawal of popular respect and support for teachers. Teachers became the enemy for those who viewed themselves as progressive. As Grant (1988) noted in his excellent book, *The World We Created at Hamilton High,* teachers were ordered to pay for generations of societal racism.

In fact, this process of "blaming the teacher" was inadvertently abetted by the federal government (and teacher unions as well—a factor discussed later in this chapter). As conditions in inner cities worsened and as the perceived failures of urban education began to dominate the agenda of civil rights leaders and their supporters, the federal government decided to help by sponsoring a plethora of well-intentioned reforms. "It was the severity of the 'urban problem' that brought about change in the traditional view that education was a local and state responsibility and that the federal government had no business 'meddling' into what was a parental-local-state affair" (Sarason, 1982, p. 92). Among other changes wrought by the influx of federal monies was the creation of additional bureaucratic layers within school systems and the addition of educational specialities of all varieties into school buildings. Although these efforts were intended to lessen the burden of the average classroom teacher, the results were, predictably, far from exclusively positive. In many cases, these additional personnel served to further undermine the already eroding authority and autonomy of the classroom teacher, creating an even more cumbersome bureaucracy and engendering a sense of role confusion in classroom teachers.

But of still greater consequence, federal government intervention into schools turned the national spotlight even higher on teachers and left them blamed severely when ill-conceived reforms failed. That these efforts were doomed to fail because reformers had little or no knowledge of the culture of the school in which change was to occur was convincingly argued by Sarason (1982). Too often, educational reform was formulated by those outside of school systems (university professors, government officials) and thrust upon those (teachers) whose advice or needs were rarely sought or respected. Educational "experts" soon joined the ranks of those who were convinced that teachers *were* the problem and that teachers' intransigence was the major impediment to successful school reform. "Faced with failure these well-intentioned proponents for change could only understand school personnel in terms of personality traits, e.g., rigid, paranoid, unmotivated" (Sarason, 1982, p. 3). And because these experts were far more influential in affecting public opinion than teachers themselves, their acerbic views only reinforced an already declining public faith in schools and school personnel. Such attitudes toward teachers are still apparently operative; during the years 1986–1987 former Secretary of Education William Bennett frequently accused teachers' unions of sabotaging efforts at school reform.

The "transformation of blame" that deemed all school failure, especially that of minority children, to be the fault of teachers was an enormously painful process for teachers to endure during this earlier era. In the 1950s and early 1960s, teachers, though grossly underpaid, were widely respected and regarded as competent professionals; even as late as 1969, the Gallup Poll indicated that 75 percent of this nation's parents would like their children to become public school teachers, a figure that as of 1980 had dropped to 48 percent. During the era of popular support, if a child was not doing well in school it was the child's "fault" and the parents' shame; the teacher was considered sacrosanct. But in an era of social awareness and protest, an era when "the system" became the focus of abuse, critical changes in attitudes occurred. Violence in schoolchildren was now seen as the inevitable product of an unresponsive, morally bankrupt nation; the onus of educational failure began to shift from the child to the teacher. Teachers no longer received the same kind of respect and admiration, and now, if a child was not doing well in school, it was regarded as the fault of an uncaring, incompetent, and possibly even racist teacher. The child was now the highly respected and often sacrosanct institution; a child's failure was now considered the school's fault and the teacher's shame. This trend rightfully exonerated children but it missed the point—that the racism that pervades this society has created an underclass whose needs cannot be met even by "good teachers." It is ironic and unfortunate that many of the same educators, critics, and concerned citizens who applauded the demise of the "deficit model" of the child—a model ascribing the failures of urban education to cultural, emotional, and intellectual deficiencies in the child—were now substituting a deficit model of the teacher, contending that school failures were primarily the result of teacher deficiencies. The wholesale adoption of this model by a public eager to scapegoat some group for educational failures certainly drove—and continues to drive—teachers into an embittered isolation.

Many who entered teaching in the sixties were supportive of the civil rights movement and felt confused, betrayed, and angered by the ubiquitous accusations in the latter part of that decade that teachers were subverting the needs of minority children. The perceived insult (as well as irony) of this situation was exacerbated for many Jewish teachers in larger cities, like New York, where condemnation of teachers was tinged with an unmistakable dose of anti-Semitism. Raised in liberal homes, seeped in liberal sentiment, experienced in the ways of marches and demonstrations, many young Jewish teachers felt overwhelmed by antiteacher, anti-Semitic sentiment in their school communities. In fact, it was a bitter shock to many teachers who entered the urban educational system in the sixties—white, black, Jewish, Christian, or otherwise—to find themselves treated as members of a vilified group.[1]

Although many teachers—new and old—were sympathetic, at least in principle, with the underlying grievances of black leaders, most were neither prepared for educators to relinquish control of the schools nor willing to endorse the vituperative indictments made against teachers by community leaders, antiestablishment journalists, or "progressive" educators. A commonly heard charge of community activists in the late sixties was that blacks and other minorities were being subjected to a policy of "genocide" directed by school boards and implemented by white teachers. Nat Hentoff's book *Our Children Are Dying* (1966) was only slightly less incendiary. Jonathan Kozol (*Death at an Early Age*, 1967), writing from his own experience working in an inner-city school, felt that the only thing he could learn from other teachers in his school was "how to suppress and pulverize any sparks of humanity or independence or originality in children" (p. 14).

Did these voices of protest have something valid and important to say about the state of education in America in the sixties, particularly the state of minority education? Clearly and unequivocally. There were (and still are) racist teachers and reactionary school boards with archaic attitudes and injurious policies, all of which needed (and still need) to be brought to the public's attention. The Boston public schools that Kozol was writing about were, by all accounts, run by a school board oblivious to the needs of minority children. And, arguably, many teachers did need to be sensitized to the special circumstances and problems of inner-city children. The problem though was that little or no attempt was made to discriminate among vast numbers of teachers. If distinctions were made at all, they were of the grossest sort—good versus bad, racist versus liberal, progressive versus reactionary. The sixties, especially the late sixties, was an era of polarization and of "brutal simplicities" (Morrow, 1988) and teachers were among those cast as "bad guys."

Most teachers began their careers thinking of themselves as helpers, innovative helpers at that, and while they were willing to learn and to be criticized, most weren't ready to buy either the generally prevailing message that teachers were ineffectual or the more radical message that as teachers they were part of an "oppressive machinery" that intentionally destroys the minds of minority children.

We cannot lose perspective on the extraordinary achievements that came about as the result of the civil rights movement. Neither, however, should we write about this era without remembering how uncivilly teachers were often treated, particularly after

1968 ("the year that shaped a generation," *Time* would note twenty years later). Among the events that occurred in 1968 to stir the nation's consciousness and conscience were the Tet offensive in Vietnam, the publication of Eldridge Cleaver's *Soul on Ice,* the announcement by Lyndon Johnson that he would not run for president, the seizure of campus buildings by Columbia University students, the assassination of Robert Kennedy, the poor people's march on Washington, riots at the Chicago Democratic convention, the election of Richard Nixon, and, most notable for its impact on education and school politics, the assassination of Martin Luther King, Jr. His influence was waning at the time of his death. His pacifistic style, according to Lance Morrow, "came to seem to many blacks to be irrelevantly noble, archaic, out of touch with the sharper realities" (1988, p. 23), and more "radical" black leaders such as H. Rap Brown and Stokely Carmichael were emerging; Watts, Detroit, and Newark had already erupted in riots. But these trends notwithstanding, King's assassination was a tragedy of enormous proportion, shattering our nation's dreams and plunging cities and schools into a chaos that we have yet to entirely recover from.

> James Baldwin said later that white Americans would never understand the depth of the grief that blacks felt at that moment. America was swept for a week by riots. . . . In all, there was violence in 125 cities. . . . What died with Martin Luther King Jr. and later, in great finality, with Robert Kennedy, was a moral trajectory, a style of aspiration. King embodied a nobility and hope that all but vanished. With King and Kennedy, a species of idealism died—the idealism that hoped to put America back together again to reconcile it to itself. In the nervous breakdown of 1968, the word idealism became almost a term of derogation. Idealism eventually tribalized into aggressive special interests . . . doing battle in a long war of constituencies (Morrow, 1988, pp. 23–24).

Indeed, the idealism that so marked educational philosophy in the mid-sixties (and was slowly winding down) came to a crashing halt with Dr. King's death. In its stead came confrontations with far angier, more violent, and more alienating overtones. Militant leaders became increasingly powerful figures in their communities and increasingly more active in attempting to make the educational system "more responsive to the needs of minority children"—a benign and even laudable phrase in its literal meaning but one that often presaged efforts to oust nonminority principals from urban schools and to make nonminority teachers feel unwelcome. The argument invoked was that nonminority teachers, unaware of and unsympathetic to minority culture, were more easily frustrated in the classroom and more prone to giving up on the education of minority children. Only minority teachers and administrators, it was contended, could deal with the challenges of urban education in a sympathetic, effective manner. Many beginning teachers perceived themselves as distinct from older teachers by virtue of their idealism and liberalism, but they were often treated by the community as simply new members of a traditionally unfriendly, unhelpful profession; more experienced teachers were sometimes made to feel directly responsible for urban poverty and racial bias.

This new, more confrontational phase in the fight for racial equality had dramatic consequences for many teachers, even those who didn't teach in inner-city neighborhoods. Two examples—one of a new teacher feeling the need to "choose sides" in an inner-city school, the other of a more experienced teacher in a predominantly white school—should serve to further illustrate this point.

In the fall of 1967, Diane, age twenty-three, was in her second year teaching English in a large, urban, predominantly black middle school in the Northeast. As a college student she had regarded herself as "liberal," a term that held meaning for her in regard not only to the books she read and the people she was friendly with but also in terms of her antiwar sentiment, her support of the civil rights movement and open admissions to colleges, and her desire to teach underprivileged children. She felt that the traditional methods of teaching these children were not working, mostly because teachers in these schools were too narrowly focused on mainstream, by-the-books academics and were unconcerned with or unaware of the psychological reality of these children's lives. She wanted to understand them and wanted to assign books that could help them understand more about themselves. Her students were going to read *Sounder* (the story of a black child growing up in the South) rather than *The Yearling* (the story of a young white boy's attachment to his horse).

Diane's first year as a teacher was marked by the typical discoveries that teaching was more difficult than she had imagined, that no one was going to herald her arrival or congratulate her on her accomplishments, that she was going to have little to say in terms of her class assignments, and that, although all her colleagues were nice enough, virtually all went home immediately after work. But what was most uncomfortable to her the first year was the racial tension at the school: black and white teachers disagreeing angrily over the choice of the next assistant principal, black and white students seeming to go their separate ways, black parents more frequently coming to school than white parents to protest a disciplinary suspension, a perceived slight, or a grade on a report card.

Issues of politics, race, and education all became more volatile the following school year (1967–68) and made her acutely uncomfortable and confused. "If you're not part of the solution," she was repeatedly reminded by several parents and colleagues, "you're part of the problem." But it was unclear to her how this phrase was to be translated into what she did in her classroom. She felt as if she was already "part of the solution," as she had already infused much of her teaching with issues that she imagined would be "relevant" and interesting to her students. She also felt that she was making a genuine attempt to understand the lives of her students and felt committed toward helping them understand themselves better and develop skills that would serve them well in the world. But because there was much anger and rage in the streets and there were students in her classes who were not doing well, she felt unsure of herself. Perhaps she was to blame; perhaps all teachers were. She felt as if she had to choose between two equally implausible propositions: One, embodying the ethos of the prevailing community position, was that all student behavior, feelings, and attitudes were "legitimate," worthy, and beyond reproach; and two, embodying the prevailing position of professional educators, was that teachers like herself, even those who were born and educated well outside the bounds of this community, were the experts, the only ones who truly knew what was best for all children.

She was able to balance these positions, if precariously, in her choice of what to teach. She deviated freely from the prescribed curriculum and substituted what she considered to be more relevant to her students' lives. What was considerably more difficult, though, was to find appropriate ways of dealing with disruptive behavior in her classroom. Feeling that minority students were already subject to much misunderstanding and even abuse at the hands of adults, she felt uncomfortable and even somewhat racist "coming down hard" on those who misbehaved. On the other hand, ignoring their behavior and talking to some of these students individually didn't seem to work well and she felt that it was unfair to the other students in her classes for such misbehavior to continue. She also felt helpless and less professional when she couldn't control her class or when students would insult or curse at her. And, as both the frequency and vehemence of these attacks increased during the course of the year, she realized that, though she could intellectually understand this rage, she was less able to endure it personally.

The climate of the school was beginning to wear on her and coming to work began to feel much less appealing. She realized that she was angry at the feelings that were being directed at her, the school, and teachers in general by a growing number of her students and the community at large. Although she recognized the shortcomings of her profession (for example, bureaucratic incompetence) and could acknowledge inadequacies in herself and her colleagues, she also felt that neither she nor her profession deserved the treatment they were being subjected to. She still cared for the children in her classes but felt that the community's anger at teachers was often misdirected. Teachers, she felt, somewhat protectively, were often the most reliable helpers in poor communities. She and her colleagues shouldn't be blamed for the chronic lack of jobs, housing, and adequate child care that plagued this and other neighborhoods. The choice she made—and it only became clear in retrospect, years later—was to disinvest her energies from the entire situation. Her anger at being blamed didn't stop her from caring for the children in her class, but it did stem her enthusiasm. She was still a teacher but less ardently so.

Jim had been teaching sixth grade in the same working-class, predominantly white neighborhood for nineteen years, beginning shortly after his discharge from the army in 1947. He enjoyed the work and prided himself on being a good, solid, no-nonsense teacher. He was, by his own admission, "a meat-and-potatoes man," intent on teaching the students in his class the "basics," the three R's; he was not especially interested in learning about the latest educational ideas or about new curriculum materials. He was widely respected in the neighborhood, a fact he appreciated. And he was the kind of teacher that would be visited, years later, by former students eager to share with him their own success stories.

To understate the case, he was not prepared for the changes that the sixties would usher in: not the new clothes, not the new music, not the antiwar, anti-America sentiment, and certainly not the charge that American education was failing abysmally and in need of a major overhaul. He surprised himself by getting used to the longer hair and wilder clothes of his students, but he never could accept the essential iconoclasm of these years, the disrespect for authority. He was used to being treated with respect and indeed thought he had earned it. His pay was meager and he struggled to pay bills but he, along with his family and friends, was proud of his college education and professional status. He was not generally sympathetic to the political protests that had begun to proliferate around the country, but he didn't feel particularly affected by them either. What infuriated him was reading about sit-ins in principals' offices, physical assaults on teachers, and the need for commissioned reports on the state of education in this or that city or the entire country. Furthermore, he felt betrayed by the lack of support shown for teachers in the wake of such invective; though many parents and even newspaper editors voiced protests over the tactics of those attacking educational institutions, few seemed to actually come to the defense of teachers. How quickly it seemed everyone had forgotten all the years of good work and all the classes of successful students that he and his colleagues could legitimately point to with pride.

Everyone from parents to newspaper editors seemed to be intimating that the teaching profession needed a major overhaul; to Jim, a tune-up was all that seemed necessary. Though he remembered a similar public outcry over the quality of American education in 1957, following the Soviet Union's launching of Sputnik, that earlier outcry seemed to him to be less focused on teachers per se and more on the need for new teaching methods and a greater nationwide emphasis on math and science education. This newer wave of criticism was more questioning of the basic abilities and sensibilities of teachers themselves, a charge that Jim thought of as "basic character assassination." He felt he had been sold out by the press and the public, and though he knew he still had the support of the parents in his neighborhood, he wondered where parental support for teachers nationwide had gone. Teaching for him had become, for the first time, a misunderstood and lonely profession.

Whether community control of schools is a good or bad thing, whether black teachers and administrators are necessarily better for black children, and whether it is the conditions of the home or the school that contribute most to the probability of educational success are all debatable issues. What seems incontrovertible is that acrimonious debate over these issues, as well as hasty attempts to solve them, precipitated a crisis in education that left many teachers—mostly white but some black as well—feeling that their credibility, ethics, and professionalism were being doubted or even scorned. Looking at the situation retrospectively, the antiestablishment, individual-rights orientation of the sixties, in conjunction with the civil rights movement per se, set into motion an ineluctable chain of events that left many teachers feeling disenfranchised. The teachers most immediately affected by this new ethos of "blaming the teacher" were those who taught in poor, urban schools. But although this group was the initial target of widespread criticism, others did not remain immune from attack for long. The tendency to homogenize groups of individuals who are linked by a common factor or characteristic apparently affected those who were thinking and writing about teachers, and soon a whole profession was summarily regarded as incapable of meeting the needs of students. The headline used by *Time* magazine in a 1980 cover story conveys the feelings toward teachers that had been snowballing since the late 1960s: "Help: Teachers Can't Teach."

So many ironies are contained in such antiteacher sentiment. First, many of those individuals and institutions who were willing to generalize from the existence of incompetent and racist teachers to the assumption of an incompetent and racist profession were among those fighting the hardest to combat prejudice of this very sort along racial lines (dispelling generalizations about blacks and crime, for example). Second, the way teachers were blamed for their putative failures (in terms of their intransigence, incompetence, lack of vision) was remarkably similar to the notion of "blaming the victim"—a phrase usually invoked to describe the supposed attitudes of public servants, like teachers, toward *their* clients. The urban poor were (and are) certainly far worse off than the average teacher, but both groups have struggled to hold on to their self-esteem while enduring harsh and unsympathetic treatment by a public far more interested in finding character defects than in understanding the nature and historical circumstances of their current position. And a last irony: Many young, idealistic teachers who had earlier criticized older teachers were now being lumped with these teachers into one discrete mass by those who had come to regard the entire teaching profession as outdated and incompetent.

The Influx of Men into Teaching

To a great extent, the war in Vietnam galvanized the mood of the sixties, influencing virtually every political and social facet. Its effect on higher education was conspicuous and left hardly a campus untouched by protest. But its effect on public education, at least urban public education, although not as immediately noticeable, may have been even more enduring. In an era where vast numbers of young men vehemently opposed the war and refused to be drafted or to even serve six months' active duty in the military reserves, a male college graduate not wanting to flee to Canada or fake a disability had an intriguing new option available to him: Avoid being drafted by becoming a teacher in a Title 1 (disadvantaged) school. The nation needed teachers in disadvantaged school districts and was willing to grant draft deferments for those willing to teach there.

What had happened? Tremendous pressure on both federal and local governments to improve schools led to plans to reduce the size of classes and increase the numbers of teachers and support staff; suddenly a solution to the nationwide shortage of teachers had to be found. And a near "perfect" solution could be found. Rather than spend an enormous amount of time and money in an impossible and politically divisive attempt to prosecute a whole cohort of educated, assumedly idealistic, draft-resistant young men, the government could allow them to "defer" their military duty as long as they taught in an impoverished community that needed their services. And so, in New York and many other cities in the late sixties, one could qualify for a temporary teaching license with as few as twelve undergraduate credits in education (some of which could even be in related disciplines such as psychology).

Many men entered the educational system this way, sexually integrating a traditionally "feminine" occupation. Some stayed in teaching only until their twenty-sixth birthday, at which time they became more or less immune to the draft. But many others, who anticipated leaving at twenty-six, found themselves at this age with no other compelling occupational plans, little or no desire to go back to school to learn a new profession, and a sense that teaching was at least a decent career with some very substantial benefits (most notably, summers off). And so they stayed and their presence made a difference. Because men's voices were then (and perhaps still are) heard more loudly than women's and because teaching could no longer be considered just "woman's work" or just a second job, teachers began to demand more from work. As Brenton (1970) pointed out, there is "more than coincidence to the fact that the drastic rise in teacher militancy . . . occurred contemporaneously with the equally drastic increase in the number of males teaching" (p. 110). These same men (and often women too) who, when they first entered teaching in the sixties were willing to work for so few rewards, who asked for so little back, didn't stay this way forever. When the mood of teachers started turning (in the late sixties and early seventies), when they began feeling ever more isolated and unsupported, the fact that teaching was no longer "just a woman's job" helped empower the entire profession. The influx of male teachers into the system resulted in increased demands for autonomy and improved salary schedules; it provided more powerful ammunition for increased militancy on the part of teachers and their unions. The number of teacher strikes nationwide rose steadily from 5 in the 1963–64 school year to 114 in the 1967–68 school year to 242 in the 1979–80 school year. The trend has abated since then but primarily as a result of worsening economic conditions.

Teacher burnout is not, of course, an exclusively male phenomenon (though, as noted in Chapter Two, men are somewhat more likely than women to experience high degrees of stress or burnout). The point is, rather, that the more defiant stance adopted by this new group of draft-resistant, nondeferential, antiestablishment young men in the sixties helped set the tone for teachers' newfound willingness to aggressively demand what they felt was their due (for example, higher pay), to make public their grievances (note that, with the exception of Bel Kaufman's humorous *Up the Down Staircase* (1964), virtually all other first-person accounts of the difficulties of teaching have been written by men), and to make burnout a rallying cry for better conditions for teachers. In fact, the 1980 *New York Times* poll explicitly noted the existence of "one especially disenchanted group of teachers . . . men who entered the profession between 1966 and 1968 as a way of avoiding military service in Vietnam" (Fiske, 1982, p. A52).

Unions and Teacher Militancy

Many teachers went into teaching in the sixties with a number of positive feelings toward the job and came out feeling "burned," as students, communities, school boards, reformers, and the media began turning on them. Not only were teachers dealing with "racial conflicts, discipline problems, overcrowding, antiquated facilities, citizen pressures, and inadequate administration" (Campbell, Cunningham, Nystrand, and Usdan, 1980, p. 28) but somehow, somewhat incomprehensibly to them, they lost the support of the public during these difficult years. Intrinsically, teaching is a lonely profession; it has been made lonelier in the past two to three decades by the abandonment of teachers by vast segments of the American public.

What transformed teachers' angry feelings of nonsupport into a force that would further alienate the public and alter society's traditional views of them? In addition to the influx of men into the profession, the whole introspective, "consciousness-raising" tone of the sixties made teachers more aware that they, like so many other groups around them, could protest and demand more of society. Many teachers seemed ambivalent about asserting their rights and needs earlier in the decade—younger teachers because their belief systems mandated that others' needs should come first, older teachers because their belief system held that, as professionals, they shouldn't adopt a blue-collarlike pose. (Many teachers were opposed—and still are—to the American Federation of Teachers because of its insistence on maintaining close ties with the AFL-CIO.) But teachers' initial ambivalence toward asserting their needs and politicizing their cause seemed to fade dramatically in the wake of increasingly bitter attacks upon them.

"Pride" and "power," two of the more popular slogans of the sixties, began to be seen as the rightful province of teachers as well. Those currents in society that gave rise to a black power movement destined to bitterly lock horns with teachers in the late sixties also gave rise to the increased possibilities for empowerment that teachers began to demand. Still, teachers needed to become a cohesive force in order to be truly heard, and having more men in their ranks and laying claims to political slogans of the time would simply not be enough. It was the emerging strength of teacher unions (facilitated by these social changes) that provided teachers a strong voice to their feelings during this and subsequent eras. Without such a collective voice, individual expressions of discontent can be, and usually are, easily dismissed. It seems likely, then, that the emergence of teacher burnout as a critical social issue—one that could not be ignored by either teachers or the public—was made possible by the growing strength of unions. Teacher militancy and union strength clearly went hand in hand during the sixties, the one feeding off the other.

In addition to stressful working conditions and an atmosphere conducive to the expression of individual rights, a number of other historical and demographic factors influenced the growth and increasing militancy of teacher unions in the sixties. One was a strike waged by New York City teachers in 1962. Led by Albert Shanker's United Federation of Teachers (UFT, the local arm of the AFT), this action occurred in defiance of New York State law and the bargaining agreement between the union and the board of education. As Campbell, Cunningham, Nystrand, and Usdan noted:

"The strike in New York City was indeed a landmark because not only did teachers discover that they could strike successfully without suffering dire consequences, but they also found that militancy yielded dividends at the bargaining table" (1980, p. 283).

Another historical development that aided in the growth of teacher unions was an executive order signed by President Kennedy in 1962 that established the right of federal employees to organize and negotiate with the agencies for whom they work. This action, prompted by demand from the growing number of professional employees within the federal government, encouraged collective action by public employees at the state and local levels. Several other factors facilitating increased teacher union aggression in the 1960s were noted by Campbell and his collegues, including the fact that "more teachers were better educated and thus less tolerant of paternalistic school boards and administrators," and that, with 75 percent of the population living in urban areas, "romantic notions concerning the virtues of rugged and unbridled individualism . . . were vanishing" (1980, p. 284). Brenton (1970) summarized these factors well in describing how the contemporary teacher of 1970 arrived at a stage of militancy: "His loyalty to the school has lessened as the school has grown increasingly bureaucratized. Finding himself at the bottom of a professional hierarchy, lacking a sense of identification or continuity with the community, better educated and expecting the status of the educated person, leavened by the greater aggressiveness and pragmatism of the young men who have come into the teaching ranks, feeling insecure about or cornered by his many duties—the teacher still sees himself as a second-class citizen, underpaid, without the esteem or autonomy that confirms the full functioning professional. What he sees makes him angry. The superficial support many communities give their school makes him angrier still. . . . He recalls what the history of teachers has been like. He's affected by the climate of protest and action that characterizes other groups' efforts to shake off second-class citizenship" (p. 112).

These factors converged until the entire structure of teacher unions changed in the late 1960s. For many years the National Education Association (NEA)—significantly larger but traditionally less militant than its major competitor, the American Federation of Teachers (AFT)—comprised more than thirty autonomous national education associations representing virtually the entire spectrum of educational professionals, including teachers, principals, and school superintendents. The NEA's relatively unassertive stance on behalf of teachers can be traced to its belief that everyone engaged in professional educational activities (teachers, administrators, other management-level school personnel) is a member of the same team and should be encouraged to work together for the sake of the profession as well as for the sake of students; moreover, for many years much of the central political structure of the NEA was dominated by school administrators. Rising teacher militancy, however, led to internecine struggles within the NEA and "in the course of a few years . . . all remnants of even the illusion of a unified education profession were shattered" (Campbell, Cunningham, Nystrand, and Usdan, 1980, p. 282). Furthermore, faced with the loss of membership to the more aggressive AFT, the NEA began to advocate more aggressive policies. In 1968, the NEA led and supported a statewide teachers' strike in Florida, suggesting to some that the NEA had become by then virtually as militant as the AFT.

The most infamous and significant of nationwide teacher strikes occurred in New York City during the late sixties, specifically in 1967-68. Nationally, blacks were demanding more control over their lives, their communities, and their schools, and anger over these issues seemed to be rising. Locally, community leaders were infuriated by the United Federation of Teachers' (UFT) insistence on controlling and limiting the transfer of teachers into different districts, a policy that resulted in a disproportionate number of inexperienced teachers in inner-city schools. They were also in the course of establishing three community-controlled school demonstration centers, a process that would have brought them into direct conflict with two organizations not easily disposed to share power—the UFT and the New York City Board of Education.

The New York City Board of Education, which operates less than smoothly in even the best of circumstances, reacted to the threat of community control by becoming even more bureaucratically rigid and obstructive. And the UFT began to flex its muscles against both the board and the demonstration districts. The first strike was called in the fall of 1967 over issues pertaining to money, policies regulating the treatment of disruptive students, and the board of education's commitment to support an educational model that featured small classes and great numbers of support staff in inner-city schools. The walkout lasted three weeks, engendered much hostility in the black community, and resulted in Albert Shanker's being jailed for having violated the state's antistrike law. Most critically, though, it set the stage for subsequent confrontations between the union (and its now-martyred leader) and the black community—confrontations that would ultimately lead to an ever more bitter and protracted strike the following year: "Charging that the teachers had been 'fired,' claiming due process violations with respect to involuntary transfers, and brandishing 'mob rule' signs (which the black community saw as racist code words), the UFT struck. . . . Fifty thousand teachers (out of about 55,000) stayed out of school, along with the administrators and—a couple of weeks later—the custodians, who shut off boilers and changed door locks in an effort to keep nonstriking teachers, parents and students from entering locked schools. . . . A few schools were forced open and kept open, though most white parents supported the UFT. Thus, more than 1,000,000 schoolchildren were deprived of a month of school" (Brenton, 1970, pp. 122–123).

Clearly, this power struggle harmed students, teachers, and racial relations in New York City. To Mayer (1969), the 1968 strike had a more detrimental social effect than a major race riot. But the ramifications of this strike extended well beyond New York City borders. It cast a general pall over teachers and community-teacher relationships in this country that continues to haunt teachers today. It signaled an end to an image of teachers (as honorable, if passive, public servants unaffected by and uninterested in political influence) that, while never entirely accurate, was nonetheless a source of pride for many teachers and grounds for respect from much of the public. And it provided teachers with a new image, powerful and influential enough to distress and threaten many parents, former supporters, and some old-line teachers as well. Although welcomed by most teachers, this new image thus threatened the traditional grounds for public respect.

By the late sixties or early seventies, both the NEA and AFT had reached a surprising level of militancy, demanding not only sizeable pay increases in new contracts but also a voice in such traditionally management-dominated areas as class size, personnel transfers, and curriculum development; moreover, both organizations were prepared (perhaps even eager) to lead strikes when their demands were not met in ways they deemed reasonable. Teachers now wanted this militancy from their unions who, in turn, were only too anxious to comply. As Brenton (1970) noted, teachers needed to express their anger and frustrations, to "dispel the image and reality of second-hand citizenship," and to force the world to acknowledge their importance (pp. 114–115).

My sense is that over the last twenty to thirty years teachers have been only partially successful in achieving these goals. They have certainly succeeded in negotiating far more favorable contracts with far greater professional perks, and their personal and professional lives have become substantially less controlled by external power groups. Yet these victories have not come without a price. Teacher strikes and boycotts have not only created divisions within the teaching profession but have at times alienated much of the public as well. As Campbell, Cunningham, Nystrand, and Usdan observed, the public is oblivious to the distinctions between the NEA and AFT; strikes, sanctions, and boycotts all look alike to taxpayers (1980, p. 285). The respect once accorded teachers on the basis of their purported dedication and public service has now seemingly yielded to a begrudging respect based on teachers' new-found power. Moreover, as a result of this increased power and influence, teachers now have to contend with yet another burden: public resentment. An era that began with so many intimations of substantial educational change ended with this particular group of change agents feeling unappreciated and often inconsequential, attacked by a variety of constituencies, and intruded upon by ill-conceived reforms. Teachers expected much from their work and the public expected much from teachers, but neither expectation was fulfilled successfully. Current expressions of teacher burnout, then, must be seen in the context of two or three decades of "blaming the teacher" and seen too as a function of the discrepancy between the idealism of the sixties and the failure of educational reform to improve the lives of either teachers or students.

   In short, the events of the sixties wrought changes in teachers
and teaching that indelibly altered the image of the profession to
those both inside and outside the field of education. The balance
sheet is hard to calculate precisely, but the rising identification
among teachers with the concepts of stress and burnout suggests
that the sixties left a complex, troubling legacy.

Note

1.   Although new black and Hispanic teachers were sometimes
     exempt from this treatment, it would be a mistake to imagine
     that this was always the case. My experience was that some of
     the bitterest though least publicized battles of this era occurred
     among black teachers, black parents, and black community
     leaders and that it was not at all uncommon for black teachers,
     both new and old, to quietly express greater allegiance to
     teachers than to militant black leaders who were demeaning the
     profession and demanding community control of schools. Vir-
     tually all black teachers were solidly middle class, either by
     birth or through achievement, and were decidedly less sympa-
     thetic to some of their underclass students and their parents
     than was, or is, commonly imagined. And they were also far
     from sympathetic to the charges that teachers as a group were
     responsible for the current plight of poor, minority children—
     a belief that left some black teachers caught in a very uncom-
     fortable predicament, given the mood of the time.

6

Through the Looking Glass:
How the Media Reflect, Distort, and
Influence Our View of Teaching

IN CHAPTER FIVE, I ARGUED THAT SIGNIFICANT CULTURAL changes in the 1960s laid the foundation for the emergence of teacher burnout as a significant educational phenomenon. The great social unrest of those years focused on the related issues of economic and educational inequity, and much public pressure was brought to bear on teachers to remedy long-standing social problems. The call was for "quality education" and "equality of educational opportunity," although as Passow (1971) commented, neither phrase was clearly defined.

The task of providing quality education, especially if defined in terms of ensuring equal educational *outcomes,* was enormous and destined to take decades; we continue to confront these same challenges today. Nevertheless, the initial intensity and enthusiasm with which most of the country approached the task of overcoming past injustices blinded us to the realities of the change process. Change—whether social or educational—takes time, involves multiple constituencies, and rarely proceeds in a linear, orderly fashion (see Sarason, *The Culture of the School and the Problem of Change,* 1982, for a thorough discussion of this issue). Teachers did not and

Note: This chapter was written with the collaboration of Leonard D. Wechsler.

could not dramatically change reading or SAT scores or high school dropout rates overnight. But the public was impatient, out of either a sense of moral obligation or fear of civil unrest (or both), and scholarly explanations regarding the nature and limitations of institutional change were rarely part of public discussions on the need for vast changes in our educational system. To the extent these scholarly explanations were heard at all, they were seen as evasions of a difficult problem. Old habits, patterns, and institutional regularities do indeed die hard, and change was slow, when it occurred at all. The bottom line, though, was that virtually everyone and everything connected to schools—teachers, administrators, unions, and school buildings—began to be increasingly scrutinized and criticized by the media and ever larger segments of the public.

Teachers felt attacked and ultimately threatened by those who sought to wrest control of the schools from the educational establishment. Many were embittered by the change in their public image and the increasing necessity of having to defend themselves and their profession from those who found little to praise either among individual teachers or in the entire school system. Young, idealistic teachers were unprepared to deal with the hostility unleashed against them (what had they done to deserve it?); many older teachers were outraged at this kind of "payoff" for their years of dedicated service. Thus, some teachers left the field, some took the criticisms to heart and worked even harder, some attempted to ignore the criticisms and just do their work as always, and some gave up even as they continued in their jobs. Teacher strikes, as noted earlier, further fueled public resentment and animosity, and the relationship between teachers and the public came to be increasingly characterized by an unfortunate mixture of mutual insensitivity, misunderstanding, and overreaction.

To this mixture, though, one additional inflammatory element must be added: a string of antiteacher books in the sixties and seventies that contributed strongly to public images of teachers as racist, authoritarian, and antiprogressive. Whatever difficulties teachers and their various constituencies had in understanding each others' needs during these troubled, sensitive times were exacerbated greatly by the publication of several angry best-selling books, most of them, ironically enough, written by teachers themselves.

The primary focus of the first part of this chapter is on three well-known critics of the educational system, all teachers themselves, all of whom came into prominence in the mid- to late sixties: John Holt, Jonathan Kozol, and Herbert Kohl. Although different in some respects—Kozol and Kohl emphasized the tragedies of individual children, while Holt drew our attention to what he perceived as the inanities of the entire educational system—these three authors shared a common disdain for the public school system as well as for the great majority of teachers with whom they worked. In the second part of this chapter, the focus is on the way teachers have been portrayed over the years in television and movies.

Teachers Portrayed in Books

John Holt. Of all the teacher-authors who have excoriated the American public school system, John Holt has been the most well-renowned and persistent critic. On his behalf, one could say that the gist of his message was that, as a nation, we need to take better care of children, particularly poor minority children. He seemed totally and passionately devoted to children's needs. On the other hand, in all his books he maligned schools and teachers in ways that consistently ignored the complex nature of educational systems. As Postman (1979) observed, critics like Holt "had a well-developed contempt for teachers and administrators" (p. 14).

Holt's books espoused romantic notions regarding the innocence of children and the evils of the adult (teacher) world that resonated strongly with the antiestablishment values of the time. His notion that "the chief and indeed only exploiters of children these days *are* the schools" (1969, p. 29, emphasis in original) was characteristic of a simplistic view of childhood, education, and society. He essentially ignored the fact that classrooms, particularly those in urban settings, can be difficult and frustrating places. He also ignored the fact that inner-city children may have different expectations and needs in the classroom, given their surroundings and developmental history. He trivialized and/or excused all inappropriate, disruptive behavior of students, invoking generalizations (for example, all students come into school equally prepared and equally ready to learn) that served to exalt children and vilify teachers. Holt's theory of educational failure in urban schools was one in which school, and school alone, essentially corrupted the integrity and intelligence of previously intact children. Holt's perspective allowed no learning-disabled, lead-poisoned, hyperactive, or slow-learning children. By his own admission, Holt had only taught "in exceptionally favorable circumstances . . . working with relatively small classes made up of children, who, if not eager, were at least docile" (1969, p. 97). Despite this, he showed no reluctance to write with an air of apparent certainty about the injustices perpetuated by teachers against students within urban settings.

Holt accused schools of promoting a "failure strategy" in children. Children adopt "the strategy of weakness, of incompetence, of impotence" (1964, p. 85) so that teachers won't blame or punish them for not being able to do their work. Thus, all children who fail at school do so only because they are afraid of their teachers. Little or no mention was made in Holt's book of the deleterious effects of single-parent families, of unsupervised after-school time, of the lack of positive role models, of emotional or physical abuse, of the lack of quiet places for children to study; there was no acknowledgment that low self-esteem or lack of faith in education might affect behavior, motivation, or learning style in the classroom. Holt's books showed no apparent awareness that too many inner-city children grow up in overburdened families and decaying neighborhoods where success is often achieved through avenues other than formal schooling. When Holt unconditionally blamed the school for "strategies of failure," he thus ignored the harshness of everyday life endured by many inner-city children; by doing so he also ignored the difficulty of the task assumed by teachers in inner-city schools.

Holt began *How Children Fail* (1964) by stating that almost all children "fail to develop more than a tiny part of the tremendous capacity for learning, understanding, and creating with which they were born and of which they made *full use* during the first two or three years of their lives" (p. 15, emphasis added). But many children, of course, do not make full use of their innate capacities even during their first two or three years, not to mention their first five or six. Again, environmental conditions ranging from nutritional insult to emotional neglect, from decaying housing to lack of appropriate and sufficient stimuli, may cause some children to begin school with grossly underdeveloped skills. And as can be expected, the immature child (in terms of emotional or cognitive development) will have difficulty socially and educationally. These children, who are often overrepresented in inner-city classrooms, are difficult to teach and the effort to educate them may add substantially to the ordinary stresses of teaching. It was callous of Holt to pretend that such issues are not part of the educational matrix encountered by teachers.

Our educational system is, of course, far from flawless, and teachers, as human beings, are necessarily imperfect. But Holt's suggestion that educational policies are deliberately nefarious exercises in futility and ignorance was grossly and needlessly overstated. Even to teachers seeking to improve their performance, Holt's accusatory rhetoric could hardly have been helpful. Certainly comments like these are misleading: "In he comes, this curious, patient, determined, energetic, skillful learner. We sit him down at a desk, and what do we teach him? Many things. First that learning is separate from living. 'You come to school to learn,' we say, as if the child hadn t been learning before, as if living were out there and learning were in here and there were no connection between the two. Secondly, that he cannot be trusted to learn and is no good at it" (1969, p. 17).

As teachers, parents, and most human service professionals well know, though, many children do not enter school with these exemplary qualities, either in the inner city or in the most affluent sections of suburbia. Many do not exhibit qualities of patience or determination at age five, ten, or fifteen. The point is that teachers have taxing jobs. Few who haven't tried it can imagine just how stressful it often is to be in a roomful of children with disparate abilities and attention spans, trying one's best to sustain their attention and interest in learning. To claim otherwise, to imply that children are an easy audience, filled only with glorious, wonderful qualities, is essentially to misrepresent the learning situation. In addition, the harsh inferences that Holt drew from a statement such as "You come to school to learn" were out of proportion to a statement that is basically innocuous as well as essentially true. To say that you come to school to learn in no way excludes or implies that learning cannot take place outside school, and certainly doesn't mean that the child hasn't learned before.

Perhaps the most controversial issue in urban schools is that of discipline and the "disruptive" child. As Chapter Two noted, research has shown that discipline problems are consistently among the highest-ranked stressors for teachers. In this regard, my sense is that nothing so inflamed those teachers who read Holt's books as his "apologist" stance in regard to disruptive behavior. Most teachers are responsible at any one time for twenty to thirty children, but one acting-out child is capable of sabotaging the learning efforts of all the others. It is true that an incompetent or inexperienced teacher may react poorly or inappropriately to disruptive behavior, further inflaming the problem; in addition, the probability of disruptive behavior arising is certainly greater in those classrooms where the teacher is incompetent. However, these children are not the product of anyone's imagination or the result of "inferior" teaching. Inadequate resources exist to deal with the problems of children with emotional or behavioral difficulties, but clearly the first realistic step is to acknowledge their existence and how difficult these children are to teach. Instead, Holt refused to acknowledge problem children, preferring to see only problem teachers. As Holt would have it, the child who is a discipline problem is a problem to "repressive teachers" but not to "creative, liberated teachers." The truth is that such a child is a problem to every teacher who has the welfare of the entire class in mind.

"When children," wrote Holt, "feel a little relieved of the yoke of anxiety that they are used to bearing, they behave like other people freed from yokes, like prisoners released . . . they cut up; they get bold and sassy; they may for a while try to give a hard time to those adults who for so long have been giving them a hard time" (1964, p. 97). Behind these glib words, though, are real children; for example, the child from a poor, overburdened, single-parent home who is angry and defiant and who, by his actions, interferes with or even physically intimidates those who do try to learn; or the child who when asked to do something lets loose with a torrent of invective that even if ignored by the teacher cannot help but provoke other children. Holt simplified the complex and all-too-typical problems of inner-city teachers into a very neat but misleading formula: Teachers and schools are bad; therefore students are justified in acting badly. Holt was foremost among those who criticized the educational establishment during the late sixties and seventies, popularizing this particular form of blaming the teacher for the behavior of children.

Holt acknowledged "that many children have a strong and critical need . . . for violent action, physical and vocal, and for intense personal interaction" (1969, p. 23). This tendency has been attributed by psychologists and others to temperament, to environmental conditions that make small children precociously aware of violence and other desperate aspects of urban living, and, most often, to specific patterns of family life (parent-child interaction) that fail to provide an emotionally safe environment for the child. Holt, however, failed to mention any of these factors as possible causal agents. Instead, he isolated the classroom. "This personal interaction need not be fighting, though in most repressed classrooms, where children are held down until they become so frantic and angry that they cannot be held down any longer, this is what it usually comes to" (1969, p. 23). Holt indeed pinpointed one of the major problems of urban education—violence—but mistakenly focused on the classroom as the cause of this phenomenon rather than as one scene of its manifestation. Holt's books undermined the teaching profession by implying that no agent other than the school participates in the transformation of healthy babies into disturbed and disturbing children and adolescents.

Holt was also indignant at the fact that many schools compel students to carry corridor passes when walking through school buildings, which to him was tantamount to restricting convicts in a prison yard. But inner-city schools are often rough places. Corridor passes, teacher aides in halls and doorways, security officers, and deans of discipline may not be "nice" things but they often are necessary to ensure the safety of children and teachers alike. One might imagine that those practices that were established to facilitate a safer learning environment in schools would be praised rather than criticized. Yet here again Holt opted for dramatic "headlines" (teachers are repressive) rather than for judicious reporting. At the same time that urban teachers were reeling from the problems of urban violence carried into their classrooms, someone who had admittedly never taught in such an environment was ridiculing their efforts to make schools safer. What is also ironic in this context is that in one of his books (*The Underachieving School*), Holt criticized "new educational reformers" on the basis that "their contact with schools is so special and artificial that they don't really know what school is like" (1969, p. 24).

Teachers were criticized for many things in Holt's books. In *How Children Fail,* Holt asserted that children are "afraid above all else, of failing . . . [adults] whose limitless hopes and expectations for them hang over their heads like a cloud" (1964, p. 16). But then immediately following this Holt stated that children are "bored because the things they are given and told to do in school make such limited and narrow demands on the wide spectrum of their intelligence, capabilities and talents" (p. 16). In successive paragraphs Holt criticized teachers for expecting both too much and then too little. Teachers, according to Holt, simply can't teach, and they are too insensitive or dense to gear their work to the appropriate level of the child.

Holt accused teachers not just of incompetence or mediocrity but of purposeful cruelty, and it was not just a handful of "exceptions" that were indicted but rather the whole profession. He stated: "The touch came first, and if, like most teachers, I had withdrawn or even flinched from this touch, that would probably have ended the possibility of further contact" (1969, p. 27). It is one thing, of course, to criticize the shortcomings of the school system or even the educational philosophy of teachers, but to accuse "most teachers" of being so insensitive as to flinch from a child's touch is especially unfair. Such a slur impugned the basic humanity of teachers and was the kind of disparaging, overly generalized assessment of the field that made many teachers feel defensive about their work. One might argue that this was but a single sentence in a single book, but the tone of this particular remark, along with others like it in Holt's books, reflected a new way of thinking about teachers—as professionals who tended toward malevolence, selfishness, and overt racism. This downward shift in public perception made teaching a less rewarding profession and certainly contributed to the difficulties in recruitment and retention that plagued the field well into the 1980s.

Holt also berated teachers for their use of gold stars, or papers marked "100%," or A's on report cards. These he claimed, in *How Children Fail,* were "petty and contemptible rewards." "Do children really need so much praise?" Holt asked. The answer, however, is "yes," at least in many cases, and Holt's difficulty in seeing this was yet another reflection of a stance toward teachers that consistently ignored classroom realities. Once more, we have here the specter of teachers creating or adopting solutions for difficult situations, only to be criticized for their efforts. Holt, as well as other like-minded critics of education of the sixties and seventies, insisted that teachers must be creative, sincere, honest, and loving in their work with children. Who could disagree with this? But while these may well be *necessary* conditions for effective learning, they are often not *sufficient.* The greatest fallacy of the popular education critics of this era was their implication that with the proper mixture of creativity, warmth, and understanding, children would easily and inevitably be tuned in to learning. Good teaching is not all that difficult, these books seemed to imply. One simply had to overcome middle-class notions about noise and orderliness and let the children's natural curiosity and abilities lead them (and the teacher) to true learning.

But while Holt condemned the use of gold stars and verbal praise, the fact is that all children (all people!) require praise and encouragement in order to prosper; moreover, the use of such reinforcements in motivating children who have had precious little in the way of praise and reward is logical, often successful, and gratifying for both teacher and pupil. To some children, teacher praise is one of the few available routes to greater self-esteem. In fact, it is the rare teacher who has not encountered children who solicit praise and encouragement after each math problem, spelling word, checker move, or reading of a sentence—"Was this right? Did I do good? How was I?" Holt implied that the school itself promotes such self-doubt, but the fact is that among many children, rich and poor, suburban and urban dwellers alike, poor self-image and self-doubt are fostered long before school begins and are perpetuated outside the school walls throughout the child's school-age years. If children are motivated and successful because they acquire praise or rewards as part of the learning process, we cannot simply discount this because it's not the way learning "should be." In no way do rewards, whether social or materalistic, obviate the need for effective communication between teacher and student; in no way do rewards reduce the importance of a creative teacher. They do, however, often help children to learn.

But, of course, logical rebuttals to Holt's specific criticisms are not really the point. As a body of work, his books, along with those whose work will be addressed shortly, attacked schools and teachers in ways that left many in the profession feeling extraordinarily embittered. Were teachers to believe Holt's writings they would have to conclude that they were entirely without virtues, that their efforts were worthless and bankrupt, that no one graduated from high school feeling that he or she had been well educated or treated decently by teachers, that public schools were responsible for no learning at all, that no creative writing or thinking ever occurred within this nation's schools, that their educational practices were indefensible and the quality of their caring was without any saving graces whatsoever.

Jonathan Kozol. Death at an Early Age, subtitled *The Destruction of the Hearts and Minds of Negro Children in the Boston Public Schools,* was published in 1967 and subsequently won the National Book Award. It was a stinging, convincing indictment of the racism within the Boston public school system in the early sixties. Its readers learned of "the injustices and depredations of the Boston school system which compelled its Negro pupils to regard themselves with something less than the dignity and respect of human beings" (p. 8). Readers learned painfully of kindnesses forbidden to the black students, of class and racial condescension, of "liberal dishonesty," of the cruelty of teachers who tear up a child's pictures while designating them as "garbage." Implicit in its depiction of the dismal conditions endured by black children in these schools was a passionate plea for a more humane educational system, one in which the values and needs of minority children are understood and respected. Kozol attacked the narrow-minded arrogance of those teachers who belittled the accomplishments of black children as well as the hypocrisy of those who claimed to be liberal even as they mocked the values and culture of the surrounding community. He criticized many teachers with whom he worked for their unthinking collusion with a racist system.

Kozol was far less sensationalistic than Holt and far less blatantly antiteacher. For the most part, his targets were individual teachers with whom he worked, not the entire profession. To be sure, Kozol was incensed at the behavior and attitudes of some colleagues. For example, his sense of the two teachers with whom he worked most closely was that he learned nothing at all from them "except how to suppress and pulverize any sparks of humanity or independence or originality in children" (p. 14). He described one of these teachers as follows:

> She seldom would merely walk into our class but seemed always to sweep into it. Even for myself, her advent, at least in the beginning of the year, used to cause a wave of anxiety. For she came into our class generally in a mood of self-assurance and of almost punitive restlessness which never made one confident but which generally made me wonder what I had done wrong. . . . If Stephen began to fiddle around during a lesson, the Art Teacher generally would not notice him at first. When she did, both he and I and the children around him would prepare for trouble. For she would go at his desk with something truly like a vengeance and would shriek at him in a way that carried terror Give me that: Your paints are all muddy! You've made it a mess. Look at what he's done! . . . Garbage! Junk! . . . I do not know very much about painting, but I know enough to know that the Art Teacher did not know much about it either and that, furthermore, she did not know or care anything at all about the way in which you can destroy a human being [pp. 2–4].

The difference in tone between *Death at an Early Age* and *How Children Fail* was notable and significant. Kozol's anger was directed at those whom he saw abusing children; if there are no passages describing good work performed by other teachers, at least

there are no passages suggesting that all teachers are cruel. Moreover, because Kozol was actually there, in the inner city, his observations had the ring of authenticity and quiet truth that Holt's
rhetoric never quite achieved.

On the whole, then, Kozol's message was far easier to accept—
and far fairer. Some teachers were, and some undoubtedly still are,
racist, caught up in the currents of an inexcusable part of American
history. Kozol's rage was at racism and the ways it manifested itself
in schools. But despite the painful truth of many of Kozol's assertions,
he too, like Holt, fell into the trap of imagining that schools are the
only influence on children's behavior. According to this view, all
inappropriate behavior manifest in schools is necessarily and exclusively the school's fault. Commenting on the plight of a sixteen- or
seventeen-year-old youth who hung around a classroom hoping that
there might be a place for him, Kozol suggested the following: "There
was nothing wrong with his motivation, and there was nothing
wrong in his home or home-life either. It was the public schools pure
and simple, which had held him back and made the situation of his
life pathetic. It is the same story for thousands of other children all
over Boston, and I believe it is the same for children in dozens of other
cities in the United States too" (p. 48).

Note the similarity to Holt's notion that "the chief and indeed only exploiters of children these days *are* the schools." But
Kozol did not know, or at least did not inform us, whether there
really might be something in this child's background to have made
schooling more difficult. Might this child have been held back by
inferior schooling? Yes, of course, this is a possibility. He might
have had a series of incompetent, noncaring, racist teachers. But the
assumption that this is necessarily true and that nothing in this
child's background, or the background of "thousands of others"
like him in the United States, has had anything to do with the
success or failure of learning to read or learning mathematical skills
is both facile and misleading. Similarly, Kozol implied that children's lack of self-esteem arises solely as a consequence of their
"incorporating the school's structural inadequacies into their own
consciousness and attributing to themselves the flaws which the
building or the system contained" (p. 92). The likelihood of such
a process occurring is not the issue; rather, it is the assumption that

this process accounts wholly for the deficits in self-esteem often seen in children raised in difficult, poverty-stricken surroundings.

"It's all the fault of the schools and/or teachers" is a dangerous fallacy. Its simplicity, of course, is appealing inasmuch as it attributes complex, long-standing problems to a single source while disregarding the impact of other variables. And while this theory gratified a good many people and allowed them to vent their rage against a system that was clearly not working well, it also alienated just that constituency (teachers) who were especially needed to implement changes. The difference between "teachers have a part in this" and "it s all the fault of teachers (or schools)" is not an insignificant one. Had a more complex equation been used by Holt or Kozol (or Kohl or others)—one that allowed for other variables in the analysis of school performance and one that recognized that many constituencies had failed in their mission to equalize the opportunities offered to minority children—more teachers may well have been able to accept partial culpability for educational failure and been able to invest themselves more fully in change. It should surprise no one that most teachers were not about to accept exclusive responsibility for the problems of minority education, and many were enraged at the suggestion that they should. And for some, the process of burnout was set in motion by the general failure of the American public and its popular authors to equitably distribute credit and blame for the general state of public education.

Kozol fell into another trap as well. Like many others writing about minority issues at the time, he tended to romanticize the poor. In a later work, *The Night Is Dark and I Am Far from Home* (1975), Kozol professed opposition to the notion of "romantic child-adulation" (p. 2), going as far as suggesting that the belief that "kids are neat" and that we should let them "grow and blossom, and explore, according to their own organic and spontaneous needs . . . strains all credibility" (p. 2). Nevertheless, in *Death at an Early Age,* his theme throughout was children's "quiet heroism," and all schoolchildren encountered in this book seemed to fit that description. He described a child's insolence toward a principal in terms of his ability to "suddenly and miraculously burst free" (p. 92). He dealt with noise and anger as "loyalty only to them for their nerve and for their defiance" (p. 162). He readily justified a dangerous and potentially fatal prank (sounding false alarms): "Outside of school he might do things like pulling a fire alarm lever and then having the satisfaction of hearing the sirens and seeing the fire engines and knowing that it was all of his own doing and to his own credit, so that at least he would have proof in that way that his hands and his arm muscles and his mischievous imagination actually did count for something measurable in the world" (p. 6). As a rule, Kozel saw children as innocent and benign, transformed only when they entered a school building: "The difference between the real child and the child in the chair at school was immense in all cases. It was the difference, specifically, between somebody artificial and somebody real" (p. 117). The problems he pointed out were tragic, deserving our most serious attention; yet the simplistic demarcation between good (children) and evil (teachers) in *Death at an Early Age* mars this otherwise important book. It is difficult to believe that Kozol was the only caring teacher in the schools in which he worked, or even that there were no acts of true kindness performed by any teacher other than him. The lines drawn are too neat and the distinctions too simplistic.

Herbert Kohl. The third member of the influential triad of teacher-authors writing in the sixties about their experiences in public schools was Herbert Kohl. His book *36 Children* was published in 1967 to the same sort of acclaim that Holt and Kozol's books received. In fact, this book bears a striking resemblance to Kozol's *Death at an Early Age*. Both books are essentially diaries of novice, middle-class, white teachers working in the inner-city elementary schools; both are poignant and touching in their descriptions of children who seem to blossom educationally and emotionally when finally treated sensitively and respectfully by caring teachers; and both books are powerful and inflammatory, making most readers feel incensed at the ways in which poor, minority children are dealt with by the system. In comparison to Kozol's work, Kohl's book focused more extensively on the lives of the individual children in his class, but he too recounted the tragic impact of dilapidated schools, untended classes, antiquated and irrelevant texts, missing supplies, and, of course, most centrally, uncaring and insensitive teachers on the lives of ghetto children.

For all its virtues, though, Kohl's book suffered from some familiar tendencies. For one, Kohl saw teachers and their "preconceived notions" of children as primarily responsible for whatever individual differences there are among children: "It is amazing how 'emotional' problems can disappear, how the dullest child can be transformed into the keenest and the brightest into the most ordinary when the prefabricated judgments of other teachers are forgotten" (1967, p 13). Kohl, like many other social critics of that era, assumed that inner-city classrooms operated on the principle of self-fulfilling prophecy, the so-called "Pygmalion Effect" (Rosenthal and Jacobson, 1968), wherein children live up to (or down to) the expectations of their teachers. To Kohl, it was no wonder that most inner-city children didn't do well in school, given the prejudices, insensitivity, and low expectations of their teachers. Moreover, teachers weren't just insensitive, but they also tended to be "dull and uninspiring" (Kohl, 1967, p. 54). According to Kohl, "the teacher doesn't understand much of what he is teaching, and worse, doesn't care that he doesn't understand" (p. 54).

But it is not only my sense that these were unfair charges against the entire teaching profession; a good deal of research has failed to confirm these assumptions. For example, Carew and Lightfoot (1979), two black researchers, spent a year observing the behavior and speech of teachers in two racially integrated urban schools. They found little evidence of racial (or sexual) discrimination but found instead that most teachers *rejected* stereotyped judgments of their students and even disputed others' estimates of their students' IQ. Their observations also indicated that teachers worked hard and adapted their classroom behavior in accordance with each child's abilities and needs.

Predictably, too, Kohl attributed student misbehavior to teacher incompetencies: "Discipline problems developed as the pressure of uninteresting and alien work began to mount over the weeks. . . . Alvin's malaise or John's refusal to work were natural responses to an unpleasant environment; not merely in my class but a cumulative school environment which meant nothing more to most of the children than white-adult ignorance and authority" (1967, pp. 28-29). Conversely, the solution to virtually all problems—from behavioral to academic—was, according to Kohl, teacher creativity and sensitivity: "She was considered a 'trouble-maker' by some teachers, 'disturbed' by others. Yet when offered something substantial, a serious novel, for example, or the opportunity to write honestly, she blossomed" (p. 185).

The same objections, then, may be raised in regard to this book as in response to the works of Holt and Kozol. If we were to take the sentiments of these books at face value, we would be left to believe that in the mid-1960s there were no children with problems outside of the school environment and that there were but three virtuous and dedicated white teachers, all men, in all of the nation's public schools. Unfortunately, taken together, these books may well have had just such an effect on the public, establishing or at least reinforcing the perception that schools were malevolent places, run by authoritarian and gloomy caretakers who cared little about children in general and even less about black or Hispanic children. It is important, though, to make the following distinction. I am not suggesting that these authors were inaccurate in the descriptions of the horrors they saw—in fact, it may be argued that they performed an invaluable service in raising the consciousness of this country to the plight of minority children. My objection, rather, is to their singular attribution of blame (the schools/the teachers) for a remarkably complex set of problems; to their consistent overgeneralization in regard to the characteristics, intentions, and morals of teachers; and to the sanctimony of tone in these books, a tone that implied that only one way of teaching was right and that there could be no disagreements among reasonable people as to the cause of or solutions to the described problems.

Herndon and Silberman. Two other books of this era should be mentioned as well. One is James Herndon's book *The Way It Spozed to Be* (1965), an account of teaching in an impoverished junior high school similar in style to those of Kohl and Kozol, and the second is Charles Silberman's work *Crisis in the Classroom* (1970), a more scholarly look at the state of American education in the late 1960s.

In comparison to the other books referred to in this chapter, Herndon's book was mild in tone. The school in which he taught was in California, and the feelings evoked in the book are in many

ways consistent with stereotyped notions of that state. Herndon's
anger at schools and teachers in these pages seemed more of the
"tcch-tcch" variety than the outraged/incensed/this-is-unforgivable
tone favored by the other authors discussed. What also made Herndon's
book somewhat distinctive among those of this genre was his
willingness to acknowledge that outrageous behavior can be exhibited
by students as well as teachers. He was certainly critical of the
racism of some of the teachers in his school and condemned the
intransigence of virtually everyone connected with the schools—the
ways in which everyone, including students, clung to some mythical
notion of the way schools were "spozed to be"—but he also
realized that teaching in an inner-city school could be "exhausting"
and that students could behave in difficult, unreasonable, and even
racist ways. Herndon had an intuitive understanding of burnout as
well, hoping that he could hold out long enough for "something"
to happen in his class and fearing that his teaching would make no
difference in his students' later lives (1965, p. 142).

Herndon's main point was that teachers and schools were too
obsessed with order. "Why do you let them fuss so?" asked a student
in Herndon's ninth-grade class. "I said I thought if they could ever
get it all out of their systems, they might stop. Otherwise, I said,
they'd never really stop it; they'd just be waiting until I let go a
second and they'd be at it again" (p. 151). According to Herndon,
we try too hard to limit children's freedom. Teachers and administrators
should, he believed, be more tolerant of chaos and apparent
unruliness: "We legislate against running, yelling, eating, tardiness,
cosmetics, transistors, classroom parties and free elections. We
invent penalties for transgressors; then we must invent another set
of penalties for those who won't abide by the first" (p. 187). So what
if there's noise, Herndon argued. Eventually the classroom will
calm down and learning will occur. The attempt of adults to create
order simply exacerbates the situation and sets up an adversarial
struggle that rarely abates. Herndon believed that schools were basically
places where children were "bottled up for seven hours a
day" and where their real desires were "not only ignored but actively
penalized." "Maybe you can do it," said Herndon, referring
to the ability of students to stay in school and endure the mindless-

ness and rigidity of the classroom, "and maybe you can't, but either way, it's probably done you some harm" (p. 188).

Herndon's solution to educational failure was "liberty," calling to mind Hook's (1966) and Sarason's (1982) notion of the "well-intentioned but untestable abstraction." These are usually virtuous "should be" statements with no operational criteria designated, no clear way of testing whether and how an ideal is being met. In fact, one of Sarason's examples of an untestable hypothesis bears a remarkable resemblance to Herndon's call for liberty: "School systems in general, and classrooms in particular, are authoritarian settings. The *democratic spirit* must become more pervasive" (Herndon, 1965, p. 37, emphasis in original). It is hard to argue with the goal of "liberty"—one wonders though whether Herndon ever considered that liberty might mean different things to different students and that for some it might even mean the freedom to learn in a safe and orderly environment.

In comparison to the works of Holt, Kohl, Kozol, and Herndon, Silberman's book reflects an entirely different strand of educational criticism. Funded by the Carnegie Corporation, Silberman spent three and one-half years in research and writing a book about "what is wrong and what needs to be done" (1970, p. vii) in remaking American education, in the process collaborating with many of the most eminent educators and educational scholars in the world.

Silberman was of two minds about teachers. On the one hand, he was openly sympathetic. In his foreword, Silberman stated the following: "What I hope distinguishes my indictment of the public schools from that of other critics is an empathy for the far greater number of teachers who work hard and long at one of the most difficult and exacting of jobs, but who are defeated by institutions which victimize them no less than their students" (p. x). Most teachers, claimed Silberman, were "decent, honest, well-intentioned people who do their best under the most trying circumstances" (p. 142). He agreed with Sarason's observation that teaching was a lonely job and that teachers were rarely treated in a professional manner. He noted that teachers rarely have offices of their own, that their lounges were often no more than shabbily furnished rooms, that they were typically held in low regard by the rest of the community, that media stereotypes of the profession tended to be consistently unflattering, and that their inadequate salaries were all too accurate a reflection of the public's attitude. He also noted the following: "There is the atmosphere of meanness and distrust in which teachers work; they punch time clocks like factory workers or clerks and are rarely if ever consulted about things that concern them most, such as the content of the curriculum or the selection of textbooks. And there are the conditions of work themselves: teaching loads that provide no time for reflection or for privacy, and menial tasks such as 'patrol duty' in the halls or cafeteria that demean or deny professional status" (p. 143).

For the most part, then, it was not teachers who were the objects of Silberman's criticism but rather the entrenched and mindless policies of schools and school boards. Teachers were seen by Silberman as pawns in a scheme much larger than themselves. Silberman even expressed his appreciation to a colleague who rescued him "from the arrogance and intellectual and social snobbery toward teachers that has become almost a hallmark of contemporary critics of education" (p. x). Silberman was explicitly critical of many of these critics.

> To read some of the more important influential contemporary critics of education—men like Edgar Friedenberg, Paul Goodman, John Holt, Jonathan Kozol—one might think that the schools are staffed by sadists and clods who are drawn into teaching by the lure of upward mobility and the opportunity to take out their anger—Friedenberg prefers the sociological term ressentiment, or a kind of free floating ill-temper—on the students. This impression is conveyed less by explicit statements than by nuance and tone—a kind of "aristocratic insouciance" as David Riesman calls it, which these writers affect, in turn reflecting the general snobbery of the educated upper-middle class toward the white-collar lower-middle-class world of teachers, social workers, civil servants, and policemen. . . . They seem unable to show empathy for the problems of the lower-middle-class teacher whose passivity and fear of

violence they deride as effeminate and whose humanity they seem, at times, almost to deny [pp. 141–142].

Perhaps most distinctively, Silberman was able to view the
process of education within a greater social context, understanding
and acknowledging other influences, apart from schools and
teachers, on children's school performance. "It would be unreasonable, perhaps, to expect absolutely equal results from different
schools. Lower class youngsters start school with severe educational
deficiencies for which the school cannot be blamed; moreover, the
school, as we have already argued, is only one of a number of educating institutions and influences that affect a youngster's academic achievement" (p. 62). Thus, teachers were not singled out by
Silberman, as they were by the other authors discussed in this chapter, as the sole impediment to educational success. He alone seemed
cognizant of the results of the Coleman report (U.S. Office of Education, 1966) and the U.S. Commission on Civil Rights (1967),
both of which clearly point to the effect of "the interaction of family, neighborhood, and school on the academic and affective growth
of children" (Passow, 1971).

On the other hand, Silberman could not quite extricate himself from the spirit of the times in which he wrote, which is to say
that he too occasionally fell into the teacher-bashing mode that was
so fashionable in the late sixties and early seventies. When he posed
the question "What is it in the schools that leads to failure?" (1970,
p. 83), his answer was "low teacher expectations." (No mention was
made of low expectations of underclass student performance expressed by parents, peers, or the media.) Although teachers were not
portrayed as purposely venal and racist, they were seen as doing
little to interest their students in learning, even to the point of
actively discouraging achievement in their lower-class students. As
examples of the ways in which teachers typically patronized and
disparaged their students, Silberman invoked the observations of
Herndon and Kohl. He felt, as did Holt, that schools destroyed
"students' curiosity to think or act for themselves" (p. 134). Silberman did eventually describe several schools in which teachers
treated their low-income students respectfully, but his message was
clear: Teachers who respected their students, who created joyous,

happy classrooms, were indeed rare. "Because adults take the schools so much for granted, they fail to appreciate what grim, joyless places most American schools are, how oppressive and petty are the rules by which they are governed, how intellectually sterile and esthetically barren the atmosphere, what an appalling lack of civility obtains on the parts of teachers and principals, what contempt they unconsciously display for children as children" (p. 10). Thus, despite his intention to avoid the usual belittlement of teachers, Silberman at times created a caricature of teachers that was not all that dissimilar from those with whom he professed to differ.

Effect of Books on Teacher Burnout. At this point the obvious question is, to what extent did the message and tone of these books affect teacher stress and burnout in the late 1960s and early 1970s? My sense is that these books did, indeed, increase the stress on teachers during these troubled times. Being the object of derision and contempt in a series of popular books was hardly what teachers of this era needed, given the enormity and assumed immediacy of the task with which they were challenged, the political brouhahas within which many teacher organizations were entangled, and the chaotic state of many classrooms. Critics, of course, might argue that teachers were attacked for just these reasons—that is, that they were not doing the educational work that so urgently needed doing, were too busy protecting their political and power bases, and were not functioning effectively in the classroom. But it must be acknowledged that the message we, as a society, were giving teachers was rather an odd one, something on the order of: "We need you desperately to right the past wrongs of education, we want you to accomplish this difficult task almost immediately—and by the way, we think most of you, if not all of you, are essentially incompetent and morally unfit for this undertaking." Actually, the message was at times even more vexing, because many of the critics of education were unsure whether to label the task "difficult" or not—the potential charge of racism confounding the definition of the task. The bottom line, though, is that the wholesale derogation of the profession made it more difficult for teachers to enlist the cooperation and trust of parents and school boards, not to mention of students themselves, many of whom could not have helped picking up on the prevailing cynical attitude toward teachers' competence and authority. Without question, working effectively and confidently in such circumstances became increasingly difficult.

Grant (1983) ascribed the decline in teachers' status in this country to the general erosion of the social bases of authority that occurred in the sixties. He felt that the loss of teachers' esteem could not be "wholly or even largely blamed on the romantic writers or neo-Marxist critics of the recent past" (p. 601), although he did suggest "that a great libel was committed" (p. 601). Although I agree with Grant that books such as Holt's, Kohl's, Kozol's, Herndon's, or Silberman's did not, by themselves, cause the decline in public respect for teachers, the view here is that the "great libel committed" did not fall onto deaf ears. The books noted in this chapter were not esoteric, high-brow literature; they were popular, "high-profile" works. If these books did not create the tone for disrespect for teachers, they certainly exacerbated an already established tendency. They contributed to a cultural milieu in which it became increasingly difficult for teachers to feel good about what they were doing or to feel they were contributing to the social welfare of this country.

Contrast, if you will, the impact of these books on teachers' motivation, self-esteem, and social standing with the potential impact of a series of similarly popular books praising the diligent, if flawed, efforts of teachers, acknowledging explicitly the difficulty of their work, reminding them of the critical role they play in the social change process, and imploring them to rise to the challenge of the changing needs and directions of the times. The books did not, by themselves, cause any teacher to give up or burn out; it is doubtful that any teacher resigned as a direct result of reading any of them. These books did, however, constitute yet another source of stress for teachers, another unwelcome burden. Burnout is a phenomenon defined in large part by feelings of uselessness and inconsequentiality—and these books contributed in some small but meaningful way to this feeling.

Teachers on Television and in the Movies

Television. The "sixties books" just discussed are perhaps the most conspicuous examples of antiteacher sentiment expressed through popular media. But criticism of teachers continued throughout the 1970s and 1980s and was expressed in other forms as well. Raywid (1984) argued that the media, especially the popular press, have played a significant role in undermining the public's confidence in schools. "People obtain a less positive picture of schools from the media than direct contact generates" (p. 208).

Images of teachers over the last thirty years, in both television and the movies, have depicted teachers either as saints or, more recently, as one of two foils for the saints: buffoons or tyrants. In the 1950s, consistent with society's view, the media depicted teaching as a female profession that dealt effectively with innocuous childhood problems. These teachers were extraordinarily dedicated and naturally gifted—like mothers—at developing young minds and values. Like nurses and secretaries (the only other professions easily open to women), teachers were there to take care of others. And while teachers couldn't actually be stupid, the job seemed to require more patience and nurturance than intelligence. Nothing that was taught seemed that difficult to learn and teaching itself seemed a pretty straightforward business.

For example, "Our Miss Brooks" was a TV saint who worked hard to help every one of her students. She had two favorites in her class but exhibited unfailing patience with even her most difficult students. Because teaching, like other women's careers, was regarded as a way to fill a few years before marriage and family, Miss Brooks was single and spent much of her time plotting to trap her friend, Mr. Boynton, into marrying her. Miss Brooks was not only kindly toward her students but was also a woman of complete virtue. The fifties, of course, was a time when any real deviance or radical behavior on the part of teachers could lead to dismissal.

"Mr. Peepers," another TV show of the fifties, presented the star as well-meaning and able to positively influence his students but as a Casper Milquetoast, not quite a "real man." Slight in stature, with glasses and a soft voice, Mr. Peepers was a stray in a woman's world. The image is benign but the message clear: Teaching is women's work; real men don't teach; teaching is a mostly cheerful, not-very-difficult job.

The tradition of TV teachers as saints has continued in a virtually unbroken lineage since Miss Brooks and Mr. Peepers, with

"Lucas Tanner," "Mr. Novak," "The White Shadow," "The Bronx Zoo," "Welcome Back, Kotter," "Room 222," "Fame," and "Head of the Class." Each teacher on these shows accomplishes weekly miracles through "good humor, a bit of devious manipulation and the application of common sense" (Gunderson and Haas, 1987). Actually, in this regard, it might be argued that the image of the TV teacher is less that of "saint" than of a slightly eccentric, well-meaning, highly dedicated, and very effective camp counselor. Nevertheless, each, almost unfailingly, creates happy endings. Even in the 1970s and 1980s, when students on TV shows became more belligerent, a teacher's intervention was all that was necessary to transform all into Boy Scouts or Girl Scouts within the half-hour or hour. Teachers in these shows rarely, if ever, give up on students; rarely, if ever, have administrators that even approach a minimum level of competence; and rarely, if ever, have colleagues that care about students 1/100th as much as they do. In fact, the odds against finding a good teacher in these TV shows in infinitesimally small— typically there's only one in each school. The balance of teachers (and virtually all administrators) are the bad guys, either buffoons or tyrants. Ultimately, what we learn from TV about teachers is that they are either saintly and dedicated or uncaring and incompetent.

TV teachers, at least the heroes and heroines, are notable for spending evenings and weekends socializing with their students. In fact, as Gunderson and Haas (1987) observed, on television "teaching is presented as a sidelight to the important things the teacher accomplishes outside the classroom environment" (p. 30). The teachers on "Fame," oblivious to danger, walk through crime-ridden neighborhoods to reach out to needy students. The White Shadow, a former professional basketball player now working in an urban high school, constantly intervenes in his students' lives to teach them the importance of getting an education. Mr. Kotter's students treat his apartment as an extension of theirs. The implicit message is that teachers who really care spend twenty-four hours a day worrying about and tending to their students, not lesson planning, perhaps, but always available to students on a personal basis. For teachers on TV, out-of-class time with their students seems to substitute for a personal life. No other profession, with the exception of the clergy, is similarly depicted. In a few months' time, these dedicated teachers seem able to make up for years of educational failure, as well as for years of economic deprivation, parental oversight, and racism.

So why is all this a problem? After all, TV is fantasy, not reality, and TV shows follow the rules of character and drama. Furthermore, the teacher in these shows is a superhero—a positive role model, a molder of character, a person of great importance, patience, and accomplishment. Teachers, it might be argued, should be thrilled with this characterization. The problem is that there seems to be no room for a solid, good teacher who helps some, but not all students; who likes some, but not all students; who is effective with some, but not all problems; who is energetic and helpful on some, but not all days. On TV, there seem to be no problems that can't be solved in one show's time by a good-enough teacher. On TV, all students eventually learn to read, all learn to control their behavior, all learn to apologize when they offend, all learn to appreciate the value of education. Even the Sweathogs on "Welcome Back, Kotter" (purportedly a group of disturbed misfits) are, underneath it all, really nice kids amenable to the kind ministrations of their teacher. The tough guy is never seen shaking down or assaulting smaller students. Everyone just says he's tough and jokes about the smell of the socks in his gym locker. The public rarely sees a television teacher trying to teach a difficult student and failing, or struggling to get his or her points across in a lesson marred by interruptions, or intervening to protect a student from getting jumped, or becoming furious at the lack of supplies at the beginning of a school year. It all seems so easy on television, a view that can only give parents and the public a distorted sense of the true nature of a teacher's work.

Because media depictions of any profession influence how vast numbers of people in society feel and behave toward these professionals, images of teachers affect their personal and professional self-esteem more than we might imagine. Teachers are saddled with this strange, contradictory image: of being able to solve problems that no other social agency seems able to solve and of having an easy job. Neither image is fair or accurate; neither helps teachers in their work. The contradiction is often reconciled on TV (or in the movies, for that matter) by vastly underplaying the difficulty of solving chronic educational or social problems. The message we get is that if a teacher really cares, a little bit of extra work—which is no big deal, given a teacher's easy schedule—will make things better. A teacher's job, of course, is far more difficult and time consuming than TV allows and far less certain of success. Public appreciation of these facts would help teachers feel more respected and supported; its absence is yet another source of frustration.

Movies. Movies have always grappled more with real life than TV sponsors would allow, and it was Hollywood that introduced the American public to an image of schools far removed from the neighborhood of "Our Miss Brooks." *Blackboard Jungle* (1955) was the first of many postwar movies to depict a dedicated teacher pitted against troublesome, rowdy students. In this movie, the hero (Glenn Ford) teaches at a school where kids are expelled for misbehavior before they can graduate, where a gang of kids lie in wait to beat him and slash his briefcase, where one student tries to rape a female teacher. Ultimately, in true Hollywood fashion, the teacher reaches the students with his earnestness and creativity: He shows them a cartoon of Jack and the Beanstalk, which segues into an impassioned discussion on values. He awkwardly befriends Sidney Poitier, a somewhat rebellious but nonetheless reasonable student, who tells him, "In the beginning I tried to learn, but I quit trying." They make a pact—that neither of them can quit—and together they triumph and redeem the other misguided, misunderstood students. The portrayal of teachers other than the hero is notable: Many have given up and are ineffectual, but all, from the maimed veteran with the Purple Heart to the lonely single woman, are seen as well intentioned.

Within the decade, Sidney Poitier was recast from rebelling teen to teacher hero in *To Sir with Love* (1967). But in many other ways these films are remarkably similar. Like *Blackboard Jungle,* this film deftly bypasses the moral and political dilemma of portraying black students as difficult; in *To Sir with Love* the teacher is black and the London working-class kids are white. Both films also use the energy and rebelliousness of the emerging rock 'n' roll era to provide the context for student defiance of teachers. In fact, *Blackboard Jungle* introduced the now-classic Bill Haley and the

Comets hit "Rock Around the Clock," one of the earliest bona fide rock 'n' roll songs. (The song in *To Sir with Love,* performed by Lulu, has the same title as the movie and is a mild, rather soppy ballad, but the tone of the movie itself is more hard-edged.) In both films, the teachers, with the exception of the hero, are ineffective and helpless. Most remain well intentioned, however, except for the gym teacher in *To Sir,* who is a cruel "marine sergeant" type. Finally, the administrative staff in both films is hopelessly naive but essentially benign.

To Sir continues the refrain that a good teacher can overcome all problems and that all kids are basically good kids. Both films acknowledge the difficulties of working in a classroom, but they are essentially *Rocky* films for teachers. From both films we learn that a good teacher can reach problem students with creativity, persistence, hard work, and kindness, in the process making up for all the injustices the students have suffered at the hands of society and parents for the previous sixteen years or so.

Incidentally, as on TV, teacher-heroes in the movies have been almost universally male, although the reality is that in this century females have always far outnumbered male teachers. One exception to this rule is *Up the Down Staircase* (1967), a movie based on Bel Kaufman's novel of the same name. Here we see a young female college graduate (Sandy Dennis) attempting to teach English in an inner-city high school. But this movie is essentially just a sweeter version of the same basic plot laid out in *Blackboard Jungle, To Sir with Love,* and later on *Fame* (1980), in which a caring, idealistic teacher struggles to feel effective in a school that features angry, hard-to-reach students and a host of apathetic teachers. In this particular version, the denouement occurs when one of Dennis's students, a shy Puerto Rican boy, blossoms during a mock trial. Realizing that she has truly reached someone and made a real difference, she abandons her plans to leave the field and commits herself to a life of teaching.

By the end of the 1980s, Hollywood depictions of schools had changed dramatically. The teacher-hero remained noble, but the surrounding world was depicted as considerably tougher. Administrators moved from a position of benign neglect to intrusive incompetence; society became a source not just of injustice and racism but of drugs, punks, and serious crime; and parents were no longer simply ignorant and misunderstanding but neglectful and even abusive toward their children. Even students were depicted as more apathetic and dangerous than ever. But most important, the non-protagonist teachers in the school-oriented movies of the seventies and eighties—virtually the entire professional staff of schools—began to be cast not merely as passive and mediocre but as actively harmful to their students. Far more teachers than the 20 percent who may actually be burned out were depicted as noncaring, exhausted, and cynical. The image created was of a teacher force almost uniformly composed of crass, nondedicated educators whose salaries seemed entirely unjustifiable.

What Hollywood's harsher view of schools did was to increase the drama of these movies; the odds against any single teacher succeeding in an environment of unrelenting cruelty, incompetence, and apathy rose to new heights. The exceptional teacher in these films—the non–burned-out hero—became even more heroic, and the nonhero—the average teacher—became even more pathetic and contemptuous. The not-very-subtle message has been that in these troubled, extremely difficult times, we *really* need dedicated, caring teachers and we really don't get them. Occasionally, if we're lucky, we get one such teacher per school, or maybe just one per community.

One of the most popular teacher films of the 1980s was *Stand and Deliver* (1987), the true story of Jaime Escalante, an extraordinary Hispanic math teacher in East Los Angeles who works with underprivileged and often unmotivated high school students. When we first meet up with these students in the movie, they are acting out, calling out, and shooting spitballs at the teacher. There are graffiti on the blackboard and the school hallways are noisy. The students rig the bells so that classes end earlier than they should. "I don't need no math" are the words of one student and apparently the attitude of virtually all the others. But through a combination of caring passionately and enforcing standards rigidly, Mr. Escalante instills in his students pride, ambition, and a good deal of mathematical knowledge. He teaches these students advanced math so well that they are suspected of cheating on the college achievement tests. Virtually all pass the test, and we are left with the thought that many of these students will now "make it"; they will go on to college and jobs that they had never previously thought possible.

Stand and Deliver was a powerful and moving film. It offered the public the image of an impassioned, highly effective teacher who beat all the odds (incompetent administrators, cynical colleagues, apathetic students) in order to make a difference. It may be surprising to noneducators to find that many educators, from Albert Shanker to the vast majority of the teachers interviewed for this book, had very ambivalent feelings toward this movie. Why? Quite simply, because the film insinuated that if Jaime Escalante could do it, so could—and *should*—any teacher worth his or her salary. Are Escalante's standards the ones by which we should be judged, ask teachers? Should I now be expected to work a minimum of sixty hours a week, to teach night school for free, and to devote my whole life to my students, even at the expense of my spouse and children? Do lawyers judge their skills by comparing their work to Felix Frankfurter or Louis Brandeis? Do baseball players consider themselves mediocre because they don't hit as well as Babe Ruth or pitch like Nolan Ryan?

Teachers like Escalante are heroes because they are depicted as being able to do what other teachers cannot—educate children effectively in a fair and humane way. These teachers are heroic in comparison to most of their more ordinary colleagues. That is why educators are ambivalent toward most films with teacher-heroes. These films (and many TV shows also) seem all too willing to sell out an entire professional group to glorify the exceptional individual among them.

Perhaps most insidiously, though, the message of *Stand and Deliver* seems to be that in order to be considered a good teacher, one must work oneself nearly to death. Being caring (*Blackboard Jungle, To Sir, Fame*) is no longer enough. Escalante's work ethic disrupts his marriage and engenders a heart attack that nearly kills him. Still, he refuses to slow down, even fails to take time off to fully recuperate. But these events are simply held up as evidence that he *really* cares. Work around the clock and sacrifice everything else— that apparently is what a good teacher does.

Indeed, Escalante is the only humane person in the school—

a familar refrain in the media's treatment of teachers. His colleagues are tired and vaguely racist. One math teacher in his school, objecting to Escalante's plan to teach calculus, states that "you can't teach logarithms to illiterates." The female head of the department is depicted as smug and closed-minded. Only Escalante cares, and ultimately his caring makes a great deal of difference. *Stand and Deliver,* then, is another ode to the "Pygmalion" theme, but one in which the Henry Higgins figure is no longer just kind (where no one else will be) but willing to put his life on the line for those who haven't had a decent chance of their own. That this is admirable and worthy of Hollywood treatment is a given, but the unstated expectations this film leaves us with make teachers understandably uneasy.

Like Escalante, the hero in *Lean on Me* (1988)—real-life ex-high school principal Joe Clark—browbeats students until they perform, and like Escalante, underneath his baseball-bat-wielding stance is the proverbial heart of gold. And, much like in *Stand and Deliver,* the teachers in *Lean on Me* tend to be either worn out or destructive to the kids (or both). Clark's message is similar to Escalante's: We have to demand more from undereducated, unaspiring students. But Clark's venom is directed not only at teachers who don't require much of their students but also at unmotivated, misbehaving students who make learning impossible for the rest. Clark's method is one of triage: Work with those who want to learn and throw the rest out. Escalante, we suspect, would do his best to salvage all his students.

Both *Stand and Deliver* and *Lean on Me* had educators as heroes, but they differed in terms of assigning "blame" for poor educational outcome. Although both took pokes at indifferent teachers with low expectations, *Lean on Me* more forcefully insisted that a major part of the problem of low-functioning schools could be attributed to the presence of unruly, disruptive students. In this sense, it was a more even-handed movie. Although it was simpleminded in its own way, offering a tough superhero as the solution for complex problems, at least the film recognized that the current educational crisis is not purely the result of faulty teaching. Furthermore, the teachers in *Lean on Me* were discouraged and demoralized as a result of the conditions they faced, rather than because they inherently lacked moral courage or compassion.

In a similar vein to the two movies noted above, other, less notable movies of the 1980s offered the image of larger-than-life educators who could take on a whole school (*The Principal*) or even a whole school system (*Teachers*). *The Principal* (1988) was a formula action film that seemingly aspired to greater profundity through its setting (a school) and conflict (tough principal versus rowdy students). Its message—one messianic educator can turn a whole school around—was not much different from that of *Lean on Me*. In *The Principal*, we see frightened teachers pleading with the tough teacher-turned-principal (Jim Belushi) of the worst school in the district not to force the drug dealers out of the bathrooms and back into the classrooms. To do so, these teachers contend, will make it impossible to educate even the "good" kids. The principal admonishes them that they can't "teach the easy ones and throw the rest in the garbage." To prove his point, he comes in early and stays late to tutor one of the "throwaways," a poor, illiterate teenage mother. In due course, and with much posturing, including a scene where he rides a motorcycle up a school staircase, the principal triumphs over the "evil" leader of the gang. And, of course, in the end, even the nastiest, most violent kids become motivated students. From an esthetic perspective, the movie was seriously flawed by a sense of unreality and exaggeration; its dramatic moments often seem inane. From an educational perspective, its flaw was in implying that all we need is a few more seriously tough administrators to "clean up" the schools and then everything will be all right. *The Principal* also suggested that teachers cavalierly give up on too many kids who are really "good" underneath their veneer of anti-social behavior.

Teachers (1984), starring Nick Nolte, was yet another film that depicted teachers other than the protagonist as depraved. In this particular version, teachers are boring, humorless, drunk, lecherous, and only still teaching because of the evils of tenure and the fact that they are too stupid to do anything else. One teacher who typically sleeps through his class while the students complete mimeographed materials actually dies without anyone noticing for a full day. Administrators are concerned not with learning but with

avoiding bad publicity. The students here are victims, denied their
rights, respect, and the opportunity to learn.

Nolte himself is underpaid, unappreciated, and embarrassed
to tell people he's a teacher. But once he affirms that the schools are
there not for the parents, administrators, or teachers but to teach the
kids, everything falls into place. Teaching is redeemed as a noble
profession because the hero realizes that kids really do want to learn
and will learn, once adults stop getting in their way. The last line
of the movie is Nolte's proud "I'm a teacher!" shouted to his ad-
miring students, bewildered co-workers, and defeated administrators. In *Teachers*, then, we were confronted with the same black-
and-white message offered in *Stand and Deliver:* Students are innocent, teachers are harsh and selfish victimizers, and the sooner we
realize these facts the sooner we can truly educate our children. Both
these movies also presented the standardized image of the uncaring,
burned-out teacher; neither offered the possibility that at least some
of these teachers had previously worked enthusiastically for years
without a great deal of success or recognition.

These "serious films" aimed at the general viewing audience
perpetuated the dual myths that (1) most teachers are lousy and have
always been and (2) despite this, one good, strong, virtuous teacher
or administrator can right all past wrongs for all students. These
films did, however, cling to the idea of teaching as a respectable
profession. By contrast, "teen movies" during the 1980s, such as *Fast
Times at Ridgemont High, Ferris Bueller's Day Off, Porky's,* and
Private School, depicted teachers as fools. As teenagers have come to
account for a steadily increasing percentage of box office revenues,
Hollywood has rushed to provide images that teens want to buy. As
a result, the images of teachers in these films are caricatures, although
perhaps no more so than those of parents or other adults. Teenagers
naturally make fun of adults. But the way we make fun of people
reflects our sense of their flaws and idiosyncrasies. Thus, the depiction of teachers in these recent movies as malicious, lecherous, apathetic, or mentally ill may well reflect the basic lack of respect society
has for teachers' commitment, intelligence, and virtue.

Effects of Media Presentations. As Gunderson and Haas
(1987) noted, media stereotypes serve "not so much as an indicator

of reality, but as an indicator of 'reality' as seen by the public"
(p. 28). Furthermore, media stereotypes do more than reflect reality—they create it as well. The media sculpt the way we view our
world. The media promote, enforce, and perpetuate attitudes toward events, political figures, or professional groups that invariably
reflect an exaggeration of certain facts and a dismissal or minimi-
zation of others. In regard to teachers, one exaggeration has typically centered on the ability of the good teacher to solve—and solve
rather quickly—virtually any problem that is brought into the classroom or school. The good teacher—whether it's Miss Brooks, Kotter, Charlie Moore ("Go to the Head of the Class"), or Jaime
Escalante—is shown to be successful at everything from relatively
trivial peer-related problems (the guy or girl with no date to the
prom; the student with no best friend) to family problems (moms
or dads who fail to support their child's education) to more deep-
rooted educational or psychological problems (students who can't
read; acting-out, aggressive students who vandalize and prey on
others) to chronic social problems (racial prejudice). Invariably,
these teachers come up with creative, effective solutions to student
problems. Another type of exaggeration operates in the opposite
direction and concerns the number of teachers who are burned out
or otherwise afflicted with emotional disorders.

What is typically minimized or dismissed in media depictions is the time spent by any teacher on academic tasks in the
classroom and preparation outside the classroom. Based on watching television and movies, one would imagine that teachers spend
most of their time in school solving personal problems of students,
kidding around with colleagues or students, working on school
plays, and interrupting planned lessons to lead spontaneous discussions of ethical and moral issues. And if teachers are portrayed
teaching at all, it is in front of a class, never in small groups. This
image is such that few in the public imagine that teachers spend any
time at all preparing lessons at home, individualizing assignments,
marking homework, filling out reports, or reading dozens of student essays over weekends. Teachers, then—at least "good"
teachers—are seen as both more pervasively effective and powerful
than they really are and less involved in the specifics and minutiae
of teaching than they really are.

In the end, our acceptance of the first stereotype, of super-teacher as hero, is dependent upon our acceptance of a far more dangerous stereotype: that most teachers are anything but heroic. It's become far too easy then for parents or politicians or school superintendents to want or demand the first (the omnipotent and omniscient superhero) and, not getting it, to assume the latter (teacher as failure). For most teachers, of course, the truth lies in the middle: They are neither superheroes nor failures. And the expectation that they must be one or the other may contribute to stress and vulnerability to burnout. It is certainly hard to feel consequential and effective when anything less than a perfect outcome leads to public or parental derision.

7

The Erosion of
Public Respect for Teachers:
A Historical View

In the end, the quality of American education can be
no greater than the dignity we assign to teaching.

(Boyer, 1988, p. 11)

IT IS MY CONTENTION THAT THE PUBLIC'S VIEW OF TEACHERS
took a dramatic change for the worse during the late sixties, affecting teacher morale and vulnerability to stress. Influenced by vocal
critics of public schools, by the media, and by a series of widely
publicized books condemning the state of American education, the
public became less respectful and less supportive of teachers. The
teaching profession's reaction to this state of affairs was increased
militancy and the adoption of a defensive posture in response to
outside critics, both of which served to provide a measure of self-
respect for classroom teachers but provoked even greater public
resentment and a further loss of support.

Public resentment toward teachers and schools continued to
flare in the 1970s and 1980s. Here's how one prominent educator,
P. Michael Timpane, president of Teachers College, Columbia
University, viewed the fate of education in the 1970s:

The seventies were a time when the numbers of pupils
in our schools began to stabilize or decline for the first
time in a generation. Real costs per pupil rose by
twenty-five percent during the decade, and were reflected in smaller classes or additional specialists or
both. Meanwhile, performance, as measured by several

189

national achievement tests, began to decline for the
first time in the generation. Soon, there emerged widespread belief, and more than a little evidence, that the
curriculum was being watered down in many of our
schools, or at least loaded down with unnecessary ex-
tras. Many schools became the scenes of daily violence.
Drop-out rates in our high schools, which had fallen
for a generation, stopped falling. Colleges began
remedial programs for the first time in living memory.
Teachers organized collectively through the nation to
secure their welfare; but they ended the decade more
ill paid and feeling more beleaguered than they had
started. Public confidence in the schools eroded steadily and contained by the end of the decade a substantial, middle-class backlash, a feeling that the resources
and attention that had gone to the poor and minorities
had been at the expense of other children. . . . Spending limitation movements were spreading in the
states, fueled by the popular conviction that education
was neither efficient nor accountable [1982, pp. 2–3].

As the 1990s begin, there are signs that the trend toward
public denigration of teaching may be abating as more college students express an interest in teaching, as school boards seem more
willing to grant teachers significant salary increases, and as educational reform continues to be a focus of national concern. But the
devaluation of teachers that occurred in the 1960s (and later) had
serious consequences: From the mid-1960s to the late 1980s, students
were less inclined to enter the teaching profession, public ratings of
teachers became less favorable, and fewer parents were in favor of
their children becoming teachers. These changes were, of course,
attributable to several sources, among them a growing awareness
that more professional options had become available (especially for
women) and that many public schools had become more dangerous
places to work. Still, as Grant (1983) noted, the decline in public
respect for teachers played a major part in these trends.

Actually, the notion that teachers suffered a dramatic loss in
public respect during the sixties is somewhat misleading, implying

that prior to this time teachers were generally held in high esteem. More accurately, loss of respect for teachers during the sixties was judged relative to an unusual period in American history—the post–World War II era when education and teachers were regarded highly and "enjoyed a rare degree of community support" (Sarason, 1982, p. 93). This chapter, then, focuses on the ways that teachers have historically been treated in this country; the emphasis is on the changes that have occurred in teaching from World War II to the present. In addition, three prime aspects of the general lack of respect accorded contemporary teachers are discussed: public opinion; low salaries; and day-to-day treatment by parents, students, and administrators.

A Short History of Teachers' Social Status

According to some scholars, teachers' place in American society has traditionally been "little better than wretched" (Brenton, 1970, p. 60). From this perspective, the history of teachers in this country has been marked by denial of rights, expectations of servile behavior, dreadful wages, and political repression. Other scholars, although not adopting this extreme a stance, feel that teachers have always held a rather ambiguous position in the social order, a place that Lortie (1975) labeled "special but shadowed," "proximate but peripheral," and "special but nonstellar": "The services performed by teachers have usually been seen as above the run of everyday work, and the occupation has had the aura of a special mission honored by society. But social ambiguity has stalked those who undertook the mission, for the real regard shown those who taught has never matched the professed regard" (p. 10).

The history of teachers in the United States certainly suggests that both their job description and public image have left much to be desired. "In 1776, the *Maryland Journal* reported that a ship had arrived in Baltimore from Belfast and Cork with a cargo that included 'various Irish commodities, among which are beef, pork, potatoes and schoolmasters'" (Fiske, 1989a, p. B6). Early in our nation's history, any individual possessing "acceptable moral character" was considered qualified to teach. Wages received were comparable to those of a farmhand. In the early colonial days, teachers had to clean classrooms, shovel coal, ring churchbells, provide religious instruction, run community errands, fill in for ailing pastors, and even dig graves (Elsbree, 1939). They were also "boarded round," that is, sent to live with different families each week as a way of reducing community expenses. Essentially, they were servants of the community, with few rights, who could not deviate in their personal or professional behavior from the roles prescribed by their employers. Community boards supervised their behavior closely, treating them by implication as not much better or more trustworthy than the children they taught. Most teachers during this time were men, many of whom aspired to the clergy and viewed teaching as "an apprenticeship to be discarded after [acquiring] credentials for a more significant position" (Lortie, 1975, p. 11). To both Lortie and Charters (1963), these teachers were valued members of their local communities but "could not command deference when they competed with men of broader cosmopolitanism and prominence" (Lortie, p. 11).

During the nineteenth century, teaching evolved as a profession as the nation became secularized, industrialized, and urbanized. The Common School Crusade, led by the likes of Horace Mann and Henry Barnard, fostered the establishment of free, tax-supported, compulsory education in nearly every state by the end of the century. How, we might ask, did these reforms affect public attitudes toward or respect for teachers? On the one hand, teachers were seen as playing key roles in the establishment and maintenance of a more humane and industrialized society. Horace Mann saw education as the "great equalizer of the conditions of men" and as "the most effective and benign of all the forces of civilization" (1847, p. 112). And, as technology rapidly improved and factories proliferated, schools were increasingly needed to select and train children for their future vocations. Teachers, of course, were the conduit through which these social changes were to occur. In the days of the one-room schoolhouse, it mattered little if students learned no more than the alphabet and how to make change, but as society changed, teachers were needed to prepare individuals for new roles. According to Elsbree (1939), educational reform during these years abounded, with new schools, curriculum advances, educational journals, and teacher training institutes.

On the other hand, as the need for teachers increased, and as teaching increasingly became a feminine occupation (men were needed for and attracted to newly created factory jobs), the prestige of teaching declined. Teachers remained "for the most part among the worst trained, lowest paid, and most shabbily treated of professional workers" (Brenton, 1970, p. 63). Women's salaries were often not even half those of men, and men's salaries were often not even half those of skilled workers such as blacksmiths, painters, and carpenters. Even during a time of egregious racial prejudice, the weekly salary of women teachers ($2.50) in at least one Boston suburb in 1867 was exceeded by that of black cooks ($3.00) in the same area (Brenton, p. 64). But because teaching was often seen as the most (and, in some instances, the only) respectable profession for a woman (Lortie, 1975), women teachers were expected to bear the low pay, responsibilities, and stresses of the job without complaint. Normal schools, created in 1839 to train women to become teachers, often required their charges to live extraordinarily austere lives. Both male and female teachers continued to pay the price for their purportedly "exalted" social role: Loyalty oaths were often required; annual competency examinations, often administered by those knowing virtually nothing about teaching, were commonplace; and, in general, teachers' behavior continued to be scrutinized and prescribed at every turn. According to one diarist, being a teacher in 1862 meant dealing with paradoxes: living in a humble sphere yet having an "elevated" mind; being inferior in station, yet "content" because teaching enabled one to do good (cited in Grace, 1978).

Much of this ambivalence—this public sense of teacher as unfortunately necessary, as both defender of community values and potential corrupter, as dedicated professional but also as common and undeserving of decent remuneration—continued into the twentieth century. In 1926, the average annual salary of teachers, principals, and superintendents in U.S. public schools was $1,276, while trade union members were earning $2,402 and "high-grade clerical workers" $1,908 (National Education Association, 1927). Communities continued to resent the fact that teachers and schools cost money. Teachers also continued to be regulated in both their personal and professional lives. "As late as the 1920's, teachers who smoked had a hard time getting jobs in California, Tennessee, parts of Illinois, Massachusetts, and other places. . . . Politically, as rigid state laws in New York, Ohio, Michigan, Tennessee, and many other states made pointedly clear, teachers were to tread . . . a path that left no room to question any aspect of established American life, either politically or socially" (Brenton, 1970, p. 67). Teaching was still widely viewed by both those within and outside the profession as a transient occupation, with men leaving for better jobs and women for marriage or motherhood.

But the twentieth century did bring important changes to the profession. Educational associations, originally (but abortively) organized in the early decades of the nineteenth century, began to reappear. The National Education Association grew from 10,000 members in 1919 to 220,000 members by 1932 (Elsbree, 1939); state teacher associations increased their membership from 15 percent of all teachers in 1910 to 70 percent by 1937. Present estimates are that 90 to 95 percent of teachers in this country belong to a union.

Another change that has gradually occurred during this century is the easing of social restrictions on teachers. As the nation has grown increasingly urbanized and as the moral climate has relaxed, monitoring of teachers has grown more difficult. No longer would we expect, or teachers tolerate, contracts such as the one required of women teachers in 1927 in a small southern town, which included the promise to abstain from dancing, dating, and falling in love, as well as to "consider [oneself] at all times the willing servant of the school board and the townspeople" (Waller, 1932, p. 43).

Although as late as 1964 only 40 percent of teachers believed that they were as free as other citizens to take sides on political issues (Brenton, 1970), many more teachers than ever before were entering politics, writing books, and taking strong and open positions on social issues. This trend increased dramatically as the mood of the sixties intensified and as a new group of idealistic and outspoken teachers entered the profession.

The Shift in Public Attitudes and the Rise of Teacher Burnout

The growth of teacher unions, the easing of social restrictions on teachers, and the increased role of the federal government in education since the late 1950s all influenced the nature of teachers' professional and personal roles. But to understand why many teachers' reactions to the events of the 1960s were so intense and why teacher burnout became so prominent an issue during those years, the focus must be on something less tangible than the growth of unions or the amount of money the federal government spent on education. The most relevant issue here is the attitude of the public toward teachers and schooling in the era preceding the sixties, the era that began following the end of World War II.

This post-World War II era was marked by a vastly increased emphasis on the need for and value of education. Much of the impetus for this view came from the passage of legislation (the GI Bill of Rights) that provided federal funds for the further education of millions of veterans. As Sarason (1983) noted, this bill dramatically changed public attitudes toward education. Schooling was now considered the royal road to success, the best means to a good life for both children and adults. "In the late 1950s one began to hear, from parents and others, that children growing up in the post-World War II period . . . were and would be the best educated generation the world had ever seen. . . . The significance of this parental view was, first, the emphasis that it placed on schooling or, more correctly, on *increased* schooling. Education was salvation for the individual, the society, and the world" (p. 95).

This is not to say that schools or teachers weren't criticized during this era. Criticism of education, in one form or another, has been a constant throughout our history, in large part because "society expects so much and so many different results from schooling" (Sarason, 1983, p. 36). But it is important to remember that, despite criticisms, most Americans in the post-World War II period were strong believers in the power of education and strong supporters of the efforts of individual teachers. In contrast to what was later to happen in the sixties, the criticism of the educational system that occurred during this time—in academic and government circles, for example—seemed not to directly influence public respect for teachers. In most households, there was no question but that the teacher's authority was absolutely legitimate; teachers might be wrong, or old-fashioned, or unfair, but they were to be listened to, learned from, and respected. Children understood these rules, even if they didn't like them. For most children, disrespect for a teacher was out of the question, and if it occurred at all it was considered a serious offense. If a child talked back to a teacher, he or she could

well expect that parents would quickly be summoned for a conference with the teacher and/or principal, and could equally well
expect that some parental punishment would be forthcoming. But
even to say that parents were *expected* to support the teacher's authority is somewhat misleading, for it implies that they perceived
some external pressure to do so; the fact is that parents themselves
generally subscribed to the same set of values as both the teacher and
the principal. Schooling was "the way" and adherence to teachers'
rules was an indisputable aspect of education. Parents might disagree with a teacher's style or perhaps look forward to the day when
their child would have a different teacher, but their stance toward
their child would usually be "OK, he [or she] is not the best teacher,
but *he [or she] is still the teacher and you have to listen.*" Debates
about curriculum and methods and appropriate goals might rage
outside the school and arouse passionate pleas for change, but the
implicit consensus was that inside the classroom the teacher
reigned. In *The World We Created at Hamilton High,* Grant (1988)
noted that during this era schools were orderly, lateness to class was
a rarity, and seldom did students need more than a stern glance from
the teacher to correct misbehavior.

It was this attitude, this sense of respect and support, that
most teachers in the 1950s and early 1960s experienced. To be sure,
this aura was tinged with a "shadowed" side that allowed the public
to grossly underpay its teachers and otherwise regard them as not
quite as bright or honorable as most other professionals. But the
importance of this "specialness" cannot be overestimated. Not only
do public respect and support serve as reinforcers for teachers' efforts in the absence of more tangible (financial) rewards, but, as
Grant (1983) noted, they also serve as the foundation of teachers'
authority within the classroom. As the sixties were soon to show,
teaching is nearly an impossible job without public support and
cooperation. Classroom discipline invariably erodes, administrative
help proves more difficult to secure, friction within a school mul-
tiplies as different factions compete to please (or further antagonize)
school critics, and teaching becomes even lonelier.

To say that public respect and support compensate for the
many ills and poor salary that teachers are forced to endure is to
grossly oversimplify a series of complex relationships. It would be

more accurate to suggest that for much of the postwar period until the mid-1960s, these qualities provided the foundation for many other, often more frequently articulated rewards of teaching, such as working effectively with students and performing a socially important role. Teaching and teachers might be criticized by academics, curriculum reform might be planned with little or no input from teachers, salaries might continue to barely provide a living wage, and insidious putdowns of teachers ("those who can, do . . . those who can't, teach") might be part of the American culture, but despite it all, most teachers had sufficient community support for their work that they could derive satisfaction from the most essential aspect of teaching—the student-teacher relationship.

But social conventions changed dramatically in the late 1960s and 1970s. The authority of teachers was eroded on several fronts. Grant (1983) argued persuasively that the authority of teachers is derived from four sources: the esteem granted them by the general public, the acceptance offered them by the community they serve, the attitude and support of other educators with whom they work, and the general status of adults within society. Each, he suggested, underwent a significant decline in the sixties.

First, teaching was no longer as esteemed a profession. Attacks, suggestions, and "constructive criticism" emanated from governmental agencies at all levels, from academics, from social critics, from community groups. All contributed to the sense that, at the least, teachers didn't know what they were doing and, at worst, might be harming those whom they were charged with educating. Meanwhile, the baby boom generation, coming of age in the late 1960s, often had "higher" aspirations than teaching. They saw law, medicine, and psychology as providing more prestigious means of achieving social good.

Second, organized parent groups as well as individual parents and other community members seemed no longer to be consistently supportive of teachers' efforts or prerogatives. Rather than actively supporting teachers, an increasing number of parents seemed eager to use legal and political means to combat them. As Goodlad (1984) commented: "The almost unquestioned supportive relationship between home and school that characterized earlier periods deteriorated substantially. The child spanked in school one hundred and even fifty years ago was spanked again at home. The child spanked in school in 1975 frequently became the pivotal figure in a suit against the school brought by his parents" (p. 7). Few will wax nostalgic over the benefits of spanking children per se, but, of course, spanking is not the point. An implicit though critical bond between the school and the community was being altered in ways whose ramifications none could foresee. Ostensibly, many of the changes wrought by legal challenges, public demands, and the like were meant to extend and strengthen the rights of children; few considered the potential impact of these changing social attitudes on teachers' ability to function within the classroom. The basic assumption on which teachers had been proceeding for decades—that classroom rules were set by teachers and, unless egregiously unjustified, supported by parents—was no longer operative in many communities. Teachers could no longer proceed from the assumption that students knew who was in charge. The impulse to challenge authority—as old as the first oedipal conflict—was no longer held in check by community prohibitions.

Third, Grant noted, as I did in Chapter Five, that teachers who were college-educated in the sixties often came into schools questioning values and traditional practices. Steeped in the beliefs that "competition was amoral and hierarchies of any kind were to be avoided," this new generation of teachers contributed to a "new note of uncertainty within schools" (Grant, 1983, p. 604). Although it might be argued that a diversity of opinion on such matters as discipline, testing, and homework is healthy to the functioning of a school, research (for example, Coleman, 1981) suggests that both discipline and student test scores are better in those schools where there is a general consensus on these matters among teachers and between teachers and administrators. As Grant stated, "the authority of any one teacher in the school is affected by the consensus or lack of it achieved by teachers in that setting" (1983, p. 604). The influx of young, idealistic teachers upset the traditional order, the "way it spozed to be." This, of course, was not unintentional—many new teachers were entirely aware, and proud, that their values were discrepant with those of older, more experienced teachers. The major points are these, however: Beginning in the 1960s, significant internal disagreements over educational rules and values diminished teachers' authority both within a given school system and in society in general; and these disagreements interfered with the establishment of collegial bonds that often serve to mitigate the impact of stress.

And fourth—an issue discussed in detail in Chapter Five—is that during the sixties there was a general assault on authority. As Grant stated, the assumption of adult prerogatives and rights was no longer pervasive among broad segments of society. Simply put, the fact that teachers (or anyone else in authority, for that matter) "said so" was no longer good enough reason to believe or act in a prescribed way.

I add one additional item to Grant's list. As noted earlier, teachers' authority was also eroded in the sixties because there was considerable social pressure to refocus the attribution for educational failure. Such failure, previously attributed either to student lack of ability or to the unfortunate consequences of cultural deprivation, began to be seen instead as the result of teacher inadequacy. The general public sentiment in regard to students was: "All must have prizes." Everyone was to be "above average" and to the extent that someone was not, either the teacher, the school, or the criteria for this judgment (standardized tests, for example) were derogated. Along with the view that each child deserves a future in the "new" America came the need for a new scapegoat when it became clear that delivering that future wasn't so simple. In short, public and political pressure to immediately compensate for generations of educational neglect of minorities precipitated widespread criticism of teachers' efforts, talents, tools, and commitment. Teachers were blamed for the disproportionate rate of educational failure among minority children, accused of conservative, even injurious educational practices, and seen as an inextricable part of an unyielding power establishment.

Taken together, these trends dramatically lessened teachers' power and standing. Without general public support, without parental support, without the support of teachers within their school, and without the traditional mantle and protection of adult status, teachers felt more alone and emotionally drained than ever. The erosion of these supports, coupled with increased, often unrealistic expectations of pupil achievement (both from inside and outside the profession), left many teachers feeling that the satisfactions of teaching were no longer commensurate with the stresses. Feeling unappreciated, attacked from all sides, and often inconsequential, more and more teachers became burned out.

Beginning in the 1950s and continuing to this day, teachers have occupied a more prominent and more conspicuous place in American society than ever before. In part, this explains why teachers reacted so strongly to the attacks upon them during the sixties. At a time when they were just beginning to experience a sense of professionalism and public acceptance, the public's attitude seemed to change precipitously, and rather viciously at that. My sense, then, about the timing of teacher strikes and of the incipient perceptions of burnout among teachers in the mid-1960s is analogous to Alexis de Tocqueville's theory about the French Revolution: The oppressed don't revolt until their oppression is lifted somewhat and their expectations are aroused. A chronic history of public disrespect and indifference in regard to teachers abated a good deal in the fifties and early sixties and raised the expectations of teachers.

The Dade County Studies

Data to support many of these contentions can be found by comparing attitudes of teachers in 1964 with attitudes held in 1984. In 1964, Lortie surveyed over 6,500 Dade County (Florida) school teachers; these data formed the basis of his seminal work, *Schoolteacher* (1975). Lortie chose Dade County, with its culturally homogeneous population of both teachers and schoolchildren, as a "better-than-average" setting for investigating the attitudes of teachers toward a wide range of educational issues. In order to provide a historical perspective on many of these issues and attitudes, Kottkamp, Provenzo, and Cohn (1986) surveyed over 2,700 Dade County teachers twenty years later.

They found the 1984 teachers older, more experienced, and better educated than their 1964 counterparts. They also found that a number of attitudes and perceptions had changed over the years. In 1964, 81 percent of Lortie's sample felt satisfied with teaching as a job—that is, they endorsed any of the three top choice points ("very satisfied," "satisfied," "more satisfied than not") on a seven-point scale. In 1984, 76 percent of Kottkamp and his colleagues' sample expressed this level of satisfaction, an indication to the authors of "a slight decline." Another way of looking at these data, though, is from the bottom up rather than from the top down. From this perspective, the number of teachers either "dissatisfied" or "very dissatisfied" with their jobs nearly doubled, from 2.9 percent in 1964 to 5.5 percent in 1984. The number of teachers satisfied with their schools (rather than their jobs per se) declined from 80 percent in 1964 to 68 percent in 1984. Viewed from the bottom-up perspective, however, the number of teachers *dissatisfied* with their schools increased significantly—rising from 2.5 percent to 10.2 percent. Although the percentages of dissatisfied teachers may still appear to be relatively low and some of these numerical shifts may be due to normal sampling error, these percentages have still increased substantially; moreover, even small numbers of seriously disaffected teachers may adversely influence the functioning of a school.

The type of rewards that teachers view as most important has also changed over the years. Lortie (1975) posited three categories of rewards: extrinsic (salary, prestige, power over others); ancillary (job security, schedule, "fit" between person and job demands); and psychic (opportunity to master a discipline, reaching a group of students, developing relationships with children). Most relevant here is that substantially fewer teachers in 1984, in comparison to 1964, viewed "the respect [they] receive from others" as the most satisfying extrinsic reward of teaching. While "salary earned" remained stable in terms of the percentages of those endorsing it as the most satisfying extrinsic reward (about 14 percent), the number of teachers who viewed "the respect I receive from others" as their most satisfying extrinsic reward declined from 36.6 percent to 26.3 percent. Even more significant, the number of teachers stating that they received "no satisfaction at all from these [extrinsic] things" more than doubled, increasing from 13.0 percent in 1964 to 27.8 percent in 1984. To the extent that these findings are valid, this represents a remarkable shift—with more than a quarter of a recent sample of teachers contending that they received *no satisfaction* from any of the extrinsic rewards of teaching. It is also of note that the ancillary reward that gave most teachers the greatest satisfaction was their schedule—"the ability to spend time *away* from work" (Kottcamp, Provenzo, and Cohn, 1986, p. 565, emphasis in original).

The kind of students Dade County teachers preferred working with also changed over these two decades. As Kottcamp and others noted, "Dade County teachers in 1984 were more likely than their 1964 counterparts to seek students who would not drain them physically, intellectually, and emotionally" (p. 563). Reacting, I suspect, to the specter of burnout, the percentage of teachers whose first choice of students would be "nice kids from average homes, who are respectful and hard-working" rose from 36.2 percent in 1964 to 46.6 percent twenty years later.

Lortie's (1986) understanding of these changes parallels mine to a great extent. He too views the decline in the status of teachers as resulting from years of social and educational turbulence and from years of public criticism of education. In regard to the former, he points to the influence of involuntary transfers, salary erosion, crises and scandals involving school boards and administrators, and desegregation, "a much-needed medicine [that] occasionally produced side effects . . . that confused teachers' career lines" (p. 570). In regard to the latter, he notes, as I have repeatedly, that "time and again, national and local media trumpeted 'the failure' of the schools, and they were not reluctant to blame the teachers" (p. 570).

Teachers and the Public: Surveys Show
How Each Views the Other

The results of two annual surveys (the Metropolitan Life Survey of the American Teacher that began in 1984 and the Gallup Poll of the public's attitudes toward the public schools that began in 1969) provide further data to support the contentions that teachers suffered a loss of respect following the sixties and that the issues of public respect and support are still critical issues for teachers. Taken together, the results of these surveys lead to the following conclusions regarding the views that teachers and the public have toward each other.

Public attitudes toward education grew increasingly negative in the decade between 1974 and 1983. "Between 1974, when the question was first asked [by the Gallup Poll], and 1983, the percentage of people rating their local schools A or B (i.e., excellent or good) dropped from 48% to 31%. There was a corresponding increase in the lower ratings: from 11% rating their local schools D or F in 1974 to 20% in 1983. Even allowing for some sampling error, these figures represent a negative change of opinion by 25 to 30 million people. . . . It is a significant change indeed" (Elam, 1984, p. 3). My contention is that public attitudes toward education and public schools had begun to change before 1974, but data to confirm this belief are not available. Although the Gallup Poll of the public's attitude toward public schools began in 1969, respondents were not asked about "attitude changes" or the grade they would assign their local public schools until several years later.

The downward trend toward negative evaluations of schools and teachers seems to have ended in 1983. Evidence for this trend comes from at least three areas: public ratings of local schools, attitudes toward salaries of teachers, and feelings about one's child becoming a public school teacher.

As Table 7.1 indicates, in 1984, the percentage of individuals rating their local public schools as either *A* or *B* rose to 43 percent—the highest figure since 1976. Since then, the percentage of those grading their local public schools this highly has stayed in the 40 to 43 percent range through the balance of the 1980s. Ratings of local teachers have also become more positive during this time frame. Furthermore, in the 1981 Gallup survey, 36 percent of those surveyed felt teacher salaries were too low; by 1986, 49 percent felt this way.

The downward trend in the numbers of those who want their children to become teachers also seems to have ended in 1983. From 1969 to 1983, there was a steady drop in the numbers of parents who said they would like their children to become teachers—from 75 percent in 1969 to 45 percent in 1983. Gallup attributed this decline to the lack of available teaching positions in the 1970s and 1980s but noted too the influence of several other factors, including low salaries, the increase in career options for women, and the growing awareness of the phenomenon of teacher burnout. In 1984, the trend began to reverse, as 50 percent of those interviewed said they would

Table 7.1. Public Attitudes Toward Teachers and Schools in the 1980s.

	1989	1988	1987	1986	1985	1984	1983	1982	1981	1980
Ratings Given to the Public Schools Nationwide										
A/B	22	23	26	28	27	25	19	22	20	
D/F	19	16	13	15	15	15	22	19	21	
Don't know	12	13	19	16	15	11	21	15	16	
Ratings Given to Local Public Schools										
A/B	43	40	43	41	43	42	31	37	36	35
D/F	15	14	13	16	14	15	20	19	20	18
Ratings Given to Local Public School Teachers										
A/B			49	41	49	50			39	
D/F			9	16	15	10			15	
Would You Want Your Child to Become a Teacher?										
Yes		58					45		46	48
No		31					43		40	40
Don't know		11					11		12	12

Source: Annual Gallup Polls of the public's attitudes toward the public schools (1981–1989).

like their daughter to become a teacher and 46 percent said they would like their son to enter this field. In 1988, 58 percent of those interviewed felt they'd like to have their child take up teaching.

Although the downward trend toward negative evaluation of schools and teachers ended in the early to mid-1980s, this has not yet culminated in attitudes that are as positive toward education as they were in the late 1960s and even early 1970s. The data noted above reflect this fact. Ratings of public schools in the late 1980s still were not as high as they were in the early 1970s and the percentage of those parents in the 1980s who wanted their children to become teachers has never even approximated the 1969 figure.

The public tends to rate local public schools much more favorably than public schools nationally. In 1981, the Gallup Poll began asking respondents to give grades not only to their local public schools but to the public schools in the nation as a whole. As Table 7.1 indicates, from 1981 to 1989 there has been, on average, a sixteen-percentage-point discrepancy in the numbers of those rating the public schools nationally either an *A* or *B* and those rating their local schools this favorably. In 1989, local schools were rated

A or *B* by 43 percent of the sample; schools nationwide were rated *A* or *B* by 22 percent of the sample. Commenting on these results, Gallup and Elam (1989) suggested that "the more firsthand knowledge one has about the public schools (i.e., knowledge that does not come from the media), the better one likes them. This is a rare case of familiarity breeding respect" (p. 50).

In comparison to other occupational groups, teachers are judged by the public as having a low status. When respondents were asked in the 1981 Gallup Poll to give their impressions of twelve different occupational groups, teachers were ranked third in terms of their contribution to the general good of society (after clergymen and physicians), second in terms of the amount of stress or pressure they face (after physicians), and eighth in terms of prestige or status (after physicians, judges, clergymen, bankers, lawyers, business executives, and public school principals). The public perceived teachers' status as being higher than only three other occupational groups noted in this survey: local politicians, advertising practitioners, and realtors. The public's respect for teachers, then, is not commensurate with their understanding of the contributions teachers make or the pressures they face.

Teachers' feelings about important aspects of schools are in many ways quite different from the public's attitude. Teachers, for example, rate the schools and their own performance considerably more favorably than does the general public. In 1984, when 50 percent of the public graded teachers *A* or *B*, 78 percent of teachers gave themselves and their peers these high grades. Teachers are also considerably more concerned than the public is with the lack of money available for education: More than twice as many teachers (27 percent) as nonteachers (12 percent) feel that "lack of proper financial support for the schools and teachers" is among the biggest problems that confront the public schools (Elam, 1989).

Another rather curious difference between teachers and the public is that a greater percentage of the public than of teachers want their children to become teachers. As noted above, in 1988, 58 percent of the public said that they would like a child of theirs to become a teacher; by contrast, only 48 percent of teachers wanted their daughters to follow in their footsteps and only 38 percent wanted their sons to. What we must remember is that the public has

always had a dual image of teachers: as having both an extraordinarily difficult job (of containing and educating children) and as
having a relatively easy job (in terms of number of hours per day
and number of weeks per year spent working). For teachers, therefore, the balance sheet on the attractiveness of teaching as a career
is not as positive as it is to the general public.

One reason is that teachers believe there is a significant difference between their value to society and their status in society.
"Teachers tend to regard themselves as martyrs. Overwhelmingly,
they believe that they are unappreciated and underrewarded" (Elam,
1989, p. 785). Consider that in both the 1984 and 1989 Gallup Polls
teachers ranked themselves first in value and last in status among
twelve occupations listed. Teachers' perception of their own status
is even lower than that of the public. As noted earlier in this chapter, the public ranked teachers third in value and eighth in status.

Most parents rate most aspects of schools favorably. According to the 1987 Metropolitan Life survey, a substantial proportion
of parents are favorably impressed with their child's school and
teachers. More than 50 percent of parents gave "good" or "excellent" marks to thirteen of fourteen items that surveyed various aspects of schooling. Parents' most favorable response was to "the
availability and responsiveness of teachers when you need to contact
them." Other items receiving high grades from parents included the
degree to which most teachers seem to care about their students, the
qualifications and competence of teachers in their child's school,
and the overall quality of education that their child received. Parents reserved their lowest grades for items relating to educational
outcome, for example, "the success of the school in preparing students for jobs after high school" (only 44 percent favorable).

Most parents respect teachers. Most parents (nearly two-
thirds) feel that, as a group, they do respect teachers (Harris and
Associates, 1987). Remarkably enough, even a greater proportion of
teachers (over three-fourths) agree. "Parents themselves don't perceive any lack of respect from their end. Moreover . . . teachers don't
actually feel a lack of respect from their own students' parents (as
opposed to from society at large)" (Harris and Associates, 1987,
p. 18).

Although there has been a critical mass of disenchanted parents and scornful media commentary—and this mass grew from the mid-1960s to mid-1980s—keep in mind that most people did not then (in the sixties and seventies) and have not now (in the eighties and early nineties) given up on the public schools. Timpane (1982) reminded us that "schools are still among the most popular institutions in our country, in an age when all institutions are less popular than they were" (p. 3). Timpane's source for this statement was probably the 1980 Gallup Poll. In this survey, the church was the institution that the public seemed to have most confidence in, but public schools were second in a list of eight, ahead of the courts, local, state, and national government, labor unions, and big business. Judgment of public attitudes toward teachers needs to be tempered by this understanding.

A substantial minority of parents do not respect teachers or the job that they are doing. Do most parents respect teachers and view most aspects of schools in a favorable light? Yes, the data are clear on this. But what cannot be discounted is the fact that 20 to 35 percent of the parents in the Metropolitan Life survey did not highly esteem teachers or the job they were doing. These parents felt that teachers were doing only a "fair" or even "poor" job in terms of how much they seemed to care about their students, regarded the qualifications and competence of teachers in their child's school as either fair or poor, and felt that the overall education their child received was only fair or poor. It should be clear that strong minority opinions may have a significant impact upon the feelings and self-regard of any professional group.

Furthermore, 35 percent of those surveyed by the Gallup Poll and 38 percent of the parents surveyed by Metropolitan Life felt their child's education was worse today than when they themselves were in school. Finally, what cannot be overlooked is that in all Gallup Polls in the 1980s, a significant minority of individuals graded even their local public schools D or F. This figure ranged from 13 percent in 1987 to 20 percent in 1983; the 1989 figure was 15 percent.

The authors of the Metropolitan Life survey suggested that "this critical minority [of detractors] provides a strong constituency for reform and change" (Harris and Associates, 1987, p. 18). What these authors did not consider, though, is that this critical minority may serve not as a force for educational improvement but instead as a force to undermine teachers' morale and efforts. The distinction between constructive and destructive criticism may well lie in the eyes of the beholder.

Still, these figures do indicate that it is a minority of parents who fail to show respect for teachers or schools and that teachers themselves recognize this fact. These data suggest that from a teacher's perspective "lack of public respect" has two distinct references: the lack of respect that emanates from a seemingly large and anonymous segment of the general public (often reflected in media caricatures of teachers) and the lack of respect that comes from a small but influential minority of parents who are familiar with neighborhood schools.

From teachers' perspective, lack of parental support is a major educational problem. Determining the number of teachers who feel unsupported (rather than disrespected) by parents is problematic. According to the Carnegie Foundation (*The Condition of Teaching,* 1988a), 90 percent of all teachers nationwide report that lack of parental support is a problem in their school. On the other hand, when the Metropolitan Life survey (Harris and Associates, 1987) asked teachers to rate the amount of support for their school shown by parents, 22 percent checked "excellent," 36 percent "good," 31 percent "fair," and 11 percent "poor." According to this sample of teachers, those parents who live in suburbia, who have college degrees, and who have children in elementary school are the most available and responsive to teacher input. In part, the wide differences in numbers may reflect the fact that one survey (the Carnegie Foundation) relied on mailed questionnaires while the other (Metropolitan Life) employed personal telephone interviewing, a method that may have tempered the tendency of teachers to denounce parents. The disparity in these percentages may also reflect the specific nature of the questions posed. Thus, it is entirely possible that most teachers feel that parental support for their efforts is generally good or excellent but that there are some parents in the school (the critical minority) whose lack of support poses a major problem for schools and teachers.

Yet another angle was provided by the 1984 and 1989 Gallup Polls of teachers' attitudes toward the public schools. In both surveys, the school problem most frequently mentioned by teachers was not discipline or drug-related problems (the public's view) but rather lack of parental support and interest. In 1984, 31 percent of teachers viewed the lack of parental support as among the most important problems facing schools while only 19 percent mentioned school discipline and 54 percent use of drugs; in 1989, 34 percent of teachers noted parents' lack of interest and support, 27 percent mentioned lack of discipline, and 13 percent mentioned drug use. Lack of parental support and interest had a variety of meanings to these respondents. According to Elam (1989), "some said they have 'no backing from parents on discipline.' Others charged that 'parents don't help students realize the importance of preparing for the future.' Some pointed to 'parental apathy,' while others said that 'parents lack faith in the school system'" (p. 786). For the most part, then, teachers tend not to respect the job that parents are doing. When asked what grade they would give to the parents of students in the local public schools for bringing up their children, the highest proportion of grades given (45 percent) was C (Gallup, 1984). Only 2 percent of teachers rated these parents an A. Teachers are less impressed with parents' abilities than vice versa.

Parent-teacher relations are a critically important determinant of teachers' work satisfaction. As Table 7.2 indicates, teachers who report excellent parent-teacher relations indicate a greater degree of satisfaction in their work than others. Note particularly that

Table 7.2. Job Satisfaction of Teachers Connected to Relations with Parents.

Relations Between Parents and Teachers (According to Teachers)	Degree of Teacher Satisfaction			
	Very Satisfied	Somewhat Satisfied	Somewhat Dissatisfied	Very Dissatisfied
Excellent (n = 178)	67	28	5	0
Good (n = 527)	40	46	12	1
Fair or Poor (n = 294)	24	53	28	6

Source: The Metropolitan Life Survey of the American Teacher (Harris and Associates, 1987). Complete report available from the Metropolitan Life Insurance Company.

67 percent of teachers who report excellent relations with parents are very satisfied with their jobs, whereas only 24 percent of teachers who report fair or poor relations feel very satisfied. Similarly, the poorer the state of parent-teacher relationships, the greater the chance that teachers have considered leaving the profession or intend to do so within the next five years. For example, 60 percent of teachers who report either fair or poor parent-teacher relations have considered leaving teaching, but only 36 percent of those who report excellent relations have considered this possibility.

Living in a Material World: Teachers, Salaries, and Public Respect

Apart from general issues of public opinion, when teachers speak about the lack of respect or support accorded them, they are most often referring to their salaries and/or the ways in which they're treated by students, parents, and administrators.

To many current teachers, the pitiful size of their salaries is the most palpable indication of the public's lack of respect. Historically, of course, teachers have been poorly remunerated, even when, beginning approximately one hundred years ago, education began to be widely perceived as socially valuable. Low salaries in education are a reflection of both the "special but shadowed" status of teachers in general and the unfortunate lack of respect traditionally accorded to women workers. The prevailing cultural assumption has long been that teaching is neither full-time nor fully professional work and therefore not deserving of a pay scale consistent with jobs performed by more talented, resourceful, or hard-working individuals. Moreover, the predominance of women in teaching has kept salaries down. For many years, the annual availability of a plentiful supply of young women graduating from teaching institutions helped limit salaries; in addition, women's salaries in general were, until quite recently, not expected to be equal to those of men. A teacher's salary, it was assumed, had only to provide for the meager needs of a single woman or serve as a modest supplement to the income of the primary wage earner in the family.

The desire to help others is an influence that far outweighs monetary returns for those who choose teaching (Lortie, 1975), but when the pursuit of this satisfaction becomes encumbered by complex social issues and a general attitude of antiteacher sentiment—as it clearly did during the later sixties and for years thereafter—then other satisfactions are pursued. For many teachers, then, the prevailing attitude became, "If I can't be the highly respected professional I was once considered, at least I'll demand to get paid decently for what I have to put up with." Ironically, though, despite the plethora of teacher strikes in the late 1960s and early 1970s, the 1970s produced at least a 17 percent decline in teacher purchasing power nationwide (Ornstein, 1980).

But teachers' salaries have begun to rise. The average teacher salary in the United States in 1989–90 was $31,315, nearly double the 1980 levels of $16,100 and nearly triple the $9,705 teachers earned in 1972. Feistritzer (1985), in a Carnegie Foundation report, *The Condition of Teaching*, makes the point that "salaries of teachers have been outstripping the inflation rate since 1981–1982, reversing decades of lagging behind inflation" (p. 35). In addition, her data suggest that teachers have not been as grossly underpaid as has been claimed. Taking 1982 as an example, she notes that the average starting salary for teachers then ($14,000) was more or less comparable to the starting salaries of others whose jobs require a bachelor's degree: accountants ($18,700), architects ($12,000), psychologists at the federal level ($14,500), and public relations specialists ($11,500). Still, even the public believes that teachers are underpaid; 80 percent of those surveyed in the 1988 Gallup Poll indicated as much. And not surprisingly, most teachers agree; according to the 1989 Gallup Poll of teachers' attitudes, 82 percent consider themselves underpaid. Most teachers seem to believe that recent increases in salary barely begin to make up for years and years of being economically shortchanged.

Moreover, even if one were to concede that teachers' starting salaries are in the "reasonable range" (a position I would not take), the fact remains that teachers' average salaries, as well as peak salaries, tend to be well below those of comparable occupations. In 1986, the average teacher's salary was $25,257, just over half the median income of an electrical engineer. The opportunity to significantly increase one's income in teaching remains quite limited. In a related vein—and perhaps even more important from a psychological perspective—teachers have few, if any, opportunities for advancement. For the most part, young teachers who stay in education simply become older, more experienced teachers.

Gujarati (1985) described the feelings of many women who, having played by all the rules governing promotion in the business world, find themselves unable to progress beyond middle management. Their frustration often becomes evident when they realize that nothing they can do will bring the prestige and remuneration they feel they deserve. Teachers face this problem as soon as they enter the field. They quickly learn that their salaries are based on established schedules that are uninfluenced by their own competence. Gujarati suggested that plateaued workers should "explore" their feelings, refocus their frustration on more "constructive outlets," and reexamine career goals. If teachers were to adopt this suggestion, many more would leave for more lucrative positions in careers offering serious opportunities for advancement.

Apart from frustration, anger, and resignation from the profession, a common response of teachers to inadequate salaries is moonlighting. According to a 1985 survey done by Louis Harris and his associates for Metropolitan Life Insurance, 28 percent of all teachers work at other jobs after normal school hours. The prime second occupation of these teachers is, broadly speaking, other school work. Many work as coaches, tutors, or teachers in special remediation programs. This type of work often sharply increases the workload of the individual, leading not infrequently to added stress, resentment, and a diminished capacity to teach well. For these individuals, doing other work after school taxes an already too burdened system.

Several teachers interviewed for this book claimed that the degradation of having to do extra work was as damaging as the work itself. They felt strongly that teaching alone should afford them an adequate salary. Many felt that working summers as a way of supplementing their income was reasonable but that the necessity of working after school was an "outrageous" burden for a professional to have to assume, one that ultimately damaged the education of the children they were responsible for.

Daily Doses of Disrespect

If salary issues form the "ground" of a teacher's vision, issues of daily disrespect constitute the "figure." Salary issues are never too far from a teacher's consciousness; monetary decisions, after all, must be dealt with regularly by all of us and under stress many teachers wonder whether their salaries justify what they have to put up with. Still, teachers can and often do perform their work without focusing on their finances. In contrast, teachers are rarely oblivious to the way they are treated on a daily basis by students, parents, and administrators. It is the ongoing tone of the classroom, the ongoing nature of parent-teacher contacts, and the ongoing professional atmosphere within the school that most directly influence a teacher's perception of the respect he or she receives. "Teachers . . . are expected to work miracles day after day and then often get only silence from students, pressure from the principal, and criticism from parents" (Boyer, 1988, pp. 8–9).

Student Disrespect. What is it that teachers are reacting to when they complain of student disrespect? The stereotypical image is of students insulting, threatening, or talking back. Unfortunately this stereotype is not simply the product of the media's tendency toward sensationalism. For many teachers we spoke with (especially those at the junior high or high school level), school discipline issues are never too far from their consciousness. A high school history teacher in Texas had this to say:

> I often feel stuck. Typically, I'm in the middle of teaching a lesson when I see something going on in the back of the classroom. Let's say two kids are talking—all right, I'll usually ignore this. They may just be making plans for lunch or gossiping about who's going out with whom. But sometimes their talking is so loud that others, including me, become distracted. Or sometimes they'll be doing more than talking— insulting each other or someone else, threatening each other or someone else, taunting—that kind of thing.

If I step in and tell them to cut it out, I've interrupted my lesson and let them know that they've got the power to decide what the class is going to attend to. They become the focus. Of course, this may be necessary because if I don't step in, I may soon have a fight on my hands—or at least some pretty angry verbal exchange where each of them just has to have the last word. On the other hand, again, if I do step in everything may just escalate with me in the middle. It's true that every once in a while an angry look or angry word will be enough to stop what's going on. More typically, though, each of the kids involved will blame the other for "starting it." Or worse, I'll be told that "it's none of my business" or that I should "back off." I know that at that point I should just stop but sometimes I can't—I'm too mad then 'cause the lesson's been ruined, my control of the class has been usurped. So, I'll start shouting. You know, the "how dare you stop other kids from learning" type of thing. Of course, then I'm likely to get back, "Who gives a damn about your stupid class anyway?"

And I can't pretend it doesn't get to me. It does. It takes a lot out of me. And I'm not sure sometimes whether I'm more disgusted with myself for the fact that I couldn't control myself or the fact that once again, I was threatened by a fifteen-year-old kid . . . sometimes friends will try to console me by telling me that it's not personal. That kids this age have no respect for anyone or anything, including themselves. I know that. But you know it's easy for them to say— meanwhile I'm the one who's taking this crap every day—sometimes too I wonder why I can't console myself by remembering all the good stuff that's gone on. I don't know, though, maybe it's just human nature, but for most of us [teachers] the disrespectful stuff puts an awful taste in your mouth that's not so easy to wash out.

AN OPEN LETTER TO NEW TEACHERS

Welcome!

We entrust you to our brats. We expect you to discipline them where we have not. But do it in a way that won't make us angry.

Keep our children entertained. They are bound to get restless. They watch a lot of television so they aren't very good at entertaining themselves. School bores them because they can't flip channels.

Some of us are ardently against abortion. Others of us are ardently pro choice. Some of us demand school prayer. Others demand no school prayer. Some of us are Christians and hate atheists. Some of us are atheists and hate Christians. Please reinforce the correct moral views to our children who are in your care.

Feed our children well. We don't have time to give them breakfast at home so they are quite hungry when lunchtime rolls around.

We understand that teachers are human beings and have days when they are depressed, not feeling well and just plain have the blues. Never show that side of yourself to our children. We want them to believe the world is always a happy place. Smile.

Teach our children that America is always right, has always been right and is the best place to live in the entire world and that now is the best time to be alive in the entire history of man. Of course we don't believe this stuff anymore ourselves, but we want our children to believe it. They will read enough negative things in the newspaper.

Remain in control at all times. Our children will yell at you. We will call you up on the phone and yell at you. We will go to the school and yell at the

Source: "An Open Letter to New Teachers" is reprinted from an Ann Landers column of August 24, 1985, with permission from Harris Enterprises, Inc.

principal about you. Please stay calm. Someone has to.

Accept the great responsibility that has been given to you. If our children don't learn to read, it will be your fault. If they come out of high school having no idea what they want to do in life, it will be your fault. If they go to college and flunk out, it will be your fault. If they can't find a job, that will also be your fault.

Be perfect. Lord knows our children see enough imperfection in their homes. Somebody has to set an example.

And please don't gripe about money. Really now, you get three months of vacation away from the brats. We have to have them around all year long.

Yours truly,
The Parents

Parent Disrespect. This letter, originally written in 1985 by Randy Attwood, then managing editor of the *Olathe* (Kansas) *Daily News,* apparently represents the truth (about parents) as many teachers perceive it. According to Attwood, he received hundreds of letters reacting to the column from teachers all over the United States and abroad, all of whom concurred with its sentiments.

The statistics cited earlier in this chapter showed that it was only a minority of parents that failed to respect teachers. Nevertheless, small numbers of difficult and unreasonable parents can have a major impact on teacher morale.

The interviews conducted for this book suggest that for suburban teachers, disrespect most often takes the form of "superior attitudes" adopted by parents: These parents, because they have been as well or better educated and because they typically earn far more than teachers, know more about education and what's best for the children in their community. At the far end of this continuum are those parents who set themselves up as experts on everything from the right books to read to the correct proportion of time that should be spent on College Board preparation to the relative merits of multiple-choice versus essay-type exams. Again, most parents are not like this, but if enough feel impelled to share incontestable opinions with a teacher on a regular basis, one may well imagine the impact this might have on a teacher's sense of autonomy. Few teachers resent genuine parental input, but few can tolerate constant challenges to their authority, knowledge, or professional preroga-tives, or lack of faith in their abilities. "I had a parent come in a few weeks ago who basically told me that her child was 'gifted,' and wondered why the school wasn't doing more to enable her to grow to her potential. In fact, her child was bright; she read well—about a grade level ahead of herself—wrote well, and was decent, if not talented, in math. And she's a likable child, too—gets along well with all her classmates. My feeling is we're doing terrifically with this kid. She's self-assured, learning well, socially comfortable, seems to like school, and so on. What ticks me off is that this mother, rather than recognizing what a good job I'm doing and how much I'm contributing to her child's well-being, was essen-tially accusing me of keeping her back, and of not doing enough. She was too sophisticated to be directly rude to me but I sensed that she really felt her daughter was being shortchanged."

Suburban teachers, then, to the extent they feel a sense of disrespect from parents, perceive they are being challenged by the following question: "Are you really capable enough to help my child reach his potential?" In contrast, urban teachers do not feel that their capabilities are being questioned but rather their invest-ment. For the most part, the challenge hurled at these teachers is "Do you care enough about my child?" "Are you truly invested in seeing that he or she gets a good education?" These questions, it may be argued, are not disrespectful at all but rather necessary and indicative of parental involvement. Parents have the right and ob-ligation to insist that their children's teachers be caring and highly motivated. Moreover, based on the history of our educational sys-tem, there is more than good reason for parents of minority children to be wary of public school teachers' efforts to educate their chil-dren. Questions and legitimate concerns, however, may be raised in a variety of ways, varying in tone from the insistent yet respectful inquiry pursued in interviewing a potential pediatrician to outright suspicion and hostility. From the perspective of many teachers in urban schools, too many parents undermine their efforts as well as sense of respect by either attacking their integrity or failing to support their ideas or efforts.

> I like when parents come in to talk with me about their children's assignments or general progress or whatever. It makes my job easier when parents are involved. What I don't like is hearing that parents are talking behind my back. I also don't like when a parent comes in just to attack me, not at all interested in my side of things. For example, the other day a parent came to my room just when school was starting and began to yell at *me* because her child failed a test. She was complaining that the test wasn't fair, and that if I was a better teacher her child would have done better on the test. She implied that I really didn't care about teaching Ed [her child]. I tried telling her about my approach, what I had done to prepare the students for the test, and why I thought tests were important. I also wanted to focus on Ed's preparation for the test, his work habits and all, but she kept interrupting me. She finally left, saying she was going to have to talk to the principal about the fact that her child simply wasn't getting a good education.

There are alternative ways of thinking about this issue of respect for teachers. One of my colleagues, who is involved in training teachers, claims that if he were superintendent of schools, his first act would be to issue a proclamation stating that any teacher talking disrespectfully to a parent will be dismissed. His contention is that teachers too often assume that parents are the enemy and not to be trusted. Teachers, he claims, learn early in their careers (from peers and union leaders) that "power" is to be carefully guarded and that expertise lies only in the hands of the teacher. From his point of view, teachers provoke power struggles and bitterness by their failure to truly encourage dialogue with parents. Disrespect toward teachers, he suggests, is the inevitable result of teachers' reclusive and ungenerous attitude toward parents.

I disagree with this view, though I do recognize the fact that some teachers, like some professionals in all fields, are arrogant and patronizing. I also recognize that some teachers are more defensive than they need to be about protecting their professional prerogatives. But my sense is that most teachers encourage parental (and administrative) input, though they, like virtually all professionals, do reserve for themselves the right of deciding what is ultimately best for the clients they serve. It is when suggestions from others become mandates, and when conversations become opportunities for belittlement, that teachers recoil. The lack of respect, or worse, active disrespect, that teachers experience in their dealings with parents remains a primary factor in teachers becoming dissatisfied or burned out.

Although I've used the terms *respect* and *support* almost synonymously, it is possible to differentiate them. Lack of parental respect for teachers (personal attacks on the integrity, motivation, or competence of the teacher) tends to occur relatively infrequently and, while highly stressful, can generally be contained. On the other hand, lack of active support for teachers or education in general (parental apathy) tends to be a major problem because it is widespread and constantly interfering with teachers' ability to feel effective. Of course, these two may co-occur and the effect is then cumulative, enhancing teachers' perceptions that their efforts are inconsequential and that leaving the profession as soon as possible would be the wisest decision.

Administrative Disrespect. The last part of this triad, and one that some teachers find the most onerous, is teachers' ongoing relationships with school administrators. Dealing with disruptive or uncooperative students may be rationalized as part of one's job. And, for most teachers, dealing with entitled, sanctimonious, or contemptuous parents is fortunately not an everyday event. But dealing on a daily basis with officious administrators and otiose bureaucratic regulations is enough to try the patience of most teachers. Administrators, at least, are supposed to be on the same side as teachers, supposed to be supportive and facilitative rather than adversarial and obstructive. In this vein, a math teacher in North Carolina said: "I don't think burnout is caused by the children. Usually it is the administration. No one strokes you enough" (Tifft, 1988, pp. 62–63).

Several themes resonated throughout the interviews conducted with teachers. One was that administrators had little respect for teachers. Maeroff (1988a), in a book documenting the acrimony between school administrators and teachers, observed that principals often treat teachers as though they occupied a niche only slightly higher than that of students. A second, related theme was that administrators had little respect for the "sanctity" of the classroom and would barely think twice before either interrupting on-going classes with announcements or messengers or shuffling classroom schedules for special events. In this vein, Albert Shanker (1986a) related the following story: "Several years ago, a high school teacher told me that in the middle of one of his most difficult classes, a gorilla suddenly burst into the room. Of course, it actually was a student in costume advertising an upcoming school show. But the interruption turned the class into a shambles. When the teacher complained, he was told that some spontaneity was needed to jazz up the school day. But when you get the 'feel' of teaching . . . you know that an administrator's first job is to keep gorillas out of classrooms" (p. E7).

A third theme was that too many administrators were willing to "sell out" teachers in order to protect their own positions. Teachers felt that they served as convenient scapegoats for administrators when schools weren't performing as well as the school board, the public, or the parents expected. A fourth theme was that administrators too often bypass teachers in the decision-making process; changes in the school's structure, focus, or curriculum occur with little or no input from teachers themselves. One teacher related the following anecdote: "Our sixth-grade reading scores were down last year—actually for the second year in a row—and our principal was angry and somewhat fearful [of community reaction]. In conjunction with the vice-principal, he decided to call all the fourth-, fifth-, and sixth-grade teachers together to decide whether we should adopt a new reading system. There was much debate and discussion and the teachers thought it would be best to continue to meet before we decided to do anything different. A week later, before we had even met again, we found that a whole new reading system had been ordered and that a consultant was going to be coming in a month to brief us."

This leads to the final complaint of teachers—that administrators are blind to all but the most obvious indicator (test scores) of student success. As Daniel Duke (1986) observed, administrators all too often are out of touch with what teachers are trying to accomplish in their classes. Too many administrators fail to acknowledge social improvement in individual students, or improved classroom attendance, or improvements in self-esteem, or even academic improvement that isn't measurable on standardized tests. In short, teachers too often feel that administrators have deprofessionalized them by eliminating them from decisions that affect profoundly the nature of their work and dehumanized them by reducing teaching to a technical quest for improved test scores. Both can surely lead to the feeling of inconsequentiality in teachers.

In this section I have focused primarily on the disrespect and lack of support felt by teachers in their daily contacts with students, parents, and administrators. Each of these groups, though, could easily assemble a persuasive set of grievances. Mutual recriminations constitute a significant part of most school cultures. Thus, while teachers complain that too many parents fail to support education in any meaningful way, parents complain that too many teachers are second-rate and uncaring and that teacher burnout is simply an excuse, an abdication of teachers' responsibility to their students and society. While teachers complain that their school administrators are primarily concerned with petty stuff like the right forms and procedures and care little about helping teachers or enforcing discipline, these same administrators may well be confiding to their colleagues that too many of the teachers in their school are just interested in their paychecks and not terribly interested in improving their pedagogical skills. Similarly, although teachers often feel that in the classroom "nobody listens and nobody cares" (Weinstein, 1988), students levy the identical charge against their teachers. And, of course, administrators suggest that their jobs would be far easier if more parents were better parents, while parents are wondering why it is that school leadership seems to provide so little for their children. Finally, according to many parents, teachers, and administrators, students in this day and age are entitled, materialistic, selfish, impulsive, and difficult to discipline and teach; from the perspective of students, none of these adult groups begins to understand their problems, concerns, or needs. These differing perspectives complicate the task of education for everyone. Indeed, teachers are not alone in complaining that they feel burned out in trying to perform their jobs effectively—parents, administrators, and even students voice similar complaints.

Effect of Public Attitudes on Burnout

What can we conclude about public respect for teachers from the plethora of images, facts, and figures? That a strong majority of the public (especially those with their own children in school) respects teachers and supports their efforts but that a substantial minority—possibly in response to media influence—undervalues and denigrates teachers; that teachers feel that lack of public support for their efforts undermines their work; and that teachers feel they're doing better in their jobs than do parents. In short, the public does respect teachers—but not all of the public, not as much as they do other professionals, and not as much as teachers feel they deserve.

The loss of public respect and support, the increase in public expectations and resentment, the disrespect they feel emanating from administrators and students—all of this has undermined teachers' authority and self-respect, lessened the attraction of teaching for current as well as prospective teachers, and increased teachers' vulnerability to the variety of dysfunctional conditions that we know generically as teacher burnout.

8

Teaching in an Urban Setting:
Stories from the Classroom

OBSCURED BY ALL THE STATISTICS ON STRESS, BURNOUT, SAT-
isfactions, dissatisfactions, and attrition rates are the daily experiences of teachers, from commuting in the morning to working with
a multitude of different personalities to leaving at 3 P.M. (or 4 or 5)
and dealing with personal responsibilities and the next day's lesson
plans. Even a comprehensive listing of the factors contributing to
stress, burnout, and premature retirement cannot capture the phe-
nomenology of a teacher's workday with its rapidly mounting pressures and variety of intense, sometimes contradictory feelings.
Providing a sense of the texture of a teacher's work may make these
phenomena more clearly understood. Thus, in this chapter an attempt has been made to compose a typical "day in the life" of an
urban teacher. Chapter Nine describes a typical day for a suburban
teacher and, in addition, examines the experiences of teachers working in rural, private school, and special education classrooms.

Several caveats regarding these two chapters come to mind.
First, these descriptions could certainly have been organized around
different themes: gender lines, racial lines, geographical lines, experience, age, or marital lines, size of school, subject taught, or level

Note: This chapter was written with the collaboration of Leonard D.
Wechsler.

of schooling (elementary, junior high, senior high). Each way of looking at teachers is valid; each distinction offers a unique perspective. Elementary school teachers and high school teachers view their work differently, as do men and women teachers, young and older teachers, black and white teachers, or even teachers of Latin and teachers of physical education. I chose what was arguably the broadest possible distinction among teachers. Second, in a given level in a given school in a given community, different teachers—even those bound by common demographic traits—view their work differently. Third, any given day of a given teacher's workday is unique to him or her; each day brings its own batch of problems, rewards, and surprises. In both this and the next chapter, my sense of teachers' experiences in their various settings is embellished with comments, quotations from interviews with teachers, excerpts from accounts of teaching published elsewhere, and some additional statistics.

In talking with teachers or reading accounts of their experiences, several consistent themes appear. First, classrooms are typically in flux and disorder is the rule of the day ("unpredictabilty is the norm in school life"—Duke, 1986); second, a sense of isolation from other adults is a prominent aspect of teachers' daily work experience; third, in many urban schools, despair and hopelessness seem pervasive, seemingly intractable parts of the system; fourth, work and work-related feelings don't end at the close of the school day; fifth, thoughts of quitting are never far from many teachers' minds, even those who know that this is not a realistic option; sixth, feelings of anger or frustration occur frequently throughout the workday; and seventh, satisfactions, while relatively few in number, are often experienced intensely.

Following is a look at one day in the life of an urban high school teacher; actually, apart from some added details and some minor demographic alterations, this "day" is modeled closely on the reported experiences of one of the teachers interviewed for this book.

Walt Collins's alarm wakes him at 6:00 A.M. His wife and two kids, who do not have to get up for another hour and a half, lie sleeping. He tiptoes out of his bedroom into the bathroom. By 6:40 he is showered, shaved, and dressed for work. After a quick breakfast that includes two cups of coffee, he is out the door.

This is Walt's twentieth year as a high school teacher in an urban setting in the Midwest. He has worked in three schools, once transferring to be closer to home, another time switching as a result of staff reductions. He has a bachelor's degree in history and a master's degree in education. Walt's salary in 1988 was slightly above $40,000. He frequently complains that he is a victim of the "pewter handcuffs" syndrome. Although he earns more than he could by starting over in another field, and although many people in the United States would envy his salary, he takes home less than $25,000 after taxes. High inflation has cut into his buying power, and his living expenses continue to rise. His wife's job enables them to live a middle-class lifestyle.

Walt carries his briefcase to the car and hurries to get in before the alarm goes off, an event that occasionally wakes the neighborhood. Ten minutes later he arrives at the local shopping center to meet the rest of his carpool and begin the morning commute. There is not much conversation; at this early hour he and his two companions do not yet feel entirely awake. The comments that do pass among them tend to be amusing ancedotes about their students, sarcastic jibes aimed at any one of several school administrators, or mildly self-deprecating remarks about their willingness to endure the indignities of their job. Their destination is an urban high school with an enrollment of 3,500. Students range in age from fourteen to twenty-one; approximately 60 percent are Hispanic and 40 percent are black. Over half of these students' families receive some form of public assistance. There are few major disciplinary problems, although approximately 100 relatively minor infractions are reported each year. There are over 300 workers at the school, about one-third of whom are minority group members.

This morning the traffic is light, and Walt and his colleagues arrive early and find a parking spot right in front of the school. He barely glances up at the graying old school building. By now he is almost entirely oblivious to the garbage strewn on the streets and to the decaying rows of apartment houses across from the school. He does, however, glance quickly down the street to make sure there are no drug addicts nearby looking for their next round of victims. The carpool was instituted four years ago following the mugging, around the corner of the school, of one of his fellow commuters, a young woman teacher.

At 7:20, they all walk into the school building. Walt says a quick hello to his favorite school secretary and to some other early arrivers, then walks with another teacher down the hallway to the social studies office to run off mimeographed copies of materials for his classes. The pungent odor of the copy fluid and a bit of purple stain on his hands are reminders to wash up in the men's room. He then heads for the teacher's cafeteria to join the regular group of early arrivers for another cup of coffee.

At the table an irate colleague is complaining about a written evaluation of his work that he found in his mailbox that morning: "Can you believe this? That [obscenity] wrote that my lesson was too 'teacher-dominated,' that I did most of the talking, and that my questioning was weak." Another teacher, close to retirement, counsels: "Forget it. There's no point in getting angry. He has to criticize teachers because he feels that's how he earns his salary. In the thirty years I've been teaching I've never had a write-up that just said I taught a good lesson. What I'd really like to do is write an evaluation of him and let him know how useless he is around here." Another teacher is talking to a friend about one of her students who she suspects is both using and selling drugs in the school. Another is complaining about the lack of easy-reading textbooks to teach science. These conversations reflect many of Walt's feelings about his profession, and he thinks to himself: "This whole system is absurd. Supervisors write reports filled with suggestions that teachers ignore; teachers write lessons that students ignore; students cry out for help from their parents that parents ignore; and the educational process goes nowhere. Meanwhile I'm still here, I'm still trying—most of the time at least—and I'm not sure why."

He walks slowly to his classroom, giving himself a pep talk all the while ("let's make this a good day"). He becomes aware of a rising level of noise as students begin to arrive in school. He is aware of but consciously chooses to ignore the many petty quarrels and taunts. Instead, he picks out in the crowd of students one eleventh-grade student whose presence in class he particularly enjoys, gives her a smile and a "hi," and, on this note, enters his classroom.

Anticipating the arrival of his students for a senior-level class in American history at 8:07, Walt writes the homework assignment, instructions to the students to read the mimeographed handout and answer several questions, and the aim of the lesson on the board. The bell rings and he stands in the front of the room as a few students drift in, pick up papers, and begin their work. Hardly anyone greets him, with the exception of those who approach him with explanations of why they have not done their homework. Students continue to drift in slowly until, by 8:25, most of the class has appeared. Walt sticks his head out of the classroom door, notices several students loitering in the hallway—none of his—and returns to his class. The room is noisy and beginning to feel chaotic. Walt takes a deep breath, calls out a loud, commanding "good morning, ladies and gentlemen, let's settle down," and begins to explain the finer points of the class assignment.

Two minutes into his explanation, a monitor comes to his door with a message from the principal (a reminder that school census forms have to be handed in by the end of the day). During the thirty seconds that he's opened the door for the monitor, read the message, and said "thank you," the class has grown noisy again as two boys in the back have begun to tease a girl sitting in front of them and as several of their classmates have begun to take sides in the dispute. Getting the class back to a reasonable noise level takes another minute or two, for one of the boys in the center of the confrontation seems intent on continuing the teasing rather than focusing on the task at hand. Nevertheless, Walt does quiet the class and has them work on the assignment for several minutes. He then asks his students to consider, based on their homework from the night before and today's handout, the ideological differences between Theodore Roosevelt and Woodrow Wilson. Specifically, he asks them to summarize the basic policies of both men regarding monopolies and business regulation and control of banks and railroads. There is silence for several moments. Then, following an attempt by him to rephrase and simplify the question, one student begins to answer, only to be drowned out by someone in the back who's whispered, loud enough for everyone to hear, an obscenity-filled answer that provokes much laughter. Trying not to be provoked, Walt redirects the attention of the class to the previous responder.

For several minutes a good dialogue is kept up with at least a few students participating in the discussion. Walt feels heartened and energized by the attention paid by a few of his better students. But as he probes further, he begins to feel the class slipping away and realizes that both he and the class are becoming increasingly frustrated. The classroom buzzes with obscene comments—some as part of ongoing conversations between students, some in response to Walt's questions. Some students begin to wander around the class. Although Walt began this class as a dialogue, it ends up as a short lecture. As he collects the written exercise, he realizes that only a few of the class have attended to it in a serious way. Some have done no more than write their names on the paper; some have not even bothered with this. At the end of this class period, when the bell rings, Walt takes a deep breath and is already beginning to feel somewhat drained and discouraged. He sits down at his desk and quickly looks over his notes as his next class begins to make its way in.

For his second class period, a sophomore class in the history of the Third World, Walt writes an in-class exercise on the board. He instructs students to read a section of a handout he's prepared and to answer some questions based on this reading. Students slowly file in, sit, and begin to look over what he's distributed. "What's this?" some want to know. One student loudly proclaims, "Oh, man, I don't want to do this." Some chat with each other, and some begin to read the assignment. As the class settles into a rhythm, Walt takes attendance. Twenty minutes later he begins to go over the work, only to be interrupted almost immediately by an announcement that comes over the public address system (for a teacher to come to the office). Reflexively, several students respond to the announcement with their own fantasies about why this particular teacher needs to come to the office. Another deep breath and Walt tries to redirect their attention to the lesson at hand (European colonization in Africa). With the input from the handful of students who are regular active participants, the lesson goes well for a while. But again, twenty-five minutes into the lesson, things begin to lag. Three students have their heads down on the desk and another small group are talking among themselves. Although there is no major discipline problem, Walt feels he's losing momentum as the boredom and listlessness of a few begin to affect the others. The lesson seems to drone on, kept barely alive by a handful of responsive students. Walt begins to think of lunch, a welcome reprieve just two periods away.

In this school, teachers are assigned to hall patrol once every three terms. Security guards are on the lookout for drug traffic and serious infractions, but they tend to hover around major exits and thus hall discipline is left mostly to teachers. This is how Walt spends his third period—urging loitering students to return to their classes, breaking up a disagreement that verges on a fist fight, and consoling a sobbing student who has had an argument with her boyfriend. At worst, hall patrol can result in personal injury; at best, it is a resented chore. Occasionally, although happily not on this day, Walt gets into a confrontation with a recalcitrant student. He does not like to admit it, but there have been times when he has been afraid. Moreover, he resents having to play the role of security guard and, like many teachers considers it a violation of his dignity as a professional.

Fourth period is essentially a repeat of second. Again, Walt launches into a discussion of European colonization of Africa only to find students in this class even less responsive than those during second period. In general, he has found the students in the second period to be academically inferior to those in the fourth, although on paper the classes are purportedly equal. He is relieved that fifth period is lunch and looks forward to rest, relaxation, and moral support from his fellow teachers. Meanwhile, though, this class period is not yet over and one of the students is beginning to give him a hard time about staying seated and quiet. "I can talk if I want to. It's nobody else's business." Walt remembers being down this road before and can even replay the rest of the dialogue.

"Yes, Kevin, it is somebody else's business if your talking interferes with those who are trying to learn."

"I'm not stopping anybody from learning. They can learn all they want."

"But it's hard to learn if you're talking and carrying on."

"Nobody's learning anything in this class anyway. We'd all be better off selling some stuff and making some money."

But Walt decides he doesn't want any part of this dialogue this morning. It's disruptive and also vaguely unsettling to Walt, inasmuch as he believes that Kevin may be at least partially right. So this morning, Walt simply replies with "OK, Kevin, I'd just appreciate it if you'd keep it down." And after a gruff and somewhat sarcastic "OK, man, I'll keep it down," he does, in fact, lower his voice somewhat. Several minutes later, though, someone else challenges him: "This is boring." Several students snicker; some agree. Walt decides to ignore the remark entirely. He makes it through the next few minutes, occasionally reflecting on the veracity of the "boring" comment, and feels thankful for the bell ending the period.

Lunchtime. He leaves the classroom and hurries past a group of students. Some wave nonchalantly in his direction as he passes, and two girls yell out "Hi, Mr. Collins," in a tone that could be either genuinely friendly or mocking. He's never quite sure. Several older boys stand together in the hallway near the doors looking somewhat menacing to a casual observer. It is clear that many students are going out of their way to steer clear of this group. Walt says nothing, but wonders whether these boys—some of whom look as if they're in their early twenties—are really students in the school. He wonders too whether this group is the "ruling caste" of the student body. He thinks to himself what it would be like if Joe Clark were principal of this school.

Lunch with his group of colleagues, all veteran teachers who hold administrative jobs in addition to their teaching duties, feels like a psychological necessity to Walt. The first thing he and his buddies do upon receiving their teaching program each term is to search for a common period for lunch. In addition to the daily meetings in the teachers' cafeteria, group members get together once a month in a local restaurant. They're often joined by former members who have retired or left the school. Today's lunchtime diatribe is directed against paperwork. Laughter, as well as obscenities, occurs frequently. One of Walt's colleagues suggests that they mark attendance sheets in invisible ink; another wonders whether there should be a college course for ed majors focusing exclusively on "filling out forms"; a third imagines that all the forms go straight from the school office to the local landfill.

Feeling somewhat energized by his lunchtime break, Walt returns to the classroom for sixth period. Once again he is to teach a lesson on the colonization of African countries, this time with an especially slow group of students, many of whom can barely read. About one-third of the class roster never show up for this or any social studies class. Despite the fact that he'd put in extra time the night before trying to find creative ways of presenting this material, almost everyone in the class seems baffled by his questions and resistant to his efforts to engage them in the lesson. Students regularly request the bathroom pass, often interrupting Walt in the middle of questions. Some students, he notices, are doodling in their notebooks, some gazing out the window, some tilting back on their seats with an air of nonchalance. There is a familiar plodding rhythm to this class, one that Walt has reluctantly learned to accept. What happens today, though, to break this rhythm is something he has a harder time accepting. One of the girls mocks the correct answer of another by commenting in a sing-song voice: "She thinks she's so smart. She thinks she knows everything." Immediately, Walt turns to her and sharply calls her name: "Darlene!" Almost immediately another student cries out, "Yeah, Darlene, why don't you shut up?" Walt replies, "Thank you, but I don't need your help." "Yes, you do" is the answer that laughingly comes from several students at once. "OK," says Walt, "let's settle down." "I'm gonna get you later," whispers Darlene loudly to the student she mocked. "Just you try" is the answer, and again Walt has to intervene. He does manage to restore control but the lesson feels ruined and no one, it seems, will now venture an answer to any of his questions. He feels demoralized and he silently rejoices at the sound of the bell announcing the end of the period. Assurances from his colleagues (and wife) that he is a good teacher and valued by the school, kudos from supervisors, and the gratification of seeing many of his more talented students succeed serve as important rewards but they cannot obliterate the frustration and helplessness he feels when he is faced with a class that seems not to learn.

In contrast to sixth period, seventh is a joy: an American history class of bright, college-bound students. Walt anticipates (correctly) that almost everyone will hand in homework and will respond to his questions. As expected, students arrive on time, listen attentively, take notes, and participate in the class discussion. He even has some time at the end of the period to consider the broader implications of the theories of political reform and party ideology he has outlined in the lesson. Walt feels encouraged by the motivation and accomplishments of these students. He also thinks of the students he has tutored for the SATs and encouraged to achieve their goals and for whom he has written college recommendations. He is finally reminded of why he was attracted to teaching in the first place.

Although Walt has completed his teaching for the day, he is required, as is all staff, to remain in school for eighth period. He goes to the social studies office to mark homework. Had all the students handed in their assignments, he could not have completed marking them all at school. Slower classes, however, average only about ten homework papers a day (until the crush for passing grades at the end of term). Walt waits till he gets home to prepare his next day's lessons.

Normally, Walt leaves with his regular carpool after eighth period, at 3:00. Wednesdays, however, he works overtime in an after-school tutoring program and remains at school until 4:30. Walt is paid per session for his tutoring, that is, strictly by the hour, with no extra compensation for the preparation necessary to do the work. Also, the pay scale for tutoring is that of the average teacher, much lower than Walt's usual pay, which is based on seniority. Again, Walt vents to himself about how per-session teachers are the only workers in the country to get paid less for overtime than their normal hourly wage. Still, he tends to find this work much less stressful than regular class-room teaching, and the fact is he does find the extra pay useful. Although he is not an English teacher, Walt tutors a group of students who were not able to pass standardized English composition exam-inations. Most are well motivated and Walt derives a good deal of satisfaction in helping them learn the language. The students use computers to develop composition and editing skills.

At 4:45, Walt punches out on the time clock and leaves school with another teacher involved in the tutoring program. Although heavy traffic can sometimes delay his arrival home by over an hour, traffic today is relatively light, and at about 5:15 his friend pulls up to the shopping mall where Walt left his car. On the way back, both have acknowledged feeling exhausted, and Walt echoes this senti-ment once again as he leaves his friend.

In the house, he greets his eleven-year-old son, who perspi-caciously asks, "Tired, Daddy?" "A bit," Walt replies. "You know," he says to his son for at least the 100th time this year, "it's tough being a teacher!" At the kitchen table, over snacks and cold drinks, they chat for a few minutes before going their separate ways. Walt changes into some work clothes and goes out to trim some bushes in the front yard—a chore he's been putting off for weeks. Moments later a neighbor drives by and calls out to him in a half-serious, half-kidding tone: "I wish I could get home as early as you do. Teaching is something, isn't it, working only half days?" Walt smiles but inwardly resents the fact that even intelligent people continue to think about teaching in distorted ways.

Walt's wife comes home around 6:00. Together they prepare dinner while discussing their respective days. "Anything exciting happen today?" his wife asks. "Not really, a pretty typical day. My 'smart class' went really well, the others were fair, and Darlene ruined another lesson. It was all right. I think I've got some good ideas for tomorrow." His short answer to his wife's questioning is also typical, a product of his feeling somewhat irritable and tired at the moment, and also a product of his not wanting to talk too much about work. Too much talking or thinking about it makes him edgy, that is, makes him wonder whether he's really made the right career move and whether he'll ever regain the inspiration he once had for teaching. After talking about his day, he often finds himself envious of his wife's nine to five job. So he switches the conversation around to his wife's day and it's only much later that he'll fill in some of the blanks and recount in greater detail some of the highlights and outrages of his day.

After dinner Walt skims the evening paper and then retires to his basement office to prepare the next day's materials for class. He switches his computer on, writes an outline for each lesson, and thinks of questions and current events that will help students analyze and apply the factual information contained in their text. Next, he turn his attention to preparing handouts to complement the task.

At 9:30, Walt puts his work away and heads upstairs to spend about a half-hour looking over his kids' homework or watching television with them. Later, he picks up a book from the coffee table but finds that he's too tired to read. Instead he heads for the bedroom, chats briefly with his wife, and watches the news. "I feel exhausted," he tells his wife. "Burned out?" she asks. "No, I don't think so," he replies. "It's just that there are days that I don't get enough back. Today one class was responsive. That was it. I dunno. It wasn't a hard day and it wasn't a great day. But right now I just feel empty. I guess it'll be OK tomorrow but I just wish I could feel like I was getting through to more of them. I'll be OK," he reiterates. "A temporary crisis of faith." He is asleep by 11:00.

The two forces that combine to produce burnout—too many stressors and too little positive feedback—are both operative here. Yet despite feeling stressed, Walt seems not to be burned out. The stressors are annoying to him but not intolerable; the rewards are disappointing but not entirely negligible. While some teachers in this school are undoubtedly burned out, the school seems to function reasonably well. Many urban schools are far worse, and many urban teachers are not just stressed (like Walt) but truly worn out with little left to give.

According to the Carnegie Foundation for the Advancement of Teaching (1988b), the innovative reforms of the middle and late 1980s have been largely irrelevant to the great proportion of black and Hispanic schoolchildren in our urban schools: "The harsh truth is that the reform movement has largely bypassed our most deeply troubled schools." Hopelessness, says the report, continues to engulf children who grow up in these environments.

What are the factors that explain why urban teachers are particularly prone to feeling stressed or burned out? Certainly all the factors noted in earlier chapters, including too much paperwork, bureaucratic incompetence, low salaries, and administrative and parental disrespect, are part of the explanation. Decaying surroundings are also an unfortunate part of the urban teachers' environment, and as Rangel (1987) notes, "teaching in a school that has steadily deteriorated in the last 20 years takes a toll" (p. B3). Urban teachers also seem to feel they have less control over decision making than teachers in other schools. For example, 36 percent of those in urban schools feel they have no control over selecting textbooks, whereas only 12 percent of those teaching in other schools feel this way (Carnegie Foundation for the Advancement of Teaching, 1987). But two issues are primary for the urban teacher: student violence and the academic difficulties of poverty-stricken students. Both make the task of feeling consequential enormously difficult for those who teach in inner-city schools.

Student Violence

"Day in and day out, in almost every school of the city, crime and violence send students and teachers home angry, confused, frustrated, demoralized, physically exhausted and emotionally spent. For many, just getting through the day becomes the primary goal. Never mind learning and teaching—it has come down to survival!" (Saltzman, 1988, p. A27). There has been no federal study since 1978 documenting the level of crime and violence in schools, but in 1988 the director of the National School Safety Center suggested that, while the number of violent incidents in schools has probably not increased, the severity of these crimes—given the impact of drugs and gangs—probably has. Metal detectors, policemen, and/or security guards are prominent in many urban high schools. Some have instituted weapons searches; others have declared a ban on beepers in an attempt to discourage in-school drug trafficking.

As Table 8.1 indicates, in comparison to teachers in suburban and rural neighborhoods, teachers in urban neighborhoods are considerably more likely to view their schools as having problems with a variety of discipline-related behaviors. Proportionately, the number of teachers in urban schools who view vandalism, theft,

Table 8.1. Teacher Ratings of Discipline Problems at Their Schools.

	Percent of Teachers Reporting Behavior "a Problem"	
	Urban Schools	Other Schools
Student apathy	81	66
Absenteeism	78	51
Student turnover	58	25
Disruptive class behavior	53	30
Drugs	53	48
Vandalism	52	26
Alcohol	51	56
Theft	48	23
Violence against students	32	9
Racial discord	19	5
Violence against teachers	13	3

Source: Carnegie Foundation for the Advancement of Teaching, 1987.

violence against other students, and racial discord as problems in their schools is at least twice that of teachers in other environments. In addition, a greater percentage of teachers in urban schools (40 percent) than in other schools (31 percent) believe that their principal's performance is "below average" in terms of support for teachers. Thus, many teachers feel powerless and unsupported by school administrators in the face of threats and violence. Despite gross attempts by administrators to cut down on the number of weapons brought into schools, teachers continue to feel that administrators have been egregiously neglectful in dealing with the day-to-day problems of student violence.

The issue of student discipline is rarely far from the minds of teachers in urban schools. Consider, for example, this young teacher's account of his experience teaching in an inner-city junior high school in New York:

> [S]tudents career in and out of doors and hallways, screaming, pouncing on people, starting fights; during class, students get up and walk around or out of the doors, fight and sing and dance, bang out the radio's bass beats on their desks; boys make their raps on girls the focus of the class, girls counter with screaming retorts. You find out pretty early there's not a thing you can do about most of it. . . . It's simply emotionally devastating to be regularly threatened with violence from mugging to murder for telling students anything from "Sit down" to "Break it up." I would soon realize that here violence is the only path to honor in day-to-day life, and that everyone is hungry for a fight—hoping to distinguish himself for one moment of one day that, like the rest, is leading nowhere quickly and violently. . . . All the horror-story urban statistics are reality here.
>
> Students are generally from welfare-imposed one-parent households. Violence of all kinds—domestic, fun-related, cash-related—is the social norm. . . . The most frustrating lesson I learned was that lessons break down even if students *are* interested in the mate-

rial. Not that students don't *want* to read better (in fact, my students cited reading as the only subject they consider important for their lives) or that they lack the intelligence. The problem is that students don't trust anything that goes on in school. So when I used bits from Eddie Murphy movies or lines from the latest hiphop hits, the students refrained from the usual classroom anarchy *until* they realized that I wanted these things to be *part of the learning process.* . . . My students and I eventually did forge some sort of understanding—as people, not as teacher and students. For example, they trusted me to hold their pens, money, jewelry, and jackets (so the stuff wouldn't be stolen). They began joking with me because they respected me for coming in day after day. . . . But no teaching goes on. . . . I now work as a word processor operator at twice the pay with none of the stress [Dinerstein, 1985, pp. 18, 23].

Most teachers recognize the "racially inflicted economic, cultural and psychological damage" (Wilkins, 1989, p. A23) that minorities, particularly blacks, have suffered in this country. Most are aware too that the inner-city poor live under constant stress, often with little or no support. Virtually all know of the drug scourge afflicting the inner cities and of the damage that this has done to families. Most would agree with Roger Wilkins's assessment that "children born into this chaos are victims at birth and on their way to becoming societal burdens or menaces at 15" (p. A23). And most teachers, I suspect, would agree with the following two propositions: first, that if we as a society really want to solve the educational problems associated with poverty, including the problem of school violence, we can do so with a large influx of additional funds; and, second, that the likelihood of such an occurrence is minimal because society would rather sacrifice both teachers and the education of poor children than spend the money necessary.

But there is another point here. It is the feeling that many teachers have that when it comes to dealing with discipline problems in inner-city schools they are the victims of racial guilt—of a

system that can't or won't deal effectively with minority students
who are violent or emotionally troubled. Giving credence to this
view is William Julius Wilson's (1987) suggestion that "many of
those who represent traditional liberal views on social issues have
been reluctant to discuss openly, or, in many instances, even to
acknowledge, the sharp rise in social pathologies in ghetto
communities."

Society may—and often does—ignore the wounds, the ills,
and the violence of inner-city neighborhoods but teachers cannot.
They are forced to cope with these issues on a daily basis. Discipline
becomes harder to enforce in schools as fewer adults, including
school-based administrators, are willing to play the necessary roles
and as fewer students feel an obligation to listen. Teachers spend
increasing amounts of time attempting to establish order in the
classroom and decreasing amounts of time engaged in teaching per
se. "Teachers can't handle more than one, at most two, disruptive
students in a class. With four, my class is unteachable. I wrote long
evaluations about each boy, explaining that they are misplaced. I
tried to get counseling for them. In desperation, I even referred them
to the dean's office for instruction in classroom behavior. Nothing
was done. Now a whole class learns nothing" (Weinstein, 1988,
p. 17).

As disciplinary problems increase in a classroom, professional roles which were once incidental become prominent. And for
many who teach in urban schools, the satisfactions of teaching become ever more elusive.

Pedagogical Problems

One child in four under the age of six in this country lives
in poverty, a figure that is closer to one in two in large cities. By
the time many poor children enter school they are already far behind their more advantaged peers, both academically and socially.
Poor prenatal nutrition has been linked to learning difficulties during a child's school years. Children grow up in depressed and violent neighborhoods, in crumbling apartments, in large families
with a single parent, on streets where drugs and crime offer constant
temptation: all factors that make learning more difficult for chil-

dren and teaching more difficult for teachers. The needs of the student population in many schools are overwhelming. In fact, in one survey (Corcoran, Walker, and White, 1988), the first priority of urban teachers was for more support personnel such as counselors, social workers, and nurses.

To state the obvious: All inner-city schools do not reflect the worst problems of the chronically poor underclass. But those teachers whose inner-city assignments do put them in contact with underclass students and their parents face a particularly difficult situation. These teachers work in classrooms that often seem chaotic; with students who are far behind academically; with a student population that is often transient; with parents whose own age, limitations, or afflictions limit their value to their own children. A detailed explanation for the rise in numbers of the underclass in this country goes beyond the scope of this book. The interested reader is referred to Wilson's book *The Truly Disadvantaged* (1987). In short, the argument advanced by Wilson is that considerable numbers of newly successful blacks and Hispanics left inner-city neighborhoods in the 1960s and 1970s, depriving these communities of stability and successful role models. Furthermore, successful employment in the inner city grew more difficult: There was a large exodus of manufacturing jobs from northern cities, the nation's economy shifted from manufacturing to service industries, the number of jobs requiring less than a high school education declined, and affirmative action programs, while laudable in their intentions, seemed to help those who already had skills and education.

Regardless of the reasons—and there are those such as Christopher Jencks (1988) who argue that both economic and cultural factors need to be considered—the underclass has grown. It is a segment of society that, as Richard Nathan (1989) argued, "is not just a function of being poor. It involves geography and behavior. It is a condition of alienated people living in communities in which antisocial activities are the norm" (p. A31). As noted earlier, though, there is still a wide gap between acknowlegment of the social pathologies that exist in inner-city neighborhoods—drugs, crime, random violence—and the recognition of their impact on teaching and teachers. Depression, anger, and aggression may be understandable by-products of racism and deplorable living conditions, but they still have a significant adverse effect on classroom learning. Too often, the public and its politicians just want to know the bottom line—typically, test scores. Their attitude toward teachers and administrators seems to be "Don't bother us with your difficulties, just tell us how many students in your school are reading above grade level." For many teachers, this is a cruel and crude benchmark of success, one that fails to acknowledge partial successes acheived through hours of hard work.

If inner-city underclass students constitute a group with a great number of social, economic, behavioral, and academic problems, then homeless students make up a subgroup of this population with even greater problems. In 1989, the Department of Education estimated the number of homeless school-aged children in this country at 220,000, of whom 30 percent (65,000) do not attend school on a regular basis. These figures are considerably lower than those reported in 1988 by the National Coalition for the Homeless, which suggested that there were between 500,000 and 750,000 homeless children of school age, 57 percent of whom do not attend school regularly. Even those students who do attend school, however, often do not attend the same school long enough to adjust either socially or academically. Many of these children are depressed, or aggressive, or both; many also have learning difficulties that require specialized, intensive attention.

In what is clearly a massive understatement, the director of research for Advocates for Children of New York, Yvonne Rafferty, was quoted in the *New York Times* as saying that "homelessness is not conducive to becoming educated." Some of these children, she notes, have been in as many as six schools per year. "These kids are being bounced from school to school as the family is bounced from shelter to shelter. How can they be expected to succeed?" (cited in Wells, 1989, p. B11). And, I might add, how can teachers be expected to succeed with them? Among other problems confronting teachers and administrators in trying to aid homeless children are the fact that these children and their parents are understandably reluctant to acknowledge their condition, the fact that academic and health records are sometimes lost in the frequent shuffles between schools, the fact that these students tend to have high rates of absenteeism, and the unfortunate fact that these students tend to be far behind in their schoolwork.

Another rapidly rising, tremendously needy group includes children with AIDS. In the early 1990s, teachers in urban centers will have yet another major crisis to contend with: the first wave of children prenatally exposed to crack. Research has indicated that these children suffer from neurological, behavioral, emotional, and learning-related problems. School and teachers are scarely prepared to deal with these two groups.

For teachers in some urban schools another major pedgogical problem lies in dealing with a large influx of students from other countries. The 1970s and 1980s featured massive immigration of children from Latin America, the Caribbean countries, and Southeast Asia. In Dade County, Florida, alone, over 18,000 children from Cuba and Haiti entered the public schools between April 1980 and January 1982. Nationwide, some 3.4 million children lack sufficient English language skills to succeed in school (Dolson, 1985). Educational issues that must be dealt with include the lack of sufficient numbers of bilingual educators, the social integration of these students into the schools, and, most prominently, the lack of basic skills some of these children bring with them to this country. All this is a legitimate part of a school's function, of course, but there can be no mistaking that the lives of individual teachers can be extremely taxed by large numbers of non–English-speaking students and low numbers of support personnel.

An especially vexing problem encountered by teachers in underclass communities is the undervaluation of education by some students. In the depiction of a typical day in Walt Collins's career as a teacher, I recounted a classroom argument between two students in which one taunted the other for, essentially, doing classwork correctly. In the Dinerstein article quoted earlier in this chapter, students were willing to cooperate with their teacher until they realized he was trying to get them to learn something, at which time they rebelled. The point here, and it is again a sensitive, often ignored issue, is that "learning" or "success at school" is a value that the peer culture at some schools rejects. Perhaps school success is considered unacceptable as a goal because it represents the values of a culture historically repressive and insensitive to the needs of minorities; perhaps it is seen as "toadying" to a system that has given precious little back to minority group members. Regardless of the reasons, as Fordham and Ogbu (1986) point out, there is enormous peer pressure against academic success in some black high schools. It's considered "acting white." We may well lament the implications of this stance for scores of minority youth as well as society in general. It should also be noted, though, that to the extent this attitude exists in a school, teachers will necessarily be more frustrated in their work and find their satisfactions that much harder to secure.

Although even in the most distressed school there are students who work hard, who strive to learn and to achieve, many do give up. Politicians and educators alike have been confronted by alarming high school dropout rates, estimated to be as high as 40 percent in some urban school districts. Ethical, legal, and even economic interests have spurred the creation of numerous programs to curb the high dropout rate. Virtually everyone concerned with education agrees that, as a nation, we have an obligation to increase the percentage of minority youth graduating from high school; some have also noted the vital economic need for more skilled and literate workers. Yet while these programs offer teachers increased opportunities for a particular kind of reward—seeing high-risk students succeed—they may also inadvertently be promoting teacher stress and burnout. Working with students who are at high risk for dropping out means a need for more individualized attention, for more services, for more supplies—for more of everything that is already in short supply, especially teachers' patience and ability to deal with an already overstimulating and needy environment. This is not to argue that such programs shouldn't be continued, even increased; it is to say that, if we are truly interested in the success of these programs, we need to be more aware of the needs and difficulties of those teachers involved in them.

Many teachers in urban settings have strong feelings toward a system in which a great proportion of students drop out or fail. Some blame the students themselves, some the students' families and homes for not providing them with middle-class values, some the junior high and elementary schools for not teaching students basic skills, some the whole process of education in this country for not being sufficiently creative or motivated to meet the needs of millions of children, and some the government for not being aggressive enough in combating poverty and all its attendant problems. But even with this intellectual understanding of the complexity of the problem, some teachers blame themselves and other teachers for not being good or strong enough to do what is required.

Most teachers, though, do not hold themselves accountable for student failure. They do what they can and no longer expect miracles or even significant changes. For the most part, individual teachers recognize that their efforts to make changes affect but a short period of the student's life; they understand how limited their influence is. Adopting this attitude is, in one sense, realistic and helpful; past a certain point of moderation, however, it may lead some teachers to give less to their students and expect less of them.

In regard to the relationship between social problems and teachers, the points I emphasize are as follows:

1. The problems associated with poverty necessarily and continuously impact upon the teaching experience of virtually everyone working in inner-city schools.
2. Serious social problems (violence and drug abuse, for example) that have been shaped by generations of poverty and racism in this country, and that have been refractory to the best efforts of other social agencies, are too often expected by the public to be effectively managed by teachers.
3. There is still a noticeable hesitancy among politicians and even educators to examine the implications of social problems for the educational *process* (that is, the nature of student-teacher or student-student interactions).
4. This reluctance has resulted in a nearly exclusive focus on *educational outcome* ("minority children are receiving a bad education," "urban schools are failing," "teachers are doing a poor job") that too glibly denigrates teachers and their efforts.

The Non–Burned-Out Urban Teacher

In Chapter Two, I noted that almost 22 percent of urban teachers reported that they felt "frequently" burned out. That study

(Farber, 1984b) also showed that an additional 22 percent of urban teachers reported that they "occasionally" felt burned out. Nearly 48 percent of urban teachers rarely or never felt that they were receiving adequate emotional rewards for their efforts. A significant number of urban teachers (42 percent) also tended to feel that they had been inadequately prepared for the stresses of teaching. Furthermore, urban teachers tended not to feel supported in their work: 75 percent believed that parents rarely or never made their jobs easier for them, 77 percent said they rarely or never received support from their principals, and a whopping 91 percent reported finding administrative meetings rarely or never helpful. Colleagues, at least, got somewhat better ratings: Although 30 percent of urban teachers felt they rarely or never had rewarding contacts with colleagues during the workday, 30 percent also reported frequent rewarding contacts with their colleagues.

What we shouldn't forget though is that the majority of urban teachers continue to feel committed to teaching. Most still feel that they can easily create a relaxed classroom atmosphere with their students, understand how their students feel about things, and deal very effectively with student problems. Many of these teachers thus still work effectively, and some even joyfully, under seemingly impossible conditions. Take, for example, the following school: "The blackboards are so badly cracked that teachers are afraid to let students write on them for fear they'll cut themselves. Some mornings, fallen chips of paint cover classrooms like snow. A boy's locker room smells of urine because of backed-up plumbing. Teachers and students have come to see humor in the waterfall that courses down six flights of stairs after a heavy rain . . . the landscape [is] of hopelessness: burned-out apartments, boarded windows, vacant lot upon garbage-strewn vacant lot" (G. Martin, 1988, p. B29). The teachers working in such an environment must be stressed. Yet in 1988, in this school building, teachers donated their own money to present the first Shakespearean play to be put on in this school in eighteen years. These teachers, like many in urban environments, do continue to care greatly about their school and their students.

Urban classrooms, then, are often extremely stressful. It is true that a significant minority of urban teachers are burned out; this is a tragedy that affects a number of individuals both inside and outside the school system. But it's also true that most teachers, even in the most depressing of urban environments, endure the stresses, find rewards, and avoid burnout. This latter group is surely deserving of more encouragement and admiration than society currently grants them.

9

Teaching in Other Contexts: Suburban, Rural, Private, and Special Education Classrooms

ALTHOUGH STRESS AND BURNOUT ARE PHENOMENA MOST PROM-
inently associated with teaching in urban school systems, they afflict teachers across a variety of settings. Many of the same factors
that are stressful to teachers in urban settings are stressful to those
in other settings as well. Teachers in suburbia are disturbed by
apathetic and unruly students, by incompetent and insensitive administrators, by massive amounts of paperwork, by a sense of public
and parental disrespect. On the other hand, the frequency or intensity of certain stressors (for example, student violence) may vary
greatly depending on the community, and some stressors (for example, writing individualized educational plans for special education
students) are unique to specific types of educators. In this chapter,
the focus is on those experiences of suburban, rural, private, and
special education teachers that may lead them to feelings of stress
or burnout.

Suburban Schools

First, let us examine a day in the life of one suburban elementary school teacher.

Note: This chapter was written with the collaboration of Leonard D.
Wechsler.

Gail Williams, thirty-five, is married (to a banker), has two school-age children (a boy aged seven, a girl nine), and lives in a modest three-bedroom ranch-style house located ten miles from the school in which she has been teaching fifth grade (with a break for maternity leave) for the past eight years. An education major in an excellent liberal arts college, she has grown increasingly disenchanted with the state of education in this country, specifically with the treatment accorded teachers. And, as she has grown older and seen her contemporaries succeed in more prestigious lines of work, she has become envious of their more high-powered careers. Periodically she reminds herself that teaching has afforded her the time to be with her children a great deal, an opportunity that friends in most other careers have not had. Intellectually, she is thankful for this opportunity; on an emotional level, though, she still resents the low status and relatively low pay of her job and, perhaps most of all, the cavalier way she feels she is often treated by school administrators and parents of students.

A day in November. Gail is out of bed by 6:30 A.M. Her husband leaves for work shortly afterwards. In addition to getting herself ready for work, she assumes the primary responsibility for getting the children ready for school, including waking them, pushing them to get dressed, helping them with breakfast, and making their lunches. It's little solace to her knowing that this is a normative state of affairs in this country—that in dual-career families it's still the wife who does most of the child care and daily household chores. As usual, the morning feels rushed. And, as if preparing her for what she will soon face in school, the kids begin to bicker over possession of a favorite cereal box. Gail has to separate them and urge them to eat their breakfasts quickly in order to be on time for the school bus. As they finish up, she finds their jackets, puts their bookbags by the door, kisses them goodbye, and watches them walk to the corner to wait for the bus. Gail then returns to the kitchen, puts some dishes in the sink, gulps down the last of her coffee, and hurries to her car.

Gail's school is a fifteen-minute car ride away. She parks in a lot behind the school and locks up, though to her knowledge only one teacher's car has been broken into during the past ten years. Because of her morning responsibilities, she is always among the last of the teachers to arrive. She is thankful that no administrator has ever questioned her (or the other latecomers) about consistently arriving at school five to ten minutes late. She clocks in, gives a hurried hello to the school secretary and the new assistant principal, and hurries to her classroom to prepare for class. Her second-floor classroom is large, well lighted, well furnished, and well maintained. It is attractively decorated with children's artwork, book reports, and posters (which she's paid for out of her own pocket). There are the standard chairs and desks for each of her students. There are also several discrete sections to the room: Next to the window in the back are easy chairs for the "reading corner"; nearby are an aquarium and hamster cage; in the front of the room, near her desk, is a "computer center." From the window next to her desk, Gail can see many of her students in the playground. A quick glance at her watch reminds her that she has but ten minutes before they'll start walking into class.

Her schedule for the day is already on the blackboard, put up yesterday afternoon before she left. Now she looks over her lesson plans, reads the memos that were in her mailbox this morning, opens the attendance folder, and jots down a few items on her "to do" pad, including "call Bobbie's mother," "call custodian to replace fluorescent light," "check with health plan re kids' benefits," "check with Don [a colleague] about fifth-grade field trip," "make an appointment with Ann [school psychologist]," and "order more art supplies."

The class files in quickly after the bell. There are twenty-five students registered for the class and all are present today. These students are predominantly white (with two blacks, three Asian-Americans, and one Hispanic student) and middle to upper-middle class. At least two-thirds, figures Gail, are college bound and some, she thinks, will disappoint their parents by not getting into Ivy League schools.

Gail greets her students as they walk in, admonishes two of the boys to "calm down," and tells the class that they are to start on their reading assignments immediately following the Pledge of Allegiance and school announcements. With the exception of two or three of the slower boys who typically resist reading assignments and who are still arguing about their favorite baseball players, the rest of the class begins to get to work. A walk to the desk of the baseball fans quickly calms them down and they too begin to read silently. Gail prefers to begin each class with a quiet reading assignment because she knows from experience that this exercise sets a good tone for learning.

Each of the three groups is reading from basal readers. Several years ago Gail considered assigning more contemporary works but decided against it after what happened at the local high school. One of the English teachers there assigned *Catcher in the Rye,* precipitating a series of acrimonious school board meetings that left most of the teachers in the community shaken. The compromise solution eventually adopted now forces teachers to clear all controversial curriculum material with a committee composed of teachers, administrators, school board members, and a local "concerned" parents' group.

Gail begins to work individually with each reading group in turn, going over their comprehension of the material and their written answers to the questions posed by their reading book. Occasionally, she pauses to quiet some of the students down, ask others whether they have completed the assignment, and remind still others what their options are if they have finished the work. She enjoys teaching reading and considers this her forte. When pushed she'll acknowledge that working with the most advanced reading group gives her the greatest degree of satisfaction, but she also points out that it's quite satisfying to see the slowest readers making progress and learning to enjoy books. What annoys her are those students who constantly complain that the reading assigned to them is either "too hard," "too easy," "too long," or "boring"—the latter being the current most popular word of complaint among students in her school.

In fact, the tendency of some of her students to facilely assign the word *boring* to a host of activities is indicative to Gail of a major problem in this school's community, namely, the sense of entitlement she feels characterizes a small but vocal minority of the parents and students with whom she works. This sense of entitlement gives rise, Gail feels, to the assumption on the part of some parents that their son or daughter is a genius—or at least a near-genius—worthy and deserving of specialized attention and to the assumption that they, rather than professional educators, are the true educational experts. All this becomes a complicated issue. Gail realizes that sometimes parents do know best, at least about the needs of and best approaches to their own children, and she often welcomes their input.

What she resents, though, is the tendency of some parents to confuse their financial success with an advanced degree in education. Running a successful business or having expertise in another profession (for example, law or medicine) generally doesn't translate into a practical knowledge of how to run a fifth-grade classroom and serve the needs of twenty-five children with disparate needs and abilities. Moreover, Gail feels strongly that the tendency of some of these parents to question her decisions, to insist constantly on offering their input, and to nearly always assume that student problems are the fault of the teacher serves to denigrate her sense of professionalism and expertise.

After the reading groups are finished, Gail checks students' homework. One boy can't find the work and is scrambling through his looseleaf and desk. "I probably left it home," he offers, and she reassures him that it'll be OK if he brings it in tomorrow. He looks relieved, though still somewhat embarrassed. Two boys sitting nearby tease him with sarcastic comments: "Sure, you forgot it." "I'll bet the dog ate it." Gail quiets them down easily enough and begins to go over the homework, a series of math problems (multiplying complex fractions). Several students are eager to show off their answers to some of the more complicated equations and Gail calls them to the board to demonstrate their skill. "Does everyone understand this?" she asks. Though no one admits to it, she knows from past experience and the puzzled looks on their faces that several students in the class haven't caught on yet. She again explains the steps involved in the process.

10:30—time for the class to go to "phys ed" and time for Gail to take her prep period. She escorts her class to the gym and then walks to the teachers' lounge for some coffee and company. Several other teachers walk in over the next few minutes and begin discussing the new assistant principal, someone brought in from outside the district. The consensus is that there were several competent people from within the school district who should have been offered the job and that, once again, the administration has failed to respect its own teachers. Except for one teacher who is very active in the union local, the rest of the group looks more annoyed and frustrated than truly angry. Gail herself is of two minds. She feels that the administration was indeed insensitive in the way they recruited for (and announced) the new position, but she feels too that it barely matters who was hired as an assistant principal since no one she has ever known in that capacity has ever been particularly helpful. She quickly flashes on an interaction she had with the previous assistant principal, who, after months of promising her new software for the computer, finally admitted that the likelihood of her actually receiving it was quite low. "Budget problems," he said. And then another image: of this same AP (assistant principal) trying to influence the school psychologist not to declare one of the children in her class in need of remedial services. Gail stays in the lounge for just a few minutes, electing to return to her classroom to do some paperwork.

She has procrastinated for several days and feels she can no longer put off completing several forms and surveys that the administration has requested. She resents these tasks enormously and silently curses at this aspect of her job. Among her mildest oaths: "What the hell does this have to do with teaching?" She quickly makes her way through one of the survey forms ("Which children bring lunch from home?") and is halfway through another (monthly attendance) when she realizes it's time to collect her students from their gym class. She reminds herself to bring home several other forms that are due that week.

Her students are a bit wild—they always are after gym—and she allows them some leeway in walking back to their classroom. Once in the class, though, she wants them to settle down and resume work on their social studies projects. The class divides up into four groups. Each group has been assigned a different country in either South or Central America and has questions to answer regarding customs, currency, imports, and the like. Gail very much enjoys going around the room and acting as a resource for each group. She kids around with some of her students and cajoles others to get to work. She helps each group organize the charts it needs to prepare for the assignment. She feels helpful and good that she's able to create a relaxed atmosphere: The class is a bit noisy, but in a busy, productive way.

Lunchtime comes quickly. Gail has a date to go to a local diner with a friend who teaches sixth grade. On the way to her car with her friend, Gail waves to many of her current and former students. She has a good feeling about her students; in fact, they are the best part of the job. It's the administrative hassles, the paperwork, the lack of status in teaching, and the still inadequate pay that make Gail wonder how long she'll stay in the field.

Lunch is a nice combination of laughter and sober reflections on work. Gail's friend Joan is wise as well as funny, and Gail again appreciates the fact that she has a number of such colleagues whom she likes and respects a good deal. During lunch, though, Gail admits to Joan that she feels burned out. Her explanation is that teaching, although rewarding, is too emotionally exhausting and that she feels "fed up" with the attitude of virtually everyone (except her colleagues) toward teachers and teaching. Joan has heard this before—from Gail and others. "Are things worse now?" she asks. "Is your class giving you a hard time?" "No," Gail admits, "it's a good class and I like most of the kids. And I know I'm doing a good job—although probably almost anyone could do a decent job with this class. It's just that I don't get enough back. The kids like me—I know that and maybe that should be enough, but it's not. Too many hassles from too many other people, and too little appreciation. You know that. There are too many people out there who just assume that no teacher does a good enough job. Parents think we don't know anything; the school board thinks we get too much money; the administration thinks we complain too much about paperwork and should just accept it as a part of our job. My next door neighbor is an attorney. A couple of days ago we started chatting about the pool club she belongs to. I sort of hinted around that I might be interested in joining and all of a sudden she got evasive. I got the feeling she was trying to let me know that a teacher wouldn't fit in with all the hot shots at her club. I don't know, but I compare myself with some of my friends out in the real world and they're treated quite differently. Maybe they do work longer hours, but they're also treated like adults. For the effort I put in, I should be feeling better about what I get from this job, and I don't. When I was younger, the satisfactions that happened right in the classroom, like working with the kids, were enough to keep me going. Now I guess I want more—I want respect, appreciation, status, and opportunities for promotions. And they're not there." "You're not going to quit, are you?" asks Joan. "No. I'll keep working and keep feeling burned out."

After lunch, Gail gives a science lesson (on adaptation in animals), assigns a composition (on adaptations people make to seasonal changes), and winds up the day with a short current events lesson, an innovation she began several years ago and has continued to find quite enjoyable. A different student each day brings in either a local or national news article that he or she summarizes, following which the class discusses the major points. She feels this allows her to get to a different aspect of her students, even their burgeoning political beliefs. Gail assigns homework (a creative writing assignment: "Write a short story on the time that severe winter storms closed schools for a week"), asks her students to tidy up their desks, and dismisses them. The students have, for the most part, been cooperative and she's had to raise her voice only a few times during these afternoon lessons. (One time two of the boys were teasing a third for "a dumb play" he allegedly made in a weekend soccer game; another time several of the girls were passing notes back and forth on the latest gossip regarding "who likes whom.")

Gail feels tired and wishes she could lie down somewhere for a while but forces herself instead to walk down to the lounge for a diet soda. She waves goodbye to some of her students, says hello to some of the parents, and is about to enter the teachers' lounge when one of the parents stops her to "ask a quick question." "I'm wondering why Erica isn't in the advanced math group. . . . She feels left out because all her friends are in the group and if you could help her with the work a bit, maybe give her some extra individualized attention, I'm sure she'd do fine." Gail's immediate feeling is irritation but, suppressing this, she wonders whether she should ask this mother to make an appointment, invite her to come to her classroom now to discuss the matter in greater detail, or answer her here and now. Her decision is to give the mother a brief answer now and invite her to make an appointment to discuss the matter in greater detail.

"I can understand Erica's disappointment. But my feeling, based on the diagnostic tests I gave all the children in the beginning of the year and on the math homework, was that Erica is best suited for the middle math group and that she isn't ready for the higher group. Maybe she will be later on in the year, and we can certainly monitor how she's doing and make adjustments later on. But I think that putting her in the higher group now wouldn't be a good idea for her."

"What would you think about trying it and seeing how she does?"

"I think it'd be better if she worked her way up. If she does well where she is now, we can think about the other group next marking period."

"Well, all right, but she's really disappointed."

"I'll talk to her about it, OK?"

"OK. Thanks."

Gail lets out a deep breath and shakes her head as she enters the teachers' room to buy her soda. She thinks to herself: "I'll tell you what, Mrs. Clark; why don't we let Erica skip elementary math altogether and just go straight to advanced calculus?" She gets her soda, takes it to her classroom, and sips it while working on the next day's lesson plans. An hour later, she writes the day's agenda on the board, then walks to the office to clock out. After a couple of quick good-byes to a few other teachers, she gets in her car to pick up her children at their after-school programs. She realizes with irritation what's awaiting her at home: breakfast dishes, cooking dinner, a trip to the supermarket, twenty-five compositions to correct, her own children's homework to look over, and phone calls to several parents (all of whom she knows will be "pleasant enough" but some of whom will also be cloyingly and falsely deferential). She imagines she wouldn't feel this exhausted if she were in another occupation.

Gail is similar to other suburban teachers in that her sources of satisfaction are experiences that make her feel sensitive to students' needs and helpfully involved with their education. In an earlier study I did of suburban teachers (Farber, 1984a), the highest-ranked survey items included "I could easily create a relaxed atmosphere with my students," "I could easily understand how my students feel about things," "I have dealt very effectively with the problems of my students," "I have felt I was positively influencing students' lives through my work," "I have accomplished many worthwhile things on this job," and "I have felt exhilarated after working closely with my students." An additional source of suburban teacher satisfaction found in this survey involved rewarding contacts with colleagues during the school day. I found—contrary to the experience of Gail—that most suburban teachers felt they had time and energy for friends, family, and outside activities.

This study also found that, rather than discipline problems or the need to work with great numbers of students who lack basic skills, the primary sources of stress for suburban teachers are excessive paperwork, the lack of advancement opportunities in the field, and the lack of parental or administrative support. Like their urban counterparts, these teachers feel generally dissatisfied with the extent of support granted them. As Table 9.1 indicates, a total of 66 percent never or rarely feel that parents have made things easier, almost 87 percent think that administrative meetings never or only rarely prove helpful in solving their problems, 63 percent think they rarely or never receive support or encouragement from their principals, and 61 percent never or only rarely feel there is a sense of community in their schools. Moreover, suburban teachers do not feel well regarded by society: 80 percent rarely or never have felt satisfied with teachers' standing in society.

It is certainly unsettling to consider that almost 87 percent of suburban teachers surveyed felt that administrative meetings are unhelpful in solving the problems of teaching. This corroborates Cichon and Koff's (1978) finding that "management tension" is a significant source of stress for teachers, and also it lends support to the idea that one of the critical factors in the teacher burnout process is a lack of organizational support (Fibkins, 1983; Ianni and Reuss-Ianni, 1983). Fibkins, for example, contended that teacher burnout is the result of the school organization's lack of responsiveness to the increasingly complicated and burdensome nature of teachers' work. And the comments of some teachers polled by the Carnegie Foundation (cited by Hechinger, 1989a, p. B11) offered additional agreement with this point of view. Said one experienced teacher in a suburban section of Connecticut, "Money is available for administrative conferences, expense accounts, 'perks,' while teachers buy everything from Kleenex to crayons to journals." According to another educator, a first-grade teacher for twenty-one years: "No administrator ever says 'thanks.' No comments on the quality of teaching, only about PTA fund raisers, attendance registers, and supply lists." In my study, the comments that some teachers included on their returned survey forms suggested that administrators,

Table 9.1. A Comparison of Urban and Suburban Teachers' Attitudes
Toward Their Profession.

Item	Percent Endorsing "Frequently"		Percent Endorsing "Never" or "Rarely"	
	Urban	Suburban	Urban	Suburban
I feel burned out from my work.	21.6	10.3	56.7	70.3
I feel my physical health has deteriorated because of teaching.	16.2	5.9	70.7	85.4
I feel that teaching has increased my irritability outside of school.	18.4	13.3	62.9	64.4
I have been angered by the insolence of students.	23.7	9.1	48.5	67.7
I feel satisfied with teachers' standing in society.	6.3	6.2	81.8	79.9
I feel that parents have made things easier for me.	8.4	5.7	75.5	66.1
I feel that administrative meetings prove helpful in solving problems.	2.3	3.1	90.6	86.9
I have received support and encouragement from my principal.	9.1	12.8	76.7	63.4
I feel there is a sense of community in my school.	11.8	15.2	69.2	60.8
I have had rewarding contact with colleagues during the workday.	30.1	42.4	29.7	25.0
I can create a relaxed atmosphere with my students.	51.1	57.9	15.1	9.2
I have felt I was positively influencing students' lives through my work.	31.7	43.5	32.5	23.4
I have accomplished many worthwhile things in this job.	35.0	40.9	31.7	20.2
I gain suitable emotional rewards, given the effort I put in.	27.4	33.9	47.9	36.2
If I had to do it again, I would choose to be a teacher.	25.9	32.5	55.5	47.6
I feel the benefits of teaching outweigh the disadvantages.	23.6	31.4	45.4	35.1

including principals, are not perceived as being on the "same side" as teachers, and that the administrators are more interested in protecting their own images and positions than they are in improving school conditions for either teachers or students. Administrators, some teachers feel, prefer teachers who "don't make waves" and don't have problems. It may be that administrators are caught in the dilemma of either being active in the school (thereby risking charges of intrusiveness) or staying in the background (thereby risking charges of neglect of duties). It certainly bears keeping in mind that administrators are also vulnerable to their own versions of stress and burnout. Still, these data suggest that administrators have swung too far to the background and are perceived as being uninvolved or, at best, only perfunctorily and nonhelpfully involved in the daily work of teachers. It may be that, as some teachers suggest, administrators, having once been teachers themselves, have "turned their backs" on their former colleagues to safeguard their own positions. However, alternative explanations of teachers' unflattering views of administrators are equally plausible. For example, a form of psychological displacement may be occurring: Just as some parents have unrealistic and unfair expectations of what teachers can accomplish for their children, so do some teachers have somewhat unrealistic and unfair expectations of what administrators can accomplish for them.

According to the Metropolitan Life Survey of the American Teacher (Harris and Associates, 1988), there are at least two other major stressors for suburban teachers. One is working with students who have either alcohol or drug problems, a problem that is growing increasingly severe and has begun to affect even elementary school teachers. "Frankly," said one sixth-grade teacher interviewed for this book, "I expected this to be a problem in city schools, and maybe even a bit of a problem in some suburban high schools around here, but sixth grade? There are kids in this school who are getting high every weekend and who are telling their friends how great it is. It's becoming a major issue and parents are screaming at each other, and at us, to do something about it."

For some teachers, particularly those currently in their forties who came of age in the 1960s and who spent at least a part of their youth experimenting with drugs, this problem takes on a special and ironic quality. "It feels more than a little bit strange to come down hard on my students or to act moralistic with them about drugs given my own history. It's true that I wasn't doing drugs in high school, but by my first year in college I was getting stoned constantly. To a certain extent, I can justify my position because today's drugs are much more potent and because the kids who are trying them seem to be getting younger and younger. . . . We're trying to stop kids from drinking or using drugs, but I don't think it's working that well. The drug program in this school seems good and I guess it 'saves' some kids from trying drugs. But there's so much around. My own feeling is that what it does best is to prevent kids from driving or doing crazy or really dangerous things when they are high. But it's certainly not funny. They're messing themselves up and there's not that much we can do about it. It's frustrating and frightening."

The other, often overlooked problem in both suburban and rural schools concerns apathetic students. According to the Metropolitan Life Survey of the American Teacher (Harris and Associates, 1988), the percentage of students acknowledging that they really don't like going to school is higher in rural (25 percent) and suburban (24 percent) than in urban schools (19 percent).

Despite such problems, most suburban teachers do not feel burned out. As a group, these teachers have not lessened their involvement in their work, do not feel that teaching has hardened them emotionally, and do not experience any deterioration of their physical health. Most point to the intrinsic satisfaction of teaching as their reason for staying. One woman, an English teacher in an affluent suburb in Westchester, New York, had this to say about her profession at the end of the school year: "I want to say that I can't imagine any better job. I know there's a need for doctors and arbitrage people (whatever they do), and that not everyone can be as lucky as me. As I file away my lesson plans for the year just passed I forget all the non-homework doers and negative stuff, and I remember the epiphanic moments" (cited in Fisk, 1988, p. 26).

Nevertheless, there is a wide diversity of feelings among suburban teachers as to whether they gain suitable rewards from teaching, given the effort they put in: 36 percent either never or rarely feel this way, 30 percent occasionally feel this way, and 34 percent frequently feel this way. Similarly, there is virtually an even distribution of opinion as to whether the benefits of teaching outweigh the disadvantages: 35 percent rarely or never think so, 33 percent occasionally think so, and 31 percent frequently think so.

But there are teachers in suburbia who are burned out: about 10 percent indicate that they "frequently" feel burned out; another 19 percent acknowledge that they "occasionally" feel burned out. Suburban teachers at greatest risk for burnout are those in the thirty-four-to-forty-four-year-old age group and those who teach at a junior high or middle school. As noted earlier, teachers in this age group are most vulnerable to doubts about the wisdom of their career choice and find it most difficult, given their family and financial situations, to look for alternative careers. Teachers at a junior high or middle school must deal with the more serious acting-out behaviors of adolescents.

As Table 9.1 indicates, the percentage of suburban teachers who frequently feel burned out or "damaged" as a result of their work is indeed less than the percentage of urban teachers who feel this way. And far fewer suburban teachers frequently feel angered by the disrespect shown them by their students. Conversely, a greater percentage of these suburban teachers frequently feel that they have rewarding contact with colleagues, that the benefits of teaching outweigh the disadvantages, and that they are positively influencing their students' lives through their work. This last factor—that it is easier for suburban teachers to feel effective—is paramount in understanding their lesser vulnerability to burnout. In part, of course, this is because many urban teachers are consumed with handling student discipline problems, which, as pointed out in Chapter Eight, are likely to impair teachers' ability to feel effective.

Teachers in urban settings or in underpaid private schools often look at teachers of mainstream students in the suburbs as the "lucky ones," the teachers with few problems. Suburban parents tend to agree. Suburban schools seem to "work"—that is, children in these schools seem to receive a good education, or at least to score well on standardized tests. Urban schools, on the other hand, seem not to work and their problems are naturally given greater attention. Actually, the assumption that teachers in the suburbs have few, if any, problems may itself serve as a stressor, since this attitude often leads to a failure to take seriously the concerns and issues that exist for these teachers.

Rural Schools

In many ways, the problems and stressors of rural schools mirror those of surburban schools. As is true of suburbia, student discipline problems and serious academic problems are less prevalent here than they are in urban centers. Compared to 27 percent of inner-city teachers who contend that "constant discipline problems" constitute a "very serious" issue for their school, only 11 percent of suburban and 10 percent of rural teachers feel this way. Whereas 38 percent of inner-city teachers acknowledge that the number of students lacking basic skills is a very serious problem in their schools, only 12 percent of suburban and 13 percent of rural teachers endorse this view (Harris and Associates, 1988). But, as in suburbia, drug and alcohol problems are considered very serious by a sizeable percentage of rural teachers. In fact, a greater percentage of teachers in rural schools (38 percent) than in inner-city schools (32 percent) feel that student alcohol abuse is a very serious problem. In both suburban and rural schools, 50 percent of teachers say they know ten or more students with a drinking problem; only 37 percent of urban teachers make the same claim (Harris and Associates, 1988).

Other problems that beset rural schools revolve around the fact that they are typically small. Between 9 and 10 percent of both the elementary and secondary schools in this country contain fewer than 100 students and, even a late as 1987–88, there were still 729 schools in this country with only one teacher. Teachers in small rural schools may have to teach several different subject areas and prepare lessons for several different grades. And, because of the monetary problems afflicting some rural schools, teachers are underpaid, textbooks are old, supplies are scarce, and the physical plant is in need of repair (Berger, 1989).

Other problems for rural teachers are familiar to all teachers: the fact that there are children from overburdened single-parent homes or from two-parent, indigent, poorly educated homes. Teachers in rural schools complain that too many parents are not sufficiently invested in their children's education, that too many assume that their children's futures will not include the need for a high school diploma or beyond. Some parents fear that advanced education will spur their children to leave the area for opportunities unavailable in their own communities.

Finally, in rural communities, schools—and teachers' lives— tend to be strongly dominated by local school boards. Not only do rural school boards have strong opinions about what teachers should and shouldn't do (both in and out of the classroom) but they

consider themselves independent, even in relationship to governmental rules and regulations. "The paramount principle in rural
areas . . . is local control, a 'don't tell us what to do' attitude"
(quoted by Berger, 1989, B8). Teachers in small rural districts, more
than in other types of communities, may be subject to a great degree
of personal and professional scrutiny.

On the other hand, there are those rural school communities
where teachers are accorded the kind of professional respect and
support that is often dreamed about in teacher journals. Aware of
the serious problem of recruiting and retaining teachers in rural
areas, some communities have actively and successfully attempted
to improve the lot of teachers. One school, for example, implemented the following changes: tuition reimbursement for graduate
courses; release time for working on curriculum or visiting other
classrooms; summer remuneration for attending institutes or establishing new curriculum; arrangement with a local university to
offer graduate courses in specific curriculum areas or educational
topics; and the institution of several conferences on outcome-based
learning and several new in-service courses (Matthes and Carlson,
1986). A teacher in this school (which, not surprisingly, has earned
the reputation of being a good place to work) said: "We feel as
though we are professionals and the board of education and administrators treat us that way" (p. 11).

Those attracted to teaching opportunities in rural schools
may have different values from those who teach elsewhere. Matthes
and Carlson (1986) found that beginning teachers in rural districts
rated the pace of living, the cost of living, and the size of the school
as more important than those in suburban and urban schools.
These researchers concluded that "those accepting teaching positions in rural school districts were more concerned about settling
into the community, whereas their counterparts in suburban and
urban settings seem to be more concerned about their 'professional'
future—that is, issues related to professional autonomy, salary, and
the like" (p. 8). In addition, rural teachers seemed more intent on
garnering the support of parents, whereas teachers in urban and
suburban communities seemed more interested in administrative
support.

No figures are available regarding the percentages of those in rural schools who may be burned out. Rural teachers, though, tend to be similar to suburban teachers in regard to the percentages of those who feel it very likely or fairly likely that they will leave teaching within the next five years: 24 percent of suburban teachers, 26 percent of rural teachers (Harris and Associates, 1988).

Private Schools

According to a 1987 report commissioned by the Center for Education Statistics, *Private Schools and Private School Teachers,* there are about 28,000 private schools in this country employing 400,000 teachers and educating 5.6 million pupils. These schools constitute 25 percent of this nation's elementary and secondary schools and represent 12 percent of total student enrollment. As the report notes, "private schools may be viewed as increasing the number of options for parents who feel their children have special needs" (p. 1). Approximately 80 percent of private schools have a religious orientation; these sectarian schools, nearly half of which are Catholic, enroll 86 percent of private school students. With an average enrollment of 234 students, private schools tend to be small. The average number of teachers in private schools is also small—14. Teacher-pupil ratios range from 10 to 1 in nonsectarian schools to 15 to 1 in non-Catholic religious schools to 21 to 1 in Catholic private schools. Most (76 percent) of the teachers in private schools are female and most (92 percent) are white. In 1987, the mean base salary for this group was $14,400, ranging from $13,900 at Catholic schools to $16,500 at nonsectarian private schools. Slightly less than one-quarter of these teachers (23 percent) receive some form of in-kind income, for example, housing, meals, transportation, or reduced tuition for family members.

There is much to be said about the advantages of teaching in private schools. These teachers feel that there is a great deal of cooperative effort among staff members (88 percent agree with this statement), that staff members maintain high standards of performance for themselves (93 percent agreement), that the principal is interested in new ideas (85 percent), and that the school administration's behavior toward the staff is supportive and encouraging (84 percent). There is also widespread consistency of opinion regarding school discipline problems and drug use. Eighty-six percent disagreed with the following statement: "The level of student misbehavior and/or drug or alcohol use in this school interferes with my teaching." However, even within the context of these generally positive trends, about 8 to 10 percent of private school teachers seem disenchanted with their schools. Members of this group consistently "disagree" or "strongly disagree" with those survey items indicating positive feelings about student behavior, administrative support of teachers, principals' responsiveness to new ideas, and collegial relations. Apparently, at least 10 percent of teachers are burned out regardless of the setting in which they are working.

Financial woes are among the major problems of private schools, and teachers are obviously affected by this situation. The salaries of private school teachers are typically 25 to 33 percent lower than those of their counterparts in public schools. According to a survey done of nonsectarian private school teachers (Goldman, 1988), nearly half would consider transferring to a public school and 40 percent are thinking about a career change. Beginning teachers in nonsectarian private schools plan on spending only three years in their current position before moving on to jobs either in industry or in the public school system. That they are willing to teach at all for considerably less remuneration is due to the fact that the atmosphere in independent schools is considered to be far less stressful. Independent school teachers appreciate the academic freedom in their schools, the relative absence of bureaucratic nonsense, the fewer number of students (and the far fewer number of seriously troubled students), the achievement motivation of most of their students, and the congenial working conditions. Their contributions are often recognized and appreciated, at least by other staff members.

Two short profiles—one of a teacher in a church-affiliated school, the other of a teacher in a secular school—may illustrate the range of satisfactions and stressors that exist for private school teachers.

Vicky, a married, thirty-eight-year-old mother of three, teaches seventh grade in the local Catholic school, only a few blocks from her house. The school, in a solidly middle-class area in a suburban outskirt of a small city, houses both elementary and middle school programs. Students here can complete the eighth grade before going on to high school; most will attend the regional Catholic high school. There are approximately 500 students in the school, with each grade from K through eight divided into two classes of about 30 students each. Although virtually all the students are Catholic, they come from a wide variety of ethnic groups.

As her students enter her classroom, Vicky greets each by name and all wish her a good morning. Some pass messages on from their mothers, women Vicky knows from church. Although at times Vicky feels her personal and professional lives are merging into one, she recognizes that her social contacts with many of these parents enable her to maintain a stricter yet less oppressive environment in her class. Students act up less when they realize the closeness of the relationship between teacher and parents. Rarely do her students fail to do their homework, and when a student does poorly on an exam, a conference between parent and teacher is a virtual certainty.

Vicky follows a curriculum that has been set by others in the church hierarchy. Although given some leeway in her methods of teaching, her choices in regard to literature and her stance in regard to the teaching of history are expected to demonstrate church-accepted values.

Vicky has been teaching for four years, ever since her youngest child started attending school. She and her husband often discuss whether she should leave her school and apply for a position in the public schools. Her husband tends to take the position that she should leave, citing the fact that her income would immediately be increased by almost 50 percent and her benefit package also increased substantially. Vicky, on the other hand, feels that her husband earns a high enough income that her low salary does not pose an extraordinary hardship to the family. Moreover, she feels a moral commitment to the school, which, after all, is educating their own children. She believes that the children at her school are far better off than those at the local public schools. She admires the values taught, the importance placed on morality and spiritual beliefs. Another advantage, she feels, is the disciplinary code at the school. Students are expected to dress and behave appropriately. Every student knows that a major disciplinary infraction could lead to a response ranging from a warning to permanent expulsion. Although there are a handful of students each year who are suspended for various lengths of time, Vicky realizes that she does not have to deal with many of the serious problems that commonly arise in public schools. She is fascinated yet outraged by newspaper accounts of school violence, drugs, and student failure in the schools, even those in the suburbs. Each report further convinces her that her choice to work in a nonpublic school is correct.

Vicky spends most of her day in the classroom. She has a break only at lunch and when her students go to physical education, or the priest comes in for religion classes. She has thirty-two students in her room and has to move around quickly trying to meet all their needs. Classes tend to be recitations, as Vicky asks students to respond to many specific questions about the work they have prepared. The day passes quickly. There are almost no disciplinary problems, and these are usually minor infractions like whispering or note-passing.

Although some of the teachers in the school are required to stay late and work at extracurricular activities, as the mother of three children, Vicky is allowed to leave at 3 P.M. to supervise her own children. She brings her youngest child with her on her errands, then heads home to begin dinner. While it is cooking, Vicky sits in the kitchen marking papers and working on lesson plans for the following day. Having taught seventh grade for several years in a school that embraces the concept of stable and enduring values, Vicky only has to make minor changes in her lesson plans.

All in all, the day goes smoothly. There are no major stressors. She is somewhat tired but not exhausted; she experiences a sense of satisfaction that the day has gone well and that she has done a good job. Were someone to ask her if she were burned out, Vicky would likely reply, "No, not really." Yet were she asked if she intended to stay on the job for several more years, she'd likely say that she wasn't sure. "I like what the school is doing for the kids, but I have no freedom to be creative in my teaching and at this point I'd really like that. I've got some ideas but I know they wouldn't be accepted. I also feel annoyed at how much I'm getting paid. I deserve more and I could get more in the public school system. Salaries of public school teachers have gone up tremendously the last few years but mine hasn't. I feel I'm doing a lot of good but I also feel I deserve to be getting more for my efforts."

Ronni, a teacher in a private secular school, usually sets her alarm clock for 6 A.M. to be able to get to school early. Her roommate, who works in an office, is able to wake up later and Ronni envies this prerogative. She walks quietly through the small apartment, trying to get her things in order. She resents having to share an apartment but her salary is so low that she could not survive well on her own.

Ronni lives in a large city and takes a bus to work. Her school is a progressive, independent school where classes are very small and tuition is very high. Parental expectations regarding their children's achievement are also very high. Because of the fees, most of the students are from wealthy families, except for a couple of teachers' children and some children from working- and middle-class families receiving modest scholarships.

Ronni's classes are small, none above fifteen students. Her subject area is physical education and her specialty is swimming. There is only one other female physical education teacher in the school, unfortunately someone whom Ronni does not care for that much. As a result, Ronni does sometimes find herself feeling isolated, knowing that there are few people around to whom she can turn for help.

She enjoys her work, though, and likes and respects most of her students. The great majority of them are hard-working, well-intentioned, high-achieving, good kids. Those whom she has the most difficulty with are the spoiled, "entitled" ones. These students, Ronni has found, often react poorly to disappointments, have great difficulty in hearing even the mildest of criticism, and are catty and sarcastic toward their classmates. (After she meets their parents, it is no surprise to Ronni that these students act as they do.) Still, these students (and their parents) are in the minority, and they pose more of an annoyance to Ronni than a major source of stress. Ronni enjoys teaching phys ed and her classes generally go well; she also enjoys coaching and has achieved a good deal of success with her teams.

In Ronni's case (like Vicky's), the major stressor is not the teaching itself but rather the poor salary she receives for the amount of work she does. As part of her contract, Ronni is required to coach at least one sport each term. In fact, she coaches three sports each year to earn the small amounts of extra money involved. In addition, there are constant evening activities at her school, many of which teachers are required to attend. Ronni spends, on the average, two evenings a week working for the school. Occasionally, too, she has to give up a weekend to take a team to a tournament.

The school prides itself on conveying values of personal worth and dignity to students. It is unabashedly liberal in its social and political philosophy. Each student is expected to perform some form of community service each term; some students, for example, spend time tutoring in nearby inner-city community centers. Classes are largely unstructured and students, especially the older ones, are given a good deal of freedom to pursue their own areas of interest. Many assemblies are convened to address issues of current importance. Ronni's own political beliefs were once entirely consonant with those of the school, a synchrony that propelled her originally to take the job. When she was first offered the job, she was especially impressed with how much input she'd have into phys ed curriculum. But now the school's values seem ironic and somewhat hypocritical to Ronni in light of school policy toward teacher salaries. Moreover, Ronni is not as enamored of a liberal stance toward politics or education as she was eight years ago when she began teaching here. She's begun to feel that many of the students in the school need more structure in their lives. And, as a result of the problems besetting the neighborhood she lives in, her beliefs about drugs and crime have become decidedly nonliberal. For some of her colleagues, the school's mission offers a strong sense of purpose and engenders a sense of community; for others, though, like Ronni, it has become both burdensome and alienating.

As a result primarily of her poor pay and her declining belief in the school's philosophy, Ronni often contemplates leaving her job. She feels she is going nowhere, on a treadmill leading to her own cycle of poverty. She has earned a good deal of respect in her area and thinks about transferring to a public school. It is an idea that may or may not reach fruition, but it disturbs Ronni greatly that she even has to think about it seriously. She once felt she might stay in this school till retirement. But despite the good feelings she has for most of her colleagues and students, and despite, too, the fact that the

administration seems to appreciate her work, Ronni feels it unlikely
that she will stay where she is for more than a few more years.

Most researchers in the field of occupational stress have contended that workers become burned out or quit when they can no
longer generate the satisfactions necessary to continue. Among others, Kanner, Kafry, and Pines (1978) found that the lack of job
motivators (phenomena that promote feelings of personal growth,
self-actualization, and recognition) are far more powerful predictors
of professional stress than is the presence of "hygiene factors" (oppressive working conditions). Salary conditions of private teachers,
however, may be perceived as so onerous as to constitute an exception to this general rule. On the other hand, one could argue that
in cases such as Ronni's, the salient factor is not salary deprivation
per se but rather the loss of a primary motivator, such as a strong
sense of community. In any case, the popular image of the private
school teacher remains clear in the minds of many—that of the
individual who will forgo economic compensation for the satisfaction of teaching highly motivated and high-achieving students in
small, collegial schools. One wonders, though, whether this proto-
type will remain valid if salaries in private schools fail to keep
relative pace with the escalating salaries in the public domain.

Special Education

About 11 percent of this nation's schoolchildren—4.4 million in all—receive some kind of special education. While children
with sensory handicaps (visual, hearing) and physical handicaps
have always been relatively identifiable, in the last three decades
there has been an increasing number of students entering special ed
programs with mild or moderate handicaps, particularly in the do-
mains of speech problems, mental retardation, learning disabilities,
and emotional handicaps.

According to a government study, in 1985–86 the cost of educating the average special education student was $6,335, or 2.3
times the cost for regular classroom students. The extra money spent
on special education, however, has not served to inoculate teachers of
these children against the effects of stress. Like their colleagues in

regular education, many special ed teachers have soured on their jobs. Over 58 percent of special ed teachers have developed more negative views of their jobs over time (Fimian, Pearson, and McHardy, 1986), and over 8 percent have sought professional counseling for reasons related to job stress (Fimian and Santoro, 1983). In Bradfield and Fones's (1985) study of special education teachers, 10 percent reported a high level of stress as a result of teaching, 75 percent reported a moderate level, and only 15 percent a low level.

Teachers of students with special needs constitute a group of educators that are in many ways distinct from regular teachers. Furthermore, each group of teachers within special education has satisfactions and stresses unique to their specialty area. In this regard, Zabel and Zabel (1982) found that teachers of emotionally disturbed students had higher levels of burnout than teachers of the learning disabled, educable mentally retarded, trainable mentally retarded, gifted, visually impaired, hearing impaired, and multiply or severely handicapped. This, of course, should be no surprise. As Bloom (1983) pointed out, almost all adults become nervous around emotionally disturbed, acting-out youth; teachers who work with these children typically feel helpless, full of rage, fearful, impotent, and despairing. Many have given up hope that they can make a difference.

Crane and Iwanicki (1986) found that special ed teachers in self-contained classrooms exhibited significantly higher levels of burnout on all subscales of the Maslach Burnout Inventory than did resource room teachers, and that teachers younger than forty-six and with less than ten years of experience also exhibited significantly higher levels of burnout on all subscales. The first finding—that teachers in self-contained classrooms were more prone to burnout than resource room teachers—was opposite to that of Bensky and others (1980). Crane and Iwanicki explained this discrepancy by noting that their sample, in contrast to that of Bensky and others, consisted of many teachers working in large urban school systems where the severity of behavior and learning problems in classrooms could be expected to be high. Zabel and Zabel (1982) also reported that special ed teachers at the junior high level had the highest burnout scores on the MBI, and that preschool teachers, while reporting relatively high levels of emotional exhaustion, derived the greatest amount of personal accomplishment among special ed teachers at different school levels. In addition, they found that older, more experienced teachers were less vulnerable to emotional exhaustion and depersonalization and were able to derive a greater sense of satisfaction from their work than younger, less experienced teachers. "It is unclear," they noted, "whether older, more experienced teachers have developed better skills and coping strategies, whether their expectations have become more realistic, or whether teachers who have experienced greater job-related stress have left the profession" (p. 262). Consistent too with a notion that has been emphasized throughout this book, these authors found that teachers who reported higher levels of support from administrators, colleagues, and parents had lower scores on the emotional exhaustion and depersonalization subscales of the MBI and higher scores on the personal accomplishment subscale. Similarly, Fimian, Pearson, and McHardy (1986) found that lack of administrative support was linked to job stress in special ed teachers.

Surprisingly, the literature has consistently shown that special educators, taken as a group, are no more stressed or burned out by their work than regular educators (Barner, 1982; Meagher, 1983; Wechsler, 1983). Barner, in fact, found that a greater percentage of special ed teachers (74 percent) than regular teachers (62 percent) felt they were making progress with most of their students. Her sample of special ed teachers, however, was quite small and her results, although interesting, must be considered preliminary.

Compared to other human service professionals, including regular classroom teachers, college professors, social service workers, physicians, nurses, psychologists, and police officers, the scores of special education teachers on the MBI tend to be moderate. Using the norms established by Maslach and Jackson (1981), Crane and Iwanicki (1986) found that their sample of special education teachers scored in the 47th percentile for emotional exhaustion but only in the 33rd percentile for depersonalization and the 32nd for personal accomplishment. These data suggest that special education teachers are, in comparison to other human service professionals, moderately emotionally exhausted by their work but not especially demoralized or lacking a sense of personal accomplishment, indicating that special education teachers feel that their efforts, though personally taxing, are paying off.

Factors Affecting Stress and Burnout in Special Education Teachers. There are a number of stressors that special educators face. Weiskopf (1980), for example, pointed to the enormous workload of these teachers: "implementing an individualized education program [IEP] for each student, conferring with each child's parents, attending meetings, counseling parents, instructing students, and holding discussions with regular educators" (p. 19). Special educators' vulnerability to burnout, said Weiskopf, is due to their tendency to focus on students' problems rather than their strengths or successes.

Research indicates that the sources of stress for special education teachers, except for that engendered by the need to write IEPs, parallel quite closely those of regular classroom teachers. Crane and Iwanicki (1986), whose sample of teachers was heavily drawn from urban districts, pointed to lack of administrative support, excessive time demands, and increased regulatory paperwork as the major stressors impinging on special ed teachers. Fimian, Pearson, and McHardy (1986), whose sample of special ed teachers was more evenly distributed among urban, suburban, and rural school systems, found major stressors to include inadequate salary, inadequate time and energy available for personal needs, the need to monitor pupil behavior, teaching poorly motivated students, and the lack of recognition for effective work. In a sample of special educators disproportionately composed of learning disabilities teachers, Bradfield and Fones (1985) located the primary sources of stress in parent-teacher relationships, time management, and intrapersonal conflicts.

Several of the factors enumerated above are interrelated and seem to have, as a common denominator, the extra work and demands required by PL 94-142 (the Education for All Handicapped Children Act). Previous to the passage of this bill, which was passed in 1975 to take effect in 1977, relatively little was done on the federal level for handicapped children. The differing amounts of aid and support given by the states to handicapped children provided a goad to parents in many states to demand that the federal government require equal treatment for these children. The basic purpose of PL 94-142 was to ensure a free, appropriate education for all handicapped children. Its provisions include the following:

1. States and local districts must ensure that all handicapped children are identified, located, and evaluated.
2. Parents and children are given due process safeguards, including the right to review educational records, obtain independent evaluations, receive written notices of all actions, and request a hearing in order to appeal a decision.
3. A comprehensive educational assessment, performed by a multidisciplinary team, is required, with reevaluation every three years.
4. An individualized education program (IEP) must be written and updated annually. This plan must include current performance, short- and longer-term goals, and methods of evaluation.
5. Children must be placed in the least restrictive environment that will allow them to learn.

Several authors (for example, Bensky and others, 1980; Crane and Iwanicki, 1986) suggested that the stressors on special ed teachers have increased significantly since the passage of this bill. The point is that, apart from the undeniable benefits this law has provided to children, there have been a number of unforeseen consequences, chief among them the extraordinary amount of extra work—chiefly paperwork—this law has meant for special education teachers. Said one teacher interviewed for this book: "Filling in IEPs may not seem like a major problem to people who are not involved. But I spend dozens of hours in September and October working on students' long-term goals and several hours each week after that revising their short-term goals." Another teacher noted that the favorite expression among special ed teachers in his district was: "What we lack in students, we make up for in paperwork."

Other teachers spoke of the increased tension between parents and teachers as a result of mandated parental involvement in the curriculum and placement of children. A teacher of a class for the educable mentally retarded said: "Parents now feel that they have the right—and, in fact, they do—to oversee virtually every decision I make about their child. Some come in every week to question this or that piece of work I've assigned or want to know what other remedial services may be necessary or available for their child. I understand it, I can sympathize with it, but I also know that their concerns are often obsessive and repetitive. And their expectations of what I or the school can provide or do for their child over the course of a year are often remarkably unrealistic."

Of course, not all parents come to school to make unwarranted demands. There are many who support their children's teachers totally. These parents come to meetings, ask intelligent questions, and often act as important mediators of stress by treating teachers with respect and asking the same of their children.

The frequency of evaluations has also increased following the implementation of PL 94-142. "Everyone," said one teacher we interviewed, "wants to know how I'm doing. It begins with the COH [Committee on the Handicapped] and extends right through the principal, the assistant principal, the parents, and even the assistant school superintendent for the district. Some of these people are fine and quite professional but others are intolerable. I never know when I'll be second-guessed by the 'second team'—some of the COH members who have great twenty–twenty hindsight."

Apart from work overload, the problems of role conflict and ambiguity may contribute significantly to burnout in special education teachers. Role conflict, as explained earlier, occurs when the information available to a teacher to do his or her job is sufficient but conflicting. Role conflict may occur when there are incompatible demands from two or more supervisors ("The school psychologist told me I should be more sensitive with Fred, allow him some extra leeway in the classroom; meanwhile the assistant principal told me I better crack down on his behavior if I didn't want him suspended from school"), when personal or professional resources are lacking to perform certain aspects of one's job ("I don't know enough about cognitive therapy to teach my impulsive students 'how to think' "), or when performing one's job adequately requires breaking rules or ignoring policy ("I make up the numbers on some of these reports because if I did them all letter-perfect, I'd have no time to teach or plan at all"). Sometimes the job of a special education teacher seems to consist exclusively of contradictory aspects:

"If I just taught English in a regular high school class I could just come in and talk about grammar or spelling. In this job, I also have to be mommy and friend and toughguy."

Role ambiguity occurs when the information available is nonconflictual but nonetheless insufficient to perform a job adequately, for example, when school administrators fail to brief teachers on how to complete certain forms, or when teachers remain unclear regarding the extent of their responsibilities or authority vis-à-vis those of administrators or pupil personnel staff. Crane and Iwanicki (1986) found that, in a sample of special education teachers, role conflict explained a significant proportion of the variance in both the emotional exhaustion and depersonalization subscales of the MBI, and role ambiguity accounted for a significant amount of the variance in personal accomplishment. These findings are consistent with those of Bensky and others (1980), who found that organizational factors relating to role expectations accounted for a significant proportion of the variance in stress among special education teachers, and to those of Fimian and Blanton (1986), who found that role conflict and role ambiguity contributed significantly to burnout in both special education trainees and first-year teachers.

Lack of appreciation is another stressor for special ed teachers. Several teachers interviewed suggested that parents appreciated their skills and efforts far more than did school administrators or colleagues who tended to view their jobs as "easy" and full of perks (for example, classroom aides). One teacher commented: "Most of the parents [of the non–special ed kids] have no idea what we do. They feel we just babysit our students. But what's really intolerable is the ignorance some of my colleagues have toward what special ed is about. They should have to examine our detailed plans, our behavioral objectives, our IEPs. Most of the teachers in the mainstream can just teach subject matter to their classes. They present the material they feel is important, test the students on it, and never worry whether the work is appropriate for each student. . . . A student is held accountable for learning all the work and it's his problem if he can't pass. Special education is different. Our lessons have to reflect student ability and prelearned knowledge first, then move toward broader goals. Each student has an individualized curriculum. We, the special ed teachers, are accountable for student progress to a far greater degree than any other staff members in the school."

Supervisory style may also have a significant impact on levels of burnout among special ed teachers. In a study of two schools for severely retarded children, Cherniss (1988) found that the principal with fewer burned-out teachers was significantly more supportive of teachers and spent more time discussing personal, work-related issues than did his counterpart; in addition, this "low-burnout" principal interacted significantly more often with other administrators and clerical staff.

Finally, what can't be forgotten is that the work itself with these children can be extraordinarily difficult. Even those not teaching classes of emotionally disturbed children are faced with severe emotional or physical or cognitive problems that often defy the most creative minds or indomitable will. The technology of teaching or behavior change has not caught up with some of the problems that special educators face, and while a recognition of this fact can lead to the formulation of more realistic goals, it cannot ease entirely the frustration that inevitably comes with lack of success.

The exception to this, of course, is that some special educators work with the gifted. But, as Swicord (1987) reminded us, these teachers too are vulnerable to burnout. They experience a severe energy drain as a result of the nearly constant pressure upon them to excite, challenge, and motivate their students. Because many work in multiple schools, they have to adapt to several special ed teams and arrange their schedules to meet the needs of several schools within a district. They are often called upon to lead workshops or attend committee meetings. They have to individualize much of the work, frequently update curriculum, and provide regular updates to parents and other teachers. Gifted students may drain teachers both intellectually and emotionally. In this regard, however, Zabel and Zabel (1982) found that teachers of the gifted had high levels of emotional exhaustion but also reported the highest degree of personal accomplishment.

Teachers of the gifted may also have to spend time with administrators or parent-teacher groups justifying their own positions or the financial outlay for their programs. Many feel that their program is viewed as an unnecessary luxury by administrators, other teachers, and parents of the nongifted, and that supplies and space granted them are begrudgingly and inadequately provided. As a result, many teachers remain perpetually concerned that their position will be the first to be eliminated in the face of budget cuts. Many also feel unappreciated and believe that the means to effectively judge the quality of their work are lacking. Many feel isolated and without collegial support.

Mediators of Stress. If, in comparison to regular classroom teachers, special education personnel face a greater number of stressors with no proportionate increase in burnout or other dysfunctional symptoms, the role of mediating variables must be considered.

Earlier, I noted the added burdens that IEPs place on special education teachers. However, carefully done and realistic IEPs move lessons toward specific, achievable learning experiences and may serve as a form of inoculation against the greater disappointments felt by mainstream teachers. As one teacher noted, "All of us in special education learn to focus precisely on what we want our students to learn. My sister, who teaches mainstream kids, feels forced to push her students to keep up with the curriculum. Lots of times, lots of her students can't keep up. I try to match the students with an individualized curriculum and I succeed more of the time. When my students learn something, I know about it right away. My sister can only hope her students are keeping up. She feels terribly frustrated when her students fail tests, feeling that she has been the real failure." Consistent with this notion, Beck and Gargiulo (1983) found that teachers of moderately retarded children were less burned out than those with more educable students. For these teachers, realistic expectations helped prevent long-term, severe stress.

Another mediating factor for special ed teachers is small class size. With fewer students, teachers get to know each one, each becomes important, and the specialness of each becomes more obvious. As one teacher we interviewed remarked, "By the end of the year these children are a part of me. And even though I can feel their pain, I can also celebrate their success." Another noted: "Because I can spend more time with each child, and can walk around the class giving a hand, I'm always around to give a hug and a 'good work' to everyone. I usually can make sure that every kid gets some form of positive feedback every lesson. They feel good about that and so do I."

Many special ed classrooms also have paraprofessionals or aides. The added presence of an adult figure serves both to help students and to reduce teacher isolation. Classrooms function better with greater individualized attention, and potentially volatile situations may be dealt with before things get out of hand. Not atypically, trouble can break out in one end of the classroom while the teacher is working at the other. The presence of an aide means that a classroom can continue to function while one of the adults attends to the crisis. In short, an aide can decrease stress and isolation in the classroom while facilitating success.

Finally, these teachers' intense commitment to their students is a factor in their ability to sustain motivation and avoid burnout. Although I know of no empirical data to validate this impression, my sense is that many special ed teachers have friends or relatives who themselves have children with special needs. Certainly, many of these teachers come into the field with a strong sense of purpose and a mission to help children with certain handicapping conditions. Although Freudenberger, among others, suggested that those highly committed to a field are most vulnerable to burnout, other observers, notably Cherniss and Krantz (1983), commented on the ability of those strongly committed to a cause to alleviate impending burnout by renewing their sense of purpose. The following profile illustrates a frustrated but functioning high school special ed teacher.

Steve is a forty-five-year-old high school special ed teacher who's been teaching in an urban school system for nineteen years. He feels that he is not burned out, although he does admit often feeling "frustrated, overworked, and underappreciated." When asked why these feelings don't add up to burnout, he replies that "burnout to me means acting like a shadow of oneself. Even with the frustrations, I still feel mostly intact." He also tends not to blame students for the problems they bring into the classroom. Instead, he focuses his anger on the social injustices impinging upon his students, and on the parents of these students as well. From his perspective, many of the parents he deals with are "concerned but truly incompetent. Even though many of them care, they do not know how to talk to their kids or how to discipline them." His other major gripe is with the IEPs (individualized educational programs) he's mandated to write for each of his students. According to Steve, neither he nor any of the other special ed teachers takes the task seriously, believing that there's essentially "no relationship between them and education. The IEPs are purely an administrative task. . . . I just have to concern myself with using the right words and the right style." Classrooms, contends Steve, are considerably more unpredictable than IEPs assume.

Steve has an interesting, somewhat unusual perspective on the classroom that enables him to function effectively as a teacher: He views the intensity of the classroom and of student-teacher interactions as an effective way of shutting out other problems and concerns in his life. He is able to view the classroom as a sanctuary.

His impression of others around him who do seem burned out is that they act erratically and are often "enormously sarcastic to everything and everyone connected with education." He also feels that many teachers labeled "burned out" are simply incompetent, unable to deal effectively with the exigencies of the job.

My sense, gleaned from talking with a number of special educators, is that both satisfactions and stresses may be more intense for this group of teachers than for their regular education colleagues. The fact that special educators work with smaller numbers of students over longer periods of time (often working with the same students for two or more years) provides opportunities for them to get to know their students (and their families) especially well, to work individually with them more often, and to follow their progress on a day-to-day basis. The other side of this, though, is that these teachers must constantly deal with student problems that may feel intractable, and that progress with these students (except the gifted) is typically slower and more erratic than in regular education. Many special ed teachers feel a responsibility toward and affinity with their students that seem to transcend the normal teacher-student bond developed in regular classrooms; this sense of responsibility generates strong feelings of intimacy and may motivate increased effort but it may also cause resentments and disappointments that linger beyond the boundaries of the workday. Many special ed teachers who were interviewed likened the special ed classroom to a family, noting the intensity, closeness, hurts, and deeply felt obligations that occur in both situations. Indeed, the analogy of the family can be extended further. When these teachers complained of conditions in their schools, the tone of their remarks suggested that they were especially bitter over the ways that children—*their* children—were hurt by bureaucratic indifference or petty rules.

10

Dealing with Teacher Burnout: Some Solutions and Their Problems

THE PROBLEMS HAVE BEEN DESCRIBED THROUGHOUT THIS BOOK: Teachers of every type are dissatisfied, stressed, worn out, frenetic and overcommitted, underchallenged, and leaving the field. Solutions dealing with these problems can be classified under three headings: broad-based school reform that, in part, aims to increase teacher empowerment and further professionalize the field; individual coping strategies such as relaxation training, time management, and social support; and school-based solutions such as teacher centers and school-based management teams.

This chapter will discuss these approaches, including the limitations of each. Teacher reform, for example, has often led, paradoxically, to a lessening of teacher empowerment; individual coping strategies, although helpful as temporary mediators of stress, fail to address the need for significant structural changes in schools to better meet the needs of teachers; and school-based solutions are often the most difficult to implement and sustain. Finally, it will be noted that many of the suggestions made for dealing with teacher stress and burnout, as well as many of the ideas proposed under the general mantle of reform, have failed to consider the long-term consequences of these changes. I will underscore Sarason's notion that the likelihood of unintentional consequences of these well-intentioned proposals is quite high and that, therefore, the future of the teaching profession, even given the current state of concern and action, is still unknowable.

The Reform Movement

It seems that once again we are in a time in American history when education has become a prominent public issue, a "crisis" that must be addressed promptly, forcefully, and innovatively. This attitude toward public education—that it is inadequate, overbureaucratized, antiquated in theory and practice, and failing its students—is neither new nor unique to this era, but this fact has been overlooked in our frantic attempts to combat the "tide of mediocrity" that is said to characterize our educational system.

The school reform movement of the 1980s began as a means of improving the academic performance of our nation's schoolchildren. The fear was that, as a nation, we were losing our competitive edge in the world and that our economic future was being compromised by the poor achievement of our students. Teachers were important in the early days of reform only as a means of improving student performance. "Almost forgotten is the fact that, when the renewal movement first began, teachers were sharply criticized in several states that quickly introduced teacher tests. There was a clear signal that teachers were the problem, rather than the solution" (Boyer, 1988, p. 10).

Still, as the reform movement picked up steam, the issue of teacher empowerment was increasingly incorporated into policy statements and recommendations. Many teachers became encouraged by the potential for the reform movement to enhance their lives by improving their salaries and working conditions, granting them greater autonomy and decision-making powers, and, in general, further professionalizing the field. Indeed, the changes in the profession that appeared forthcoming as a result of the reform movement seemed to augur a future in which significantly smaller numbers of teachers would leave or become burned out. That these changes have not occurred, that significant numbers of teachers are still demoralized and burned out, offers yet further testimony to the incredible difficulties in altering the fundamental nature of institutions and their policies.

The current reform movement is typically traced back to the publication of *A Nation at Risk* in 1983. Issued by the National Commission on Excellence in Education, this report was the first of many during that decade—at least eighteen, according to Orlich (1989)—to call for fundamental changes in the ways that both students and teachers in this country learn and are evaluated. More than 275 education task forces were organized in the United States (Orlich, 1989) and more than 700 state statutes affecting some aspect of education were enacted (Timar and Kirp, 1989). Actually, despite the tendency to date the beginning of the current reform movement to 1983 and the publication of *A Nation at Risk*, efforts to change the educational system had begun years earlier. School improvement programs at both the state and local levels, focused primarily on elementary education, were widespread in the 1970s and early 1980s. These programs were aimed at improving the instructional skills of teachers, developing new curriculum, enhancing the leadership abilities of school administrators, creating classroom environments consistent with ideas promulgated by the "effective schools" line of research, increasing parental involvement in schools, widening the scope of student competency testing, and tightening up teacher certification procedures.

Nevertheless, the reports of the 1980s were remarkably influential in spurring further and more far-reaching reform efforts and in generating national attention to the needs of this nation's schools. The first wave of popular reforms inspired by *A Nation at Risk* included measures such as strengthening graduation requirements, increasing the amount of student testing, tightening teacher evaluation and certification procedures, raising teachers' salaries, and implementing career ladder or master teacher programs. These changes have been called "top down" inasmuch as they are driven by bureaucratic regulations from above. The second wave of reform focused on the teaching process per se and led to reviews of curriculum and teacher training. For example, the Carnegie Task Force plan for national certification urged policy makers to find ways (other than higher salary) to create a more professional environment for teachers. And, as this book goes to press, a third wave of reform is being discussed in which measures would be aimed at making not incremental changes in the schools but rather changes in the fundamental nature of school structure.

Since 1983, school reform has touched virtually every state. Most have raised high school graduation requirements and many have passed comprehensive educational reform bills mandating higher teacher salaries and more stringent disciplinary codes. School reform even became part of the political agenda in the 1980s. President Reagan, whose administration commissioned *A Nation at Risk,* reportedly did not read the report (Fiske, 1988, p. B10). "But within a few weeks, when polls started showing that the report had struck a responsive chord with American voters, Mr. Reagan turned his attention to the real message of the document and began to make effective political use of the issue of educational reform" (Fiske, 1988, p. B10). The Reagan administration's chief spokesperson for its policy of educational conservatism was the secretary of education, William J. Bennett, who attributed the decline in American school performance to "hedonistic college students, power-hungry teachers, unions, and what he called 'the blob,' the establishment of school administrators" (Hechinger, 1989b, p. B9). Several years later, the issue of school reform played a major role in the presidential election. In accepting the Democratic nomination for the presidency in 1988, Michael Dukakis announced that "we are going to make teaching a valued and honored profession." Not to be outdone, George Bush vowed to become "the education president."

The issue of educational reform may have reached its zenith in 1989, when President Bush convened an "educational summit conference." According to the president, inadequate education was threatening to undermine "the very leadership position of America in the next century" (Fiske, 1989d, p. B10). Only twice before had an American president assumed the prerogative of inviting the governors of all states to discuss an important national issue (Theodore Roosevelt on conservation; Franklin Delano Roosevelt on the Great Depression). At this summit, the president praised the reform movement for its well-articulated criticisms of the schools, noted a continued need to experiment and try new things, and suggested that our schools need fewer rules and bureaucratic regulations. He called for accountability on the part of both teachers and principals, including the articulation of national education goals, but he also stated that "indifference toward good educators" would not be tolerated. "Society," said the president, "has no greater benefactors than outstanding teachers and principals" (quoted in Shanker, 1989, p. E7). Moreover, Bush noted, "our teachers already are giving their heart and soul to their jobs" (Fiske, 1989b, p. B8).

The Reform Reports

Since 1983, there have been dozens of reform reports that have addressed the state of public education in this country. Most suggested sweeping changes in teachers' preparation, certification, evaluation, and remuneration. I will focus on the following nine reports, briefly examining the content of each, the common themes among them, and the putative impact of their recommendations on the lives of teachers:

1. *A Nation at Risk* (1983), issued by the National Commission on Excellence in Education
2. *Action for Excellence: A Comprehensive Plan to Improve Our Nation's Schools* (1983), issued by the National Task Force on Education for Economic Growth
3. *High School* (1983), by Ernest L. Boyer of the Carnegie Foundation for the Advancement of Teaching
4. *Educating Americans for the 21st Century* (1983), issued by the National Science Board Commission on Precollege Education in Mathematics, Science and Technology
5. *A Place Called School* (1984), by John I. Goodlad
6. *Horace's Compromise: The Dilemma of the American High School* (1984), by Theodore R. Sizer
7. *A Nation Prepared: Teachers for the 21st Century* (1986), by the Carnegie Task Force on Teaching as a Profession
8. *Tomorrow's Teachers: A Report of the Holmes Group* (1986)
9. *Turning Points: Preparing American Youth for the 21st Century* (1989), by the Carnegie Corporation of New York

A Nation at Risk was the seminal reform report issued in April of 1983 by the National Commission on Excellence in Education. This short (thirty-five-page) report condemned much of our educational system, stating that "if an unfriendly foreign power had attempted to impose on America the mediocre educational performance that exists today, we might have used it as an act of war" (p. 1). The report was not only hyperbolic in tone but also "pointedly ignored evidence from . . . files that standardized test scores had already been rising for several years" (Fiske, 1988, p. B10). Despite the overblown rhetoric—or more likely because of it—this report "touched enough nerves among Americans to become the most visible symbol of the need to improve primary and high schools since the Russians put Sputnik into space" (Fiske, 1988, p. B10). *A Nation at Risk* asserted that our commitment to quality education is compromised by the "multitude of often conflicting demands we have placed on our Nation's schools and colleges. They are routinely called on to provide solutions to personal, social, and political problems that the home and other institutions either will not or cannot resolve" (p. 6). The implication drawn is that schools must be committed strictly to children's academic needs and that other agencies should address other aspects of students' lives. In this respect, *A Nation at Risk* differed from the later reports of Goodlad, Sizer, and Boyer, all of which called for smaller, more personalized schools able to attend to students' nonacademic needs. For the most part, *A Nation at Risk* called for schools to do more of the same things they had been doing for years: more testing, more homework, more rigorously enforced conduct codes, more hours in a school day, more days in a school year.

Action for Excellence: A Comprehensive Plan to Improve Our Nation's Schools was published in 1983 by the National Task Force on Education for Economic Growth. It focused primarily on the roles that states and business should play in reforming education. This report recommended that each governor develop an action plan for improving education, including the establishment of specific goals for improvement and timetables for achieving these goals. It also recommended the formation of partnerships between schools and the business community. Finally, the report urged drastic improvements in teachers' recruitment, training, and compensation.

High School, by Ernest L. Boyer, president of the Carnegie Foundation for the Advancement of Teaching, was published in 1983. It was based on two years of observation at fifteen different high schools across the country. According to Boyer, high schools "lack a clear and vital mission"; they are institutions "adrift." This report, emphasizing the needs of children rather than the needs of our nation, was quite different in tone from *A Nation at Risk*. Boyer pointed to the central role of language and communication skills in children, including reading, writing, speaking, and listening. His message was to teach students to think critically and communicate effectively. He felt that principals are excessively burdened by administrative duties and given too little authority. He also felt that teachers work under conditions that often preclude effective or sustained teaching; his suggestion was that teachers be freed of nonacademic burdens and have reduced loads to allow more time for class preparation and record-keeping. Teachers, he thought, should have more control over instructional material. Teacher excellence should be rewarded through financial rewards and recognition. Boyer envisioned a career path for teachers that would take them from "associate" to "full" to "senior" teacher. In general, Boyer was sympathetic to teachers: "The working conditions of teaching must improve. Many people think teachers have soft undemanding jobs. The reality is different" (p. 307).

Educating Americans for the 21st Century was another report issued in 1983. This document urged a "national commitment" to educational excellence and called for efforts to provide quality education to all students. According to this report, the federal government should partially finance 2,000 exemplary schools which would serve as catalysts for educational change. The report also suggested better compensation for teachers, especially highly qualified math, science, and technology teachers, whose pay should be comparable to that of professionals in other sectors.

A Place Called School, a study of elementary and secondary public schools in thirty-eight states, was written by John Goodlad and published in 1984. Goodlad believed that many educational problems could be attributed to the common practices of teachers: dealing with classes as a whole; engaging in "either frontal teaching, monitoring students' seat-work, or conducting quizzes"; seldom permitting students to learn from each other or initiate activities; infrequently praising or correcting students; and limiting students to a circumscribed set of activities (listening, writing responses to questions, and taking tests) (pp. 123-125). Goodlad also criticized teachers for conducting classes with a neutral or flat emotional tone, relying too much on lecturing (85 percent of the time!), monopolizing discussions (talking three times as much as all their students combined), and spending too much time on basic skills rather than higher-order thinking. Goodlad's alternative to these anachronistic practices was to identify and use techniques that would effectively address students' need for concrete experience as part of the learning process. He felt that the whole system of teacher preparation should be reexamined so that schools of education and school personnel could work together to examine current practices in order to create better solutions. He also felt that principals should be trained to create positive learning environments in their schools, that teachers should have some authority in the allocation of educational funds, that a career ladder for teachers should be instituted, and that the school year should be lengthened to 200 days. Arguably his most important suggestion, though, was his advice to establish schools-within-schools and to have the same set of teachers accountable for the educational progress of a cohort of students through a cluster of grades.

Theodore Sizer's *Horace's Compromise: The Dilemma of the American High School* was published in 1984. Based upon an analysis of secondary schools, both public and private, this book proposed that the central mission of high schools should be to teach students how to think and that teachers should have the freedom to determine how to teach. According to Sizer, bureaucratic hierarchies—with direction moving from the peak of the pyramid down—get "in the way of children's learning" (p. 206). Power and accountability, he felt, should be based at the individual school rather than at the district level. Like Boyer, Sizer felt that teachers face an impossible task: They necessarily compromise their teaching skills, expectations, and standards because they work for too little money, are expected to cover too much material with too many students, and experience frequent interruptions during class hours. Thus, teachers and students engage in a "conspiracy of the least," seeking an orderliness that is without academic substance. Solutions, according to Sizer, lie in improving conditions of teachers: granting teachers more autonomy, holding them accountable for the mastery exhibited by their students, reducing the number of students for which each teacher is responsible, reducing the amount of curriculum to be covered, varying work responsibilities, decentralizing authority to levels much closer to students, and providing steeper salary schedules and safer places for teachers to work.

A Nation Prepared: Teachers for the 21st Century was published in 1986 as a report of the Carnegie Task Force on Teaching as a Profession. Teachers, this report argued, should be a fully professionalized group—carefully selected, highly trained, subject to high standards of certification, and well paid. The report called for the creation of a National Board for Teaching Standards that would set standards for teacher certification. It suggested that teachers assume more authority but also greater responsibility for student progress. Teachers' salaries should be competitive with those of other professions but also tied to indices of student performance. The report also called for new forms of school management, with some schools to be managed entirely by a new class of highly paid, highly professional "lead" teachers. Schools would also move away from the lecture method as the dominant mode of instruction, instead making greater use of newer forms of instructional technology.

Tomorrow's Teachers: A Report of the Holmes Group (1986) was crafted by many of the same individuals who worked on *A Nation Prepared;* many of the ideas in these two reports, then, are similar. The goals of the Holmes Group included differentiated staffing (with teachers moving from being "instructors" to "professional teachers" to "career professionals"), the establishment of "professional development schools" where young educators can hone their skills, increased minority enrollment in schools of education, the general restructuring of teacher education, the revival of a "science of education" through increased research, and, perhaps most important, the establishment of a network of cooperating universities to implement all of the above.

In 1989, the Carnegie Corporation published another report, *Turning Points: Preparing American Youth for the 21st Century,* in which recommendations were made to radically decrease the size of schools. Similar to Goodlad's idea, schools would be divided into small units or cottages in order to better teach and counsel young adolescents. Each student would have an adult mentor and direct access to a wide range of community services. The focus would be on caring for "the whole child," an approach that goes back to the time of John Dewey.

Stedman and Jordan (1986) pointed out several overlapping themes that these reports have in common: High school reform is imperative given the country's declining competitive position in the international marketplace; students' academic performance is poor and needs improvement; academic standards, especially requirements for high school graduation, need strengthening; teachers' working conditions, including salary benefits, need to be upgraded; teachers and administrators should be granted more prerogatives and authority at the individual school level; and schools are unnecessarily isolated from other agencies and institutions, including business establishments, within the community.

Many of the reports explicitly noted such day-to-day stressors of teachers as performing nonacademic duties (including monitoring halls and cafeterias), having class lessons interrupted frequently by nonessential announcements or visits, and being responsible for too many classes with too many students. Many of the reports proposed that teachers should undergo more training, be certified under more rigorous standards, be better compensated for their work, be supported to a greater extent by aides and volunteers in their classrooms, and be granted greater decision-making powers and autonomy. These reports acknowledged what teachers have long known—that "despite the critical role they play in educating youth, [they] are given little responsibility in the educational process and few of the privileges associated with a profession" (Stedman and Jordan, 1986, p. 21). Teachers have often complained that everyone else in the educational community—parents, administrators, the school board, often even students—seems to have more of a say in determining school policy than they. Many of the reform reports recognized this fact—that powerlessness, the inability to influence or change those factors that cause stress, is in itself a major cause of stress.

School Reform: Problems and Limitations

Several criticisms of these reports can be leveled. First, and most significantly, the effect of these reform reports has been minimal. Reform has worked to some extent—more students in some states (California, for example) are taking math and science courses, SAT scores have improved somewhat in many districts, teachers' salaries have risen, and teacher participation in setting school goals and shaping curriculum has increased. On the other hand, teacher career ladder plans have often been met with hostility (New Jersey, for example, abandoned its master teacher plan when teachers refused to participate), dropout rates have increased in some states as educational standards have been raised (Florida, for example), and reform efforts have dissipated in some districts as money has become scarce or as education-minded politicians have left office. Moreover, many of the changes wrought by reform have been purely cosmetic, with no significant impact on instructional strategies or school organization (Orlich, 1989, p. 513). In general, students are still going to the same classes with the same friends in the same school, being taught by the same teachers in the same manner. As Stedman and Jordan (1986) noted, "The likelihood is great that a casual observer would see little difference in the daily operation of a pre-reform and a post-reform school" (p. 52). Similarly, John Goodlad noted as early as 1984 that reform was failing to produce changes at the most critical level: the individual classroom. Perhaps this was to be expected. Educational reform has a long history and, for the most part, this history is greatly suggestive of the French proverb, "the more things change the more they remain the same." It should be no surprise, then, if teachers are as stressed or as burned out now as they were before reform began to take shape.

A second criticism is that teachers have typically not been involved in the planning or implementation of reforms. "Reforms typically have focused on graduation requirements, student achievement, teacher preparation and testing, and monitoring activities. But in all these matters, as important as they are, teachers have been largely uninvolved" (Boyer, 1988, p. 11). A 1985 Harris Poll (Harris and Associates, 1985) found that 63 percent of teachers surveyed felt that reforms had been implemented without their input. No teachers were invited to Bush's educational summit. Furthermore, although most of the later reports suggested that educational decision making be brought down closer to the level of the individual student and teacher, most of the actual changes in school policies to this point have come as a result of state directives. States are increasing their share of power by asserting their prerogative over local school districts (Stedman and Jordan, 1986, p. 49). Again, we see a repeat of history here, for the reforms proposed in the sixties and seventies also were initiated by outside sources without teacher input.

Third, many of these reports—specifically the political ones issued by the commissions and corporations—overemphasized student testing. In an attempt to build in accountability, these reports proposed schools that are rigid and test-oriented. Critical thinking on the part of students has been deemphasized; instead, students and teachers are held to specified, standardized objectives. Backed by state and local legislation, educational bureaucrats have, in many districts, mandated testing regimens within specific areas. Since schools and teachers are evaluated on the degree to which they meet these testing standards, teachers are pressured to create a homogenized, simplified curriculum that can be readily regurgitated by their students. Thus, reform-driven schools sometimes end up looking very much like prereform schools—only with the addition of more quizzes, more in-seat work, more drills, and often more student dropouts. In addition, accountability assumes that teaching and learning can be conceptualized in terms of inputs and outputs and that a teacher's performance can be measured in terms of productivity—assumptions that teachers disagree with (Cohn, Kottcamp, McCloskey, & Provenzo, 1987). Furthermore, the emphasis on accountability, according to teachers, is making teaching a more problematic and less attractive profession: "Teachers told us in a loud and single voice that the current attempt to improve instruction through greater regulation and accountability is impeding instruction rather than improving it, and at the same time, is making the profession less 'professional' and therefore less desirable to bright and creative thinkers who need autonomy and time to do their best work" (Cohn, Kottcamp, McCloskey, and Provenzo, 1987, p. 52).

Fourth, there is little reason to believe that school reform is having or will have any impact on minority and disadvantaged students—those who should be benefiting most from change. In fact, the emphasis on testing may well increase the alienation of these students and exacerbate the mismatch between their needs and what schools can provide. The reform movement, said Terrel Bell, who as secretary of education commissioned *A Nation at Risk,* has benefited about 70 percent of students but has had no significant impact on the other 30 percent, primarily those who are low-income minority students (Reinhold, 1987). Similarly, Albert Shanker asserted that school improvements have only touched those "who are able to learn in the traditional manner—sitting still, listening to teachers talk and learning from books" (Fiske, 1988, p. B10).

Fifth, suggestions made to improve teachers' salaries, as well as to improve the attractiveness of the profession, have often focused on merit pay, master teacher, and career ladder programs. The problem with these programs is that they benefit only a small minority of teachers. Moreover, most teachers are greatly opposed to these ideas, especially merit pay. In 1989, 61 percent of teachers polled by Gallup opposed the idea of merit pay (Elam, 1989). Most argued that it is too difficult to obtain fair evaluations of teaching performance and that those who are most likely to receive such evaluations are those who either "grandstand" or become personal favorites of principals or other evaluators. In addition, many teachers felt that merit pay causes morale difficulties and competitiveness among a professional staff.

Sixth, recommendations for changes in teacher training and licensure proposed by *A Nation Prepared* and also by *Tomorrow's Teacher: A Report of the Holmes Group* (both 1986) might well have the unintended consequence of further reducing the number of individuals from minority groups in the teaching force. Despite the fact that both these reports suggested preparing more minority teachers, a six- or seven-year program of higher education leading to a teaching certificate would cost new teachers one or two years' worth of lost wages as well as a year's worth of extra tuition. More stringent standards for licensing teachers might well discourage those minority college students who score poorly on standardized tests. "Implementing the proposal of these two groups would have the same undesirable effect: reducing the number of minority teachers from few to virtually none" (Orlich, 1989, p. 514).

Seventh, cooperative partnerships between schools and business—a prime aspect of later reports—is of limited value, especially in rural settings, which typically do not have local businesses with the interest or resources needed to support major cooperative ventures (Stedman and Jordan, 1986). And although in urban areas these partnerships seem to have some promise, there is also an understandable concern that, as time goes on, businesses may want more of a say in their investment and more evidence of results. Teachers are sure to be the losers if this occurs. In addition, to the extent that reform is driven by private sector corporate interests, positive outcome of reform measures may come to be conceptualized in terms of effective, mechanistic preparation for the work world rather than in the broader, more humanistic terms that teachers generally articulate.

Eighth, it is unlikely that efforts to grant teachers greater autonomy and decision-making powers will proceed without a good deal of confusion and strife. Allowing teachers more control over their environment means less power for administrators and school board members, a course both groups have opposed and will continue to oppose. As Hechinger (1988) stated, "sharing power and responsibility with teachers alarms many principals. Letting individual schools run their own affairs threatens the state education authorities and schoolboards. . . . Urban boards of education still will not give principals the money and authority to order their own supplies" (p. B7). In addition, neither teachers nor principals have been trained to think about the interpersonal or professional implications of new forms of school management or power sharing. It would hardly be surprising, therefore, if, in gaining more control over their jobs, teachers lose some degree of cooperation and support from administrators.

Ninth, the reform movement has, for the most part, neglected the most essential aspect of teaching: the classroom relationship between student and teacher. As James Comer, a psychiatrist who leads a highly touted intervention program in two inner-city schools in New Haven, noted: "All of the education-reform talk and reports of the last few years ignore child-development and relationship issues. And yet when schoolteachers and administrators are asked what is wrong, they say, 'a lack of respect, discipline, motivation'—all relationship issues" (1988, p. 29). Actually, Comer is not exactly right, for Sizer, Goodlad, and Boyer all called for smaller classes and smaller schools in which students and teachers might better relate to each other. Still, reform has not especially focused on all those classroom problems—discipline included—that often interfere with learning as well as teacher satisfaction. As Fiske (1986) asserted, "Sooner or later, the door closes on the classroom and it is individual teachers and students, not business leaders or governors or state legislators, who determine whether learning will occur or not" (p. C7).

Last, the reform movement may ultimately backfire on teachers. Once teachers are given higher pay and more autonomy, the public may well have unrealistic assumptions about the magnitude or timing of "results." "In one of the more exciting social experiments of the year, Rochester [New York] decided to pay as if urban teaching were an important job—up to $70,000 a year. But already there is uneasiness. Adam Urbanski, union president, says wherever he goes, people say, 'it's four months. Has the dropout rate gone down yet?' " (Sarason, quoted in Shanker, 1988, p. E9). Related to this is the "wall chart" approach begun by Terrel Bell, President Reagan's first education secretary, and continued by President Bush's first secretary of education, Lauro F. Cavazos. This chart lists the fifty states and the District of Columbia and provides statistics on what each is doing in terms of graduation rates, SAT scores, achievement scores, pupil expenditures, and the like. In 1989, Cavazos's conclusion was that American education was stagnant. "We are standing still," he announced, "and the problem is that it has been this way for three years in a row. We cannot be satisfied with mediocrity and so it's time to turn things around" (Johnson, 1989, p. A1). As Sarason wisely observed, "Few things are as effective as the combination of virtuous intent and missionary zeal in producing an unrealistic time perspective" (Sarason, quoted in Shanker, 1988, p. E9). The obvious implication is that in the next few years the public's patience may wear out, leaving teachers more isolated and condemned than ever.

In short, the changes proposed by many of these reports were born of good intentions, often in the hopes of increasing the professional and financial status of teachers. But many problems clearly remain in both the conceptualization and implementation of the reform suggestions. What needs to be noted too is the stressful nature of all change, regardless of directionality; the strong likelihood of unintended consequences of even well-intentioned changes; and the strong possibility that at least some of the changes will be short-lived, dissipating over time either as money runs out and the nation refocuses its priorities elsewhere, or as the educational bureaucracy gradually incorporates changes within its structure without truly yielding power.

Teachers' Views of Reform

How do teachers feel about school reform? According to the 1989 Gallup Poll, "Most teachers are not convinced that schools in their communities have improved over the last five years, a period of much talk about and considerable action directed toward reform" (Elam, 1989, p. 797). Thirty-six percent of teachers felt schools had improved, 25 percent felt they had gotten worse, and 38 percent felt they had stayed the same. Consistent with these figures, of the 13,500 teachers surveyed by the Carnegie Foundation for the Advancement of Teaching (Boyer, 1988), the vast majority, specifically 69 percent, graded school reform a *C* or less. Only 2 percent gave the reform movement an *A*. But the most disappointing finding of this report, at least in regard to the impact of the reform movement on teacher stress and burnout, was that nearly half of the teachers surveyed— 49 percent—felt that, overall, morale within the profession had substantially *declined* since 1983.

On the positive side, more than three-fourths (76 percent) of those in the Carnegie Foundation survey said that goals at their school were more clearly defined than five years ago, almost three-fourths (74 percent) reported that academic expectations for students had gone up, more than one-half (56 percent) thought more highly of the leadership role of their principal, and more than one-half (59 percent) felt that teacher salaries had improved since 1983.

On the negative side, by a 38–34 percent margin, more teachers felt that the fiscal resources now available to schools were worse rather than better, more (31–21 percent) felt that freedom from nonteaching duties had gotten worse, and a larger proportion (27– 25 percent) felt that community respect for them had gotten worse since 1983 (Boyer, 1988). A majority (59 percent) felt that political interference in education had increased as a result of school reform, and a majority (52 percent) also felt that paperwork had increased.

Boyer's sense of the reform movement was that "while new regulations have been imposed on schools, the heart of the enterprise—the teachers—has been largely overlooked" (p. 9). My conclusion is essentially the same. The reform movement, which seemed at its inception to offer the possibility of a strikingly different experience for teachers—one that might enhance autonomy, status, and self-respect and, in turn, mitigate the impact of stress—has, to this point, led to small improvements for some students and seemingly no significant improvements for the majority of teachers. As Boyer concluded, "Many teachers have remained dispirited, confronted with working conditions that have left them more responsible, but less empowered" (p. 11).

Teachers, especially those in urban classrooms, remain vulnerable to stress and burnout as a result of the conditions of their work—conditions that the reform movement has barely affected. Some of the most salient factors affecting teachers' work experience, notably those relating to classroom discipline and parental attitudes, cannot be changed by legislative or district mandate (Cohn, Kottcamp, McCloskey, and Provenzo, 1987, p. 52). As Maeroff (1988b) observed, "The situation that currently exists for many teachers, especially in problem-plagued urban school districts, produces not empowerment, but impotence" (p. 474). Reforms are well intentioned, especially as they aim to increase teachers' professionalism and autonomy. To date, though, the reform movement has not empowered teachers; nor has it been the solution to the problems of teacher stress and burnout.

Solutions to Stress and Burnout at the Individual and School Levels

A number of approaches to treating stress and burnout in human service professionals have been suggested in the literature, with specific recommendations varying most often as a function of the training and orientation of the writer. Thus, for example, those trained in a psychotherapeutic model have proposed individual or group psychotherapy for burned-out professionals. Freudenberger

(1982) has had success with a short-term, goal-limited approach, and Edelwich and Brodsky (1980) have touted the use of "reality therapy" (Glasser, 1975), in which individuals learn to develop realistic expectations for their work and enlist the support of others. Those trained in stress management techniques often suggest relaxation training, meditation, or time-management strategies to help individuals cope with work. Organizational and social psychologists emphasize the need for structural changes in the work setting: reducing client-staff ratios, shortening work hours, sensitizing administrators to the problems and stressors of staff, developing group support, allowing staff members more flexibility and autonomy, and improving pre- and in-service training programs. And community psychologists have often argued for a primary preventive approach to burnout, stressing the need for a "psychological sense of community" in which workers' needs for collaboration, support, and camaraderie are fulfilled on a daily basis. According to this viewpoint, work settings should be organized to meet the needs not only of clients but of workers as well. A psychological sense of community, it is argued, can mitigate workers' feelings of isolation and inconsequentiality and thus improve morale and productivity (Farber and Miller, 1981; Sarason, 1977).

First-Order Change Strategies. Most of the suggestions in educational journals are aimed at helping individual teachers better cope with stress. However, Pearlin and Schooler (1978), in a now classic article, found that individual coping efforts were generally ineffective in reducing work-related distress. None of the four strategies they studied—obtaining satisfaction from sources other than work, comparing one's job situation with others, attempting to change noxious aspects of work, and focusing on positive aspects of the work situation—significantly helped their heterogeneous sample of workers. Their conclusion was that most work environments are impersonally organized and hence impervious to individual coping efforts. On the other hand, Schonfeld (in press) found that some individual coping strategies were helpful for teachers. Specifically, he showed that teachers who attempted to modify aversive work conditions (for example, by trying new strategies to help students), who sought advice, and who positively compared their work with that in other fields had lower stress and higher morale than their colleagues. Schonfeld suggested that schools may be less impersonally organized than many other work settings and thus more amenable to the effects of individual coping strategies.

The most common individually oriented approaches include activities that fall within the category of stress-reduction techniques: meditation, relaxation training, jogging, swimming, and other forms of physical exercise. At least one study (Forman, 1983) focused on the effect of aerobic dancing as a means to reduce teacher stress. Other researchers (for example, Sparks, 1983) suggested that teachers change their diets and eat more healthily. Another popular approach is the use of time-management techniques: organizing and budgeting time, prioritizing goals, limiting objectives, establishing a realistic schedule for accomplishments, and setting aside at least a few moments for oneself each day. Numerous outside activities have also been offered as palliative remedies; for example, sports, hobbies, treating oneself to dinner or new clothes, or taking courses (in anything) just for the sake of learning something new. Hendrickson (1979) suggested that teachers take "mental health days"—and not feel guilty about them. For some teachers, it is important to find activities that demand participation rather than leadership; for others, it is simply important to find sources of relaxation outside of work. The common assumption here is that, with the use of appropriate techniques, work-related stress can be reduced to tolerable levels.

Another way of managing stress is through the use of certain cognitive restructuring strategies, consisting of psychological modifications of attitudes and orientations toward stressors. For example, teachers can learn to avoid certain types of cognitions, among them such self-defeating statements as "I must be perfect," "I must always try hard and be strong," "I mustn't say 'no' to people," and "I must love all my students equally and be equally effective with each." Teachers can also be taught (and it can be quite helpful) to engage in self-praising statements during the day ("I'm doing well"; "at least some of my students are learning quite a bit"; "that lesson was pretty successful"). Teachers can also learn to set realistic and flexible classroom goals (Moe, 1979) as well as praise themselves for partial successes. As many of the early researchers in the field of burnout noted (Freudenberger, for example), the tendency to regard oneself as a failure unless one is solving all problems of all those one is responsible for is a sure pathway to burnout. Teachers, as Sparks (1983) noted, need to develop a "balanced perspective." Some may profit from keeping a journal in which they record their successes as well as failures. Finally, Hendrickson (1979) recommended that teachers keep in mind their ideological reasons for deciding to teach, and McCarty (1979) suggested that teachers remember that much of the behavior that impedes their teaching is not aimed at them personally. The data of both Schonfeld (in press) and Forman (1982) bear out the value of cognitive restructuring as an effective coping device for teachers. (On the other hand, at least one study [Connolly and Sanders, 1988] found that "positive reappraisal" produced stronger feelings of depersonalization and lesser feelings of personal accomplishment in teachers. Clearly, more outcome research needs to be done in this area.)

What if a teacher's work-related stress cannot be reduced to tolerable levels through adopting any of these strategies? One view, in fact the most common one, is that these teachers should be counseled to leave the field. This strategy assumes that it serves no one's interest to have stressed or burned-out teachers continue on the job. A variant of this point of view is that teachers who are overly stressed should give less of themselves to the classroom, because psychological withdrawal places stressors at a safer distance. But the question of whether one commits more or less to the work if one feels stressed is not such a simple one. Committing less to teaching has a spiraling-down effect, with less carefully planned lessons and less concern for students inevitably leading to less return. Although distancing as a coping strategy may enable a teacher to continue functioning, he or she is operating minimally, is receiving little gratification from the job, and is at greater risk for burnout (Blase, 1982; Hanchey, 1987; Holt, Fine, and Tollefson, 1987; Schoenig, 1986). Thus, Cherniss and Krantz (1983) recommended the opposite strategy. Their suggestion is that teachers, or other burned-out professionals, recommit themselves to the job, that they find a belief or ideology that will sustain them in moments of crisis. Missionary workers, they noted, tend not to burn out because of their belief in what they are doing. The metaphor is of a burning-out fire to which one needs to add new fuel in order to keep it going. For Cherniss and Krantz, commitment to an ideology or belief is the best antidote to burnout.

A more common variant of the ideological community is the notion of social support. This concept was defined by Cobb (1976) as information leading the individual to believe he or she is cared for, loved, esteemed, and valued and "belongs to a network of communication and mutual obligation" (p. 300). Individuals with an effective social support system can marshal these resources to deal with stressful situations and dysphoric feelings. Support groups can be formal or informal, and members can be drawn solely from the work environment or from a combination of work, social, and home environments. Groups may or may not elect to have a leader; some rotate this responsibility. More formal support groups meet regularly to share information, provide emotional support, and offer encouragement and advice to members. In Chicago, public school teachers were trained to act as consultants to support groups geared to the amelioration of teachers' stress (Walley and Stokes, 1981). In a suburban section of New York, a "teacher-directed peer coaching project" was begun that includes many features of a social support group but emphasizes the aspect of professional growth. As described by Anastos and Ancowitz (1987), this project involves ten experienced teachers analyzing and critiquing one another's videotaped lesson plans. "Many participants perceived the program as an anti-burnout instrument and said that they enjoyed being in charge of the observation process, a feeling they had not experienced during routine administrative evaluations" (p. 42).

Pines and Aronson (1981) hypothesized that social support encompasses six functions: listening, professional support, professional challenge, emotional support, emotional challenge, and the sharing of social reality. They found that professional workers rated "listening" (having someone who will actively listen without giving advice or making judgments) and "emotional support" (having someone who is on our side and who appreciates what we are doing) as the most important of these social support functions. Pines (1983) found that in a heterogeneous group of professional workers, scores on the MBI correlated negatively with the availability of each of these functions, suggesting that people who have social support readily available are less likely to experience burnout. She also found that in a group of elementary school teachers, burnout was most strongly correlated (in a negative direction) with the availability of technical challenge and with the availability of technical support.

Other studies yielded similar results. Russell, Altmaier, and Van Velzen (1987) found that three aspects of lack of social support were predictive of burnout in teachers: support from their supervisor, reassurance of their worth, and "reliable alliance" (the availability of people to turn to in an emergency). Cherniss (1987) found that one of the factors that promoted positive adaptation to professional work (and decreased the likelihood of burnout) was the continued availability of intellectual stimulation, challenge, and creativity. These factors did not diminish over time they were as important for professionals twelve years into their work as they were when they first began their jobs. Schwab, Jackson, and Schuler (1984) found that higher levels of social support from teachers' colleagues were associated with lower levels of burnout, and Bridges and Hallinan (1978) found that a teacher's perception of group cohesiveness was negatively related to high absenteeism. Absenteeism was lowest in smaller schools where there was a great deal of contact among a small teaching staff, but even in larger schools, teachers who felt they played an important role in the functioning of the school were less likely to be absent. Taken together, these findings once again suggest that teaching is an isolated, lonely profession and that burnout is all too possible for those teachers who do not have available to them either colleagues or administrative supervisors who provide a gentle but supportive push toward professional growth. These findings also confirm the assumption that one subtype of burnout involves individuals who are not sufficiently challenged by their work.

In an earlier study (Farber, 1984a), I found that, in general, teachers experience rewarding contact with colleagues but not a psychological sense of community—that is, they do not feel as if others around them (parents, administrators, students) share common goals and values with them. In response, perhaps, to the perceived insensitivity and criticism of administrators and the general public, teachers have retreated and isolated themselves somewhat.

Satisfactions occur on a micro, rather than macro, level; the school and the community are not sources of satisfaction, whereas selected students and colleagues are.

From an intervention perspective, the findings of these studies suggest that social support is an effective buffer against stress and burnout and that teachers would do well to cultivate relationships—in and out of the workplace—that provide a feeling of well-being. Russell, Altmaier, and Van Velzen (1987) suggested that "supervisory personnel should be the focus of programs designed to increase the social supports available to teachers" (p. 272). They recommended that administrators be sensitized to teachers' needs for acknowledgment and support of their skills and abilities.

A number of other educators (Calabrese, 1987; Gillet, 1987; Reed, 1979; Schlansker, 1987) agreed that school administrators, particularly principals, are an essential component in alleviating stress and preventing burnout in teachers. Although not writing from a social support perspective, these writers nevertheless suggested that principals should do a number of things to foster in teachers a sense of "being taken care of." These include:

- Involving teachers in decision making
- Becoming more visible around the school
- Increasing both written and oral communication to teachers
- Providing recognition for good effort and support for what is currently working
- Encouraging faculty to try new things
- Providing clear guidelines for policy, especially disciplinary policy
- Following up on requests with action, feedback, and more action
- Protecting teachers from impossible demands from parents, politicians, or the school board
- Developing a teacher assistance team
- Encouraging additional in-service courses
- Offering teachers changes in their routines (teaching a different grade or area; team teaching)
- Encouraging the development of in-house resource centers
- Making school athletic facilities available

- Building more links between the home and school
- Offering release time for the development of innovative projects

Despite the consequences of stress and burnout for both educators and their students, there is a dearth of programs in education that address these problems. Compare the situation in public schools to that in industry, where many stress programs exist and successes abound. Many corporations have built fitness centers for their employees, including tracks, gymnasiums, and pools. Some have trained staff on hand to develop fitness programs for groups or individual employees; others have instituted employee assistance programs. It must be remembered too that the facilities built by many corporations have no intrinsic business value but are seen as a cost-effective means to increase employee productivity and morale and decrease absenteeism and sickness. On the other hand, not only do school districts routinely fail to develop programs for their employees but some actively discourage use of their facilities. It is indeed ironic that institutions like schools and hospitals that profess to nurture individuals often provide no services for employees or their children.

Perhaps the most frequently chosen institutional response to the problems of teacher stress and burnout is "the workshop." Typically, outside consultants are hired to speak either on a one-time basis at a "Superintendent's Day Conference" or for a series of after-school workshops. (It may make a great deal of difference in terms of both process and outcome if the consultant is hired by the union local, some other representative group of teachers, or the school or district administration. In the latter case, teachers often feel as if they are being manipulated—that the consultant has been hired to "fix" teachers to work better.)

Most often, stress workshops focus on the development of self-awareness (identifying stressors and acknowledging individual reactions) and the establishment of a stress management plan (including elements of meditation, attitude modification, and physical exercise). The workshops that I have conducted have included exercises that force individuals to think about the structure and organizational regularities of their particular school Questions I typically ask of workshop participants, both teachers and administrators, include:

1. In what ways does your school successfully meet the needs of teachers and other educational personnel?
2. In what ways does your school fail to meet the needs of teachers and other educational personnel?
3. How could your school best be designed to meet the needs of teachers?
4. Where along the following continuum would you place yourself: on one side, working in a self-contained vacuum, or on the other side, working as a member of a community effort with a commonly defined system of goals and values?
5. Does your school work on a crisis-oriented model or does it feature continuous helpful input among its members?
6. What is the role of supportive services in your school?
7. What opportunities are there for teachers to share and contribute expertise and advice with each other?
8. What opportunities are there for teacher input into decision making (for example, curriculum, textbooks, school policy)?
9. Who in your school is most likely to recognize when a teacher is suffering from stress or burnout?
10. Once a teacher has been informally identified as suffering from burnout-related problems, what is the typical response of your school? Ideally, what would you like it to be?

After sharing ideas and experiences and enumerating typical stressor and their consequences, I offer an overview of common stress-reduction techniques (for example, time management, use of support groups, focusing on the positive) and ask the group to brainstorm other potential remedies. Sometimes, too, I use role-playing techniques—that is, I ask teachers to conceptualize burnout, as well as formulate solutions to this problem, from the perspectives of administrators, school board members, parents, students, and their own colleagues in different schools.

Leaders warn participants that a workshop is not a panacea, that solutions at the individual level tend to go the way of diets (quick initial success but low probability of lasting impact), and that solutions at the school level rarely reach the implementation stage. Unless there is an ongoing commitment to modifying structures and procedures that contribute to staff stress—an unlikely event, in my experience—the benefits of stress workshops tend to be ephemeral. Perhaps the greatest benefit of a workshop—other than the temporary "workshop high" that is often experienced—is the opportunity it provides for teachers to realize that they are not alone in their feelings. This realization can lead to a greater sense of collegiality among teachers in a given school or district and may reduce teachers' sense of isolation.

Many of the solutions, then, to teacher stress and burnout fall under the rubric of either stress-reduction techniques or group support, both of which are likely to enable teachers to better withstand the negative consequences of stress. For example, teachers often feel gratified by the opportunity to share their work experiences in a supportive workshop atmosphere. However, these measures fall within the category of "first-order change" (Watzlawick, Weakland, and Fisch, 1974). That is, they tune up malfunctioning parts but do not alter the nature of the malfunctioning system. In fact, these changes often serve to perpetuate misconceptions regarding the origins and dimensions of the problem. These solutions may provide teachers with a quick fix of social support or teach them how to cope better with stress, but rarely do they provide guidelines for altering the sources of stress, especially those that emanate from a school environment that pays little attention to the needs of teachers. Even when such first-order change strategies fail—in this case, when teachers begin to perceive one-day workshops as essentially unhelpful—they are likely to be continued. The nature of social science problem solving is such that failure most often leads to increased use of the same or similar strategies (Watzlawick, Weakland, and Fisch, 1974).

There are several other reasons why these solutions are not likely to have any long-term impact on the incidence of teacher burnout. For example, it has long been the experience of most workshop leaders that those who attend sessions are often those who need help the least and that the most burned-out teachers are those who are first out the door at three o'clock, who want no part of anything additional associated with the school. In addition, these solutions often fail to take into account individual differences among teachers and settings, assuming homogeneity in regard to such variables as size of school and availability of administrative support. In essence, many workshops are geared to treating a label ("burnout") and not a specific set of symptoms that are necessarily embedded in a social-historical-political context. Still another limitation of typical attempts to treat teacher burnout is that they generally pay insufficient attention to how administrators, parents, the school board, and the union local affect the work experience of teachers. Focusing efforts on reducing stress within the classroom or even on creating collegial bonds with other teachers ignores the potentially vital role of parents and others in mitigating stresses for teachers. Finally, most current efforts to reduce teacher burnout focus primarily on treatment of teachers who are already affected. They have not emphasized strategies for preventing burnout, for example, by more adequately preparing teachers-in-training for dealing not only with students but with administrators and parents or by restructuring schools to meet the needs of teachers (see Sarason, 1982).

Teacher centers are often of more enduring value than workshops in reducing stress. Although the exact nature of these centers varies from locale to locale, they are generally "creative, stimulating places where a rich exchange of material and ideas can occur" (Lieberman and Miller, 1979, p. 189). Teacher centers may operate in individual schools, serving the staff of those schools, or in school districts, serving the entire district staff. Their purpose is to provide teachers with a place where they can meet to discuss common problems, pool resources, acquire new skills, and provide peer support. The Bay Shore Teacher Center in Long Island (New York) is one of the more successful of such establishments. Under the directorship of William Fibkins, this center was established in 1971 to combat teachers' feelings of isolation from the world outside the school and from each other. Lectures and workshops, many given by teachers within the school district, regularly take place in the center—a room adjoining the cafeteria of the junior high school—where teachers gather for lunch or on breaks.

Fibkins's (1983) sense of the process by which a teacher center becomes established has been well thought out and acknowledges the need to fully understand the history and needs of the multiple constituencies involved in any school district. Stage 1, says Fibkins, involves understanding the history of the setting: learning how this school within this district was started, who the leaders have been, how the community has perceived the school, how and when feelings of burnout among the staff began, and in what ways this school has served the needs of both students and faculty. "A close examination of what went wrong for staff should begin with what went right" (Fibkins, 1983, p. 181). Stage 2 involves identifying appropriate facilitators for staff development. "It is essential that a project have facilitators who have credibility with staff and who can translate the renewal needs of staff into a program" (p. 182). Stage 3 is one of assessment: making an inventory of current needs, of existing resources, of possible impediments, and of staff resistances. In doing this assessment, Fibkins concluded that all members of the staff should be encouraged to participate in the teacher center, including administrators, secretaries, and custodians. Fibkins emphasized that a crucial aspect of this third stage is the recognition that the development of a program takes time. "The building of trust and avenues for staff affirmation is not a task that can be accomplished in a month or a year in most settings. . . . It took us two years of missionary work to find and decorate a center, develop a weekly series of workshops based on staff needs, encourage, cajole, and manipulate fellow staff members to lead workshops, and most difficult of all, encourage staff to give up old habits and grievances so that they would participate in these sessions" (p. 183).

Stage 4 in this process was the creation and modification of actual programs. When in place, sessions and workshops were offered that "helped participants practice their reactions to a variety of conflict situations, talk openly about their plans for retirement and career alternatives, learn how to care for themselves with better nutrition and exercise, and seek affirmation for their projects" (p. 184). Stage 5 was one of professional outreach—of helping other teacher centers become established, and of inviting teachers from other schools to give workshops at the Bay Shore Center. The final stage, stage 6, was community outreach: "Those engaged in trying to reduce teacher burnout must be prepared to reach out to other professionals in medicine, police work, clergy, social service, and academia, whose resources and talents are hidden behind parochial institutional structures" (p. 185). Fibkins's vision was of a mutually beneficial system in which teachers, children, parents, senior citizens, and other members of the community banded together to combat common problems as well as to solve problems unique to each group.

Fibkins's vision is an exciting one. Nevertheless, two caveats are in order: First, as in many other settings, as the enthusiasm or energy of the original director (or group) begins to flag, teacher centers may quickly lose their sense of purpose or become weighted down by the divisiveness of competing interests; second—and this is true, as mentioned earlier, of workshops as well—those who tend to use the resources of the teacher center are often those who need them the least.

Second-Order Change Strategies. A second-order change strategy is one that reconceptualizes a problem in a different manner and modifies essential components of a system's functioning (Watzlawick, Weakland, and Fisch, 1974). In the case of teacher burnout, the reconceptualization and modification might well follow from the thought that schools should be places where the needs of the helpers (the teachers) are as important as those of the helpees (the students). An effective and enduring solution to teacher burnout probably requires such second-order change strategies.

How can schools be restructured to meet the needs of teachers? There are a multitude of possibilities and combinations, but the focus here will be on just three. One strategy is to augment the opportunities for teachers to work with students in more intensive, more personalized ways, thereby increasing the likelihood of their experiencing more of the intrinsic rewards of the teaching process per se. A second strategy is to provide opportunities for teachers to exercise true autonomy within a school system by, for example, establishing a teacher-led school-management team. And a third strategy, somewhat akin to Fibkins's vision, is to organize a school around the principles of a psychological sense of community.

An example of the first approach was provided by Wechsler (1983). He examined a high school that contained two separate working environments, one a fairly typical academic school, the other a vocational subsystem. A survey found that although teachers in both the academic and vocational departments were alienated from their students to a similar degree, vocational teachers were significantly more committed to teaching and significantly less burned out. And although vocational teachers failed just as many students and complained as vociferously as the academic teachers about working conditions, they were more content with their work.

Vocational teachers were recruited as craftspeople, hired off the job, and then sent to college to earn education credits. They taught block-programmed courses, usually one three-period class to tenth graders and above and one two-period class to ninth graders. No more than twenty-eight students were allowed in any class, corresponding to the number of work stations in any room. The rooms were large, well lighted, and well equipped. Students passed a course by submitting a prescribed number of projects.

Classroom interaction was different from normal academic practices. The teacher, after a brief formal presentation, spent most of the class time walking through the room, supervising students, who usually worked on their own. The teacher watched a particular procedure and made suggestions. There was almost no confrontation and very little public criticism of students. Most of the teachers, when questioned, agreed that they gained a good deal of satisfaction from these personal interactions with students.

Similar procedures might work with academic teachers as well. If English teachers, for example, could spend more time with their students, perhaps two or three periods a day, more intense interactions could take place. In fact, recently the Coalition for Essential Schools experimented with such flexible scheduling. Linda Chion-Kenney (1987) reported that teachers at several of the coalition's schools restructured the school day so that fewer students were taught for longer periods of time. As part of the plan, some teachers also taught outside their specialty area; English teachers, for example, taught both English and social studies.

There are several advantages to these changes. Teachers are able to better understand how each student learns and able to intervene earlier when a student is having a problem. They are able to schedule more activities of different sorts in longer periods. They are better able to work with a number of small groups. And teaching across normal subject lines allows educators to be more creative in their approach to the curriculum material. For example, teaching the development of the English ruling dynasties can be made clearer by having students read Shakespeare. Transference of learning is enhanced when the scope of presentation is expanded. In addition, the few teachers who see each student are able to discuss problems and strategies with each other. Most important, though, teachers who are given the opportunity to work more closely with fewer students will likely report a greater satisfaction from their work.

The Dade County school system (Florida) provides an example of a change strategy that involved restructuring schools to grant teachers more autonomy. In 1987, teachers agreed to waivers in their contracts to allow them the power to change schedules, curricula, and working conditions. The experiment was designed as a way to promote change without extra expenditures. Experimental changes included having peers instead of principals evaluate teaching, giving up free class periods in exchange for smaller classes, and eliminating supervisory positions and using the money saved to pay for after-school programs, supplies, and teacher aides. (In some schools, teachers have thus been paid extra money to help develop curriculum and aid in staff development.) These changes seem prudent but, as pointed out earlier, reform-driven changes are subject to the vagaries of numerous constituencies. In this regard, too, it is not at all certain that significant and enduring changes in school structure will be made even when teachers are making the decisions. In addition, the long-term effects of these changes on all members of the school community, including teachers, have yet to be determined. For example, the costs to individual teachers who sit on governing boards are enormous in terms of time and energy.

Another example of a reform that has allowed teachers a greater than usual degree of autonomy is the "school choice" program that has been operating since the mid-1970s in Community District 4 in East Harlem, New York. To provide choices for parents of elementary and junior high school students, teachers themselves were encouraged to create alternative schools. The district now features fifty-two schools (in twenty buildings) employing a variety of methods, curricula, emphases, and structures. This experiment has been highly touted and the director of the Central Park East second-ary school, Deborah Meier, was the recipient of a MacArthur Foundation "genius" award. And yet even in this setting, there are familiar problems. As of late 1989, bureaucratic impediments, hir-ing practices, and "budget problems, scandal and school politics" have combined to threaten the program (Fiske, 1989c, p. B8). If these problems continue—and given the history and tradition of school-ing, they certainly will—teachers in this program, who have been reported to be remarkably free of burnout, will surely begin to suffer in greater numbers from stress-related disorders.

Farber and Miller (1981) have proposed a third strategy to radically alter school structure to meet the needs of teachers. They suggested that the prevention of teacher burnout requires the devel-opment of a structurally enduring psychological sense of commu-nity. For this to occur, the environment of the school must be altered in such a way that it becomes a growth-producing, motivat-ing one for teachers and other educational personnel. Reppucci (1973) offered several guidelines for the creation of settings condu-cive to the needs of helping professionals, among them "a guiding idea or philosophy which is understandable to, and provides hope for all, all members of the institution" (p. 331); an organizational structure encouraging consistent collaboration among all levels of staff personnel; and the necessity for active community involve-ment. Based on these principles, schools in which teachers expe-rience a psychological sense of community might feature, for example, ongoing case conferences geared not only to acute student crises but to the long-term expression of teachers' needs, concerns, and interests; a team-teaching concept of education; variation in teachers' scheduled routines; consistent program- and problem-oriented contact with administrative as well as paraprofessional personnel (apart from the usual adversarial meetings); an active in-school teacher center (such as the one described above); use of school facilities for teachers after hours; recruitment and utilization of community volunteers; a school-based management team; and action-oriented committees made up of teachers, administrators, parents, and community leaders (Farber and Miller, 1981). In regard to this last point, active collaboration among all segments of the educational community reduces the institutionalization of teaching as a lonely profession; reinforces the teacher's esteem for peers, community members, and self; and rejuvenates a teacher's commitment to and investment in the children in the classroom.

The problem here, of course, is one of implementation. Assumably, no one is opposed to the notion of effective coalitions among various parties interested in education; difficulties arise when the inevitable issues of control, power, and ultimate authority have to be negotiated. The decentralization debacle in New York City is a prime example of how community involvement in schools can go awry. On the other hand, James Comer's program in inner-city schools in New Haven, Connecticut, which features active collaboration between parents and teachers, has been, by all accounts, extremely successful (in terms of achievement scores, attendance, and positive social climate) and has been adopted as a model plan by several other school districts. Similarly, the staffs of two elementary schools in northern California, as part of their participation in the "Accelerated Schools" project developed by Henry Levin of Stanford University, have actively encouraged parental support and input. These teachers view parental participation as "essential for achieving the objectives they themselves had embraced" and as "an integral part of a comprehensive plan to mobilize all available resources" (Seely, 1989, p. 47). Within this laudatory model, parental involvement is viewed as *necessary* and the school is viewed as a collaborative community learning center.

It should be clear that social problems do not have solutions in the same sense as do mathematical or biochemical problems. And though restructuring schools to better meet the needs of teachers cannot guarantee the prevention or abolition of teacher burnout within a school, solutions of this nature can, and do, offer a more comprehensive and potentially enduring strategy to this problem than the usual individually oriented, ameliorative approaches.

Still, where education is concerned, there are no panaceas. As yet, there are no studies examining either the short- or long-term consequences of these solutions—and one can be reasonably sure that the eventual documentation of positive outcomes will also note several unforeseen negative changes as well. For example, as teachers in some communities become better paid, more autonomous, and less isolated, they will likely be expected to perform educational miracles; failing to do so, they may well be the target of even greater criticism than before. Moreover, it is quite possible that no discrete set of reforms can ever be sufficient to eradicate teacher stress or burnout. Certainly, salary increases alone will not make it easier for teachers to reach students and derive the intrinsic satisfaction of a hard job well done. And, if history is a guide, current reforms of school structure (as in Community District 4 in New York) may shortly wither under economic or political pressure. Even under the best of conditions and the best of reform climates, then, teachers are likely to continue to feel stressed and burned out. Perhaps, as Cohn, Kottcamp, McCloskey, and Provenzo (1987) imply, teachers need to be on the verge of burnout—to be giving more than they are receiving—in order to be effective. "The job of teaching, if it is to be pursued with energy and responsibility for motivating the learner, is a difficult and draining one. Even with significant pay increases, it is doubtful as to whether the salary would ever equal the time and energy required to do the job well" (p. 57).

The symptoms of stress and burnout in teachers are clear: anger, anxiety, depression, fatigue, boredom, cynicism, substance abuse, psychosomatic symptoms, marital and family crises, a reduction in commitment to students. Sarason (1977) noted, too, that the detrimental implications of disillusionment in human service workers extend "far beyond the spheres of their individual existence" (p. 232). Teacher stress and burnout have affected and will continue to affect the lives of teachers and their families, administrators and their families, students and their families, and all of society. I am not so naive as to think there truly is a solution to these issues; indeed, I believe that as long as half the students in this country are in the lower half of their class, teachers will continue to be criticized and continue to be vulnerable to stress and burnout. And I believe too that without adequate financial and emotional support for teachers, without sufficient personnel to help teachers, and without adequate understanding either of the nature of teachers' tasks or the time necessary to reach socially established goals, teachers will continue to struggle to feel successful in the classroom. The hope must lie in society's eventual realization that education—and therefore teachers—are truly national priorities.

References

Adams, B. P. "Leader Behavior of Principals and Its Effect on Teacher Burnout." Unpublished doctoral dissertation, University of Wisconsin, Madison, 1988.

Altman, L. K., and Rosenthal, E. "Changes in Medicine Bring Pain to Healing Profession." *New York Times,* Feb. 18 1990, p. A1.

Anastos, J., and Ancowitz, R. "A Teacher-Directed Peer Coaching Project." *Educational Leadership,* Nov. 1987, pp. 40–42.

Anderson, M. B., and Iwanicki, E. F. "Teacher Motivation and Its Relationship to Burnout." *Educational Administration Quarterly,* 1984, *20* (2), 94–132.

Banks, J. L. "School Problems Start Long Before Children Enter a Classroom." *New York Times,* Sept. 12, 1987, p. 25.

Barnard, H. *Normal Schools and Other Institutions, Agencies, and Means Designed for the Professional Education of Teachers.* Vol. 1. Hartford, Conn.: Case, Tiffany and Company, 1851.

Barner, A. E. "Do Teachers Like to Teach?" *Pointer,* 1982, *27* (1), 5–7.

Beck, C. L., and Gargiulo, R. M. "Burnout in Teachers of Retarded and Nonretarded Children." *Journal of Educational Research,* 1983, *76* (3), 169–173.

Belcastro, P. A. "Burnout and Its Relationship to Teachers' Somatic Complaints and Illnesses." *Psychological Reports,* 1982, *50,* 1045–1046.

Belcastro, P. A., and Hays, L. C. "Ergophilia . . . Ergophobia . . . Ergo . . . Burnout?" *Professional Psychology: Research and Practice,* 1984, *15* (2), 260–270.

Bensky, J. M., and others. "Public Law 94–142 and Stress: A Problem for Educators." *Exceptional Children*, 1980, *47*, 24–29.

Berger, J. "Allure of Teaching Reviving: Education School Rolls Surge." *New York Times*, May 6, 1988, pp. A1, A17.

Berger, J. "Poignant Problems of the Nation's Rural Schools." *New York Times*, July 26, 1989, p. B8.

Bergin, A. E. "The Evaluation of Therapeutic Outcomes." In A. E. Bergin and S. L. Garfield (eds.), *Handbook of Psychotherapy and Behavior Change: An Empirical Analysis*. New York: Wiley, 1971.

Berry, B. *Why Miss Dove Left and Where She Went: A Case Study of Teacher Attrition in a Metropolitan School System in the Southeast*. Triangle Park, N.C.: Southeastern Regional Council for Educational Improvement, 1985.

Birmingham, J. "Job Satisfaction and Burnout Among Minnesota Teachers." Unpublished doctoral dissertation, University of Minnesota, 1984.

Blase, J. J. "A Social-Psychological Grounded Theory of Teacher Stress and Burnout." *Educational Administration Quarterly*, 1982, *18*, 92–113.

Blase, J. J., Dedrick, C., and Strathe, M. "Leadership Behavior of School Principals in Relation to Teacher Stress, Satisfaction, and Performance." *Journal of Humanistic Education and Development*, 1986, *24* (4), 159–169.

Blase, J. J., and Pajak, E. F. "The Impact of Teachers' Work Life on Personal Life: A Qualitative Analysis." *Alberta Journal of Educational Research*, 1986, *32* (4), 307–322.

Bloch, A. M. "The Battered Teacher." *Today's Education*, 1977, *66* (2), 58–62.

Bloch, A. M. "Conflict Neurosis in Inner City Schools." *American Journal of Psychiatry*, 1978, *135*, 189–192.

Bloom, R. B. "The Effects of Disturbed Adolescents on Their Teachers." *Behavioral Disorders*, 1983, *8* (3), 209–216.

Boyer, E. L. *High School: A Report on Secondary Education in America*. New York: Harper & Row, 1983.

Boyer, E. L. *Report Card on School Reform*. Princeton, N.J.: Carnegie Foundation for the Advancement of Teaching, 1988.

Bradfield, R. H., and Fones, D. M. "Stress and the Special Teacher: How Bad Is It?" *Academic Therapy*, 1985, *20* (5), 571–577.

Bredeson, P. V., and others. "Organizational Incentives and Secondary School Teaching." *Journal of Research and Development in Education*, 1983, *16* (4), 52–58.

Brenner, S., Sorbom, D., and Wallius, E. "The Stress Chain: A Longitudinal Confirmatory Study of Teacher Stress, Coping and Social Support." *Journal of Occupational Psychology*, 1985, *58* (1), 1–13.

Brenton, M. *What's Happened to Teacher?* New York: Coward-McCann, 1970.

Bridges, E. M. *The Incompetent Teacher: The Challenge and the Response*. Philadelphia: Falmer, 1986.

Bridges, E. M., and Hallinan, M. T. "Subunit Size, Work System Interdependence, and Employee Absenteeism." *Education Administration Quarterly*, 1978, *14* (2), 24–42.

Broiles, P. H. "An Inquiry into Teacher Stress: Symptoms, Sources, and Prevalence in Public Schools." Unpublished doctoral dissertation, Claremont Graduate School, Claremont, Calif., 1982.

Brown, J. Y. "A Study of the Relationship Between Job Stress and Burnout in Teachers." Unpublished doctoral dissertation, Teachers College, Columbia University, 1985.

Brown, N. J. "An Analysis of Stress Factors as Perceived by Elementary Teachers." Unpublished doctoral dissertation. University of Arkansas, 1983.

Burke, R. J., and Greenglass, E. R. "Psychological Burnout Among Men and Women in Teaching: An Examination of the Cherniss Model." *Human Relations*, 1989, *42* (3), 261–273.

Cadavid, V. "Locus of Control and Pupil Control Ideology as Related to the Dimensions of Burnout of Special Education Vis-à-Vis Regular Classroom Teachers." Unpublished doctoral dissertation, Southern Illinois University, 1986.

Calabrese, R. L. "The Principal: An Agent for Reducing Teacher Stress." *NAASP Bulletin*, Dec. 1987, pp. 6–70.

Campbell, R. F., Cunningham, L. L., Nystrand, R. O., and Usdan, M. D. *The Organization and Control of American Schools*. (4th ed.) Columbus, Ohio: Merrill, 1980.

Caplan, R. D., and Jones, K. W. "Effects of Workload, Role Ambiguity, and Type A Personality on Anxiety, Depression and Heart Rate." *Journal of Applied Psychology*, 1975, *60*, 713–719.

Carew, J. V., and Lightfoot, S. L. *Beyond Bias: Perspectives on Classrooms*. Cambridge, Mass.: Harvard University Press, 1979.

Carnegie Foundation for the Advancement of Teaching. *National Survey of Public School Teachers*. Princeton, N.J.: Carnegie Foundation for the Advancement of Teaching, 1987.

Carnegie Foundation for the Advancement of Teaching. *The Condition of Teaching: A State-by-State Analysis, 1988*. Princeton, N.J.: Carnegie Foundation for the Advancement of Teaching, 1988a.

Carnegie Foundation for the Advancement of Teaching. *An Imperiled Generation: Saving Urban Schools*. Princeton, N.J.: Carnegie Foundation for the Advancement of Teaching, 1988b.

Carnegie Task Force on Teaching as a Profession. *A Nation Prepared: Teachers for the 21st Century*. New York: Carnegie Forum on Education and the Economy, 1986.

Center for Education Statistics. *Private Schools and Private School Teachers: Final Report of the 1985–86 Private School Study*. Washington, D.C.: Center for Education Statistics, 1987.

Cerra, F. "Teachers Find It Hard to Cope as Rolls Drop." *New York Times*, Oct. 14, 1980, pp. B1–B2.

Chance, P. "That Drained-Out, Used-Up Feeling." *Psychology Today*, 1981, *15*, 88–92.

Charters, W. W., Jr. "The Social Background of Teaching." In N. L. Gage (ed)., *Handbook of Research on Teaching*. Chicago: Rand McNally, 1963.

Cherniss, C. *Professional Burnout in Human Service Organizations*. New York: Praeger, 1980a.

Cherniss, C. *Staff Burnout: Job Stress in the Human Services*. Newbury Park, Calif.: Sage, 1980b.

Cherniss, C. "Stress and Burnout in New Public Service Professionals: A Long-Term Follow-Up Study." Paper presented at the annual meeting of the Academy of Management, New Orleans, La., 1987.

Cherniss, C. "Observed Supervisory Behavior and Teacher Burnout in Special Education." *Exceptional Children*, 1988, *54* (5), 449–454.

Cherniss, C., Egnatios, E., and Wacker, S. "Job Stress and Career Development in New Public Professionals." *Professional Psychology*, 1976, *7*, 428-436.

Cherniss, C., Egnatios, E., Wacker, S., and O'Dowd, W. "The Professional Mystique and Burnout in Public Sector Professionals." Unpublished manuscript, University of Michigan, 1979.

Cherniss, C., and Krantz, D. "The Ideological Community as an Antidote to Burnout in the Human Services." In B. A. Farber (ed.), *Stress and Burnout in the Human Service Professions.* Elmsford, N.Y.: Pergamon Press, 1983.

Cherrington, D., Reitz, H. J., and Scott, W. E. "Effects of Contingent and Non-Contingent Reward on the Relationship Between Satisfaction and Task Performance." *Journal of Applied Psychology*, 1971, *55*, 531-536.

Chion-Kenney, L. "The Coalition of Essential Schools: A Report from the Field." *American Educator*, 1987, *11* (4), 18-27, 47-48.

Cichon, D. J., and Koff, R. H. "The Teaching Events Stress Inventory." Paper presented at the annual meeting of the American Educational Research Association, Toronto, Mar. 27-31, 1978.

Cichon, D. J., and Koff, R. H. "Stress and Teaching." *NASSP Bulletin*, 1980, *64* (434), 91-104.

Claesson, M. A. "Teacher/Mothers: Problems of a Dual Role." Paper presented at the annual meeting of the American Educational Research Association, San Francisco, Apr. 16-21, 1986.

Cobb, S. "Social Support as a Moderator of Life Stress." *Psychosomatic Medicine*, 1976, *5* (38), 300-317.

Cohn, M., Kottkamp, R. B., McCloskey, G. N., and Provenzo, E. F. *Teachers' Perspectives on the Problems of Their Professions: Implications for Policymakers and Practitioners.* Washington, D.C.: Office of Educational Research and Improvement, 1987.

Coleman, J. "Public Schools, Private Schools." *The Public Interest*, Summer 1981, pp. 19-30.

Comer, J. "The Social Factor." *New York Times*, Section 4a (Education Life), Aug. 7, 1988, pp. 27-31.

Connolly, C., and Sanders, W. "The Successful Coping Strategies—the Answer to Teacher Stress?" Paper presented at the annual meeting of the Association of Teacher Educators, San Diego, Calif., Feb. 13-17, 1988.

Cooke, R. A., and Rousseau, D. M. "Stress and Strain from Family Roles and Work-Role Expectations." *Journal of Applied Psychology*, 1984, *69* (2), 252–260.

Corcoran, T. B., Walker, L. J., and White, J. L. *Working in Urban Schools*. Washington, D.C.: Institute for Educational Leadership, 1988.

Council of the Great City Schools. *Challenges to Urban Education: Results in the Making*. Washington, D.C.: Council of the Great City Schools, 1987.

Cox, T., and Brockley, T. "The Experience and Effects of Stress in Teachers." *British Educational Research Journal*, 1984, *10* (1), 83–87.

Crane, S., and Iwanicki, E. "Perceived Role Conflict, Role Ambiguity, and Burnout Among Special Education Teachers." *Remedial and Special Education*, 1986, 7 (2), 24–31.

Cruikshank, D. R., Kennedy, J. J., and Myers, E. "Perceived Problems of Secondary School Teachers." *Journal of Educational Research*, 1974, *68*, 154–159.

Darling-Hammond, L. *Beyond the Commission Reports: The Coming Crisis in Teaching*. Santa Monica, Calif.: Rand Corporation, 1984.

Darling-Hammond, L. "Boosting Our Scientific Future." *New York Times*, May 21, 1989, p. E21.

Darling-Hammond, L., and Wise, A. E. "Teaching Standards or Standardized Teaching?" *Educational Leadership*, Oct. 1983, pp. 66–69.

Dinerstein, J. "Diary of a Mad Teacher: Why One Man Won't Go Back to School." *Village Voice*, July 30, 1985, pp. 18, 21, 23.

DiTeodoro, V. A. "Sources of Teacher Satisfactions, Stress and Burnout in a Suburban School District." Unpublished doctoral dissertation, Teachers College, Columbia University, 1984.

Dixon, P., Shaw, S. F., and Bensky, J. M. "Administrator's Role in Fostering the Mental Health of Special Services Personnel." *Exceptional Children*, 1980, *47*, 30–36.

Dolson, D. P. *The Application of Immersion Education in the United States*. Rosslyn, Va.: National Clearinghouse for Bilingual Education, 1985.

Duke, D. L. "Understanding What It Means to Be a Teacher." *Educational Leadership,* 1986, *44* (2), 26–32.

Dworkin, A. *Teacher Burnout in the Public Schools: Structural Causes and Consequences for Children.* Albany: State University of New York Press, 1987.

Edelwich, J. and Brodsky, A. *Burnout: Stages of Disillusionment in the Helping Professions.* New York: Human Sciences Press, 1980.

Eisner, E. *What High Schools Are Like: Views from the Inside.* Palo Alto, Calif.: Stanford University Press, 1985.

Elam, S. M. "The Gallup Education Surveys: Impressions of a Poll Watcher." *Phi Delta Kappan,* Sept. 1983, pp. 26–32.

Elam, S. M. *The Phi Delta Kappa Gallup Polls of Attitudes Toward Education 1969–1984: A Topical Summary.* Bloomington, Ind.: Phi Delta Kappa, 1984.

Elam, S. M. "The Second Gallup/Phi Delta Kappa Poll of Teachers' Attitudes Toward the Public Schools." *Phi Delta Kappan,* June 1989, pp. 785–798.

Elsbree, W. S. *The American Teacher.* New York: American Book Company, 1939.

Engelking, J. L. "Teacher Job Satisfaction and Dissatisfaction." *Spectrum,* 1986, *4* (1), 33–38.

Erikson, E. H. *Childhood and Society.* (2nd ed.) New York: Norton, 1963.

Erikson, E. H. *Identity: Youth and Crisis.* New York: Norton, 1968.

Farber, B. A. *Stress and Burnout in the Human Service Professions.* Elmsford, N.Y.: Pergamon Press, 1983.

Farber, B. A. "Stress and Burnout in Suburban Teachers." *Journal of Educational Research,* 1984a, 77, 325–331.

Farber, B. A. "Teacher Burnout: Assumptions, Myths, and Issues." *Teachers College Record,* 1984b, *86,* 321–338.

Farber, B. A. "The Genesis, Development, and Implications of Psychological-Mindedness in Psychotherapists." *Psychotherapy,* 1985, *22,* 170–177.

Farber, B. A., and Miller, J. "Teacher Burnout: A Psychoeducational Perspective." *Teachers College Record,* 1981, *82* (2), 235–243.

Feistritzer, C. E. *The Condition of Teaching.* Princeton, N.J.: Carnegie Foundation for the Advancement of Teaching, 1985.

Feisritzer, C. E. "Education Vital Signs: Teacher." *American School Board Journal,* 1986, *173* (10), pp. A12–A16.

Feitler, F. C., and Tokar, E. B. "Teacher Stress: Sources, Symptoms and Job Satisfaction." Paper presented at the annual meeting of the American Educational Research Association, Los Angeles, Apr. 13–17, 1981.

Fibkins, W. L. "Organizing Helping Settings to Reduce Burnout." In B. A. Farber (ed.), *Stress and Burnout in the Human Service Professions.* Elmsford, N.Y.: Pergamon Press, 1983.

Fielding, M. "Personality and Situational Correlates of Teacher Stress and Burnout." Paper presented at the annual meeting of the American Educational Research Association, New York, Mar. 1982.

Fimian, M. J. "What Is Teacher Stress?" *Clearing House,* 1982, *56* (3), 101–105.

Fimian, M. J., and Blanton, L. P. "Variables Related to Stress and Burnout in Special Education Teacher Trainees and First-Year Teachers." *Teacher Education and Special Education,* 1986, *9* (1), 9–21.

Fimian, M. J., Pearson, D., and McHardy, R. "Occupational Stress Reported by Teachers of Learning Disabled and Nonlearning Disabled Handicapped Students." *Journal of Learning Disabilities,* 1986, *19* (3), 154–158.

Fimian, M. J., and Santoro, T. M. "Sources and Manifestations of Stress as Reported by Full-Time Special Education Teachers." *Exceptional Children,* 1983, *49,* 540–543.

Fischer, H. J. "A Psychoanalytic View of Burnout." In B. A. Farber (ed.), *Stress and Burnout in the Human Service Professions.* Elmsford, N.Y.: Pergamon Press, 1983.

Fisk, P. "As Classroom Empties, Teacher Takes Inventory." *New York Times,* July 10, 1988, Section 12, p. 26.

Fiske, E. B. "Survey of Teachers Reveals Morale Problems." *New York Times,* Sept. 19, 1982, pp. A1, A52.

Fiske, E. B. "Reform Drive Turns to Classroom Itself." *New York Times,* May 27, 1986, pp. C1, C7.

Fiske, E. B. "35 Pages That Shook the U.S. Education World." *New York Times*, Apr. 27, 1988, p. B10.

Fiske, E. B. "Teachers May No Longer Be Lumped with Potatoes, but an Image Problem Persists." *New York Times*, July 19, 1989a, p. B6.

Fiske, E. B. "The Bush Compact with the Governors Shows a Sharp Turn from the Reagan Policies." *New York Times*, Oct. 4, 1989b, p. B8.

Fiske, E. B. "The Alternative Schools of Famous District 4: Accolades and Better Attendance Are Not Enough." *New York Times*, Nov. 1, 1989c, p. B8.

Fiske, E. B. "Will President Bush Pass the Test at His Education Summit Conference?" *New York Times*, Sept. 13, 1989d, p. B10.

Fleischut, J. S. "A Longitudinal Study of the Origin and Intensity of the Job-Related Stress of Elementary School Teachers." Unpublished doctoral dissertation, Temple University, 1983.

Fordham, S., and Ogbu, J. U. "Black Students, School Success: Coping with the Burden of 'Acting White.'" *Urban Review*, 1986, *18* (3), 176-206.

Forman, J. S. "The Effects of an Aerobic Dance Program for Women Teachers on Symptoms of Burnout." Unpublished doctoral dissertation, University of Cincinnati, 1983.

Forman, S. G. "Stress Management for Teachers: A Cognitive-Behavioral Program." *Journal of School Psychology*, 1982, *20* (3), 180-187.

"Former Teachers in America." *American Educator*, *10* (2), 1986, 34-39, 48.

Frataccia, E. V., and Hennington, I. "Satisfaction of Hygiene and Motivation Needs of Teachers Who Resigned from Teaching." Paper presented at the annual meeting of the Southwest Educational Research Association, Austin, Tex., Feb. 11-13, 1982.

Freed, J. C. "Teachers Who Quit Offer Their Reasons." *New York Times*, Apr. 22, 1986, pp. C1, C9.

French, J. R., Jr., and Caplan, R. D. "Organizational Stress and Individual Strain." In A. J. Marrow (ed.), *The Failure of Success*. New York: AMACOM, 1972.

Freudenberger, H. J. "The Psychologist in a Free Clinic Setting: An

Alternative Model in Health Care." *Psychotherapy: Theory, Research, and Practice,* 1973, *10* (1), 52–61.

Freudenberger, H. J. "Staff Burnout." *Journal of Social Issues,* 1974, *1,* 159–164.

Freudenberger, H. J. "The Staff Burnout Syndrome in Alternative Institutions." *Psychotherapy: Theory, Research, and Practice,* 1975, *12,* 73–82.

Freudenberger, H. J. "Counseling and Dynamics: Treating the End-Stage Burnout Person." In W. S. Paine (ed.), *Job Stress and Burnout.* Newbury Park, Calif.: Sage, 1982.

Freudenberger, H. J. "Burnout: Contemporary Issues, Trends, and Concerns." In B. A. Farber (ed.) *Stress and Burnout in the Human Service Professions.* Elmsford, N.Y.: Pergamon Press, 1983.

Freudenberger, H. J. "Burnout and Job Dissatisfaction: Impact on the Family." In J. C. Hansen and S. H. Cramer (ed.), *Perspectives on Work and the Family.* Rockville, Md.: Aspen, 1984.

Freudenbeger, H. J., with Richelson, G. *Burn-Out.* New York: Bantam Books, 1980.

Gallup, A. M. "The Gallup Poll of Teachers' Attitudes Toward the Public Schools." *Phi Delta Kappan,* Oct. 1984, pp. 97–107.

Gallup, A. M. "The 17th Annual Gallup Poll of the Public's Attitudes Toward the Public Schools." *Phi Delta Kappan,* Sept. 1985, pp. 35–47.

Gallup, A. M. "The 18th Annual Gallup Poll of the Public's Attitudes Toward the Public Schools." *Phi Delta Kappan,* Sept. 1986, pp. 43–59.

Gallup, A. M., and Clark, D. L. "The 19th Annual Gallup Poll of the Public's Attitudes Toward the Public Schools." *Phi Delta Kappan,* Sept. 1987, pp. 17–30.

Gallup, A. M., and Elam, S. M. "The 20th Annual Gallup Poll of the Public's Attitudes Toward the Public Schools." *Phi Delta Kappan,* Sept. 1988, pp. 33–46.

Gallup, A. M., and Elam, S. M. "The 21st Annual Gallup Poll of Public's Attitudes Toward the Public Schools." *Phi Delta Kappan,* Sept. 1989, pp. 41–54.

Gallup, G. "The 15th Annual Gallup Poll of the Public's Attitudes Toward the Public Schools." *Phi Delta Kappan,* Sept. 1983, pp. 33–47.

Gallup, G. "The 16th Annual Gallup Poll of the Public's Attitudes Toward the Public Schools." *Phi Delta Kappan,* Sept. 1984, pp. 23-38.

Gillet, P. "Preventing Discipline-Related Teacher Stress and Burnout." *Teaching Exceptional Children,* Summer 1987, 62-65.

Glass, D. C. *Behavior Patterns, Stress, and Coronary Disease.* Hillsdale, N.J.: Erlbaum, 1977.

Glasser, W. *Reality Therapy.* New York: Harper & Row, 1975.

Gold, Y. "The Relationship of Six Personal and Life History Variables to Standing on Three Dimensions of the Maslach Burnout Inventory in a Sample of Elementary and Junior High School Teachers." *Educational and Psychological Measurement,* 1985, *45,* 377-387.

Goldman, R. *A Profession at Risk: Eight Schools Address the Faculty Compensation Issue.* Boston: National Association of Independent Schools, 1988.

Golembiewski, R. T., and Munzenrider, R. "Active and Passive Reactions to Psychological Burn-Out? Toward Greater Specificity in a Phase Model." *Journal of Health and Human Resources Administration,* 1984, 7, 264-289.

Golembiewski, R. T., Munzenrider, R., and Carter, D. "Phases of Progressive Burnout and Their Work Site Covariants: Critical Issue in OD Research and Praxis." *Journal of Applied Behavioral Science,* 1983, *4,* 461-481.

Goodlad, J. I. *A Place Called School.* New York: McGraw-Hill, 1984.

Grace, G. *Teachers, Ideology and Control.* London: Routledge & Kegan Paul, 1978.

Grant, G. "The Teacher's Predicament." *Teachers College Record,* 1983, *84* (3), 593-609.

Grant, G. *The World We Created at Hamilton High.* Cambridge, Mass.: Harvard University Press, 1988.

Gray, J. *The Teacher's Survival Guide.* Santa Monica, Calif.: Fearon, 1967.

Green, T. F. *Work, Leisure and the American Schools.* New York: Random House, 1968.

Greene, G. *A Burnt-Out Case.* New York: Viking Press, 1961.

Greenglass, E. R., and Burke, R. J. "Work and Family Precursors of Burnout in Teachers: Sex Differences." *Sex Roles,* 1988, *18* (3/ 4), 215–223.

Grissmer, D. W., and Kirby, S. N. *Teacher Attrition: The Uphill Climb to Staff the Nation's Schools.* Santa Monica, Calif.: Rand Corporation, 1987.

Gujarati, R. "Female Burnout." *ASTD Women's Network,* July 1985, pp. 1, 7.

Gunderson, D. F., and Haas, N. S. "Media Stereotypes in Teacher Role Definition." *Action in Teacher Education,* 1987, *9* (2), 27– 31.

Hackman, J. R. "Tasks and Task Performance in Research on Stress." In J. E. McGrath (ed.), *Social and Psychological Factors in Stress.* New York: Holt, Rinehart & Winston, 1970.

Hammen, C., and DeMayo, R. "Cognitive Correlates of Teacher Stress and Depression Symptoms: Implications for Attributional Models of Depression." *Journal of Abnormal Psychology,* 1982, *91* (2), 96–101.

Hanchey, S. G. "Teacher Burnout: The Person and Environmental Influences." Unpublished doctoral dissertation, California School of Professional Psychology, Fresno, 1987.

Harris, L., and Associates. *The Metropolitan Life Survey of the American Teacher.* New York: Metropolitan Life Insurance Company, 1984.

Harris, L., and Associates. *The Metropolitan Life Survey of the American Teacher.* New York: Metropolitan Life Insurance Company, 1985.

Harris, L., and Associates. *The Metropolitan Life Survey of the American Teacher.* New York: Metropolitan Life Insurance Company, 1986.

Harris, L., and Associates. *The Metropolitan Life Survey of the American Teacher.* New York: Metropolitan Life Insurance Company, 1987.

Harris, L., and Associates. *The Metropolitan Life Survey of the American Teacher.* New York: Metropolitan Life Insurance Company, 1988.

Hay, L. "Bye-Bye Miss Beadle and You, Too, Miss Brooks." *Television and Families,* 1985, *8* (2), 1–9.

Hechinger, F. M. "About Education: Enough Reports Already, Says a New Report on School Improvements." *New York Times,* June 22, 1988, p. B7.

Hechinger, F. M. "About Education: From Frustrated Teachers Comes a Passionate Cry on Behalf of Children." *New York Times,* Jan. 18, 1989a, p. B11.

Hechinger, F. M. "About Education: The Decade Changes with Questions About How to Reach Teaching Goals." *New York Times,* Dec. 20, 1989b, p. B9.

Heifetz, L. J., and Bersani, H. A., Jr. "Disrupting the Cybernetics of Personal Growth: Toward a Unified Theory of Burnout in the Human Services." In B. A. Farber (ed.), *Stress and Burnout in the Human Service Professions.* Elmsford, N.Y.: Pergamon Press, 1983.

Hendrickson, B. "Teacher Burnout: How to Recognize It; What to Do About It." *Learning,* 1979, *7,* 36-39.

Hentoff, N. *Our Children Are Dying.* New York: Viking, 1966.

Herndon, J. *The Way It Spozed to Be.* New York: Simon & Schuster, 1965.

Herzberg, F. *Work and the Nature of Man.* Cleveland, Oh.: World Publishing, 1971.

Heyns, B. "Educational Defectors: A First Look at Teacher Attrition in the NLS-72." *Educational Researcher,* 1988, *17* (3), 24-32.

Holland, J. *Making Vocational Choices: A Theory of Careers.* Englewood Cliffs, N.J.: Prentice-Hall, 1973.

Holmes Group. *Tomorrow's Teachers: A Report of the Holmes Group.* East Lansing, Mich.: Holmes Group, 1986.

Holmes, T. H., and Rahe, R. H. "The Social Readjustment Scale." *Journal of Psychosomatic Research,* 1967, *11,* 213-218.

Holt, J. *How Children Fail.* New York: Dell, 1964.

Holt, J. *How Children Learn.* New York: Dell, 1967.

Holt, J. *The Underachieving School.* New York: Delta, 1969.

Holt, P., Fine, M. J., and Tollefson, N. "Mediating Stress: Survival of the Hardy." *Psychology in the Schools,* 1987, *24,* 51-58.

Hook, S. *Reason, Social Myths and Democracy.* New York: Harper & Row, 1966.

Ianni, F., and Reuss-Ianni, E. " 'Take This Job and Shove It!' A Comparison of Organizational Stress and Burnout Among Teachers and Police." In B. A. Farber (ed.), *Stress and Burnout in the*

Human Service Professions. Elmsford, N.Y.: Pergamon Press, 1983.

Jackson, S. "Burnout: Redefining the Issues." Paper presented at the annual meeting of the American Psychological Association, Washington, D.C., Aug. 1982.

Jackson, S. E., Schwab, R. L., and Schuler, R. S. "Toward an Understanding of the Burnout Phenomenon." *Journal of Applied Psychology,* 1986, *71* (4), 630–640.

Jencks, C. "Deadly Neighborhoods." *The New Republic,* June 1988, *198* (24), 23–32.

Johnson, A. B., Gold, V., and Vickers, L. L. "Stress and Teachers of the Learning Disabled, Behavior Disorder, and Educable Mentally Retarded." *Pyschology in the Schools,* 1982, *19,* 552–557.

Johnson, J. J. "Nation's Schools Termed 'Stagnant' in Federal Report." *New York Times,* May 4, 1989, p. A1.

Kahn, R. L. "Conflict, Ambiguity, and Overload: Three Elements in Job Stress." In A. McLean (ed.), *Occupational Stress.* Springfield, Ill.: Thomas, 1974.

Kaiser, J. "Sources of Stress in Teaching." Paper presented at meeting of New York United Teachers, Oct. 1981.

Kanner, A. D., Kafry, D., and Pines, A. "Conspicuous by Their Absence: Lack of Positive Conditions as a Source of Stress." *Journal of Human Stress,* 1978, *4,* 33–39.

Karger, H.J. "Burnout as Alienation." *Social Service Review,* 1981, *55,* 270–283.

Kaufman, B. *Up the Down Staircase.* New York: Avon 1964.

Keavney, G., and Sinclair, K. E. "Teacher Concerns and Teacher Anxiety: A Neglected Topic of Classroom Research." *Review of Educational Research,* 1978, spring, pp. 273–290.

Kelly, D. "A Call to Cut School Class Size." *USA Today,* June 26, 1990, p. D1.

Kobasa, S. C. "Stressful Life Events, Personality, and Health: An Inquiry into Hardiness." *Journal of Personality and Social Psychology,* 1979, *37,* 1–11.

Kohl, H. *36 Children.* New York: Signet, 1967.

Kohut, H. *The Analysis of the Self.* New York: International Universities Press, 1971.

Kottkamp, R. B., Provenzo, E. F., Jr., and Cohn, M. M. "Stability and Change in a Profession: Two Decades of Teacher Attitudes, 1964–1984." *Phi Delta Kappan,* 1986, *67* (8), 559–567.

Kozol, J. *Death at an Early Age.* New York: Bantam Books, 1967.

Kozol, J. *The Night Is Dark and I Am Far from Home.* New York: Continuum, 1975.

Kyriacou, C. "Teacher Stress and Burnout: An International Review." *Educational Research,* 1987, *29* (2), 146–152.

Kyriacou, C., and Pratt, J. "Teacher Stress and Psychoneurotic Symptoms." *British Journal of Educational Psychology,* 1985, *55* (1), 61–64.

Kyriacou, C., and Sutcliffe, J. "Teacher Stress: A Review." *Educational Review,* 1977, *29,* 299–306.

Kyriacou, C., and Sutcliffe, J. "Teacher Stress: Prevalence, Sources and Symptoms." *British Journal of Educational Psychology,* 1978, *48* (2), 158–167.

Lasch, C. *The Culture of Narcissism: American Life in an Age of Diminishing Returns.* New York: Norton, 1979.

Lazarus, R. S. *Psychological Stress and the Coping Process.* New York: McGraw-Hill, 1966.

Levine, M. "Teaching Is a Lonely Profession." In S. B. Sarason, M. Levin, I. I. Goldenberg, D. L. Cherlin, and E. Bennett (eds.), *Psychology in Community Settings: Clinical, Educational, Vocational, Social Aspects.* New York: Wiley, 1966.

Levine, M., and Levine, A. *A Social History of Helping Services.* New York: Appleton-Century-Crofts, 1970.

Levinson, D. *The Seasons of a Man's Life.* New York: Knopf, 1978.

Lieberman, A., and Miller, L. (eds.). *Staff Development: New Demands, New Realities, New Perspectives.* New York: Teachers College Press, 1979.

Liff, M. "Get Off My Case Teach." *New York Sunday News Magazine,* Sept. 21, 1980, pp. 14–17.

Lortie, D. *School Teacher.* Chicago: University of Chicago Press, 1975.

Lortie, D. "Teacher Status in Dade County: A Case of Structural Strain?" *Phi Delta Kappan,* Apr. 1986, 568–575.

McCarty, F. H. "Energy and Stress in the Classroom." Unpublished manuscript, 1979.

McEnany, J. "Teachers Who Don't Burn Out: The Survivors." *Clearing House,* 1986, *60* (2), 83-84.

McGuire, W. H. "Teacher Burnout." *Today's Education,* 1979, *68* (4), 5.

McIntyre, T. "The Relationship Between Locus of Control and Teacher Burnout." *British Journal of Educational Psychology,* 1984, *54* (2), 235-238.

Maeroff, G. I. *The Empowerment of Teachers: Overcoming the Crisis of Confidence.* New York: Teachers College Press, 1988a.

Maeroff, G. I. "Blueprint for Empowering Teachers." *Phi Delta Kappan,* Mar. 1988b, *69,* 473-477.

Makinen, R., and Kinnunen, U. "Teacher Stress over a School Year." *Scandinavian Journal of Educational Research,* 1986, *30,* 55-70.

Malanowski, J., and Wood, P. "Burnout and Self-Actualization in Public School Teachers." *Journal of Psychology,* 1984, *117* (1), 23-26.

Mann, H. *Tenth Annual Report to the Board of Education.* Boston: Dutton and Wentworth, 1847.

Margolick, D. "At the Bar." *New York Times,* Mar. 9, 1990, p. B6.

Mark, J. H., and Anderson, B. D. "Teacher Survival Rates: A Current Look." *American Education Research Journal,* 1978, *15,* 379-383.

Marlin, T. R. "Teacher Burnout and Locus-of-Control, Sex, Age, Marital Status, and Years of Experience Among a Group of Urban Secondary Teachers." Unpublished doctoral dissertation, Rutgers University, New Burnswick, N.J., 1987.

Martin, G. "Walls Crumble, but Morris High Retains Its Spirit." *New York Times,* Dec. 10, 1988, p. B29.

Martin, J. M. "Teacher Burnout and the Urban School System." Unpublished doctoral dissertation, Boston University, 1988.

Maslach, C. "Burned Out." *Human Behavior,* 1976, *5,* 16-22.

Maslach, C. "Burnout: A Social Psychological Analysis." Paper presented at the annual convention of the American Psychological Association, San Francisco, 1977.

Maslach, C. "The Client Role in Staff Burnout." *Journal of Social Issues,* 1978, *34* (4), 111-124.

Maslach, C., and Jackson, S. "The Measurement of Experienced Burnout." *Journal of Occupational Behavior*, 1981, *2*, 1–15.

Maslach, C., and Jackson, S. *The Maslach Burnout Inventory*. Palo Alto, Calif.: Consulting Psychologists Press, 1986.

Maslach, C., and Pines, A. "The Burnout Syndrome in the Day Care Setting." *Child Care Quarterly*, 1977, *6* (2), 110–113.

Matthes, W., and Carlson, R. "Conditions for Practice: The Reasons Teachers Selected Rural Schools." Paper presented at the 67th annual meeting of the American Educational Research Association, San Francisco, Apr. 16–20, 1986.

Mattingly, M. A. "Sources of Stress and Burnout in Professional Child Care Work." *Child Care Quarterly*, 1977, *6* (2), 127–137.

Mayer, M. *The Teachers' Strike, New York, Nineteen Sixty-Eight*. New York: Harper & Row, 1969.

Meagher, L. "Variables Associated with Stress and Burnout of Regular and Special Education Teachers." Unpublished doctoral dissertation, University of Kansas, 1983.

Meehling, D. A. "An Investigation of the Effects of Personal Locus of Control, Anxiety, Self-Esteem and Selected Demographic Variables on Teacher Stress." Unpublished doctoral dissertation, University of Maryland, 1982.

Meier, S. T. "The Construct Validity of Burnout." *Journal of Occupational Psychology*, 1984, *57* (3), 211–219.

Metropolitan Life Insurance Company. *Former Teachers in America*. New York: Metropolitan Life Insurance Company, 1986.

Miller, A. "Stress on the Job." *Newsweek*, Apr. 25, 1988, p. 40.

Moe, D. "Teacher Burnout: A Prescription." *Today's Education*, 1979, *68*, 35–36.

Moracco, J., D'Arienzo, R., and Danford, D. "Comparison of Perceived Occupational Stress Between Teachers Who Are Contented and Discontented in Their Career Choice." *Vocational Guidance Quarterly*, 1983, *32* (1), 44–51.

Morrow, L. "The Burnout of Almost Everyone." *Time*, Sept. 21, 1981, p. 84.

Morrow, L. "1968." *Time*, Jan. 11, 1988, pp. 16–27.

Nagy, S. "The Relationship of Type A and Type B Personalities, Workaholism, Perceptions of the School Climate, and Years of Teaching Experience to Burnout of Elementary and Junior High

School Teachers in a Northwestern Oregon School District." Unpublished doctoral dissertation, University of Oregon, 1982.

Nathan, R. P. "Is the Underclass Beyond Help?" *New York Times,* Jan. 6, 1989, p. A31.

National Commission on Excellence in Education. *A Nation at Risk: The Imperative for Educational Reform.* Washington, D.C.: U.S. Department of Education, 1983.

National Education Association. "The Scheduling of Teachers' Salaries." *Research Bulletin,* Feb. 1927, 5.

National Education Association. *Nationwide Teacher Opinion Poll.* Washington, D.C.: National Education Association, 1979.

Needle, R. H., Griffen, T., Svendsen, R., and Berney, C. "Teacher Stress: Sources and Consequences." *Journal of School Health,* Feb. 1980, *50* (2), 96–99.

Newell, R. C. "Paperwork: We're Fed Up and Fighting Back." *American Teacher,* Apr. 1987, *71* (7), 8–9.

New York State United Teachers Research and Education Services. *NYSUT Teacher Stress Survey.* Albany, N.Y.: New York State United Teachers Research and Education Services, 1979.

Ollman, B. *Alienation: Marx's Conception of Man in Capitalist Society.* Cambridge, England: Cambridge University Press, 1971.

Olson, L. "The Unbalanced Equation." *Education Week,* June 22, 1988, p. 19.

Olson, L., and Rodman, B. "In the Urban Crucible." *Education Week,* June 22, 1988, pp. 27–33.

Orlich, D. C. "Education Reform: Mistakes, Misconceptions, Miscues." *Phi Delta Kappan,* Mar. 1989, pp. 512–517.

Ornstein, A. C. "Teacher Salaries: Past, Present, Future." *Phi Delta Kappan,* 1980, *61,* 677–678.

Packard, V. *A Nation of Strangers.* New York: McKay, 1972.

Passow, H. *Urban Education in the 1970's.* New York: Teachers College Press, 1971.

Pearlin, L. I., and Schooler, C. "The Structure of Coping." *Journal of Health and Social Behavior,* 1978, *19,* 2–21.

Pepitone-Rockwell, F. (ed.). *Dual-Career Couples.* Newbury Park, Calif.: Sage, 1980.

Perlez, J. "New York School Buildings Scarred by Years of Neglect." *New York Times,* May 13, 1987, pp. A1, B6.

Phelan, W. T. "Teachers Under Duress: Some Effects of Declining Enrollment and District Staffing Policies." Paper presented at the annual meeting of the American Educational Research Association, New York City, Mar. 1982.

Pines, A. "Helper's Motivation and the Burnout Syndrome." In T. A. Wills (ed.), *Basic Processes in Helping Relationships*. Orlando, Fla.: Academic Press, 1982.

Pines, A. "On Burnout and the Buffering Effects of Social Support." In B. A. Farber (ed.), *Stress and Burnout in the Human Service Professions*. Elmsford, N.Y.: Pergamon Press, 1983.

Pines, A. "Who Is to Blame for Teachers' Burnout? A Case Study." Unpublished manuscript, 1984.

Pines, A., and Aronson, E., with Kafry, D. *Burnout: From Tedium to Personal Growth*. New York: Free Press, 1981.

Postman, N. *Teaching as a Conserving Activity*. New York: Dell, 1979.

Quinnett, P. "The Perfect Out." *New York Times*, Aug. 26, 1981, p. A23.

Rangel, J. "Two Who Make a Difference in New York City's Schools." *New York Times*, Dec. 25, 1987, p. B3.

Raphael, R. *The Teacher's Voice: A Sense of Who We Are*. Portsmouth, N.H.: Heinemann Educational Books, 1985.

Raywid, M. A. "Education and the Media or Why They Keep Raining on Your Parade." *Contemporary Education*, 1984, *55* (4), 206-211.

Reed, S. "What You Can Do to Prevent Teacher Burnout." *The National Elementary School Principal*, 1979, *58* (3), 67-70.

Reinhold, R. "School Reform: 4 Years of Tumult, Mixed Results." *New York Times*, Aug. 10, 1987, pp. A1, A14.

Reppucci, N. D. "Social Psychology of Institutional Change: General Principles for Intervention." *American Journal of Community Psychology*, 1973, *1* (4), 330-341.

Roberts, K. L. "An Analysis of the Relationship of Principals' Leadership Style to Teacher Stress and Job Related Outcome." Unpublished doctoral dissertation, Washington State University, 1983.

Robison, W. A. "Paperwork: The Educator's Nightmare." *Clearing House*, 1980, *54*, 125-126.

Rosenthal, R., and Jacobson, L. *Pygmalion in the Classroom.* New York: Holt, Rinehart & Winston, 1968.

Rottier, J., Kelly, W., and Tomhave, W. K. "Teacher Burnout—Small and Rural School Style." *Education,* 1983, *104* (1), 72–79.

Russell, D., Altmaier, E., and Van Velzen, D. "Job-Related Stress, Social Support, and Burnout Among Classroom Teachers." *Journal of Applied Psychology,* 1987, *72* (2), 269–274.

Ryan, W. *Blaming the Victim.* New York: Pantheon, 1971.

Safire, W. "Burnout." *New York Times,* May 23, 1982, Section 6, p. 16.

Sakharov, M., and Farber, B. A. "A Critical Study of Burnout in Teachers." In B. A. Farber (ed.), *Stress and Burnout in the Human Service Professions.* Elmsford, N.Y.: Pergamon Press, 1983.

Saltzman, H. "Put a Stop to Violence." *New York Times,* Jan. 9, 1988, p. A27.

Sarason, S. B. *The Culture of the School and the Problem of Change.* Boston: Allyn & Bacon, 1971.

Sarason, S. B. "Jewishness, Blackishness and the Nature-Nurture Controversy." *American Psychologist,* 1973, *28,* 962–971.

Sarason, S. B. *Work, Aging, and Social Change: Professionals and the One Life–One Career Imperative.* New York: Free Press, 1977.

Sarason, S. B. *Psychology Misdirected: The Social Scientist in the Social Order.* New York: Free Press, 1981.

Sarason, S. B. *The Culture of the School and the Problem of Change.* (2nd ed.) Boston: Allyn & Bacon, 1982.

Sarason, S. B. *Schooling in America: Scapegoat and Salvation.* New York: Free Press, 1983.

Sarason, S. B. *Caring and Compassion in Clinical Practice: Issues in the Selection, Training, and Behavior of Helping Professionals.* San Francisco: Jossey-Bass, 1985.

Savicki, V., and Cooley, E. "Theoretical and Research Considerations of Burnout." *Children and Youth Services Review,* 1983, *5,* 227–238.

Schlansker, B. "A Principal's Guide to Teacher Stress." *Principal,* May 1987, *66* (5), 32–34.

Schlechty, P. C., and Vance, V. S. "Recruitment, Selection, and Retention: The Shape of the Teaching Force." *The Elementary School Journal,* 1983, *83* (4), 470–487.

Schoenig, T. M. "An Investigation of the Relationships Among Burnout, Hardiness, Stressful Teaching Events, Job and Personal Characteristics in Public School Teachers." Unpublished doctoral dissertation, Hofstra University, 1986.

Schonfeld, I. S. "Coping with Job-Related Stress: The Case of Teachers." *Journal of Occupational Psychology,* in press.

Schwab, R. L., and Iwanicki, E. F. "Who Are Our Burned Out Teachers?" *Educational Research Quarterly,* 1982, 7 (2), 5–16.

Schwab, R. L., Jackson, S. E., and Schuler, R. S. "Educator Burnout: Sources and Consequences." Paper presented at the meeting of the American Educational Research Association, New Orleans, La., Apr. 1984.

Seely, D. S. "A New Paradigm for Parent Involvement." *Educational Leadership,* Oct. 1989, pp. 46–48.

Seligman, M. E. *Helplessness.* San Francisco: W. H. Freeman, 1975.

Selye, H. *The Stress of Life.* New York: McGraw-Hill, 1956.

Selye, H. *The Stress of Life.* (Rev. ed.) New York: McGraw-Hill, 1976.

Shanker, A. "New York Must Do More for Its Undereducated." Paid newspaper column, *New York Times,* Feb. 14, 1982, p. E7.

Shanker, A. "Early Retirement: Major Loss to Schools." Paid newspaper column, *New York Times,* Aug. 10, 1986a, p. E7.

Shanker, A. "Women's Options Challenge Schools: Teaching Losing in Career Competition." Paid newspaper column, *New York Times,* May 4, 1986b, p. E9.

Shanker, A. "Impatience Short-Circuits Reform: Tough Problems Need Time and Effort." Paid newspaper column, *New York Times,* Mar. 13, 1988, p. E9.

Shanker, A. "The President's Speech from the Summit: A Generous Vision." Paid newspaper column, *New York Times,* Oct. 8, 1989, p. E7.

Silberman, C. *Crisis in the Classroom: The Remaking of American Education.* New York: Random House, 1970.

Sizer, T. R. *Horace's Compromise: The Dilemma of the American High School.* Boston: Houghton Mifflin, 1984.

Slater, P. *The Pursuit of Loneliness.* (Rev. ed.) Boston: Beacon Press, 1976.

Spaniol, L., and Caputo, J. *Professional Burn-Out: A Personal Survival Kit.* Lexington, Mass.: Human Services Associates, 1979.

Sparks, D. "Practical Solutions for Teacher Stress." *Theory into Practice*, 1983, *22*, 33–42.

Spector, A. M. "The Relationship Between Coping Strategies, Locus of Control, and the Experience of Burnout Among Teachers." Unpublished doctoral dissertation, Fordham University, 1984.

Standard, E. "Why Would One, After Several Careers, Go Back to School to Become a Teacher?" *New York Times*, Sept. 6, 1987, p. 32.

Stedman, J. B., and Jordan, K. F. *Education Reform Reports: Contents and Impact.* Washington, D.C.: Library of Congress, Congressional Research Service, 1986.

Stone, J. A. "The Relationship Between Perceived Stress and Job Satisfaction, Locus of Control, and Length of Teaching Experience." Unpublished doctoral dissertation, University of Houston, 1982.

"Stress." *New York Teacher Magazine*, Jan. 27, 1980, pp. 1B–2B.

Super, D. E. *Work Values Inventory.* Boston: Houghton Mifflin, 1970.

Sutton, G. W., and Huberty, T. J. "An Evaluation of Teacher Stress and Job Satisfaction." *Education*, 1984, *105* (2), 189–192.

Sutton, R. I. "Job Stress Among Primary and Secondary Schoolteachers." *Work and Occupations*, 1984, *11* (1), 7–28.

Swicord, B. "Burnout Among Teachers of the Gifted." *Gifted Education International*, 1987, *5* (1), 38–40.

Talbert, J. E. "The Staging of Teachers' Careers: An Institutional Perspective." *Work and Occupations*, 1986, *13* (3), 421–443.

Taton, K. D. "The Causes and Levels of Teacher Stress as Perceived by Teachers, Former Teachers, and Site Administrators." Unpublished doctoral dissertation, University of Southern California, 1983.

Taylor, R. D. "Burnout Among the Isolated, Rural Teachers in Montana." Unpublished doctoral dissertation, Montana State University, 1986.

Taylor, S. E. "Health Psychology: The Science and the Field." *American Psychologist*, 1990, *45* (1), 40–50.

"Teaching in Trouble." *U.S. News and World Report,* May 26, 1986, pp. 52–57.

Terkel, S. *Working.* New York: Pantheon, 1972.

Tifft, S. "Who's Teaching Our Children." *Time,* 1988, *132* (20), 58–64.

Tifft, S. "Crusaders in the Classroom." *Time,* 1990, *136* (4), 66.

Timar, T. B., and Kirp, D. L. "Education Reform in the 1980s: Lessons from the States." *Phi Delta Kappan,* Mar. 1989, pp. 504–511.

Timpane, P. M. *The Silver Lining of the Seventies: Hard Lessons Slowly Learned About the Progress of Education in America.* New York: Teachers College, Columbia University, 1982.

Tosi, H., and Tosi, D. "Some Correlates of Role Conflict and Role Ambiguity Among Public School Teachers." *Journal of Human Relations,* 1970, *18,* 1068–1076.

U.S. Commission on Civil Rights. *Racial Isolation in the Public Schools.* Washington, D.C.: U.S. Government Printing Office, 1967.

U.S. Office of Education. *Equality of Educational Opportunity.* Washington, D.C.: U.S. Government Printing Office, 1966.

Vaillant, G. *Adaption to Life.* Boston: Little, Brown, 1977.

Waller, W. *The Sociology of Teaching.* New York: Russell and Russell, 1932.

Walley, W. V., and Stokes, J. P. "Self-Help Support for Teachers Under Stress." Paper presented at the annual convention of the American Psychological Association, Los Angeles, Aug. 1981.

Watzlawick, P., Weakland, J., and Fisch, R. *Change: Principles of Problem Formation and Problem Resolution.* New York: Norton, 1974.

Wechsler, L. "The Effects of Different Types of Stress as Perceived by Teachers in an Urban High School." Unpublished doctoral dissertation, Teachers College, Columbia University, 1983.

Weinstein, E. "High School Teacher." *New York Times,* Nov. 6, 1988, Section 4A, p. 17.

Weiskopf, P. "Burnout Among Teachers of Exceptional Children." *Exceptional Children,* 1980, *47* (1), 18–23.

Wells, A. S. "Teacher Shortage Termed Most Critical in Inner-City Schools." *New York Times,* May 10, 1988, p. A28.

Wells, A. S. "Effort to Reach Homeless Students Puts Increasing Strain on Schools." *New York Times*, Feb. 22, 1989, p. B11.

White, R. W. "Motivation Reconsidered: The Concept of Competence." *Psychological Review*, 1959, *66*, 297–333.

Wilkins, R. "The Black Poor Are Different." *New York Times*, Aug. 22, 1989, p. A23.

Williams, D. C. "The Relationship Between Teacher Stress and the Leader Behavior of Principals, Teacher Self Concept, and the Degree Level of Teachers." Unpublished doctoral dissertation, Auburn University, 1982.

Wilson, C. *Survey of Teachers in San Diego County*. San Diego, Calif.: Department of Education, 1979.

Wilson, W. J. *The Truly Disadvantaged*. Chicago: University of Chicago Press, 1987.

Wong, M. J. "Teacher Decisional Participation and Stress." Unpublished doctoral dissertation, University of Houston, 1983.

Yankelovich, D. *New Rules: Searching for Self-Fulfillment in a World Turned Upside Down*. New York: Random House, 1981.

Zabel, R., and Zabel, M. K. "Factors in Burnout Among Teachers of Exceptional Children." *Exceptional Children*, 1982, *49* (3), 261–263.

Zager, J. "The Relationship of Personality, Situational Stress and Anxiety Factors to Teacher Burnout." Unpublished doctoral dissertation, Indiana University, 1982.

Name Index

Subject Index